PRISONS AND JAILS

A DETERRENT TO CRIME?

PRISONS AND JAILS
A DETERRENT TO CRIME?

Jeffrey Ferro

INFORMATION PLUS® REFERENCE SERIES
Formerly published by Information Plus, Wylie, Texas

GALE GROUP

THOMSON LEARNING

Detroit • New York • San Diego • San Francisco
Boston • New Haven, Conn. • Waterville, Maine
London • Munich

PRISONS AND JAILS: A DETERRENT TO CRIME?

Jeffrey Ferro, *Author*

The Gale Group Staff:

Editorial: Ellice Engdahl, *Series Editor*; John F. McCoy, *Series Editor*; Charles B. Montney, *Series Editor*; Andrew Claps, *Series Associate Editor*; Jason M. Everett, *Series Associate Editor*; Michael T. Reade, *Series Associate Editor*; Heather Price, *Series Assistant Editor*; Teresa Elsey, *Editorial Assistant;* Debra M. Kirby, *Managing Editor*; Rita Runchock, *Managing Editor*

Image and Multimedia Content: Barbara J. Yarrow, *Manager, Imaging and Multimedia Content*; Robyn Young, *Project Manager, Imaging and Multimedia Content*

Indexing: Lynne Maday, *Indexing Specialist*

Permissions: Lori Hines, *Permissions Specialist*; Maria Franklin, *Permissions Manager*

Product Design: Michelle DiMercurio, *Senior Art Director and Product Design Manager*; Michael Logusz, *Cover Art Designer*

Production: Evi Seoud, *Assistant Manager, Composition Purchasing and Electronic Prepress*; NeKita McKee, *Buyer*; Dorothy Maki, *Manufacturing Manager*

Cover photo © Digital Stock.

ISBN 0-7876-5103-6 (set)
ISBN 0-7876-5402-7 (this volume)
ISSN 1536-5190 (this volume)
Printed in the United States of America
10 9 8 7 6 5 4 3 2 1

TABLE OF CONTENTS

outlined and discussed here are mediation and restitution, halfway houses and residential programs, day reporting centers, day fines, community service, treatment programs, intensive supervision probation, house arrest and electronic monitoring, work release, and boot camps.

Substance use and abuse are prevalent among offenders. An increasing number of prison inmates have been convicted of drug offenses, and numerous others are drug or alcohol abusers, making treatment programs an important prison service. Also discussed are drug trafficking and smoking in prisons.

Prisoners do not surrender all their constitutional rights and are entitled to challenge the conditions of their imprisonment if they believe their rights have been wrongfully denied. This chapter describes key court decisions pertaining to prisoners' rights and discusses the challenges of preventing frivolous lawsuits while still ensuring that prisoners are not mistreated.

PREFACE

Prisons and Jails: A Deterrent to Crime? is one of the latest volumes in the Information Plus Reference Series. Previously published by the Information Plus company of Wylie, Texas, the Information Plus Reference Series (and its companion set, the Information Plus Compact Series) became a Gale Group product when Gale and Information Plus merged in early 2000. Those of you familiar with the series as published by Information Plus will notice a few changes from the 1999 edition. Gale has adopted a new layout and style that we hope you will find easy to use. Other improvements include greatly expanded indexes in each book, and more descriptive tables of contents.

While some changes have been made to the design, the purpose of the Information Plus Reference Series remains the same. Each volume of the series presents the latest facts on a topic of pressing concern in modern American life. These topics include today's most controversial and most studied social issues: abortion, capital punishment, care for the elderly, crime, health care, the environment, immigration, minorities, social welfare, women, youth, and many more. Although written especially for the high school and undergraduate student, this series is an excellent resource for anyone in need of factual information on current affairs.

By presenting the facts, it is Gale's intention to provide its readers with everything they need to reach an informed opinion on current issues. To that end, there is a particular emphasis in this series on the presentation of scientific studies, surveys, and statistics. These data are generally presented in the form of tables, charts, and other graphics placed within the text of each book. Every graphic is directly referred to and carefully explained in the text. The source of each graphic is presented within the graphic itself. The data used in these graphics is drawn from the most reputable and reliable sources, in particular the various branches of the U.S. government and major independent polling organizations. Every effort has been made to secure the most recent information available. The reader should bear in mind that many major studies take years to conduct, and that additional years often pass before the data from these studies is made available to the public. Therefore, in many cases the most recent information available in 2001 is dated from 1998 or 1999. Older statistics are sometimes presented as well, if they are of particular interest and no more-recent information exists.

Although statistics are a major focus of the Information Plus Reference Series, they are by no means its only content. Each book also presents the widely held positions and important ideas that shape how the book's subject is discussed in the United States. These positions are explained in detail and, where possible, in the words of their proponents. Some of the other material to be found in these books includes: historical background; descriptions of major events related to the subject; relevant laws and court cases; and examples of how these issues play out in American life. Some books also feature primary documents, or have pro and con debate sections giving the words and opinions of prominent Americans on both sides of a controversial topic. All material is presented in an even-handed and unbiased manner; the reader will never be encouraged to accept one view of an issue over another.

HOW TO USE THIS BOOK

Crime is one of the big issues facing Americans today, but crime cannot be discussed in proper context without discussing the American system of prisons and jails. Much public funding is spent on the construction of new prisons and jails and the maintenance of old ones, but many people question the effectiveness of prisons and jails as a deterrent to crime. Is the purpose of institutions such as prisons and jails truly to rehabilitate criminals, or simply to punish them? Are certain races or ethnicities more prevalent in the prison population than others? Does juvenile incarceration work? What should day-today life be like for those in prisons and jails? What rights do prisoners give up, and what rights do they retain? These and other challenging questions are discussed in this volume.

Prisons and Jails: A Deterrent to Crime? consists of thirteen chapters and three appendices. Each chapter is devoted to a particular aspect of prisons and jails in the United States. For a summary of the information covered in each chapter, please see the synopses provided in the Table of Contents at the front of the book. Chapters generally begin with an overview of the basic facts and background information on the chapter's topic, then proceed to examine sub-topics of particular interest. For example, Chapter 7: Juvenile Confinement begins with a discussion of exactly how America defines a "juvenile," as that term relates to criminals. It then examines the different types of facilities, public, private, and institutional, in which juvenile criminals are confined. Later, the chapter addresses characteristics of juvenile offenders, juvenile criminals sentenced as adults and confined in adult facilities, the death penalty for juveniles, and boot camps. Readers can find their way through a chapter by looking for the section and sub-section headings, which are clearly set off from the text. Or, they can refer to the book's extensive index if they already know what they are looking for.

Statistical Information

The tables and figures featured throughout *Prisons and Jails: A Deterrent to Crime?* will be of particular use to the reader in learning about this issue. These tables and figures represent an extensive collection of the most recent and important statistics on prisons and jails and related issues—for example, the number of people in jail or prison in the United States, characteristics of those incarcerated, and the amount of money spent on the prison system. Gale believes that making this information available to the reader is the most important way in which we fulfill the goal of this book: to help readers understand the issues and controversies surrounding prisons and jails in the United States and reach their own conclusions.

Each table or figure has a unique identifier appearing above it, for ease of identification and reference. Titles for the tables and figures explain their purpose. At the end of each table or figure, the original source of the data is provided.

In order to help readers understand these often complicated statistics, all tables and figures are explained in the text. References in the text direct the reader to the relevant statistics. Furthermore, the contents of all tables and figures are fully indexed. Please see the opening section of the index at the back of this volume for a description of how to find tables and figures within it.

In addition to the main body text and images, *Prisons and Jails: A Deterrent to Crime?* has three appendices. The first is the Important Names and Addresses directory. Here the reader will find contact information for a number of government and private organizations that can provide information on the American prison and jail system. The second appendix is the Resources section, which can also assist the reader in conducting his or her own research. In this section, the author and editors of *Prisons and Jails: A Deterrent to Crime?* describe some of the sources that were most useful during the compilation of this book. The final appendix is the index. It has been greatly expanded from previous editions, and should make it even easier to find specific topics in this book.

COMMENTS AND SUGGESTIONS

The editors of the Information Plus Reference Series welcome your feedback on *Prisons and Jails: A Deterrent to Crime?* Please direct all correspondence to:

Editor
Information Plus Reference Series
27500 Drake Rd.
Farmington Hills, MI, 48331-3535

ACKNOWLEDGEMENTS

Permission to use the following quotes, photographs, illustrations, figures, charts and tables appearing in Information Plus Prisons and Jails 2001 *was received from the following sources:*

Bureau of the Census. From statistics in *Statistical Abstract of the United States: 2000.* U.S. Census Bureau, Washington, D.C., 2001. Courtesy of the Bureau of the Census.

Bureau of Justice Assistance. From a table in *Juveniles in Adult Prisons and Jails: A National Assessment.* U.S. Department of Justice, Bureau of Justice Assistance, Washington, D.C., 2000. Courtesy of the Bureau of Justice Assistance.

Bureau of Justice Statistics. From statistics in *Capital Punishment 1999.* Bureau of Justice Statistics, Washington, D.C., 2000. From statistics in *Correctional Populations in the United States, 1997.* U.S. Bureau of Justice Statistics, Washington, D.C., 2000. From graphics in "Defense Counsel in Criminal Cases," *Bureau of Justice Statistics Special Report.* U.S. Department of Justice, Washington, D.C., 2000. From tables in *Felony Sentences in State Courts.* Bureau of Justice Statistics, Washington D.C., 1996. From graphics in *HIV in Prisons 1997.* Bureau of Justice Statistics, Washington, D.C., 1999. From statistics in "Incarcerated Parents and Their Children," *Bureau of Justice Statistics Special Report.* U.S. Department of Justice, Washington, D.C., 2000. From a table in "Medical Problems of Inmates, 1997," *Bureau of Justice Statistics Special Report.* Department of Justice, Washington, D.C., 2001. From statistics in *Prison and Jail Inmates at Midyear 2000.* Bureau of Justice Statistics, Washington, D.C., 2001. From graphics in *Prisoners in 1999,* Bureau of Justice Statistics, Washington, D.C., 2000. From a table in *Prior Abuse Reported by Inmates and Probationers.* Bureau of Justice Statistics, Washington D.C., 1996. From statistics

in "Profile of State Prisoners under Age 18, 1985–97," *Bureau of Justice Statistics Special Report,* U.S. Department of Justice, Washington, D.C., 2000. From tables in the *Sourcebook of Criminal Justice Statistics 1997* and *Sourcebook of Criminal Justice Statistics 1999.* Both edited by Kathleen Maguire and Ann L. Pastore. U.S. Bureau of Justice Statistics, 1997, 1999. From a table in *State Court Organization 1998.* Bureau of Justice Statistics, Washington, D.C., 2000. From a table in *State Court Sentencing of Convicted Felons, 1996.* Bureau of Justice Statistics, Washington, D.C., 2000. From statistics in *State Prison Expenditures, 1996.* U.S. Bureau of Justice Statistics, Washington, D.C., 1999. From tables in *Substance Abuse and Treatment State and Federal Prisoners, 1997.* Bureau of Justice Statistics, Washington D.C., 1997. From a table in *Truth in Sentencing in State Prisons.* Bureau of Justice Statistics, Washington, D.C. From tables in *U.S. Correctional Population Reaches 6.3 Million Men and Women: Represents 3.1 Percent of the Adult U.S. Population.* Bureau of Justice Statistics, Washington, D.C., 2000. From a table in "Women Offenders," *Bureau of Justice Statistics Special Report,* U.S. Department of Justice, Washington, D.C., 2000. All courtesy of the Bureau of Justice Statistics.

Bureau of Prisons. From a table in "Federal prison population over time/drug offenders," U.S. Bureau of Prisons, Washington, D.C., 2000. Courtesy of the U.S. Bureau of Prisons.

Castine Research. From a table in *Overcrowded Times* by Walter Dickey and Pam Stiebs Hollenhorst. Castine Research Corporation. Reproduced by permission.

Executive Office of the President. From a chart in *The Budget for Fiscal Year 2001.* Executive Office of the President, Washington, D.C., 2000. Courtesy of the Executive Office of the President.

Federal Bureau of Investigations. From graphics *in Crime in the United States,* 1999. Federal Bureau of Investigation, Washington, D.C., 2000. Courtesy of the Federal Bureau of Investigations.

National Association of State Budget Officers. From charts in the *State Expenditure Report.* National Association of State Budget Officers, 2000. Courtesy of the National Association of State Budget Officers.

National Conference of State Legislatures. From a graphic in "State Budget Actions, 1999," National Conference of State Legislatures, Denver, CO, 1998.

National Institute of Corrections. From graphics in *Sexual Misconduct in Prisons: Laws, Remedies and Incidence.* National Institute of Corrections, Longmont, CO, 2000.

National Institute of Justice. From a table in *Addressing Correctional Officer Stress: Programs and Strategies,* National Institute of Justice, U.S. Department of Justice, Washington, D.C., 2000. From graphics in the *National Institute of Justice Journal.* U.S. Department of Justice, Washington, D.C., April 1999. Courtesy of the National Institute of Justice.

Office of Juvenile Justice and Delinquency Prevention. Statistics from *Juvenile Court Statistics 1997,* National Center for Juvenile Justice, Office of Juvenile Justice and Delinquency Prevention, U.S. Department of Justice, Washington, D.C., 2000. From graphics in *Juvenile Justice Bulletin.* Office of Juvenile Justice and Delinquency Prevention, U.S. Department of Justice, Washington, D.C., December 2000. From tables and charts in *Juvenile Offenders and Victims: 1999 National Report,* Office of Juvenile Justice and Delinquency Prevention, Washington, D.C., 1999. From graphics in the *Office of Juvenile Justice and Delinquency Prevention Fact Sheet,* #17, U.S. Department of Justice, Washington, D.C., November 2000. All courtesy of the Office of Juvenile Justice and Delinquency Prevention.

The Sentencing Project. From graphics in *Diminishing Returns: Crime and Incarcera-* *tion in the 1990s.* The Sentencing Project, Washington, D.C., 2000. Reproduced by permission.

V.L. Streib. Statistics from *The Juvenile Death Penalty Today: Death Sentences and* *Executions for Juvenile Crimes, January 1, 1973–December 31, 2000,* Ohio Northern University College of Law, 2001. Available on-line at: http://www.law.onu.edu/faculty/ streib/juvdeath.pdf. Reproduced by permission.

CHAPTER 1

HISTORY OF CORRECTIONS—
REVENGE OR REHABILITATION?

A terrible stinking dark and dismal place situated underground into which no daylight can come. It was paved with stone; the prisoners had no beds and lay on the pavement whereby they endured great misery and hardship.

— Inmate at Newgate Jail (1724)

The philosophy of punishment for crimes, like ideas on raising children, has changed over the centuries. Society's practices in most countries have evolved from avenging one's family, either by killing the accused or a member of his family (blood feuds), to written codes setting down punishments. Jails and prisons have changed from holding places for prisoners waiting to be deported, maimed, whipped, or executed, to being the actual punishment. The philosophies behind putting people in jails and prisons have included revenge, rehabilitation, and the desire to keep criminals off the streets.

ANCIENT TIMES

Many ancient cultures allowed the victim or a member of the victim's family to deliver justice. The offender often fled to his or her family for protection. As a result, blood feuds developed in which the victim's family sought revenge against the offender's family. Sometimes the offender's family responded by striking back. Retaliation could continue until the families tired of killing or stealing from each other or until one or both families were destroyed or financially ruined.

As societies organized into tribes and villages, local communities increasingly began to assume the responsibility for punishing crimes against the community and its members. Punishments could be brutal, such as being boiled in oil or eaten by wild beasts. With the development of writing societies usually listed crimes and their respective punishments. The Code of Hammurabi in Babylon (circa 1750 B.C.E.—before the common era) is generally considered the first such set of laws. The laws of Moses in the Bible also recorded offenses against the community and their corresponding punishments. Nonetheless, personal revenge was still practiced. Indeed, the Bible reports 10 cities in which an accused murderer would be safe from the victim's family. The Justinian Code (Emperor Justinian of the Byzantine or Eastern Roman Empire, 529–565) organized many of the early codes.

As empires developed the owners of large tracts of land, and later the rulers, wanted a more orderly legal system than blood feuds, and so they established courts. These courts most often sentenced the offender to slavery in the victim's family for several years as restitution for the offense. Other punishments included laboring on public works projects, banishment, or death. The rise of organized religions often brought about more severe punishments, since crimes became sins not only against the community, but also against God's will.

MEDIEVAL TIMES

As in ancient times the medieval period of Europe had very harsh punishments. Torture and death were common forms of punishment. Sometimes torture and the death penalty were combined in such terrible instruments as the rack or the Iron Maiden. The rack stretched its victims until their bodies were pulled apart. The Iron Maiden was a box in which a person was placed and, when the door was closed, spikes entered the victim from both back and front. Public execution by burning, beheading, and hanging was common.

Confinement

Those arrested were usually confined (imprisoned) until they confessed to the crime and their physical punishment took place. The medieval church sometimes used long-term incarceration to replace executions. Some wealthy landowners built private prisons to enhance their own power, imprisoning those who disputed the landowners' pursuit of power or even their whims. With the Assize of Clarendon (1166) many crimes were classified as offenses against the "king's peace" and were punished by the state and not by the church, the lord, or the victim's extended family. At this time the first prisons designed solely for incarceration were constructed.

Prisons

The only comfort prisoners had in the cold, damp, filthy, rat- and roach-infested prisons of medieval Europe was what they could buy. The prison-keeper charged for blankets, mattresses, food, and even the manacles (chains). The prisoner had to pay for the privilege of being both booked (charged) and released. Wealthy prisoners could pay for plush quarters but most suffered in terrible conditions, often dying from malnutrition, disease, or victimization by other prisoners.

THE RISE OF NATIONS

In Europe in the 1500s, while most jails still housed people waiting for trial or punishment, workhouses and debtors' prisons developed as sources of cheap labor or places to house insane or minor offenders. Those found guilty of serious crimes could be transported instead of executed. England transported many prisoners to colonial Georgia in the United States and later to Australia, while France sent many to South America. Although transportation was a less severe punishment than the death penalty, many prisoners did not survive the harsh conditions either on board the transport ships or life in the early colonies to which they were sent.

COLONIAL AND EARLY POST-REVOLUTIONARY PERIODS

Just as in Europe physical punishment was common in colonial America. Americans used stocks, pillories, branding, flogging, and maiming—such as cutting off an ear or slitting the nostrils—to punish offenders. The death penalty was used frequently. The Massachusetts Bay Colony listed 13 crimes that warranted execution. In early New York State 20 percent of offenses, including pick-pocketing, horse stealing, and robbery, were capital crimes (warranting the death penalty).

Jails were used to hold prisoners awaiting trial or sentencing or as debtors' prison, but not as the punishment itself. Puritan beliefs that humans were naturally depraved made it easier for the colonies and the first states to enforce harsh punishments. In addition, since Puritans believed that humans had no control over their fate (predestination), most early Americans felt there was no need for rehabilitation.

Pennsylvania

The Quakers, led by William Penn, made colonial Pennsylvania an exception to the harsh punishments often practiced in the other colonies. The early criminal code of colonial Pennsylvania abolished executions for all crimes except homicide, replaced physical punishments with imprisonment and hard labor, and did not charge the prisoners for their food and housing.

Ideas of the Enlightenment

The philosophy of the Enlightenment (the Age of Reason) emphasized the importance of the individual. After the French Revolution (1789), which was based on the ideas of the Enlightenment, western European countries abolished torture as a form of punishment and emphasized that the punishment should fit the individual's crime(s). Rather than inflicting pain as the main element of correction, the idea of changing the individual became the goal.

In England John Howard (1726–1790) wrote about the horrible treatment of prisoners in *The State of the Prisons in England and Wales* (1777). He thought prisoners should not be harassed by keepers who extorted from them, nor should they have to suffer malnutrition and disease. He advocated segregating prisoners by age, sex, and type of crime; paying the staff; hiring medical officials and chaplains; and supplying prisoners with adequate food and clothing.

Howard called the facilities "penitentiaries" (from the word "penitent," meaning to be ashamed or sorry about doing something bad) because he based his ideas on the Quaker's philosophy of people repenting, reflecting on their sins, and changing their ways. Public concern led the British Parliament to pass the Penitentiary Act of 1779, which called for the first secure and sanitary penitentiary. The law eliminated the charging of fees. Prisoners would live in solitary confinement at night and work together silently during the day. Nonetheless, although Parliament passed the law, it did not actually go into effect until the opening of Pentonville Penitentiary in North London in 1842.

THE REFORM MOVEMENT

The ideas of individual freedom and the concept that people could change society for the better by using reason permeated American society in the early 1800s. Reformers worked for the abolition of slavery, women's rights, and the prohibition of liquor, as well as changes in corrections.

Pennsylvania System

In 1787 in Pennsylvania, a group campaigning for more humane treatment of prisoners established the Philadelphia Society for Alleviating the Miseries of Public Prisons. Led by Dr. Benjamin Rush, this organization, which included many Quakers, campaigned for the imprisonment of criminals rather than physical and capital punishment. The Quakers thought solitary confinement could reform criminals. In such cells the offenders could think over their wrongful ways, repent, and reform. In 1790 Pennsylvania established the Walnut Street Jail in Philadelphia for "hardened and atrocious offenders."

The association continued pressuring the legislature for more prisons and, finally, in 1829, the state built the Western Penitentiary outside Pittsburgh and the Eastern Penitentiary near Philadelphia. The individual twelve feet-by-eight feet-by-ten feet cells with individual exercise yards isolated inmates from everyone so they could work, read their Bibles, and contemplate in order to be rehabilitated. The only voice the inmates heard was that of the chaplain on Sunday.

The reformers thought solitary confinement not only allowed the offenders to repent but was also a punishing experience since humans are social animals. In addition, the system would be economical since, under these conditions, prisoners would not take long to see the error of their ways and fewer guards would be needed. Many prisoners found the total isolation very difficult to endure. The jails, however, quickly became overcrowded warehouses for prisoners.

Auburn System

The Auburn System (New York, 1819) used the Quaker idea of solitary confinement at night but used a system of congregating (putting together) the inmates in a common workroom during the day. The prisoners could not talk to or look at each other. Any violation of the rules was met with immediate and strict discipline. Each supervisor had the right to flog an inmate who violated the rules.

Reformers thought the system economical because a single guard could watch a group of prisoners at work. Also, the work of the inmates would help pay for their upkeep, they would learn about the benefits of work, and have time to meditate and repent. Both the Pennsylvania and Auburn systems dictated that offenders should be isolated and have a disciplined routine. European countries tended to adopt the Pennsylvania system while most American states chose the Auburn system. While these methods made it easier to run a prison, they did little to rehabilitate prisoners.

After the Civil War (1861–1865) huge industrial prisons were built to house thousands of prisoners in the Northeast, Midwest, and California. The western states used their old territorial jails while the South relied on leasing out prisoners for farm labor.

THE CINCINNATI DECLARATION

Because many prison administrators were corrupt convicts were mistreated and used as cheap labor. However, a growing number of prison reformers were beginning to believe that the prison system should be more committed to reform. In 1870 the newly established National

Prison Association (which later became the American Correctional Association) met in Cincinnati, Ohio, and issued a Declaration of Principles. The philosophy of the Auburn system (fixed sentences, silence, isolation, harsh punishment, lockstep work) was considered degrading and destructive to the human spirit. The values in the Declaration of Principles included the following:

- The penal system should be based on reformation, not suffering, and prisoners should be educated to be industrious free citizens able to function in society, not orderly inmates controlled by the guards.

- Rewards should be provided for good conduct.

- Indeterminate sentencing (not a mandated exact sentence) should include the ability for prisoners to earn their freedom early through hard work and good behavior.

- Citizens should understand that society is responsible for the conditions that lead to crime.

- Prisoners should recognize that they can change their lives.

ELMIRA REFORMATORY

The superintendent of the Elmira Reformatory in New York, Zebulon Brockway, used some of these ideas when New York opened the reformatory in 1876 for offenders 16 to 30 years old. Brockway believed that rehabilitation could be achieved through education.

Inmates who did well in both academic and moral subjects earned early release by accumulating points. Misbehavior and doing poorly in the educational courses prolonged one's sentence. Brockway used this technique because the New York legislature had passed a law allowing indeterminate sentencing and the release of inmates on parole when they showed they had been reformed. Brockway recognized it was hard to distinguish between those inmates who had truly reformed and those who pretended in order to be paroled.

PROGRESSIVE REFORMS

By 1900 this correctional philosophy had spread throughout the nation. Nonetheless, by World War I (1914–1918), the idea of using educational and rehabilitative approaches was being replaced by the use of strict discipline. The way the facilities were built, the lack of trained personnel, and the attitudes of the guards made Brockway's ideas difficult to implement. Also, the introduction of a system of probation kept the offenders easiest to rehabilitate out of the reformatories.

Nevertheless, the reform movement survived. The progressives of the early twentieth century believed that if prisons applied the ideas of behavioral science to the inmates, the prisoners could be rehabilitated. The progressives worked to change the social environment from which criminals came and to design ways to rehabilitate individual inmates. By the 1920s reformers were strongly advocating indeterminate sentencing, parole, and treatment programs, as a way to rehabilitate offenders. This more scientific approach to corrections, however, was not put into practice until decades later.

While many of the reforms had merit, most could not be properly implemented due to inadequate funding or the unwillingness of prison officials to act. As each reform apparently failed to solve the problem of crime, many people became disillusioned. By the beginning of the twenty-first century, while most people did not want to return to the exploitation and cruelty of prisons of the nineteenth and early twentieth centuries, they did not want to hear inmates complain about their overcrowded conditions or their lack of services. After all, offenders are in prison to be punished for their actions.

PRISONS AS WORK PLACES

Despite the efforts of reformers most citizens preferred prisons to pay their own way. Prison administrators constructed factories within the prison walls or hired inmates out for chain gangs. In rural areas inmates worked on prison-owned farms. In the South prisoners—predominantly black—were often leased out to local farmers. Prison superintendents justified the hard labor as teaching the offenders the value of work and self-discipline, but economics were the true motives behind the factories and farms. Some penologists (one who studies prison management) believe that the harshness of the prisons made these inmates more vindictive against society.

With the rise of unions in the North the 1930s saw an end to large-scale prison industry. Unions complained about competing with the inmates' free labor, especially amidst the rising unemployment of the Great Depression. By 1940 the states had limited what inmates could produce. By 1970 the number of prison farms had decreased substantially because they were expensive to operate and the prisons found it cheaper to purchase food. Also, agricultural work no longer prepared inmates for employment on the outside. Since the 1970s, however, support for prison factories as a way to train inmates for outside jobs has grown. Penologists believe that working in prison factories helps keep prisoners from being bored and idle and teaches them skills. While they believe prisoners benefit from work, they also believe prisoners should not suffer the exploitation that characterized the factories of the 1920s.

REHABILITATION MODEL

The rehabilitation model of corrections began in the 1930s and reached its high point in the 1950s. Qualified staff were expected to diagnose the cause of an offender's criminal behavior, prescribe a treatment to change the individual, and determine when that individual had become rehabilitated. Group therapy, counseling, and behavior modification were all part of the approach. These techniques did not work with all inmates, most states did not budget enough money for their correctional institutions to achieve these goals, and there were too many prisoners for the prison staff to treat effectively.

COMMUNITY CORRECTIONS

Advocates of community corrections in the 1960s and 1970s thought that rehabilitation needed to be done within the community, not in the prisons. They favored probation, educational courses, and job training. Starting in the 1960s the judicial system began recognizing the constitutional rights of prisoners to live in tolerable conditions.

In 1965 President Lyndon B. Johnson's Commission on Law Enforcement and Administration of Justice, a panel of experts on crime and the justice system, recommended improvements to the correctional system and initiated the first standards for operating prison facilities. The president's task force asserted that the success of a correctional system depended upon having "a sufficient number of qualified staff."

It also recommended alternative community-based approaches, educational and vocational programs, and different treatments for special offender categories. As a result the American Correctional Association's Commission of Accreditation established standards by which it assesses correctional facilities for voluntary accreditation.

JUSTICE MODEL

As the amount of crime increased, however, more citizens argued against rehabilitation, indeterminate sentencing, probation, parole, and treatment programs. They wanted criminals behind bars for a determinate amount of time, generally the longer the better. They wanted offenders to pay their debts to society and be off the streets so they could not be committing more crimes. As a result the federal government and a growing number of states introduced mandatory sentencing and "three strikes you're out" life terms for habitual criminals, as well as limiting the use of probation, parole, and time off for good behavior.

The rising number of offenders on parole and in prisons and jails has taxed the system. Facilities have become overcrowded and states experiencing budget problems cannot build prisons and jails fast enough or supply enough treatment and educational programs.

Meanwhile, state and federal courts have put caps on how many prisoners each facility can hold and have told states that certain basic services are required. With determinate sentencing often eliminating parole, prisons have

TABLE 1.1

Attitudes toward the most important goal of prison by demographic characteristics, 1996

Question: "Once people who commit crimes are in prison, which of the following do you think should be the most important goal of prison?"

	Rehabilitation	Punishment	Crime prevention/ deterrence
National	48.4%	14.6%	33.1%
Sex			
Male	48.6	16.8	30.5
Female	48.2	12.5	35.5
Race, ethnicity			
White	47.7	16.1	31.9
Black	56.4	11.8	30.9
Hispanic	42.3	7.7	42.3
Age			
18 to 24 years	50.7	17.6	29.6
25 to 39 years	47.5	14.3	33.5
40 to 59 years	49.1	13.6	33.2
60 years and older	46.3	16.5	33.5
Education			
College graduate	54.9	11.5	28.5
Some college	50.9	14.5	32.4
High school graduate	40.4	17.1	38.3
Less than high school graduate	47.6	15.3	31.5
Income			
Over $60,000	53.3	15.7	26.2
$30,000 to $60,000	49.3	11.7	36.0
$15,000 to $29,999	47.7	15.4	34.4
Less than $15,000	47.1	18.6	30.0
Community			
Urban	54.2	8.9	31.5
Suburban	46.7	13.9	34.1
Small city	46.1	17.8	33.9
Rural/small town	48.0	16.1	32.8
Region			
Northeast	52.0	17.1	27.4
Midwest	49.6	14.3	34.6
South	44.2	14.7	35.7
West	51.0	13.3	30.9
Politics			
Republican	43.3	14.9	39.0
Democrat	53.8	13.5	30.0
Independent/other	47.5	17.0	31.5

Note: The "other," "don't know," and "refused" categories have been omitted; therefore percents may not sum to 100.

SOURCE: Kathleen Maguire and Ann L. Pastore, eds., *Sourcebook of Criminal Justice Statistics 1997*, Bureau of Justice Statistics, Washington, D.C., 1998

TABLE 1.2

Respondents' ratings of several aspects of the U.S. prison system, 2000

Question: "Next, we'd like to ask you about several aspects of the prison system in the United States. For each one, please say whether you think prisons are doing an excellent, good, only fair or poor job. How about. . .?"

	Excellent	Good	Only fair	Poor	No opinion
Maintaining high security to keep prisoners from escaping	18%	49%	23%	8%	2%
Rehabilitating inmates so they are less likely to commit crimes in the future	2	12	34	48	4
Maintaining a safe environment for inmates in prison	5	25	37	26	7

SOURCE: George Gallup, Jr. and Alec Gallup, *The Gallup Poll Monthly*, September 2000, as cited in "Table 2.0003: Respondents' ratings of several aspects of the prison system in the United States," *Sourcebook of Criminal Justice Statistics* [Online], Kathleen Maguire and Ann L. Pastore, eds. May 2, 2001 http://www.albany.edu/sourcebook/

thought that crime prevention/deterrence was prisons' most important goal. (See Table 1.1.) About half of male and female respondents favored rehabilitation; however, more males favored punishment (16.8 percent to 12.5 percent), and more females favored crime prevention/deterrence (35.5 percent to 30.5 percent). Blacks were most supportive of rehabilitation (56.4 percent), followed by whites (47.7 percent), and Hispanics (42.3 percent). Fewer Hispanics favored punishment (7.7 percent) than did blacks (11.8 percent) or whites (16.1 percent). Younger respondents were most supportive of rehabilitation (50.7 percent), while those 40–59 years of age were least supportive (49.1 percent). Only 8.9 percent of urban respondents favored punishment over rehabilitation or crime prevention/deterrence, while almost twice as many from small cities favored punishment (17.8 percent). Republicans were more likely than Democrats to see prison as a tool for crime prevention/deterrence, while Democrats were more likely to consider it for rehabilitation.

In a 2000 Gallup Poll only 14 percent of respondents thought the prison system in the United States was doing either an "excellent" or "good" job rehabilitating inmates. (See Table 1.2.) Thirty-four percent thought that prisons were doing a "fair" job rehabilitating inmates, but almost half (48 percent) gave U.S. prisons a "poor" rating for rehabilitation. Respondents rated the U.S. prisons system highest at maintaining high security, with a combined 67 percent voting "excellent" or "good." Sixty-three percent of respondents thought prisons were doing only a "fair" or "poor" job of maintaining a safe environment for inmates.

When it comes to the crime of murder, most people seem to feel that there is little or no chance for rehabilitation. (See Table 1.3.) From 1985 to 2000 at least half of all respondents to Gallup Polls indicated that they favored

turned to a system called gain-time to prevent overcrowding and keep control. Gain-time, or good time, allows prison officials to deduct a specified number of days from an offender's sentence for every month served in which the inmate breaks no rules.

REHABILITATION OR PUNISHMENT— PUBLIC OPINION

In 1996 nearly half (48.4 percent) of respondents surveyed by the Survey Research Program (College of Criminal Justice, Sam Houston State University, Texas) thought that the most important goal of prison should be rehabilitation. Only 14.6 percent saw punishment as the most important goal of prison, and one-third (33.1 percent)

TABLE 1.3

Attitudes toward the penalty for murder, 1985–2000

Question: "What do you think should be the penalty for murder—the death penalty, or life imprisonment with absolutely no possibility of parole?"

	Death penalty	Life imprisonment without possibility of parole	No opinion[b]
1985	56%	34%	10%
1986	55	35	10
1991	53	35	11
1992	50	37	13
1993	59	29	12
1994	50	32	18
1997	61	29	10
1999	56	38	6
2000	52	37	11

Note: Sample sizes vary from year to year; the data for 2000 are based on telephone interviews with a randomly selected national sample of 1,050 adults, 18 years of age and older, conducted Feb. 14-15, 2000. For a discussion of public opinion survey sampling procedures, see Appendix 4.

a Percents may not add to 100 because of rounding.
b Includes volunteered responses such as "other," "neither," and "depends."

SOURCE: Frank Newport, "Support for Death Penalty Drops to Lowest Level in 19 Years, Altgough Still High at 66%," in *The Gallup Organization* [Online] http://www.gallup.com/poll/releases/pr000224.asp [accessed June 11, 2001], as adapted by Kathleen Maguire and Ann L. Pastore, eds., "Table 2.57: Attitudes toward the penalty for murder," in *Sourcebook of Criminal Justice Statistics 1999*, Bureau of Justice Statistics, Washington, D.C., 2000

the death penalty over life imprisonment without parole—from a low of 50 percent in 1994 to a high of 61 percent in 1997. That figure has tended downward to 56 percent in 1999 and 52 percent in 2000.

JUVENILES

By the late 1700s children ages seven years or younger were presumed to be incapable of criminal intent, a concept that has carried over to the present time. In the nineteenth century a movement arose based on sixteenth-century European educational reform movements that changed the concept of a child from a "miniature adult" to an individual with less fully developed cognitive capacity. This resulted in children being separated from adult offenders in many major U.S. city prisons and jails.

By passing the Juvenile Court Act of 1899, the state of Illinois established the first juvenile court, located in Cook County. Using the British doctrine of "parens patriae" (state as parent), this act formalized the right of the state to intervene in the lives of juveniles in a way that was different from the manner in which the state dealt with adults. The focus was placed on the welfare of the delinquent child, who was seen as in need of the justice system's benevolent intervention.

By 1925 most states had passed similar legislation. Unlike the adult criminal justice system, juvenile courts dealt with young delinquents by considering both legal and non-legal factors, such as home environment and schooling. However, by the 1960s the juvenile court's success in rehabilitating young offenders was being called into question, largely due to the growing population of juveniles institutionalized indefinitely while being "reformed."

In 1974 Congress passed the Juvenile Justice and Delinquency Prevention Act of 1974, which required not only the segregation of juveniles from adults, but also the separation of juvenile delinquents (those charged with a crime) from juvenile status offenders (truants and so-called "incorrigibles"). This led to the development and expansion of community-based programs and diversion in an effort to discourage institutionalization. However, a decade later the public's perception was that serious juvenile crime was on the rise and that the system devised to protect juveniles had become too lenient. This perception led to a trend in the 1990s to exclude certain serious offenses from juvenile court jurisdiction. Juveniles charged with certain crimes could legally be tried in adult court, in some states at the sole discretion of the prosecuting agency.

According to "Juvenile Justice: A Century of Change" (1999 National Report Series, Office of Juvenile Justice and Delinquency Prevention), by 1997 most states had adopted new, stricter laws for dealing with juvenile offenders in one or more of the following areas:

- Transfer provisions—making it easier to transfer juvenile offenders to the adult criminal justice system.

- Sentencing authority—giving criminal and juvenile courts expanded sentencing options.

- Confidentiality—modifying or removing traditional juvenile court confidentiality by making records and proceedings more open.

- Victims' rights—increasing the role of victims of juvenile crime in the juvenile justice system.

- Correctional programming—allowing for the development of new detention programs for certain adult offenders and for juveniles transferred to the adult justice system.

In addition, many states have added language to their juvenile codes aimed at holding juveniles accountable for criminal behavior and imposing punishment consistent with the seriousness of the crime.

CHAPTER 2
EXPENDITURES

The money spent building and running prisons to house nonviolent offenders offers a new twist on the aphorism "spend it now or spend it later." We are spending unnecessary billions now, to no lasting effect, and will have to spend massive amounts later to address not only the social and economic causes of crime, but to correct the damages caused by unnecessary incarceration and its side effects of blighted lives, broken families, and disrupted careers.

— Michael Tonry, Professor of Law, University of Minnesota

According to the Bureau of Justice Statistics (BJS), the total amount spent on corrections at Federal, state, and local levels rose from $6.9 billion in 1980 to $41 billion in 1996, an increase of nearly seven-fold. (See Table 2.1.) During the same time period total expenditures for police protection rose roughly three and one-half times—from $15 billion to $53 billion. Total judicial and legal costs rose by roughly the same rate—from $7.8 billion in 1982 to $26 billion in 1996.

In 1996 states bore the largest share of these costs, accounting for almost two-thirds (61.6 percent) of direct expenditures on corrections while the Federal government's share was 8.5 percent. (See Table 2.2.) Local governments accounted for about 30 percent of total expenditures on corrections, as well as the largest share of spending on police protection (72.1 percent) and judicial and legal costs (41.3 percent).

Calculated on a per capita basis, in 1980 total spending on corrections cost each U.S. resident approximately $30.37. By 1996 that figure had risen to $154.98 per person, an increase of more than 500 percent. (See Table 2.3.) By comparison the per capita cost of police protection rose by slightly more than three-fold—from $66.73 in 1980 to $200.22. Judicial and legal costs per person rose by about the same margin—from $33.54 in 1982 to $98.81 in 1996.

INCARCERATION RATES RISING

The reason for the escalating costs of corrections is simple enough: More people are being sent to prison and are staying longer because of mandatory sentencing and stiffer sentences. This includes a rise in female offenders, and in juvenile offenders sentenced as adults. These factors have combined to create the paradox that, despite a declining overall crime rate from 1991 to 1998, the rate of incarceration rose during that same time period in all 50 states and the District of Columbia. (See Figure 2.1.) Texas had the sharpest rise in the rate of incarceration, at nearly 150 percent, while the crime rate in Texas declined by about 40 percent. By contrast Maine had the lowest increase in the rate of incarceration at less than 5 percent; nonetheless, the crime rate dropped in Maine by nearly 25 percent, or about five times the rate of incarceration. The average rise in the rate of incarceration among all states and the District of Columbia was just below 50 percent, with the average decline in the crime rate at about 20 percent.

FEDERAL CORRECTIONS

The U.S. budget for 2001 proposed $4.4 billion for corrections, an increase of some $600 million from 1999, when $3.8 billion was budgeted for corrections. (See Figure 2.2.) According to *The Budget for Fiscal Year 2001* (Executive Office of the President, Washington, D.C.), this increase was due to the growth in the federal prison population as the result of tougher sentencing guidelines, the abolition of parole, and minimum mandatory sentences. Drug offenders accounted for about two-thirds of the federal inmate population, which was expected to reach two million in 2000. As a result the federal prison system was projected to be operating at 32 percent over capacity by the end of 2000—up from 22 percent over capacity at the end of 1997. The 2001 budget also provided funding to enroll at least 34 percent of all federal inmates in some type of educational program. That increase represents the same number of inmates actually enrolled in federal prison educational programs in 1998.

TABLE 2.1

Justice system direct and intergovernmental expenditures by type of activity and level of government, fiscal years 1980–96
(Dollar amounts in thousands)

Level of government and fiscal year	Total justice system	Police protection	Judicial and legal	Corrections
All governments				
1980	NA	$15,163,029	NA	$6,900,751
1981	NA	16,822,094	NA	7,868,822
1982	$35,841,916	19,022,184	$7,770,785	9,048,947
1983	39,680,167	20,648,200	8,620,604	10,411,363
1984	43,942,690	22,685,766	9,463,180	11,793,744
1985	48,563,068	24,399,355	10,628,816	13,534,897
1986	53,499,805	26,254,993	11,485,446	15,759,366
1987	58,871,348	28,767,553	12,555,026	17,548,769
1988	65,230,542	30,960,824	13,970,563	20,299,155
1989	70,949,468	32,794,182	15,588,664	22,566,622
1990	79,433,959	35,923,479	17,356,826	26,153,654
1991	87,566,819	38,971,240	19,298,379	29,297,200
1992	93,776,852	41,326,531	20,988,888	31,461,433
1993	97,541,826	44,036,756	21,558,403	31,946,667
1994	103,470,564	46,004,536	22,601,706	34,864,322
1995	112,868,448	48,644,529	24,471,689	39,752,230
1996	120,194,175	53,007,425	26,157,907	41,028,843
Federal				
1980	NA	1,941,000	NA	408,000
1981	NA	2,118,000	NA	436,000
1982	4,458,000	2,527,000	1,390,000	541,000
1983	4,844,000	2,815,000	1,523,000	606,000
1984	5,868,000	3,396,000	1,785,000	687,000
1985	6,416,000	3,495,000	2,129,000	792,000
1986	6,595,000	3,643,000	2,090,000	862,000
1987	7,496,000	4,231,000	2,271,000	994,000
1988	8,851,000	4,954,000	2,639,000	1,258,000
1989	9,674,000	5,307,000	2,949,000	1,418,000
1990	12,798,000	5,666,000	5,398,000	1,734,000
1991	15,231,000	6,725,000	6,384,000	2,122,000
1992	17,423,000	7,400,000	7,377,000	2,646,000
1993	18,591,000	8,069,000	7,832,000	2,690,000
1994	19,084,000	8,059,000	8,184,000	2,841,000
1995	22,651,000	9,298,000	9,184,000	4,169,000
1996	23,344,000	10,115,000	9,459,000	3,770,000
Total State and local[a]				
1980	NA	13,424,029	NA	6,515,689
1981	NA	14,918,094	NA	7,458,133
1982	31,572,916	16,656,184	6,380,785	8,535,947
1983	34,836,167	17,903,200	7,097,604	9,835,363
1984	38,155,690	19,330,766	7,678,180	11,146,744
1985	42,284,068	20,969,355	8,499,816	12,814,897
1986	47,069,805	22,712,993	9,395,446	14,961,366
1987	51,640,348	24,731,553	10,284,026	16,624,769
1988	56,766,542	26,303,824	11,331,563	19,131,155
1989	61,745,468	27,842,182	12,639,664	21,263,622
1990	69,214,959	30,579,479	14,075,826	24,559,654
1991	75,460,819	32,801,240	15,303,379	27,356,200
1992	80,247,852	34,623,531	16,573,888	29,050,433
1993	83,112,826	36,691,756	16,896,403	29,524,667
1994	88,844,564	38,686,536	17,880,706	32,227,322
1995	96,127,448	41,096,529	19,162,689	35,868,230
1996	110,673,698	46,077,896	22,898,569	41,697,233
State				
1980	9,256,443	2,194,349	2,051,108	4,547,667
1981	10,372,682	2,479,905	2,332,434	5,179,448
1982	11,601,780	2,833,370	2,748,364	6,020,046
1983	12,785,244	2,963,067	2,949,598	6,872,579
1984	14,212,842	3,173,297	3,271,076	7,768,469
1985	16,252,377	3,468,821	3,635,984	9,147,572
1986	18,555,723	3,749,413	4,004,720	10,801,590
1987	20,157,123	4,066,692	4,339,306	11,691,125
1988	22,836,919	4,531,184	4,885,843	13,419,892
1989	25,268,915	4,780,353	5,441,743	15,046,819
1990	28,345,066	5,163,475	5,970,895	17,210,696
1991	31,484,371	5,507,249	6,754,491	19,222,631
1992	33,755,092	5,592,791	7,722,882	20,439,419
1993	34,227,194	5,603,484	7,820,251	20,803,459
1994	37,161,391	6,000,330	8,026,326	23,134,735
1995	41,196,021	6,451,364	8,675,619	26,069,038
1996	47,703,657	7,847,614	10,501,884	29,354,159

TABLE 2.1

Justice system direct and intergovernmental expenditures by type of activity and level of government, fiscal years 1980–96
[continued]

(Dollar amounts in thousands)

Level of government and fiscal year	Total justice system	Police protection	Judicial and legal	Corrections
Local, total[a]				
1980	NA	$11,398,808	NA	$2,277,257
1981	NA	12,678,955	NA	2,636,064
1982	$20,967,562	14,172,313	$3,784,285	3,010,964
1983	23,186,040	15,276,352	4,361,362	3,548,326
1984	25,154,172	16,515,727	4,627,473	4,010,972
1985	27,461,643	17,847,016	5,090,344	4,524,283
1986	30,178,432	19,355,599	5,690,544	5,132,289
1987	33,265,315	21,089,053	6,229,510	5,946,752
1988	36,097,549	22,370,517	6,826,419	6,900,613
1989	38,825,015	23,671,582	7,682,188	7,471,245
1990	43,558,671	26,097,219	8,675,732	8,785,720
1991	47,075,424	28,017,151	9,418,374	9,639,899
1992	50,115,498	29,658,955	10,052,330	10,404,213
1993	52,561,979	31,733,159	10,282,702	10,546,118
1994	55,517,277	33,364,901	11,022,716	11,129,660
1995	58,932,933	35,364,493	11,673,851	11,894,589
1996	62,970,041	38,230,282	12,396,685	12,343,074
Counties[a]				
1980	NA	2,669,497	NA	1,777,763
1981	NA	3,091,038	NA	2,066,269
1982	8,635,936	3,486,823	2,805,312	2,343,801
1983	9,791,530	3,754,693	3,238,571	2,798,266
1984	10,616,787	4,051,074	3,401,793	3,163,920
1985	11,609,827	4,400,716	3,736,030	3,473,081
1986	13,031,109	4,801,572	4,209,092	4,020,445
1987	14,530,198	5,254,562	4,611,863	4,663,773
1988	15,883,574	5,574,280	5,047,003	5,262,291
1989	17,503,442	6,099,265	5,692,464	5,711,713
1990	19,644,273	6,669,385	6,416,194	6,558,694
1991	21,913,042	7,386,260	7,074,386	7,452,396
1992	23,820,019	8,012,151	7,521,219	8,286,649
1993	24,624,542	8,520,472	7,697,938	8,406,132
1994	26,070,804	8,955,664	8,275,007	8,840,133
1995	27,917,010	9,499,807	8,804,229	9,612,974
1996	29,912,681	10,577,078	9,398,308	9,937,295
Municipalities[a]				
1980	NA	8,791,989	NA	527,060
1981	NA	9,678,462	NA	602,148
1982	12,455,487	10,765,207	981,963	708,317
1983	13,550,117	11,630,815	1,130,261	789,041
1984	14,696,313	12,565,350	1,235,073	895,890
1985	16,011,251	13,549,507	1,367,982	1,093,762
1986	17,346,101	14,685,842	1,495,968	1,164,291
1987	18,973,049	16,005,162	1,626,223	1,341,664
1988	20,449,324	16,964,757	1,788,158	1,696,409
1989	21,579,228	17,756,525	2,003,083	1,819,620
1990	24,244,122	19,674,855	2,274,164	2,295,103
1991	25,599,404	20,972,085	2,358,669	2,268,650
1992	26,770,919	22,034,381	2,546,171	2,190,367
1993	28,321,497	23,506,869	2,595,607	2,219,021
1994	29,908,762	24,766,007	2,765,164	2,377,591
1995	31,580,565	26,328,895	2,886,803	2,364,867
1996	34,292,694	28,681,330	3,037,223	2,574,141

Note: Duplicative transactions between levels of government are excluded from the total for all governments, the state and local total. Such intergovernmental expenditure consists of payments from one government to another and eventually will show up as a direct expenditure of a recipient government. The state government total for 1980 and 1981 includes a residual "other" category not displayed separately. Detail may not add to total because of rounding.

[a] Data for local governments are estimates subject to sampling variation.

SOURCE: "Table 1.2: Justice system direct and intergovernmental expenditures," in Sourcebook of Criminal Justice Statistics 1999, Kathleen Maguire and Ann L. Pastore, eds., Bureau of Justice Statistics, Washington, D.C., 2000

TABLE 2.2

Justice system direct and intergovernmental expenditures by level of government and type of activity, fiscal year 1996

Activity	Dollar amounts (in thousands)				Percent distribution		
	Total all governments	Federal Government	State governments	Local governments[a]	Federal	State	Local[a]
Total justice system[b]	$123,960,175	$27,110,000	$47,703,657	$62,970,041	X	X	X
Direct expenditure	123,960,175	21,246,000	39,903,049	62,811,126	17.1%	32.2%	50.7%
Intergovernmental expenditure	X	5,864,000	7,800,608	158,915	X	X	X
Police protection[b]	53,007,425	10,115,000	7,847,614	38,230,282	X	X	X
Direct expenditure	53,007,425	8,281,000	6,499,224	38,227,201	15.6	12.3	72.1
Intergovernmental expenditure	X	1,834,000	1,348,390	3,081	X	X	X
Judicial and legal[b]	29,923,907	13,225,000	10,501,884	12,396,685	X	X	X
Direct expenditure	29,923,907	9,459,000	8,109,714	12,355,193	31.6	27.1	41.3
Intergovernmental expenditure	X	3,766,000	2,392,170	41,492	X	X	X
Corrections[b]	41,028,843	3,770,000	29,354,159	12,343,074	X	X	X
Direct expenditure	41,028,843	3,506,000	25,294,111	12,228,732	8.5	61.6	29.8
Intergovernmental expenditure	X	264,000	4,060,048	114,342	X	X	X

[a] Data for local governments are estimates subject to sampling variation.

[b] The total category for each criminal justice activity, and for the total justice system, excludes duplicative intergovernmental expenditure amounts. This was done to avoid the artificial inflation that would result if an intergovernmental expenditure of a government were tabulated and then counted again when the recipient government(s) expended that amount. The intergovernmental expenditure categories are not totaled for this reason.

SOURCE: "Table 1.3: Justice system direct and intergovernmental expenditures," in *Sourcebook of Criminal Justice Statistics 1999*, Kathleen Maguire and Ann L. Pastore, eds., Bureau of Justice Statistics, Washington, D.C., 2000

STATE CORRECTIONS

In fiscal 1999, according to the National Association of State Budget Officers (1999 State Expenditure Report, Washington, D.C., 2000), state governments spent an estimated 3.7 percent of their funds on corrections. (See Figure 2.3.) That is nearly the same proportion of total outlays spent in 1997 (3.8 percent). However, as seen in actual dollars, the amount states spent on corrections rose continuously from 1987 to 1999. (See Figure 2.4.)

State Budget Actions,1999, published by the National Conference of State Legislatures, Denver, Colorado, reported that state general fund appropriations for corrections in fiscal year 2000 increased by 5 percent over fiscal year 1999. When general funds revenues are combined with funds earmarked specifically for corrections, that increase rises to 5.2 percent. (See Table 2.4.) The highest rate of growth in combined funds for corrections was reported by North Dakota, at 46.5 percent above the 1999 rate. The lowest rate of growth was reported by Rhode Island where the level of spending for corrections fell by 7.2 percent from 1999.

A BREAKDOWN OF STATE COSTS

According to figures released by the BJS in 1999, states spent about $22 billion on prisons in fiscal year 1996. (See Figure 2.5.) Operating expenses consumed about $20.7 billion of those dollars, or 94 percent. These expenses included prison employee salaries, wages, and benefits. Capital expenditures such as construction, equipment, and land acquisition accounted for the remaining $1.3 billion. The total outlay amounted to an annual oper-

TABLE 2.3

Justice system per capita expenditures, 1980–96

Fiscal year	July 1 population (in thousands)[a]	Total justice system	Police protection	Judicial and legal	Corrections
1980	227,225	NA	$66.73	NA	$30.37
1981	229,466	NA	73.31	NA	34.29
1982	231,664	$154.72	82.11	$33.54	39.06
1983	233,792	169.72	88.32	36.87	44.53
1984	235,825	186.34	96.20	40.13	50.01
1985	237,924	204.11	102.55	44.67	56.89
1986	240,133	222.79	109.34	47.83	65.63
1987	242,289	242.98	118.73	51.82	72.43
1988	244,499	266.79	126.63	57.14	83.02
1989	246,819	287.46	132.87	63.16	91.43
1990	249,402	318.50	144.04	69.59	104.87
1991	252,131	347.31	154.57	76.54	116.20
1992	255,028	367.71	162.05	82.30	123.36
1993	257,783	378.39	170.83	83.63	123.93
1994	260,341	397.44	176.71	86.82	133.92
1995	262,755	429.56	185.13	93.14	151.29
1996	264,741	454.01	200.22	98.81	154.98

[a] Population figures are for July 1 of each year from the U.S. Bureau of the Census, Current Population Reports. They are consistent with the 1980 and 1990 decennial enumerations. They do not include adjustments for census coverage errors. They may differ from population data taken from previous *Justice Expenditure and Employment Extracts* reports because those tables were developed when only preliminary estimates were available.

SOURCE: Kathleen Maguire and Ann L. Pastore, eds., "Table 1.6: Justice system per capita expenditures." in *Sourcebook of Criminal Justice Statistics 1999*, Bureau of Justice Statistics, Washington, D.C., 2000

ating expenditure of about $20,100 per state inmate. The five highest states in terms of annual costs per inmate were Minnesota ($37,800), Rhode Island ($35,700), Maine ($33,700), Alaska ($32,400), and Utah ($32,400). The five lowest states measured by cost per inmate were

FIGURE 2.1

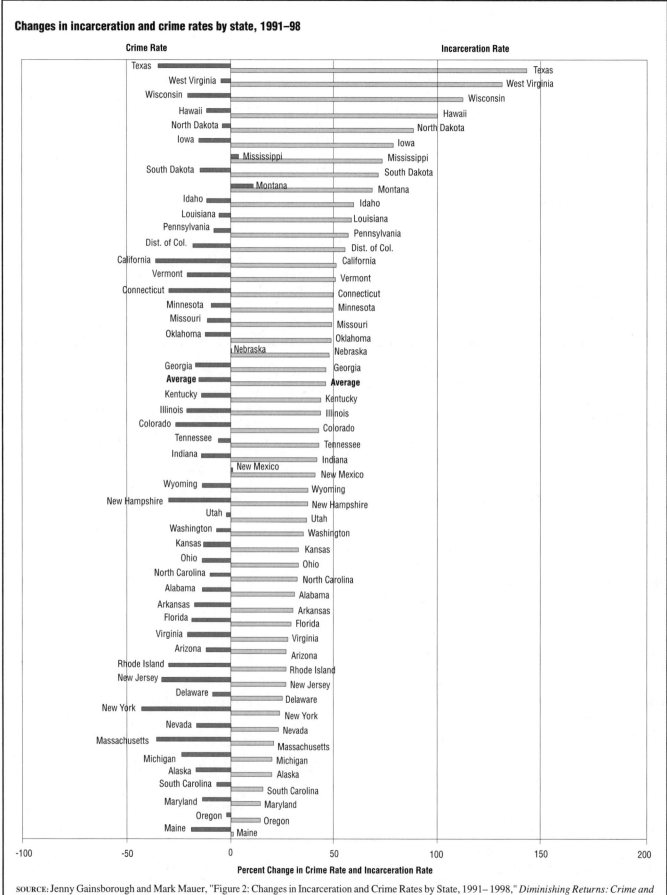

Changes in incarceration and crime rates by state, 1991–98

SOURCE: Jenny Gainsborough and Mark Mauer, "Figure 2: Changes in Incarceration and Crime Rates by State, 1991–1998," *Diminishing Returns: Crime and Incarceration in the 1990s*, The Sentencing Project, Washington, D.C., 2000

FIGURE 2.2

Federal justice expenditures, 1991–2001

Dollars in billions

Note: Data includes discretionary expenditures only.

SOURCE: *The Budget for Fiscal Year 2001*, Executive Office of the President, Washington, DC, 2000

FIGURE 2.3

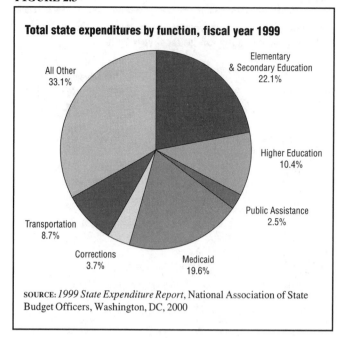

Total state expenditures by function, fiscal year 1999

SOURCE: *1999 State Expenditure Report*, National Association of State Budget Officers, Washington, DC, 2000

FIGURE 2.4

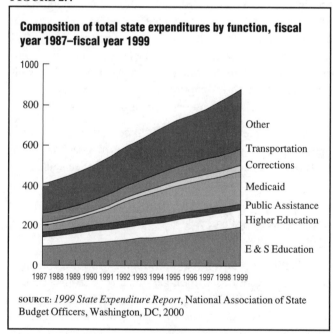

Composition of total state expenditures by function, fiscal year 1987–fiscal year 1999

SOURCE: *1999 State Expenditure Report*, National Association of State Budget Officers, Washington, DC, 2000

FIGURE 2.5

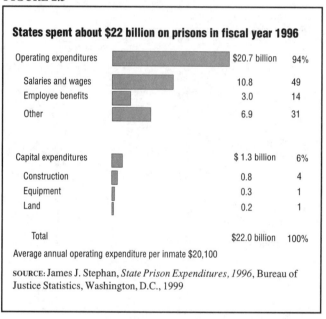

States spent about $22 billion on prisons in fiscal year 1996

Operating expenditures	$20.7 billion	94%
Salaries and wages	10.8	49
Employee benefits	3.0	14
Other	6.9	31
Capital expenditures	$ 1.3 billion	6%
Construction	0.8	4
Equipment	0.3	1
Land	0.2	1
Total	$22.0 billion	100%

Average annual operating expenditure per inmate $20,100

SOURCE: James J. Stephan, *State Prison Expenditures, 1996*, Bureau of Justice Statistics, Washington, D.C., 1999

Alabama ($8,000), Oklahoma ($10,600), Mississippi ($11,200), Texas ($12,200), and Missouri ($12,800).

Inmate medical care accounted for the highest proportion of per-inmate dollars, at $6.54 per inmate, for a total of nearly $2.5 billion nationwide. (See Table 2.5.) Food service was $2.96 per inmate, followed by utilities (water, heating, lighting) at $1.81 per inmate, and transportation costs at 52 cents per inmate. Each year a higher number of inmate health dollars is spent on inmates who test positive for human immunodeficiency virus (HIV). This number includes those who contract the virus while

in prison and inmates who were HIV-positive at the time of their incarceration, often due to prior drug use. The Correctional HIV Consortium in San Francisco, California, reports that, in 1998, the estimated annual cost of providing treatment for an HIV-positive state prison inmate was $80,396. A breakdown of these per-inmate costs includes: $38,000 for special housing and related security; $22,800 for medications; $4,750 for hospital transportation and related security; $2,800 for radiology and other tests; and $2,160 for special dietary and nutritional needs. In-patient hospital stays for HIV-positive state prison inmates averaged $1,400 annually in 1998, hazardous waste disposal and special case management each

TABLE 2.4

Percentage change in appropriations for corrections by region and state, fiscal year 1999 to fiscal year 2000

Region/State	General Fund Only	All Appropriated Funds (General fund and Earmarked)
New England	**7.7**	**8.0**
Connecticut	10.6	10.6
Maine	4.8	4.8
Massachusetts	7.7	8.4
New Hampshire	20.2	20.2
Rhode Island	-6.8	-7.2
Vermont	9.2	9.0
Middle Atlantic	**3.8**	**4.0**
Delaware	16.6	16.6
Maryland	5.4	5.4
New Jersey	4.1	5.3
New York	2.2	2.2
Pennsylvania	3.9	3.9
Great Lakes	**8.6**	**8.9**
Illinois	7.9	9.3
Indiana	2.5	2.5
Michigan	8.6	8.6
Ohio	8.9	8.9
Wisconsin	14.1	14.1
Plains	**5.1**	**5.1**
Iowa	8.6	8.6
Kansas	4.2	4.2
Minnesota	7.1	7.1
Missouri	0.7	0.7
Nebraska	8.8	8.8
North Dakota	46.5	46.5
South Dakota	2.3	2.3
Southeast	**4.0**	**4.4**
Alabama	-6.3	-6.3
Arkansas	7.8	7.8
Florida	4.1	4.1
Georgia	7.2	7.2
Kentucky	7.4	7.4
Louisiana	7.7	7.7
Mississippi	15.8	15.8
North Carolina	2.2	2.2
South Carolina	-1.3	-1.3
Tennessee	1.7	1.7
Virginia	0.8	4.8
West Virginia	6.8	6.8
Southwest	**3.4**	**3.0**
Arizona	9.2	6.9
New Mexico	3.7	3.7
Oklahoma	4.9	4.9
Texas	1.5	1.5
Rocky Mountain	**7.8**	**7.8**
Colorado	8.5	8.5
Idaho	1.6	1.6
Montana	9.7	9.7
Utah	8.5	8.5
Wyoming	0.0	0.0
Far West	**4.0**	**4.1**
Alaska	4.1	4.9
California	2.5	2.5
Hawaii	6.1	11.8
Nevada	6.2	6.2
Oregon	22.2	22.2
Washington	6.0	5.9
Other Jurisdictions		
District of Columbia	-1.1	-1.1
Puerto Rico	—Did not report—	
Total	**5.0%**	**5.2%**

SOURCE: "State Budget Actions, 1999," National Conference of State Legislatures, Denver, CO, 1998

TABLE 2.5

State prison expenditures, fiscal year 1996

Selected items	Expenditures in 1,000's*	Daily costs per inmate
Inmate medical care	$2,456,300	$6.54
Inmate programs	1,231,100	$3.28
Food service	1,112,900	$2.96
Utilities	682,028	$1.81
Transportation/travel	197,000	$0.52

*National totals are based on estimates for all States.

SOURCE: James J. Stephan, "State prison expenditures," in *State Prison Expenditures, 1996*, Bureau of Justice Statistics, Washington, D.C., 1999

RISING STATE COSTS

Measured in 1996 constant dollars, which takes into account inflation, each year from 1985 and 1996 states increased their total spending for corrections an average of 7.2 percent and their spending for prisons alone by 7.3 percent. (See Figure 2.6.) During that time the average per capita cost for total state corrections nearly doubled, from $53 in 1985 to $103 in 1996. (See Table 2.6.) The greatest increase in total per capita costs during that period was in inmate health care, which rose from $67 per person in 1985 to $123 in 1996. This was an increase of 6.6 percent annually, second only to the total per capita costs for public welfare. Next to natural resources the category that saw the lowest annual rise was inmate education, at 3.6 percent.

When separated out from total correctional costs the operating costs of state prisons have risen steadily—from $40 per U.S. resident in 1985 to $79 in 1996. (See Table 2.7.)

LOCAL JAIL EXPENDITURES FOR COUNTIES AND MUNICIPALITIES

As reported in *Sourcebook of Criminal Justice Statistics, 1999* (Bureau of Justice Statistics, 2000), the total costs for corrections at the local level rose from $2.3 billion in 1980 to $12.3 billion in 1996, a more than five-fold increase. This increase was greater than the increases in local spending on police protection and judicial/legal services. Considering that local governments bear most of the costs for police protection and judicial/legal services, the increase in corrections spending is significant. By comparison local costs for police protection rose during the same period from $11.4 billion to $38.2 billion, or about 350 percent, while local judicial and legal costs rose from $3.8 billion to 12.4 billion, a roughly three-fold increase. According to *The 2000 Corrections Yearbook: Jails* (Criminal Justice Institute, Inc., Middletown, Conn.), across the United States a total of 10 new jails facilities were opened in 1999, providing some 6,107 new jail beds at a cost of $291 million. Renovation of existing facilities added 3,056 jail beds at a total cost of $55 million.

accounted for $1,200, and the costs of medical laboratory fees and education about HIV, tuberculosis, and hepatitis, were more than $800 per inmate.

FIGURE 2.6

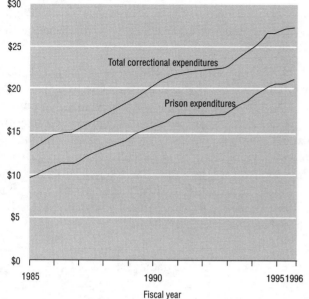

State expenditures for corrections and for prisons, fiscal years 1985–96

State expenditures in billions (1996 constant dollars)

Total correctional expenditures

Prison expenditures

Fiscal year

SOURCE: James J. Stephan, "Each year between 1985 and 1996 States increased their spending for all corrections an average 7.2% and for prisons alone an average 7.3%," in *State Prison Expenditures, 1996*, Bureau of Justice Statistics, Washington, D.C., 1999

TABLE 2.6

Annual per capita costs for selected state expenditures, 1985–96

Fiscal year	Total corrections	Prisons	Health	Education	Public welfare	Natural resources
1985	$53	$40	$67	$749	$392	$39
1990	81	62	93	861	490	46
1995	101	78	120	970	757	49
1996	103	79	123	994	738	49
Average annual percent change 1985-96	7.2%	7.3%	6.6%	3.6%	7.0%	2.9%

Note: Figures given in 1996 constant dollars.

SOURCE: James J. Stephan, "Annual per capita costs (in 1996 constant dollars) for selected State expenditures, 1985–96," in *State Prison Expenditures, 1996*, Bureau of Justice Statistics, Washington, D.C., 1999

TABLE 2.7

Expenditures for total state corrections and for state prisons, 1985–96

	Annual expenditures			
	Total State corrections		State prisons	
Fiscal Year	Total (in 1,000's)	Cost per U.S. resident	Total (in 1,000's)	Cost per U.S. resident
1985	$12,743,275	$53	$9,624,142	$40
1986	14,584,557	60	10,958,736	45
1987*	15,208,376	63	11,471,160	47
1988	16,792,796	68	13,004,578	53
1989	18,330,974	74	14,153,961	57
1990	20,099,048	81	15,563,419	62
1991	21,720,883	86	16,948,133	67
1992*	22,228,332	87	16,989,156	67
1993	22,425,272	87	17,210,562	67
1994	24,376,972	94	18,694,604	72
1995	26,608,530	101	20,511,245	78
1996	27,324,135	103	20,893,235	79

Note: Figures given in 1996 constant dollars. Correctional expenditures may be underreported. Detailed interviews of State budget officials by the Bureau of the Census for this report produced a revised estimate of $22 billion for FY 1996, 5.4% higher than the $20.9 billion reported in the 1996 Survey of Government Finances. *The Bureau of the Census conducted full censuses of State and local finances in 1987 and 1992.

SOURCE: James J. Stephan, "Appendix table. Surveys of government finances, 1985–96: Expenditures for total State corrections and for State prisons in 1996 constant dollars," in *State Prison Expenditures, 1996*, Bureau of Justice Statistics, Washington, D.C., 1999

Average Operating Costs Per Inmate

In fiscal year 1999 the overall cost per prisoner per day was $56.72, up from $54.39 in 1998 and $46.97 in 1994, the lowest annual cost per inmate since 1991. Costs per inmate per day vary from location to location. New York City jails had the highest cost per inmate per day at $228.00, due to the high cost of living there. Webb County, Texas, had the lowest cost, at $22 per inmate per day, as reported in *The 2000 Corrections Yearbook*.

THE HIDDEN COSTS OF CORRECTIONS

In *Seeking Justice* (New York, 1997), The Edna McConnell Clark Foundation, an organization seeking a "more rational, humane, and effective criminal justice system," asserted that many costs of operating and constructing prisons are not revealed by looking at budgets. For example, servicing the debt on bonds sold to construct prisons raises the price of construction, an expense taxpayers are often unaware of. According to the foundation the cost of building one maximum security bed in New York State is about $100,000. However, with interest on the debt, the price rises to about $300,000.

Some prison expenses are paid by other agencies such as mental health and education departments. These costs are not part of the corrections budgets but are part of the cost of corrections.

The National Conference of State Legislatures estimated that, with its "no parole" provision, Virginia will double its prison population and need $2 billion or more by the year 2010 to cover building costs. Researchers from the RAND Corporation, a California think tank, concluded that: "to support implementation of the law, total spending for higher education and other government services would have to fall by more than 40 percent over the eight years following implementation." In addition, imprisonment reduces the number of taxpayers and wage earners for society and creates more families on public support.

COST CONTAINMENT

With the public fearing crime and favoring a tough-on-criminals approach, costs for corrections will likely increase. However, as taxpayers have not shown themselves willing to pay additional taxes, cuts will either have to be made elsewhere, or less costly alternative ways to punish offenders will have to be found. Prisons are finding ways to cut costs by having more work programs, limiting inmate services, and charging prisoners for services. More and more jails and prisons are charging for medical care and restricting activities such as television viewing and weight training.

Some states are either considering or have signed into law bans on tennis and basketball courts. A Mississippi law allows the prisons to "hot-bunk," a system of rotating inmates through shifts of labor, sleep, and training. Some Florida county jails have removed all television sets. Although many of these restrictions were implemented to cut costs, most were designed to toughen life for the convicted and, supposedly, deter others from committing crimes.

Opponents of these restrictions argue that they will not deter anyone and will lead to strained conditions that could cause riots. However, many of the prisons where amenities were banned did not have the luxuries in the first place. For example, Mississippi banned individual air conditioners although no prisoner had one. In Louisiana, inmates could not participate in martial arts classes, even though none were offered.

Prisoners Pay a Share

Many states are looking to the prisoners to pay some of the costs. By 1995 more than 24 states had passed laws making inmates pay for some of their imprisonment. In Arizona inmates pay a utility fee for televisions or any major electrical appliance. In Texas deductions for certain services are made from inmates' wages from work outside of the prison.

In 1998 Governor Jane Hull of Arizona signed a jail-food bill into law. Arizona expects to save its taxpayers up to $2.5 million per year under the new law that permits counties to charge jail inmates $1 per day to offset the cost of feeding them. Juveniles are exempt from the law unless they are being tried in adult court. Any prisoner who cannot afford the $1 per day fee will still be fed, but any money received from friends or relatives must go to pay for that inmate's meals before he or she is able to buy extras such as snacks and toiletries.

In Little Rock, Arkansas, prisoners who ruin their jail laundry are billed for the damages, and in Cedar Rapids, Iowa, inmates who fail to pay their room and board will have their post-release earnings garnished.

Opponents of the plans to make prisoners pay often cite the fact that billing inmates can burden already low-income families, and that it is unfair that a prisoner later found innocent should be charged. However, the idea has spread with support from legislators. Court challenges to the plans have failed, and jailhouse collections have been touted as saving taxpayers' money.

CHAPTER 3
JAILS

Jail managers will be dealing with more inmates, and more of them will be long-term state inmates staying on in our jails for years. We need to plan ahead. We need to be mindful of the security realities involved in holding longer-term inmates. And finally, we need to make sure that the inmates who become motivated to change their behavior will have access to the services needed to guide those changes in socially appropriate ways.

—Richard A. Van Den Heuvel, "When Jails Become Prisons,"
American Jails, November/December, 1994

Although many people use the words "jails" and "prisons" interchangeably, they are different types of facilities. Jails are locally operated correctional facilities. Inmates sentenced to jail usually have received a sentence of a year or less. The purpose of jails is to:

• Receive individuals pending arraignment (brought into court to hear the charges) and hold them until their trials, conviction, or sentencing

• Readmit probation, parole, and bail-bond violators and absconders (those who run away or "skip bail")

• Temporarily detain juveniles pending transfer to juvenile authorities

• Hold mentally ill offenders pending their movement to appropriate health facilities

• Hold individuals for the military, for protective custody, for contempt, and for the courts as witnesses

• Release convicted inmates to the community upon completion of sentence

• Transfer inmates to federal, state, or other authorities

• Sometimes operate community-based programs with electronic monitoring or other types of supervision

NUMBER OF JAIL INMATES

On June 30, 2000, the nation's jails held 621,149 inmates, a growth rate of 2.5 percent from the year before

TABLE 3.1

Number of persons held in State or Federal prisons or in local jails, 1990–2000

Year	Total inmates in custody	Prisoners in custody Federal	State	Inmates held in local jails	Incarceration rate[a]
1990	1,148,702	58,838	684,544	405,320	458
1991	1,219,014	63,930	728,605	426,479	481
1992	1,295,150	72,071	778,495	444,584	505
1993	1,369,185	80,815	828,566	459,804	528
1994	1,476,621	85,500	904,647	486,474	564
1995	1,585,586	89,538	989,004	507,044	601
1996	1,646,020	95,088	1,032,440	518,492	618
1997	1,743,643	101,755	1,074,809	567,079	648
1998	1,816,931	110,793	1,113,676	592,462	669
1999[b]					
June 30	1,875,199	117,995	1,151,261	605,943	687
December 31	—	125,682	1,158,220	—	
2000					
June 30	1,931,859	131,496	1,179,214	621,149	702
Percent change, 6/30/99 - 6/30/00	3.0%	11.4%	2.4%	2.5%	
Annual average increase, 12/31/90 - 6/30/00	5.6%	8.8%	5.9%	4.6%	

Note: Jail counts are for midyear (June 30). Counts for 1994-2000 exclude persons who were supervised outside of a jail facility. State and Federal prisoner counts for 1990-98 are for December 31.
—Not available.
[a] Total number of persons in custody per 100,000 residents in each reference year.
[b] In 1999, 15 States expanded their reporting criteria to include inmates held in privately operated correctional facilities. For comparisons with previous years, the State count 1,136,582 and the total count 1,860,520 should be used for June 30, 1999.

SOURCE: Allen J. Beck, Ph.D., and Jennifer C. Karberg, *Prison and Jail Inmates at Midyear 2000*, Bureau of Justice Statistics, Washington, DC, 2001

as reported in *Prison and Jail Inmates at Midyear 2000* (Allen J. Beck, Ph.D. and Jennifer C. Karberg, Bureau of Justice Statistics Bulletin, March 2001). (See Table 3.1.) The increase was below the annual average of 4.6 percent since midyear 1990.

The jail inmate population rose from 163 per 100,000 U.S. residents on July 1, 1990, to 226 per 100,000 U.S.

TABLE 3.2

Jail incarceration rate, 1990 and 1995–2000

Year	Jail incarceration rate*
2000	226
1999	222
1998	219
1997	212
1996	196
1995	193
1990	163

*Number of jail inmates per 100,000
U.S. residents on July 1 of each year.

SOURCE: Allen J. Beck, Ph.D., and Jennifer C. Karberg, *Prison and Jail Inmates at Midyear 2000*, Bureau of Justice Statistics, Washington, DC, 2001

TABLE 3.3

Average daily population and the number of men, women, and juveniles in local jails, midyear 1990, 1995, and 1999–2000

	1990	1995	1999	2000
Average daily population[a]	**408,075**	**509,828**	**607,978**	**618,319**
Number of inmates, June 30[b]	**405,320**	**507,044**	**605,943**	**621,149**
Adults	403,019	499,300	596,485	613,534
Male	365,821	448,000	528,998	543,120
Female	37,198	51,300	67,487	70,414
Juveniles[c]	2,301	7,800	9,458	7,615
Held as adults[d]	—	5,900	8,598	6,126
Held as juveniles	2,301	1,800	860	1,489

Note: Data are for June 30 in 1995 and 1999-2000 and for June 29, 1990. Detailed data for 1995 were estimated and rounded to the nearest 100.
—Not available.
[a] The average daily population is the sum of the number of inmates in a jail each day for a year, divided by the total number of days in the year.
[b] Inmate counts for 1990 include an unknown number of persons who were under jail supervision but not confined.
[c] Juveniles are persons defined by State statute as being under a certain age, usually 18, and subject initially to juvenile court authority even if tried as adults in criminal court.
In 1994 the definition was changed to include all persons under age 18.
[d] Includes juveniles who were tried or awaiting trial as adults.

SOURCE: Allen J. Beck, Ph.D., and Jennifer C. Karberg, *Prison and Jail Inmates at Midyear 2000*, Bureau of Justice Statistics, Washington, DC, 2001

residents on July 1, 2000. (See Table 3.2.) The average daily jail population for the year ending June 30, 2000, was 618,319, up from 607,978 in 1999 and from 408,075 at midyear 1990. (See Table 3.3.) The number of female inmates rose by 4.3 percent during the 12-month period ending June 30, 2000, while the percent of male inmates rose by 2.7 percent. Since 1990 the average adult female jail population has grown at an annual rate of 6.6 percent compared to 4 percent for the average adult male population. Despite the increase of female jail inmates since 1990, males still comprise the vast majority of jail inmates at a rate of 1 in every 181 adult men compared to the rate of female inmates of 1 in 1,509 adult women.

REASONS FOR THE GROWING INMATE POPULATION

An Increasing Number of Arrests

Underlying the growth in the local jail population has been the rise in the number of arrests for all criminal infractions except traffic violations. Arrests grew from 12.5 million in 1986 to 14.4 million in 1999. However, despite the trend of rising arrest rates, arrests for 1999 were down from 15.3 million in 1997. The most arrests in 1999 were for drug abuse violations (1.6 million), followed by 1.5 million arrests for driving under the influence. An additional offense, drunkenness (673,400 arrests) could also be viewed, along with drug abuse and driving under the influence, within the more general category of substance abuse. (See Table 3.4.)

Jail Inmates Held for State/Federal Authorities

The nation's jail population also grew as a result of the overcrowding at state and federal prisons. According to *The 2000 Corrections Yearbook: Jails,* on any given day in jails nationwide during 1999, on average, 38 inmates were awaiting transfer to state facilities due to overcrowding in state prisons. During 1999, on average, another 80 inmates were housed in jail by contract arrangement with state or federal correctional agencies. Among the largest jail systems in 1999, New York City averaged 696 inmates awaiting transfer to state prisons, and another 677 inmates housed by arrangement with state or federal agencies. New York City was followed by Harris, Texas, with an average of 648 inmates awaiting transfer to state prisons. Maricopa, Arizona (185), Los Angeles (131) and Hillsborough, Florida (118) represented the next three jails with the largest number of inmates waiting for transfers.

Sentencing Status and Length of Confinement

According to the Bureau of Justice Statistics (BJS) on June 30, 2000, an estimated 56 percent of adult jail inmates in the United States were awaiting some type of court action on their charge. Overall, some 270,000 inmates were serving a jail sentence, awaiting sentencing by a court, or were serving time for a probation or parole violation.

As of January 1, 2000, 57.4 percent of inmates were awaiting trial, while 36.4 percent were convicted, sentenced, and awaiting placement in state corrections facilities. Another 5.9 percent were convicted and awaiting sentencing, according to *The 2000 Corrections Yearbook: Jails*. In 1999 the average length of stay of convicted and sentenced jail inmates was 91.7 days, down from 105 days in 1998 and a high of 144 days in 1994. The overall average length of confinement for jail inmates regardless

TABLE 3.4

Estimated arrests, 1999[1]

Total[2,3]	14,355,600	Embezzlement	17,300
		Stolen property; buying, receiving, possessing	124,100
Murder and nonnegligent manslaughter	14,920	Vandalism	285,000
Forcible rape	29,220	Weapons; carrying, possessing, etc.	175,500
Robbery	109,840	Prostitution and commercialized vice	92,200
Aggravated assault	490,790	Sex offenses (except forcible rape and prostitution)	93,800
Burglary	301,500	Drug abuse violations	1,557,100
Larceny-theft	1,213,300	Gambling	10,400
Motor vehicle theft	144,200	Offenses against the family and children	153,500
Arson	17,100	Driving under the influence	1,549,500
		Liquor laws	683,600
Violent crime[4]	644,770	Drunkenness	673,400
Property crime[5]	1,676,100	Disorderly conduct	655,600
Crime Index total[6]	2,320,900	Vagrancy	30,800
		All other offenses	3,809,000
Other assaults	1,322,100	Suspicion	8,000
Forgery and counterfeiting	109,300	Curfew and loitering law violations	170,000
Fraud	371,800	Runaways	150,700

[1] Arrest totals are based on all reporting agencies and estimates for unreported areas.
[2] Does not include suspicion.
[3] Because of rounding, figures may not add to total.
[4] Violent crimes are offenses of murder, forcible rape, robbery, and aggravated assault.
[5] Property crimes are offenses of burglary, larceny-theft, motor vehicle theft, and arson.
[6] Includes arson.

SOURCE: *Crime in the United States, 1999,* Federal Bureau of Investigation, Washington, DC, 2000

TABLE 3.5

Rated capacity of local jails and percent of capacity occupied, 1990 and 1995–2000

Year	Rated capacity[a]	Amount of capacity added[b]	Percent of capacity occupied[c]
2000	677,787	25,466	92%
1999	652,321	39,541	93
1998	612,780	26,216	97
1997	586,564	23,593	97
1996	562,971	17,208	92
1995	545,763	41,439	93
1990	389,171		104
Average annual increase			
1990-2000	5.7%	28,862	

Note: Capacity data for 1995-98 and 2000 are survey estimates subject to sampling error.
[a] Rated capacity is the number of beds or inmates assigned by a rating official to facilities within each jurisdiction.
[b] The number of beds added during the 12 months before June 30 of each year.
[c] The number of inmates divided by the rated capacity times 100.

SOURCE: Allen J. Beck, Ph.D., and Jennifer C. Karberg, *Prison and Jail Inmates at Midyear 2000,* Bureau of Justice Statistics, Washington, DC, 2001

TABLE 3.6

Jail occupancy as a percent of capacity

Size of jurisdiction*	Percent of capacity occupied
Total	92%
Fewer than 50 inmates	68
50-99	88
100-249	100
250-499	101
500-999	99
1,000 or more	103

*Based on the average daily population in the year ending June 30, 2000.

SOURCE: Allen J. Beck, Ph.D., and Jennifer C. Karberg, *Prison and Jail Inmates at Midyear 2000,* Bureau of Justice Statistics, Washington, DC, 2001

of their status was 47.9 days in 1999, down from 50 days in 1998 and a high of 86 days in 1994.

LARGEST JAIL JURISDICTIONS

As of June 30, 2000, the country's 50 largest jail jurisdictions held one-third of all jail inmates, accounting for a total jail population of 206,914. This was down from 208,204 jail inmates in 1999 and 211,012 in 1998.

Twenty-one states had at least one jail system that ranked in the top 50 for average daily population. States with more than one such jail system were California (11), Florida (8), Texas (6), Georgia (3), Ohio (3), Pennsylvania (2), Tennessee (2), and New Jersey (2). Some 33,300 jail inmates—or 16.1 percent of the national total—were held in Los Angeles County and New York City.

Between July 1, 1999, and June 30, 2000, the number of jail inmates decreased in 19 of the 50 largest jail systems in the United States. Jail systems with the largest decreases in inmate populations were Fulton County, Ga., down 15.1 percent; San Francisco and Santa Clara County, Calif., each down 14.6 percent; New York City, down

TABLE 3.7

TABLE 3.8

Gender, race, and Hispanic origin of local jail inmates, midyear 1990, 1995, and 1999–2000

	Percent of jail inmates			
Characteristic	1990	1995	1999	2000
Total	100%	100%	100%	100%
Gender				
Male	90.8%	89.8%	88.8%	88.6%
Female	9.2	10.2	11.2	11.4
Race/Hispanic origin				
White, non-Hispanic	41.8%	40.1%	41.3%	41.9%
Black, non-Hispanic	42.5	43.5	41.5	42.3
Hispanic	14.3	14.7	15.5	15.1
Other*	1.3	1.7	1.7	1.6

Note: Detail may not add to total because of rounding.
Conviction status in 1999 includes all inmates.
*Includes American Indians, Alaska Natives, Asians, and Pacific Islanders.

SOURCE: Allen J. Beck, Ph.D., and Jennifer C. Karberg, *Prison and Jail Inmates at Midyear 2000*, Bureau of Justice Statistics, Washington, DC, 2001

Racial characteristics of jail inmates

	Estimated count	Rate per 100,000 residents in each group
Total	621,149	226
White[a]	260,500	132
Black[a]	256,300	736
Hispanic	94,100	280
Asian[b]	10,200	80

Note: Inmate counts were estimated and rounded to the nearest 100.
[a] Non-Hispanic only.
[b] Includes American Indians, Alaskan Natives, Native Hawaiians, and other Pacific Islanders.

SOURCE: Allen J. Beck, Ph.D., and Jennifer C. Karberg, *Prison and Jail Inmates at Midyear 2000*, Bureau of Justice Statistics, Washington, DC, 2001

12.1 percent; and Shelby County, Tenn., down by 10.9 percent. Other jail systems among the 50 largest in the United States showed increases in their jail populations. These included San Bernardino County, Calif., up 17.4 percent; Travis County, Tex., up 15.9 percent; Oklahoma County, Okla., up 13.5 percent; De Kalb County, Ga., up 12.3; and Broward County, Fla., up 11.5 percent.

RATED CAPACITY

Rated capacity is the maximum number of beds or inmates allocated by state or local rating officials to each jail facility. In the year ending June 30, 2000, more beds than inmates were added to U.S. jails, bringing the rated capacity of local jails nationwide to an estimated 677,787, up by 25,466 from the 12 months ending June 30, 1999. (See Table 3.5.) As reported by the BJS, "The growth in jail capacity during the 12-month period ending on June 30, 2000, was less than the average growth of 28,862 beds every 12 months since 1990, and was considerably less than the growth of jail capacity in 1999 (39,541)." As of the year ending June 30, 2000, 92 percent of the jail capacity was occupied. In other words jails were operating at 8 percent below capacity. By comparison, during the same 12-month period, state prisons were operating from 1–17 percent above capacity, and federal prisons were 32 percent above capacity. Since 1990, when jails were operating at 4 percent above capacity, there has been a decrease of 12 percentage points in the ratio of inmates housed in jail facilities to total capacity.

At midyear 2000 jail systems with the largest average daily populations also reported the highest occupancy rates. (See Table 3.6.) The occupancy rate was 103 percent in jail systems with an average daily population of

1,000 or more inmates compared to 68 percent in jail systems with less than 50 inmates.

JAIL INMATE CHARACTERISTICS

As of June 30, 2000, local jails held approximately 1 out of every 181 adult men in the United States, and 1 in 1,509 females. Since 1990 about 9 of 10 prisoners have been male. (See Table 3.7.) However, the overall percentage of male inmates has been on a slight decline and the proportion of female inmates has risen from 9.2 percent in 1990 to 11.4 percent as of June 30, 2000, an average growth of 6.6 percent annually. When compared to rates at midyear 1999 the number of female jail inmates rose by 4.3 percent.

Most local jail inmates were minorities. At midyear 2000, non-Hispanic whites made up 41.9 percent of the jail population, up slightly from 41.3 percent at midyear 1999. Non-Hispanic blacks comprised 42.3 percent jail inmates, up from 41.5 percent in 1999. Hispanics comprised 15.1 percent, up from 15.5 percent in 1999, and other races (Asians-Pacific Islanders, Native Americans, and Alaskan Natives) made up less than 2 percent, rates which have remained fairly consistent since 1990. Relative to their proportion in the U.S. population, non-Hispanic blacks were 5.5 times more likely than non-Hispanic whites to be held in local jails, 2.5 times more likely than Hispanics, and more than 9 times more likely than persons of other races. (See Table 3.8.)

JUVENILES IN JAIL

According to the BJS from 1983 to 1998 there was a 366 percent rise in the number of juveniles confined in adult jails—from a total of 1,736 juveniles in 1983 to 8,090 juveniles in 1998. (See Table 3.9.) By comparison, during the same period, the rate of adult female jail inmates rose by 308 percent and adult male inmates rose by 153 percent. However, when viewed in terms of new

TABLE 3.9

Juveniles in adult jails, 1983–98

Year	Total Adult Inmates	All Males	All Females	Juveniles
1983	221,815	206,163	15,652	1,736
1984	233,018	216,275	16,743	1,482
1985	254,986	235,909	19,077	1,629
1986	272,736	251,235	21,501	1,708
1987	294,092	270,172	23,920	1,781
1988	341,893	311,594	30,299	1,676
1989	393,248	356,050	37,198	2,250
1990	403,019	365,821	37,198	2,301
1991	424,129	384,628	39,501	2,350
1992	441,780	401,106	40,674	2,804
1993	455,600	411,500	44,100	4,300
1994	479,800	431,300	48,500	6,700
1995	499,300	448,000	51,300	7,800
1996	510,400	454,700	55,700	8,100
1997	557,974	498,678	59,296	9,105
1998	584,372	520,581	63,791	8,090
% Change, 1983–1998	163%	153%	308%	366%

SOURCE: James Austin, Kelly Dedel Johnson, Maria Gregoriou, "Table 2: Juveniles in Adult Jails, 1983–1998," in *Juveniles in Adult Prisons and Jails: A National Assessment*, U.S. Department of Justice, Bureau of Justice Assistance, Washington, D.C., 2000

admissions, in each of the 15 years, juveniles accounted for about 2 percent of new admissions.

On June 30, 1998, an estimated 8,090 persons under the age 18 years were housed in adult jails. Approximately 8 of 10 of these juveniles had been convicted or were being held for trial as adults in criminal court. Most states define a juvenile as a person under the age of 18 years subject to juvenile court jurisdiction, but exceptions are made, usually depending upon the severity of the offense or the offender's criminal history.

ADULT CONVICTION STATUS

Convicted inmates include those awaiting sentencing, serving a sentence, or returned to jail for a violation of probation or parole. On June 30, 2000, fewer than half (44 percent) of all adults under supervision by jail authorities had been convicted of their current charges. (See Table 3.10.) This figure is down slightly from 45.9 percent at midyear 1999, and still lower than 48.5 percent in 1990. However, the number for female adult inmates increased during the same time period. As of mid year 2000, 5 percent of adult female inmates were convicted while under jail supervision, up from 4.3 percent in 1995 and 4.5 percent in 1990. The largest proportion of female jail inmates held in U.S. jails were either convicted of or facing property offenses (34 percent), followed by drug offenses (30 percent), public-order offenses such as driving while intoxicated (24 percent) and, violent crime offenses (12 percent). (See Table 3.11.) Of unconvicted adult inmates at year-end 2000, 50 percent were males and 6 percent females.

TABLE 3.10

Conviction status of local jail inmates, midyear 1990, 1995, and 1999–2000

Characteristic	Percent of jail inmates			
	1990	1995	1999	2000
Total	**100%**	**100%**	**100%**	**100%**
Conviction status (adults only)				
Convicted	48.5%	44.0%	45.9%	44.0%
Male	44.1	39.7	40.8	39.0
Female	4.5	4.3	5.1	5.0
Unconvicted	51.5	56.0	54.1	56.0
Male	46.7	50.0	48.0	50.0
Female	4.8	6.0	6.1	6.0

Note: Detail may not add to total because of rounding. Conviction status in 1999 includes all inmates.

SOURCE: Allen J. Beck, Ph.D., and Jennifer C. Karberg, *Prison and Jail Inmates at Midyear 2000*, Bureau of Justice Statistics, Washington, DC, 2001

TABLE 3.11

Offenses committed by women on probation or in jail/prison

Most serious offense*	Percent of women offenders			
	Probation	Local jails	State prisons	Federal prisons
Violent offenses	9%	12%	28%	7%
Homicide	1	1	11	1
Property offenses	44%	34%	27%	12%
Larceny	11	15	9	1
Fraud	26	12	10	10
Drug offenses	19%	30%	34%	72%
Public-order offenses	27%	24%	11%	8%
Driving while intoxicated	18	7	2	0
Number of women offenders	721,400	27,900	75,200	9,200

*Based on the offenders' most serious offense. Overall offense categories are shown with selected detail categories containing larger percentages of women offenders.

SOURCE: Lawrence A. Greenfeld and Tracy L. Snell, "Offenses of women on probation or in jail or prison" in "Women Offenders," *Bureau of Justice Statistics Special Report,* U.S. Department of Justice, Washington, D.C., 2000

CONFINEMENT STATUS

In 1995, for the first time, the Annual Survey of Jails (Bureau of Justice Statistics, Washington, D.C.) obtained the count of the number of offenders under community supervision. Respondents were asked if their jail jurisdictions operated any community-based programs and how many persons participated in them.

From midyears 1995–2000 the number of persons supervised outside a jail facility rose from 34,869 to 65,884. (See Table 3.12.) The largest number of persons supervised outside a jail facility (14,523) were sentenced to so-called "weekender programs," involving either

TABLE 3.12

Persons under jail supervision, by confinement status and type of program, midyear 1995–2000

Confinement status and type of program	Number of persons under jail supervision					
	1995	1996	1997	1998	1999	2000
Total	541,913	591,469	637,319	664,847	687,973	687,033
Held in jail	507,044	518,492	567,079	592,462	605,943	621,149
Supervised outside a jail facility[a]	34,869	72,977	70,239	72,385	82,030	65,884
Electronic monitoring	6,788	7,480	8,699	10,827	10,230	10,782
Home detention[b]	1,376	907	1,164	370	518	332
Day reporting	1,283	3,298	2,768	3,089	5,080	3,969
Community service	10,253	17,410	15,918	17,518	20,139	13,592
Weekender programs	1,909	16,336	17,656	17,249	16,089	14,523
Other pretrial supervision	3,229	2,135	7,368	6,048	10,092	6,279
Other work programs[c]	9,144	14,469	6,631	7,089	7,780	8,011
Treatment programs[d]	—	10,425	6,693	5,702	8,500	5,714
Other/unspecified	887	517	3,342	4,493	3,602	2,682

—Not available.

[a] Excludes persons supervised by a probation or parole agency.
[b] Includes only those without electronic monitoring.
[c] Includes persons in work release programs, work gangs, and other work alternative programs.
[d] Includes persons under drug, alcohol, mental health, and other medical treatment.

SOURCE: Allen J. Beck, Ph.D., and Jennifer C. Karberg, *Prison and Jail Inmates at Midyear 2000*, Bureau of Justice Statistics, Washington, DC, 2001

weekend stays in jail, some type of community service outside of jail, or a combination of both. Next were persons performing community service (13,592), persons on electronic monitoring (10,782) and persons in other work programs (8,011). For midyear 1999 the largest group of persons supervised outside a jail facility performed community service (20,139), followed by weekender programs (16,089) and persons on electronic monitoring (10,230). Persons in treatment programs fell from 8,500 at midyear 1999 to 5,714 at midyear 2000, down by nearly half from 10,425 in 1996.

PRIVATIZATION OF JAILS

One suggestion for solving the overcrowding of jails is to allow the private sector to construct, administer, and operate jails. In "Private Jails: Locking Down the Issues" (*American Jails,* vol. 11, no. 1, March/April 1997), Dale K. Sechrest and David Shichor found that proponents of privatization believe that, by following profit motives, private companies can perform most services cheaper and more effectively than the public sector. They point out that private companies can pay less for products and supplies because they do not have to deal with long-term contracts like the government does. Supporters of privatization believe that private companies are better at management and at budgeting and accounting for expenditures than civil service employees. They also feel that competition with the public sector will encourage government employees to work harder and perform their jobs better.

Those who oppose privatization, according to Sechrest and Shichor, believe that cost savings have not been proven and fear that cost cutting may lead to substandard

goods and services. They also voice concern over the issue of private companies finding qualified employees or using a smaller and less qualified workforce in order to make a profit. They point out that poorly qualified and underpaid staff can lead to a large turnover, and a stable workforce is necessary to maintain order and security in a facility that may house difficult and sometimes violent inmates, those with mental problems, and drug addicts.

There is also the issue of control. The public has elected sheriffs who are responsible for dispensing punishment, keeping the public safe, acting in accordance with local laws and regulations, taking legal responsibility for running the jail facility properly, and using deadly force when necessary. Opponents of privatization wonder how much power the government would allow a private corporation to use in order to run the jail, and how private performance would be monitored. Finally, a sheriff's department that relies on private jail management must have proper backup to take charge in an emergency situation where the use of deadly force may be required.

PRIVATIZATION OF HEALTH CARE

In *Estelle v. Gamble* (429 U.S. 97, 1976), the Supreme Court ruled that inmates had a constitutional right to adequate health services. To improve health services jail authorities turned to contract services. Although part-time doctors and dentists had already been used by jails, contracting with private firms for more health services was controversial. Opponents feared that for-profit firms would not deliver quality service. Administrators were afraid of having less control without losing the responsibility and liability. Supporters of privatization thought that the system would have better staff and would be able to retain the staff, jails could transfer legal liability to the firms, and the budget would be fixed. The generally accepted opinion arising from various court cases was that, while jail systems may lessen their liability, they cannot contract that liability away to private firms.

As long ago as 1973 Rikers Island (New York) contracted with Montefiore Hospital to provide all health services (except psychiatric, dental, and some other services not available at Montefiore). In 1978 Delaware County and Baltimore City also contracted out their health services. By the mid-1990s 110 jails in 25 states with an average inmate population of 86,950 had contracted out medical services.

A major reason for contracting health services is to save money. Before privatization appropriated funds are often scattered among various departments, so jail authorities have no accurate way of knowing the exact costs of health care. Since privatization often causes a change in the number of services offered in order to meet higher standards, it makes it harder to compare costs.

In "Privatization of Jail Health Care Services: The First Twenty Years" (*American Jails,* January/February 1995), Barbara Cotton concluded that the saying holds true that one gets what one pays for. She says that contracting for services is only one option and must fit the needs of the situation—that health services must be a team effort between health services and contract services. Cotton also believes that competition has had a positive influence on inmate health services.

PAYING FOR SERVICES

Jails in some jurisdictions are now requiring their inmates to pay for their room and board and health care. According to the National Institute of Corrections (*Fees Paid by Jail Inmates: Findings from the Nation's Largest Jails,* U.S. Department of Justice, Longmont, Colorado, 1997), at least 41 states had passed legislation authorizing assessment of inmate fees for jail services and operations. The legislation most often identifies specific functions for which fees can be collected, such as room and board, medical services, or programs.

In November 1996 the National Institute of Corrections distributed surveys to more than 130 of the nation's largest jails, with a response rate of 77 percent. About 16 jails had inmate populations of 2,500 or greater; 7 had populations of fewer than 250 inmates. Fees were imposed in four major areas:

- Medical services—collecting copayments or other fees for medical care

- Per diem fees—requiring jail inmates to reimburse the county for all or a portion of their daily incarceration costs, including housing, food, and basic programs

- Other nonprogram functions—charging for services such as bonding, telephone use, haircuts, release escort, and drug testing

- Participation in programs—imposing a fee or collecting a portion of any compensation earned by inmates in programs, such as work release, weekend incarceration, and electronic monitoring; or charging for participation in rehabilitation programs such as education or substance abuse treatment

More than three-quarters of the agencies surveyed charged fees for one or more programs and/or services or planned on implementing systems for doing so. At least seven jails initiated fees-for-services operations in 1996 or 1997. Inmates were most commonly charged fees for medical care (56 agencies) and participation in work release programs (46 agencies). Most jails charging inmates fees imposed them for more than one service or function, although 13 agencies in the survey sample charged only for medical services.

Major functions generating the most revenues in 1996 included telephone services (averaging $54,400 per year), work release programs (averaging $230,500 per year), and home detention programs (averaging $161,000 per year).

Medical Services

Fees for medical services ranged from $3 to $15 for each medical visit. The most common fee amount was $3. Most jails used a scale on which cost was determined by type of treatment. For example, a jail might charge $6 for care from a nurse or physician's assistant, $20 to see a doctor, and $12 for a dental exam. Annual revenues from medical fees tended to be modest ($22,800). This reflects the fact that, in most cases, medical fees were charged to control the numbers of visits rather than cover or offset expenses.

IMPACT OF MEDICAL FEES. Three-quarters of the agencies that collected medical fees found inmates' use of medical services declined after the fees were begun. Most of those declines were attributed to reductions in inmates' frivolous medical requests. As one respondent commented: "The demand for sick call has been greatly reduced, as fewer inmates are using this avenue as a way to get out of their cells for a couple of hours." Laramie County, Wyoming, officials noted that medical copay requirements have cut sick calls by two-thirds.

CARE FOR INDIGENT INMATES. Seventeen agencies disregarded the medical fee for inmates who could not pay. In 32 jurisdictions staff debited the inmates' accounts, creating a negative balance, and collected the fees if additional funds were received. Some jurisdictions maintained these records after the inmate was released and collected the funds if the inmate was rebooked into the jail.

Per Diem Fees

Thirteen jails in the survey charged inmates all or a portion of the daily cost of their incarceration. Since the expense of housing and caring for prisoners has traditionally been viewed as a public responsibility, charging inmates is somewhat controversial. Sixteen states have enacted laws that specifically authorize jails to charge inmates for all or a portion of the county's actual costs of room and board. Statutes in two other states authorize fees to offset "general costs of incarceration."

Ability to pay is taken into consideration in most state laws that authorize charging inmates for costs of incarceration. A Texas statute, effective September 1997, provides that if the county and inmate do not agree on the amount of the inmate's liability, either may file a civil action in a district court to determine the amount of liability. Under Florida's 1996 statute the local jail determines the financial status of inmates based on their income, assets, and obligations.

Per diem fees charged ranged from a token $2 per day in Palm Beach, Florida, to the substantial $60 per day in Oakland County (Pontiac), Michigan. Annual revenues from per diem charges ranged from $3,000 in Wayne County (Detroit metropolitan area), Michigan, to $4.9 million in Pierce County (Tacoma), Washington. Average revenues, excluding the dramatically higher Pierce County figure, were $125,000.

FLORIDA. In 1996, Florida passed a law (Florida Statute 951.033) allowing county jails to charge inmates for daily room and board (Susan W. McCampbell, "Room with a View, at a Price," *American Jails,* March/April 1997). Officials must consider the prisoners' ability to pay and establish a process by which inmates can show reasons why they cannot pay the fees. In August 1996 jail inmates in Broward County (Fort Lauderdale), Florida, began paying $2 a day for their room and board and a $10 fee for processing.

On October 21, 1996, a class action lawsuit was filed against the sheriff's office to overturn the state law and prevent the county from collecting any more fees. The lawsuit claimed that the procedures were illegal because inmates who have not yet been convicted were being charged, and that poor inmates also must pay the fee. At the time the lawsuit was filed, no other Florida jails had implemented these fees. Jail officials in many states, however, have requested information from Broward County.

JAIL INDUSTRIES

The National Institute of Justice defines a jail industry as one that uses inmate labor to create a product or provide a service that has value to a public or private client and for which the inmates receive compensation, whether it be pay, privileges, or other benefits. This defi-

nition describes a variety of activities. If a convict cuts the grass in front of the jail and thereby earns permission to watch television an extra hour, the elements of labor, service provision, value, and compensation are all present. At the other end of the spectrum are those jail inmates who work for private sector industry and earn real dollars.

Jail officials hoped these programs would develop inmate work habits and skills, generate revenues or reduce costs for the county, reduce inmate idleness, and meet needs in the community. The 1984 Justice Assistance Act (PL 98-473) removed some of the long-standing restrictions on interstate commerce of prisoner-made goods, thereby opening new opportunities for prison labor to work for the private sector. Both state prisons and county jails have entered into private-sector work programs.

In most programs inmates receive no or low wages. Their work often serves the public sector and they are usually credited with "good time." Thus the offenders pay for their crimes with public service labor, and their early release makes scarce bed space available for other offenders.

The Future of Jail Industries

The future of jail work and industries programs is bright, according to Rod Miller in "Inmate Labor in the 21st Century: You Ain't Seen Nothin' Yet" (*American Jails,* vol. 11, no. 1, March/April 1997). He sees a gradual shift toward inmate labor as the public and private sectors turn to the inmate workforce because of cost-savings and the demand that inmates work rather than be idle.

Miller predicts pretrial detainees will be put to work at the jails, while sentenced offenders work away from jails. Inmates will be involved in more diverse work projects, including high-tech projects using computers, telephones, and the Internet, which may prepare them for finding jobs after they complete their sentences. Some work will be performed 24 hours per day, seven days per week. Facility kitchens, for example, will produce goods and services for customers outside the facility.

Work assignments and activities will be related to an inmate's education and training. Eligibility for preferred programs will be based on completion of educational programs and treatment plans. Jails will begin to consider postconfinement job performance by providing employment-related programs to inmates prior to their release.

New Challenges

As the jail workforce grows, opponents and proponents of inmate work and industry programs will watch developments closely. Managers will be more accountable for the programs, and many work programs will be under pressure to become profitable, or at least self-sufficient. Inmates will raise issues with the courts including job classification, work assignments, working conditions, discipline, removal from work assignments, and fairness of work opportunities. There may be conflicts with "workfare" programs set up for welfare recipients, and some of the welfare and jail programs and activities will most likely overlap.

CHAPTER 4

PRISONS

If you cram people in prison, create forced idleness without the supervision that's needed, you can expect the situation to get out of hand. It's an unbelievable burden on corrections staff to manage people in inhumane conditions.

—Stephen B. Bright, Executive Director for Human Rights

As reported by the Bureau of Justice Statistics (BJS), in 1999 the growth in the number of state and federal prisoners was 3.4 percent, down from 4.7 percent in 1998. (See Table 4.1.) In numbers the population of state and federal prisoners grew by 43,796 inmates in 1999, as compared to an increase of 58,420 in 1998. Since 1990, the prison population has grown an average of 65,867 inmates per year, for a total increase of 592,802 from 1990 to 1999.

Prisoners with sentences of more than one year grew by 3.2 percent from 1998 to 1999. The number of sentenced state prisoners increased by 2.5 percent during that time, while the number of sentenced prisoners under federal jurisdictions increased by 10.2 percent, more than four times the rate of state prisoners. (See Table 4.2.)

RATE OF INCARCERATION

The inmate population in the United States is measured by the rate of incarceration—that is, the number of people sent by the courts to prisons and jails per 100,000 people in the general population. As reported by The Sentencing Project, Washington, D.C., in 2000 the United States became the world leader in the total rate of incarceration of its citizens, with a rate of 690 prison and jail inmates per 100,000 population. Among major nations the United States is followed by Russia, with a rate of 675, South Africa (400), the United Kingdom (125), and Canada, Australia, and Spain (each at 110).

The rate of incarceration of federal and state prisoners in the United States has risen from a low of 79 in 1925 to 476 in 1999. (See Table 4.3.) Beginning in 1925 the rate of

TABLE 4.1

Change in the state and federal prison populations, 1990–99

Years	Annual increase in the number of prisoners		Percent change
	Custody	Jurisdiction	
1990	60,000	61,555	8.6%
1991	49,153	51,640	6.7
1992	58,031	56,941	6.9
1993	58,815	64,992	7.4
1994	80,766	84,258	8.7
1995	88,295	71,172	6.7
1996	49,222	57,494	5.1
1997	48,800	58,785	5.0
1998	47,905	58,420	4.7
1999	36,957	43,796	3.4
Average annual increase, 1990–99	60,168	65,867	6.5%

Note: In years in which states changed their reporting methods, counts based on comparable methods were used to calculate the annual increase and percent change. The average annual increases were calculated on the revised counts in 1999.

SOURCE: Allen J. Beck, Ph.D., *Prisoners in 1999*, Bureau of Justice Statistics, Washington, DC, 2000

incarceration of U.S. prisoners rose steadily for 15 years to a peak of 137 in 1939. The rate declined somewhat and more or less leveled out to between 100 and 120 for the next 35 years. Then, in the late 1970s, the rate began to rise steadily. (See Figure 4.1.) From 133 in 1979 to 476 in 1999, the rate of incarceration of U.S. prisoners almost quadrupled. The rate for male prisoners climbed from 264 to 913, while the rate for female prisoners rose by almost six-fold—from 10 in 1979 to 59 in 1999. (See Figure 4.2.)

As reported in *Prisoners in 1999* (Bureau of Justice Statistics Bulletin, August 2000), since 1990 incarceration rates of prisoners in the United States rose most in the South (from 316 to 543), followed by the West (227 to 421), the Midwest (239 to 367), and the Northeast (232 to 330). Roughly 1 in every 110 males and 1 in every 1,695

TABLE 4.2

Prisoners under the jurisdiction of state or federal correctional authorities, by region and jurisdiction, year-end 1998 and 1999

Region and jurisdiction	Total			Sentenced to more than 1 year			Incarceration rate, 1999[a]
	Advance 1999	1998	Percent change, 1998-99	Advance 1999	1998	Percent change, 1998-99	
U.S. total	1,366,721	1,300,573	3.4%	1,305,393	1,245,402	3.2%	476
Federal	135,246	123,041	9.9	114,275	103,682	10.2	42
State	1,231,475	1,177,532	2.7	1,191,118	1,141,720	2.5	434
Northeast	179,758	175,681	1.5 %	171,234	167,376	1.5%	330
Connecticut[b]	18,639	17,605	5.9	13,032	12,193	6.9	397
Maine	1,716	1,691	1.5	1,663	1,641	1.3	133
Massachusetts[c]	11,356	11,799	-3.8	10,282	10,744	-4.3	266
New Hampshire	2,257	2,169	4.1	2,257	2,169	4.1	187
New Jersey[d]	31,493	31,121	1.2	31,493	31,121	1.2	384
New York[e]	73,233	70,001	2.6	72,896	70,001	2.1	400
Pennsylvania	36,525	36,377	0.4	36,525	36,373	0.4	305
Rhode Island[b]	3,003	3,445	-12.8	1,908	2,175	-12.3	193
Vermont[b]	1,536	1,473	4.3	1,178	959	22.8	198
Midwest	232,905	228,116	2.1%	231,961	227,270	2.1%	367
Illinois[d,f]	44,660	43,051	3.7	44,660	43,051	3.7	368
Indiana	19,309	19,197	0.6	19,260	19,016	1.3	324
Iowa[d,f]	7,232	7,394	-2.2	7,232	7,394	-2.2	252
Kansas[d]	8,567	8,183	4.7	8,567	8,183	4.7	321
Michigan[f]	46,617	45,879	1.6	46,617	45,879	1.6	472
Minnesota	5,969	5,572	7.1	5,955	5,557	7.2	125
Missouri	26,155	24,974	4.7	26,133	24,950	4.7	477
Nebraska	3,688	3,676	0.3	3,632	3,588	1.2	217
North Dakota	943	915	3.1	866	834	3.8	137
Ohio[d]	46,842	48,450	-3.3	46,842	48,450	-3.3	417
South Dakota	2,506	2,422	3.5	2,498	2,417	3.4	339
Wisconsin	20,417	18,403	10.9	19,699	17,951	9.7	375
South	551,284	512,271	3.7%	528,377	493,488	3.4%	543
Alabama	24,658	22,676	8.7	24,109	22,214	8.5	549
Arkansas	11,415	10,638	7.3	11,336	10,561	7.3	443
Delaware[b]	6,983	5,558	—	3,730	3,211	—	493
District of Columbia[b]	8,652	9,829	-12.0	6,730	8,144	-17.4	1,314
Florida[f]	69,596	67,224	3.5	69,594	67,193	3.6	456
Georgia[f]	42,091	39,262	7.2	42,008	38,758	8.4	532
Kentucky	15,317	14,987	2.2	15,317	14,987	2.2	385
Louisiana	34,066	32,228	5.7	34,066	32,228	5.7	776
Maryland	23,095	22,572	2.3	22,184	21,540	3.0	427
Mississippi	18,247	16,678	9.4	17,410	15,855	9.8	626
North Carolina	31,086	31,961	-2.7	26,635	27,244	-2.2	345
Oklahoma[d]	22,393	20,892	7.2	22,393	20,892	7.2	662
South Carolina	22,008	21,764	1.1	21,228	20,910	1.5	543
Tennessee[d,e]	22,502	17,738	4.5	22,502	17,738	4.5	408
Texas[e]	163,190	144,510	1.9	154,865	139,863	0.7	762
Virginia	32,453	30,276	7.2	30,738	28,672	7.2	447
West Virginia	3,532	3,478	1.6	3,532	3,478	1.6	196
West	267,528	261,464	1.9%	259,546	253,586	2.0%	421
Alaska[b]	3,949	4,097	-3.6	2,325	2,541	-8.5	374
Arizona[f]	25,986	25,515	1.8	23,944	23,500	1.9	495
California	163,067	161,904	0.7	160,517	159,201	0.8	481
Colorado	15,670	14,312	9.5	15,670	14,312	9.5	383
Hawaii[b]	4,903	4,924	-0.4	3,817	3,670	4.0	320
Idaho[e]	4,842	4,083	12.9	4,842	4,083	12.9	385
Montana	2,954	2,734	8.0	2,954	2,734	8.0	335
Nevada	9,494	9,651	-1.6	9,413	9,651	-2.5	509
New Mexico	5,124	5,078	0.9	4,730	4,825	-2.0	270
Oregon	9,810	8,981	9.2	9,792	8,935	9.6	293
Utah[e]	5,426	4,453	4.2	5,271	4,402	4.3	245
Washington	14,590	14,161	3.0	14,558	14,161	2.8	251
Wyoming	1,713	1,571	9.0	1,713	1,571	9.0	355

—Not calculated.

[a] The number of prisoners with sentences of more than 1 year per 100,000 U.S. residents.
[b] Prisons and jails form one integrated system. Data include total jail and prison population.
[c] The incarceration rate includes an estimated 6,200 inmates sentenced to more than 1 year but held in local jails or houses of corrections.
[d] "Sentenced to more than 1 year" includes some inmates "sentenced to 1 year or less."
[e] Reporting changed in 1999; percents calculated on counts adjusted for comparable reporting.
[f] Population figures are based on custody counts.

SOURCE: Allen J. Beck, Ph.D., *Prisoners in 1999*, Bureau of Justice Statistics, Washington, DC, 2000

TABLE 4.3

Number and rate (per 100,000 resident population in each group) of sentenced prisoners under jurisdiction of State and Federal correctional authorities on December 31, by sex, 1925–99

Year	Total	Rate	Male Number	Male Rate	Female Number	Female Rate	Year	Total	Rate	Male Number	Male Rate	Female Number	Female Rate
1925	91,669	79	88,231	149	3,438	6	1963	217,283	114	209,538	225	7,745	8
1926	97,991	83	94,287	157	3,704	6	1964	214,336	111	206,632	219	7,704	8
1927	109,983	91	104,983	173	4,363	7	1965	210,895	108	203,327	213	7,568	8
1928	116,390	96	111,836	182	4,554	8	1966	199,654	102	192,703	201	6,951	7
1929	120,496	98	115,876	187	4,620	8	1967	194,896	98	188,661	195	6,235	6
							1968	187,914	94	182,102	187	5,812	6
1930	129,453	104	124,785	200	4,668	8	1969	196,007	97	189,413	192	6,594	6
1931	137,082	110	132,638	211	4,444	7							
1932	137,997	110	133,573	211	4,424	7	1970	196,429	96	190,794	191	5,635	5
1933	136,810	109	132,520	209	4,290	7	1971	198,061	95	191,732	189	6,329	6
1934	138,316	109	133,769	209	4,547	7	1972	196,092	93	189,823	185	6,269	6
1935	144,180	113	139,278	217	4,902	8	1973	204,211	96	197,523	191	6,004	6
1936	145,038	113	139,990	217	5,048	8	1974	218,466	102	211,077	202	7,389	7
1937	152,741	118	147,375	227	5,366	8	1975	240,593	111	231,918	220	8,675	8
1938	160,285	123	154,826	236	5,459	8	1976	262,833	120	252,794	238	10,039	9
1939	179,818	137	173,143	263	6,675	10	1977[a]	278,141	126	267,097	249	11,044	10
							1977[b]	285,456	129	274,244	255	11,212	10
1940	173,706	131	167,345	252	6,361	10	1978	294,396	132	282,813	261	11,583	10
1941	165,439	124	159,228	239	6,211	9	1979	301,470	133	289,465	264	12,005	10
1942	150,384	112	144,167	217	6,217	9							
1943	137,220	103	131,054	202	6,166	9	1980	315,974	139	303,643	275	12,331	11
1944	132,456	100	126,350	200	6,106	9	1981	353,673	154	339,375	304	14,298	12
1945	133,649	98	127,609	193	6,040	9	1982	395,516	171	379,075	337	16,441	14
1946	140,079	99	134,075	191	6,004	8	1983	419,346	179	401,870	354	17,476	15
1947	151,304	105	144,961	202	6,343	9	1984	443,398	188	424,193	370	19,205	16
1948	155,977	106	149,739	205	6,238	8	1985	480,568	202	459,223	397	21,345	17
1949	163,749	109	157,663	211	6,086	8	1986	522,084	217	497,540	426	24,544	20
							1987	560,812	231	533,990	453	26,822	22
1950	166,123	109	160,309	211	5,814	8	1988	603,732	247	573,587	482	30,145	24
1951	165,680	107	159,610	208	6,070	8	1989	680,907	276	643,643	535	37,264	29
1952	168,233	107	161,994	208	6,239	8							
1953	173,579	108	166,909	211	6,670	8	1990	739,980	297	699,416	575	40,564	32
1954	182,901	112	175,907	218	6,994	8	1991	789,610	313	745,808	606	43,802	34
1955	185,780	112	178,655	217	7,125	8	1992	846,277	332	799,776	642	46,501	36
1956	189,565	112	182,190	218	7,375	9	1993	932,074	359	878,037	698	54,037	41
1957	195,414	113	188,113	221	7,301	8	1994	1,016,691	389	956,566	753	60,125	45
1958	205,643	117	198,208	229	7,435	8	1995	1,085,022	411	1,021,059	796	63,963	48
1959	208,105	117	200,469	228	7,636	8	1996	1,137,722	427	1,068,123	819	69,599	51
							1997	1,194,581	444	1,120,787	853	73,794	54
1960	212,953	117	205,265	230	7,688	8	1998	1,245,402	461	1,167,802	885	77,600	57
1961	220,149	119	212,268	234	7,881	8	1999[c]	1,305,393	476	1,222,799	913	82,594	59
1962	218,830	117	210,823	229	8,007	8							

Note: These data represent prisoners sentenced to more than 1 year. Both custody and jurisdiction figures are shown for 1977 to facilitate year-to-year comparison.
[a] Custody counts.
[b] Jurisdiction counts.
[c] Preliminary; subject to revision.

SOURCE: Peter Finn, "Number and rate (per 100,000 resident population in each group) of sentenced prisoners under jurisdiction of State and Federal correctional authorities on December 31: By sex, United States, 1925–99" in *Addressing Correctional Officer Stress: Programs and Strategies,* National Institute of Justice, U.S. Department of Justice, Washington, D.C., 2000

females in the United States were sentenced inmates in federal or state prisons at year-end 1999. States with the highest rates of incarceration in 1999 were Louisiana (776), Texas (762), Oklahoma (662), Mississippi (626), and Alabama (549). (See Table 4.4.) The lowest rates of incarceration by state in 1999 were Minnesota (125), Maine (133), North Dakota (137), New Hampshire (187), and Rhode Island (193).

As of midyear 2000, the BJS reported that the incarceration rate of state and federal prisoners sentenced to more than one year reached a new high of 481 per 100,000 U.S. residents.

PRISON OVERCROWDING

The American Correctional Association (ACA) guidelines call for a standard cell area of 60 square feet for inmates spending no more than 10 hours per day in their cells. In many prisons inmates are double-bunked in cells designed for one, or sleep on mattresses in unheated prison gyms or on the floors of dayrooms, halls, or basements. Some are housed in tents; others share the same bunks at different times of the day.

As room for prisoners has diminished it has become harder to segregate violent from nonviolent prisoners, causing tension and often leading to injuries. Overcrowding has

FIGURE 4.1

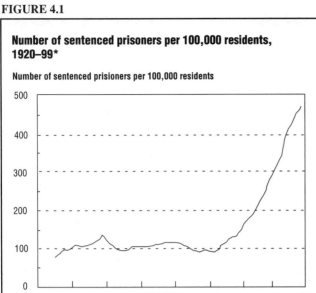

Number of sentenced prisoners per 100,000 residents, 1920–99*

Number of sentenced prisoners per 100,000 residents

Note: The rates for the period before 1980 are based on the civilian population. The civilian population represents the resident population less the armed forces stationed in the United States. Since 1980, the rates based on the total resident population provided by the U.S. Bureau of the Census.
*Data for 1999 are as of June 30.

SOURCE: "Figure 6.4: Rate (per 100,000 resident population) of sentenced prisoners under jurisdiction of State and Federal correctional authorities on December 31." in *Sourcebook of Criminal Justice Statistics 1999*, Kathleen Maguire and Ann L. Pastore, eds., Bureau of Justice Statistics, Washington, D.C., 2000

FIGURE 4.2

Sentenced female prisoners under jurisdiction of state and federal correctional authorities, 1925–99*

Female Prisoners

*Data for 1999 are as of June 30.

SOURCE: "Figure 6.2: Sentenced female prisoners under jurisdiction of State and Federal correctional authorities on December 31." in *Sourcebook of Criminal Justice Statistics 1999*, Kathleen Maguire and Ann L. Pastore, eds., Bureau of Justice Statistics, Washington, D.C., 2000

also contributed to the spread of communicable diseases such as tuberculosis. Many taxpayers do not consider overcrowding a problem because they believe that discomfort should be part of the punishment.

BUILDING MORE PRISONS—RUNNING TO STAY IN PLACE

Most states have been dealing with growth in their prison populations by building more facilities. In 1995 a BJS census found that, between 1990 and 1995, state and federal officials built 213 new prisons—168 state and 45 federal facilities—with more than 280,000 beds to try to keep pace with the growing prison population. This new prison construction resulted in an increase in the percentage of facilities less than 20 years old—from 37 percent in 1990 to more than 50 percent in 1995. Almost 40 percent of all prison inmates in 1995 were held in facilities built after 1985.

The Criminal Justice Institute (CJI) (*The Corrections Yearbook—1998*) reported that, in 1997, 15 correction agencies opened 31 new institutions, adding 25,248 beds at an average cost of $48,601.

The impact of the opening of new prison facilities on overcrowding in state prisons can been seen in recent statistics. As reported in *Prisoners in 1999,* despite the rising rate of incarceration among state prisoners there has been

a decline in the population housed as a percent of highest capacity. (See Table 4.5.) In 1990, with a rate of incarceration of state prisoners at 272, the inmate population as a percent of highest capacity was 115 percent, but by 1999, with an incarceration rate of 434, the percent of highest capacity had declined to 101 in state facilities.

In federal prisons the percent of population as a percent of highest capacity has continued to rise with the rate of incarceration. In 1995, with a rate of 32, the percent of highest capacity was 126. By 1999, as the rate of incarceration grew to 42, the population housed as a percent of highest capacity also increased to 132 percent.

Because building prisons and adding new beds is costly, states are looking for other ways to manage overcrowding, such as early release programs, electronic monitoring, keeping prisoners in local jails, paying states with less crowded prison systems to hold their prisoners for them, or paying to house them in private facilities.

STATE PRISONERS IN PRIVATE FACILITIES

At the end of 1999 a total of 71,208 prisoners under the jurisdiction of federal and state correctional authorities were housed in private facilities. (See Table 4.6.) This accounted for 5.5 percent of all state inmates and nearly 3 percent of federal prisoners. The state leading this trend was Texas, with 11,653 of its inmates housed in private facilities. By

TABLE 4.4

The 10 highest and lowest jurisdictions for selected characteristics of the prison population, year-end 1999

Prison population	Number of inmates	Incarceration rates, 1999	Rate per 100,000 State residents[a]	1- year growth 1998-99	Percent change	Growth since 1990	Average percent change[b]
10 highest:							
Texas	163,190	Louisiana	776	Idaho	12.9%	Texas	11.8%
California	163,067	Texas	762	Wisconsin	10.9	Idaho	10.6
Federal	135,246	Oklahoma	662	Federal	9.9	Federal	9.5
New York	73,233	Mississippi	626	Colorado	9.5	West Virginia	9.5
Florida	69,596	Alabama	549	Mississippi	9.4	Hawaii	9.3
Ohio	46,842	South Carolina	543	Oregon	9.2	Tennessee	9.0
Michigan	46,617	Georgia	532	Wyoming	9.0	Mississippi	8.9
Illinois	44,660	Nevada	509	Alabama	8.7	Utah	8.8
Georgia	42,091	Arizona	495	Montana	8.0	Montana	8.4
Pennsylvania	36,525	Delaware	493	Arkansas	7.3	Colorado	8.3
10 lowest:							
North Dakota	943	Minnesota	125	Rhode Island	-12.8%	Dist. of Columbia	-1%
Vermont	1,536	Maine	133	Dist. of Columbia	-12.0	Maine	1.3
Wyoming	1,713	North Dakota	137	Massachusetts	-3.8	Rhode Island	2.1
Maine	1,716	New Hampshire	187	Alaska	-3.6	Alaska	2.6
New Hampshire	2,257	Rhode Island	193	Ohio	-3.3	Massachusetts	3.0
South Dakota	2,506	West Virginia	196	North Carolina	-2.7	South Carolina	3.0
Montana	2,954	Vermont	198	Iowa	-2.2	Maryland	3.2
Rhode Island	3,003	Nebraska	217	Nevada	-1.6	New York	3.2
West Virginia	3,532	Utah	245	Hawaii	-0.4	Michigan	3.5
Nebraska	3,688	Washington	251	Nebraska	0.3	Ohio	4.4

[a] The number of prisoners with a sentence of more than 1 year per 100,000 residents in the state population. The Federal Bureau of Prisons and the District of Columbia are excluded.
[b] The average annual percent change from 1990 to 1999.

SOURCE: Allen J. Beck, Ph.D., *Prisoners in 1999*, Bureau of Justice Statistics, Washington, DC, 2000

---

proportion of prisoners at year-end 1999 New Mexico housed nearly 39 percent of its prisoners in private facilities, followed by Alaska (35 percent), Oklahoma (28 percent), Montana (25 percent), and Hawaii (24 percent). By region the South housed over 8 percent of all state prisoners in private facilities, followed by the West at 5.8 percent.

The Trend Toward Privatization Continues

In *Prison and Jail Inmates at Midyear 2000* (Bureau of Justice Statistic Bulletin, March 2001), authors Allen J. Beck, Ph.D., and Jennifer C. Karberg reported that, as of midyear 2000, 31 states, the District of Columbia, and the federal prison system reported a total of 76,010 prisoners held in privately operated facilities. These private facilities accounted for 5.8 percent of all state inmates, an increase of 5.4 percent from year-end 1999, when the BJS began collecting separate counts of privately held inmates.

Just as it did in 1999 Texas reported the most privately housed prisoners, at 14,339, followed by Oklahoma at 6,735. At midyear 2000, 41 percent of prisoners in New Mexico were housed in private facilities, followed by 34 percent in Alaska, 32 percent in Montana, and 29 percent in Oklahoma.

STATE PRISONERS IN LOCAL JAILS

At year-end 1999 a total of 63,635 prisoners in 34 states were housed in local jails or other county- or

TABLE 4.5

Trends in prison population, 1990–99

December 31	Number of inmates		Sentenced prisoners per 100,000 resident population		Population housed as a percent of highest capacity	
	Federal	State	Federal	State	Federal	State
1990	65,526	708,393	20	272	—	115%
1995	100,250	1,025,624	32	379	126%	114
1998	123,041	1,177,532	38	423	127	113
1999	135,246	1,231,475*	42	434	132	101

— Not available.
*In 1999, 6 States expanded their reporting criteria. For comparisons with previous years, the count 1,209,123 should be used.

SOURCE: Allen J. Beck, Ph.D., *Prisoners in 1999*, Bureau of Justice Statistics, Washington, DC, 2000

---

municipally-operated facilities. They accounted for 5.2 percent of all state prisoners in 1999. At 44 percent Louisiana had the largest proportion of its prisoners housed in local facilities, followed by Montana (28 percent), Tennessee (25 percent), and Kentucky (21 percent).

Although fewer in number at year-end 1999 some 6,952 prisoners from 35 states were reported housed in federal facilities or state-operated facilities other than prisons. Michigan had the most inmates held under these arrangements (774), followed by California (640), and

TABLE 4.6

State and Federal prisoners held in private facilities, local jails, or other states' facilities, by jurisdiction, year-end 1999

	Private facilites		Local jails		In other state or federal facilities	
	Number	Percent of all inmates[a]	Number	Percent of all inmates[a]	Number	Percent of all inmates[a]
U.S. total	71,208	5.2%	63,635	4.7%	6,952	0.5%
Federal	3,828	2.8	0	0.0	0	0.0
State	67,380	5.5	63,635	5.2	6,952	0.6
Northeast	2,539	1.4%	6,300	3.5%	1,301	0.7
Connecticut	0	0.0	—	—	321	1.7
Maine	22	1.3	0	0.0	55	3.2
Massachusetts	0	0.0	451	4.0	296	2.6
New Hampshire	0	0.0	34	1.5	69	3.1
New Jersey[b]	2,517	8.0	4,328	13.7	62	0.2
New York	0	0.0	1,427	1.9	0	0.0
Pennsylvania	0	0.0	60	0.2	55	0.2
Rhode Island[b]	0	0.0	—	—	42	1.4
Vermont[b]	0	0.0	—	—	401	26.1
Midwest	4,784	2.1%	2,735	1.2%	1,806	0.8
Illinois	0	0.0	0	0.0	33	0.1
Indiana	936	4.8	1,224	6.3	0	0.0
Iowa	0	0.0	0	0.0	0	0.0
Kansas	0	0.0	0	0.0	99	1.2
Michigan	301	0.6	262	0.6	774	1.7
Minnesota	80	1.3	174	2.9	165	2.8
Missouri	0	0.0	0	0.0	56	0.2
Nebraska	0	0.0	0	0.0	32	0.9
North Dakota	0	0.0	24	2.5	18	1.9
Ohio	0	0.0	0	0.0	45	0.1
South Dakota	46	1.8	0	0.0	22	0.9
Wisconsin	3,421	16.8	1,051	5.1	562	2.8
South	44,656	8.1%	46,585	8.5%	2,364	0.4
Alabama	0	0.0	1,375	5.6	432	1.8
Arkansas	1,224	10.7	703	6.2	0	0.0
Delaware	0	0.0	—	—	290	4.2
District of Columbia	4,024	46.5	—	—	1,287	14.9
Florida	3,773	5.4	0	0.0	0	0.0
Georgia	3,001	7.1	3,757	8.9	0	0.0
Kentucky	1,700	11.1	3,221	21.0	15	0.1
Louisiana	3,080	9.0	14,892	43.7	0	0.0
Maryland	131	0.6	141	0.6	52	0.2
Mississippi	3,429	18.8	3,349	18.4	...	...
North Carolina	1,395	4.5	47	0.2	0	0.0
Oklahoma	6,228	27.8	1,056	4.7	0	0.0
South Carolina	0	0.0	461	2.1	288	1.3
Tennessee	3,476	15.4	5,716	25.4	0	0.0
Texas	11,653	7.1	7,131	4.4	0	0.0
Virginia	1,542	4.8	4,084	12.6	0	0.0
West Virginia	0	0.0	652	18.5	0	0.0
West	15,401	5.8%	8,015	3.0%	1,481	0.6
Alaska	1,387	35.1	—	—	33	0.8
Arizona	1,392	5.4	17	0.1	91	0.4
California	4,621	2.8	2,826	1.7	640	0.4
Colorado[c]	0	0.0	2,675	17.1	0	0.0
Hawaii	1,168	23.8	—	—	31	0.6
Idaho	400	8.3	431	8.9	96	2.0
Montana	726	24.6	831	28.1	...	...
Nevada	561	5.9	157	1.7	206	2.2
New Mexico	1,873	36.6	153	3.0	105	2.0
Oregon	0	0.0	10	0.1	75	0.8
Utah	248	4.6	879	16.2	112	2.1
Washington[b]	331	2.3	0	0.0	73	0.5
Wyoming	281	16.4	36	2.1	19	1.1

Note: Some inmates held in private facilities may be in local jails or out of state.
—Not applicable. Prison and jails form an integrated system.
... Not reported.
[a] Based on the total number of inmates under state or federal jurisdiction.
[b] Inmates held in other state facilities include interstate compact cases.
[c] Colorado housed 2,413 inmates in private facilities under contract to local jails.

SOURCE: Allen J. Beck, Ph.D., *Prisoners in 1999*, Bureau of Justice Statistics, Washington, DC, 2000

TABLE 4.7

Reported federal and state prison capacities, year-end 1999

Region and jurisdiction	Type of capacity measure			Custody population as a percent of —	
	Rated	Opera-tional	Design	Highest capacity[a]	Lowest capacity[a]
Federal	90,075	...	...	132%	132%
Northeast					
Connecticut[b]	...	...	...	...	...
Maine	1,460	1,639	1,460	100	112
Massachusetts	...	...	9,162	122	122
New Hampshire	2,036	2,064	1,944	109	116
New Jersey	...	...	17,282	143	143
New York	61,265	66,384	53,815	108	133
Pennsylvania	25,228	32,384	25,228	113	145
Rhode Island	3,724	3,724	3,862	76	79
Vermont	1,140	1,200	1,023	95	111
Midwest					
Illinois	32,313	32,313	27,529	138%	162%
Indiana	15,383	17,944	...	96	111
Iowa	6,219	6,219	6,219	116	116
Kansas	8,860	...	...	97	97
Michigan	...	47,178	...	98	98
Minnesota	5,664	5,786	5,786	98	100
Missouri	...	27,416	...	95	95
Nebraska	...	2,963	2,371	120	150
North Dakota	1,005	952	1,005	91	96
Ohio	37,245	...	...	125	125
South Dakota	...	2,545	...	96	96
Wisconsin	...	10,951	...	139	139
South					
Alabama	21,800	21,800	21,800	97%	97%
Arkansas[c]	10,426	10,426	10,426	100	100
Delaware	...	4,206	3,192	...	...
District of Columbia	5,424	5,424	...	85	85
Florida	80,491	73,325	54,252	82	121
Georgia	...	43,808	...	89	89
Kentucky	11,947	11,707	7,421	93	150
Louisiana	19,174	19,363	...	83	84
Maryland	...	23,213	...	97	97
Mississippi/c	...	17,827	...	102	102
North Carolina	27,145	...	27,145	109	109
Oklahoma[c]	...	22,594	...	99	99
South Carolina	...	23,565	22,177	89	95
Tennessee	17,522	17,127	...	96	98
Texas[c]	155,924	152,805	155,924	97	99
Virginia	31,787	31,787	31,787	91	91
West Virginia	3,059	2,880	2,950	94	100
West					
Alaska	2,603	2,691	2,603	94%	97%
Arizona	...	24,310	24,310	101	101
California	...	154,467	80,272	101	194
Colorado[d]	...	11,230	9,424	116	138
Hawaii	...	3,406	2,481	102	141
Idaho	3,182	3,956	3,182	97	120
Montana	...	1,400	896	100	156
Nevada[c]	9,379	...	6,948	99	134
New Mexico[c]	...	5,592	5,504	92	93
Oregon	...	9,550	...	99	99
Utah	...	4,418	4,584	115	119
Washington	8,862	12,036	12,036	119	161
Wyoming	1,231	1,243	1,047	101	120

. . . Data not available.

—Not calculated.

[a] Population counts are based on the number of inmates held in facilities operated by the jurisdiction. Excludes inmates held in local jails, other states, or private facilities.

[b] Connecticut no longer reports capacity because of a law passed in 1995.

[c] Includes capacity of private and contract facilities and inmates housed in them.

[d] Excludes capacity of county facilities and inmates housed in them.

SOURCE: Allen J. Beck, Ph.D., *Prisoners in 1999*, Bureau of Justice Statistics, Washington, DC, 2000

TABLE 4.8

State prison population as a percent of capacity, year-end 1999

	State prisons[a]
Highest capacity	1,115,334
Lowest capacity	965,487
Population as a percent of capacity[b]	
Highest	
1990	115
1995	114
1998	113
1999 (comparable)	109
1999 (revised)	101
Lowest	
1990	127
1995	125
1998	122
1999	117

Note: Data reflect the highest and lowest of the three capacities reported. In 1999 California reported operational capacity for the first time; for comparisons with previous years, use 1,041,139 as the highest capacity of state prisons.

[a] Capacity figures were estimated for Connecticut in 1995, 1998 and 1999.
[b] Excludes inmates sentenced to prison but held in local jails and inmates in private facilities (unless included in the reported capacity).

SOURCE: Allen J. Beck, Ph.D., *Prisoners in 1999,* Bureau of Justice Statistics, Washington, DC, 2000

Wisconsin (562). Vermont had 26 percent of its prison population housed in federal or other state facilities, followed by the District of Columbia at 15 percent.

Sometimes states try to cope with overcrowding by sending some of their prisoners to less crowded prisons or jails in other parts of the country. Prisoner advocates criticize the transfer of prisoners to other states because it makes the lives of the prisoners and their families far more difficult. According to a spokesperson for the American Friends Service Committee in Cambridge, Massachusetts: "It's not possible for them [family and friends] to visit. Having family members incarcerated is difficult enough, but to have the person 1,800 miles away, suddenly, is absolutely devastating." In addition, the inmates complain about difficulties meeting their lawyers and arranging for work and housing upon their release.

PRISON CAPACITY

The extent of crowding in the nation's prisons is difficult to determine because of the absence of uniform measures for defining capacity. Various jurisdictions apply a wide variety of standards to reflect both available space to house inmates and the ability to staff and operate an institution. To estimate the capacity of the nation's prisons, jurisdictions are asked to supply three measures—rated, operational, and design capacities. Rated capacity is the number of beds or inmates assigned by a rating official to institutions within the jurisdiction. Operational capacity is

the number of inmates that can be accommodated based on a facility's staff, existing programs, and services. Design capacity is the number of inmates that planners or architects intended for the facility.

Of the 51 reporting jurisdictions 30 supplied rated capacities, 44 provided operational capacities, and 35 submitted design capacities. Twenty-one jurisdictions reported one capacity measure or gave the same figure for each capacity measure they reported. (See Table 4.7.) Private and contract facilities were included in the capacity counts of seven states. As a result inmates held in those facilities were added to population counts.

Most Operate Above Capacity

Prisons generally require reserve capacity to operate efficiently. Prison dormitories and cells need to be maintained and repaired periodically, special housing is needed for protective custody and disciplinary cases, and space may be needed to cope with emergencies. At the end of 1999, 26 states and the District of Columbia reported they were operating at or below 99 percent of their highest capacity.

On the other hand, in 1999, 22 states and the federal prison system reported operating at 100 percent or more of their lowest capacity. (See Table 4.8.) Rhode Island, which was operating at 76 percent of its lowest capacity, had the least crowded prison system. California, operating at 94 percent over its lowest reported capacity, had the highest percent of capacity occupied. By year-end 1999 officials estimated that state prisons were operating at 1 percent above their highest capacities and 17 percent above their lowest capacities. The federal prison system was operating at 32 percent over capacity. A closer look at the populations of federal correctional facilities at year-end 1999 reveals the tight margins between actual capacity and rated capacity. (See Table 4.9.)

This level of overcrowding in the federal correctional system not only has a negative impact on inmates, but on prison staff as well. For example, most male prison staff employees have been on the job less than nine years, while only about 2 percent have 20 years or more experience. (See Table 4.10.) Roughly the same is true for female staff members in the federal system, indicating that most male and female employees leave before reaching their 10-year mark.

RISING STATE PRISON POPULATIONS

More People Coming to Court

There are a number of reasons why the nation's state prison population has been growing. First is the simple increase in the number of prisoners. The BJS reported that, in 1996, state courts convicted 997,970 adults of a felony, 50 percent greater than the number convicted in 1988 (667,366). Since 1988 the general trend has been upward. (See Table 4.11, Table 4.12, and Figure 4.3.)

TABLE 4.9

Federal Bureau of Prisons facilities, September 1999

Facility/State	Year opened	Security level	Sex of inmates	Rated capacity	1999 1-day population count	Number of staff	Adjacent minimum security camp[a] Rated capacity	Adjacent minimum security camp[a] 1999 1-day population count
United States Penitentiaries (USP)								
Allenwood (PA)	1993	High	Male	640	989	377		
Atlanta (GA)	1902	High/Administrative	Male	1,429	1,977	690	488	476
Beaumont (TX)	1997	High	Male	960	1,531	286	350	345
Florence (CO)	1996	High	Male	640	982	347		
Leavenworth (KS)	1906	High	Male	1,197	1,795	538	414	460
Lewisburg (PA)[b]	1932	High	Male	678	997	564	352	252
Lompoc (CA)	1959	High	Male	1,035	1,579	500	276	281
Marion (IL)	1963	High	Male	482	270	478	310	283
Terre Haute (IN)	1940	High	Male	791	1,145	492	340	332
Federal Correctional Institutions (FCI)								
Allenwood Low (PA)	1993	Low	Male	992	1,302	223		
Allenwood Medium (PA)	1993	Medium	Male	841	1,189	301		
Ashland (KY)	1940	Low	Male	662	1,098	318	296	255
Bastrop (TX)	1979	Low	Male	719	1,125	254	122	147
Beaumont Low (TX)	1997	Low	Male	1,536	1,802	203		
Beaumont Medium (TX)	1999	Medium	Male	1,152	1,306	198		
Beckley (WV)	1995	Medium	Male	1,152	1,671	369	384	350
Big Spring (TX)	1979	Low	Male	468	1,023	248	144	163
Butner Low (NC)	1996	Low	Male	992	1,296	238		
Butner Medium (NC)	1976	Medium/Administrative	Male	513	785	380	296	289
Coleman Low (FL)	1996	Low	Male	1,536	1,802	200		
Coleman Medium (FL)[c]	1996	Medium	Male	1,146	1,616	251	512	430
Cumberland (MD)	1994	Medium	Male	768	1,172	308	256	255
Danbury (CT)	1940	Low	Female	508	959	278	178	191
Dublin (CA)[c]	1974	Low; Administrative[d]	Female; Male	810	1,148	275	299	321
Edgefield (SC)	1998	Medium	Male	960	1,380	409	256	276
El Reno (OK)	1933	Medium	Male	820	1,204	381	216	232
Elkton (OH)	1997	Low	Male	1,536	1,826	320	256	302
Englewood (CO)	1940	Medium/Administrative	Male	476	881	336	111	104
Estill (SC)	1993	Medium	Male	768	1,078	315	256	238
Fairton (NJ)	1990	Medium/Administrative	Male	849	1,186	335	65	87
Florence (CO)	1994	Medium	Male	840	1,232	322	416	309
Forrest City (AR)	1997	Low	Male	1,536	1,860	308	128	189
Fort Dix (NJ)	1993	Low	Male	3,331	3,824	621		
Greenville (IL)	1994	Medium	Male	752	1,160	296	256	259
Jesup (GA)	1990	Medium	Male	744	1,070	320	508	532
La Tuna (TX)[e]	1932	Low	Male	556	1,120	296	246	204
Lompoc (CA)[b]	1970	Low	Male	472	811	234		
Loretto (PA)	1984	Low	Male	473	758	219	93	94
Manchester (KY)	1992	Medium	Male	744	1,134	327	512	443
Marianna (FL)[c]	1988	Medium	Male	805	1,122	363	296	324
McKean (PA)	1989	Medium	Male	784	1,085	315	292	237
Memphis (TN)	1977	Medium	Male	597	912	349	296	278
Miami (FL)	NA	Medium	Male	586	890	292	260	321
Milan (MI)	1933	Low/Administrative	Male	1,021	1,409	361		
Morgantown (WV)	1969	Minimum	Male	935	1,005	184		
Oakdale (LA)	1986	Medium	Male	820	1,137	302		
Otisville (NY)	1980	Medium	Male	665	1,045	320	100	103
Oxford (WI)	1973	Medium	Male	586	1,058	324	156	194
Pekin (IL)[c]	1994	Medium	Male	752	1,178	303	256	295
Petersburg (VA)	1932	Low	Male	828	1,129	348	296	294
Phoenix (AZ)[c]	1985	Medium	Male	740	1,266	322	272	251
Ray Brook (NY)	1980	Medium	Male	737	1,067	269		
Safford (AZ)	1964	Low	Male	421	809	175		
Sandstone (MN)	1939	Low	Male	473	826	246		
Schuylkill (PA)	1991	Medium/Administrative	Male	729	1,122	336	296	261
Seagoville (TX)	1945	Low/Administrative	Male	866	1,260	286		
Sheridan (OR)	1989	Medium/Administrative	Male	923	1,367	373	512	446
Talladega (AL)	1979	Medium	Male	644	953	342	296	408
Tallahassee (FL)	Late 1930s	Low; Adminstrative[d]	Female; Male	692	1,133	325		
Terminal Island (CA)	1938	Medium	Male	478	1,014	309		
Texarkana (TX)	1940	Low	Male	747	1,366	304	220	320
Three Rivers (TX)	1990	Medium	Male	784	1,014	310	256	304
Tucson (AZ)	1982	Medium; Administrative[f]	Male; Both	392	830	225		
Waseca (MN)	1995	Low	Male	710	1,058	225		
Yazoo City (MS)	1997	Low	Male	1,536	1,865	283		

See notes at end of table.

TABLE 4.9

Federal Bureau of Prisons facilities, September 1999 [CONTINUED]

Facility/State	Year opened	Security level	Sex of inmates	Rated capacity	1999 1-day population count	1999 1-day Number of staff	Adjacent minimum security camp[a] Rated capacity	1999 1-day population count
Federal Prison Camps (FPC)								
Alderson (WV)	1927	Minimum	Female	838	924	179		
Allenwood (PA)	1952	Minimum	Male	567	722	119		
Boron (CA)[g]	1979	Minimum	Male	324	203	87		
Bryan (TX)[b]	1988	Minimum	Female	720	725	151		
Duluth (MN)	1983	Minimum	Male	881	575	106		
Eglin (FL)	1962	Minimum	Male	800	765	130		
El Paso (TX)	1989	Minimum	Male	308	195	51		
Montgomery (AL)	NA	Minimum	Male	920	715	122		
Nellis (NV)	1990	Minimum	Male	561	479	72		
Pensacola (FL)	1988	Minimum	Male	424	479	86		
Seymour Johnson (NC)	1989	Minimum	Male	576	489	94		
Yankton (SD)	1988	Minimum	Male	655	551	104		
Metropolitan Correctional/ Detention Centers (MCC/MDC)								
Brooklyn (NY)	1996	Administrative	Both	564	1,231	355		
Chicago (IL)	1975	Administrative	Both	411	756	222		
Guaynabo (PR)	1993	Administrative	Both	897	1,118	282		
Los Angeles (CA)	1988	Administrative	Both	728	940	272		
New York (NY)	1975	Administrative	Both	507	898	287		
San Diego (CA)	1974	Administrative	Both	612	962	260		
Federal Medical Centers (FMC)								
Carswell (TX)	1995	Administrative	Female	833	969	405	148	226
Devens (MA)[h]	1999	Administrative	Male	564	548	344	40	35
Fort Worth (TX)	1971	Administrative	Male	1,132	1,505	408		
Lexington (KY)[c]	1974	Administrative	Male	1,106	1,609	528	193	216
Rochester (MN)	1985	Administrative	Male	674	802	439		
Springfield (MO)	1933	Administrative	Male	912	1,155	657		
Federal Detention Centers (FDC)								
Miami (FL)	1976	Administrative	Both	1,283	1,544	291		
Oakdale (LA)	1990	Administrative	Male	630	884	239	118	138
SeaTac (WA)	1997	Administrative	Both	695	674	249		
Federal Transportation Center (FTC)								
Oklahoma City (OK)	1996	Administrative	Both	1,074	1,360	301		
Administrative Maximum (ADX)								
Florence (CO)	1995	Administrative	Male	490	356	333		

Note: Administrative facilities are institutions with special missions, such as the detention of noncitizen or pretrial offenders, the treatment of inmates with serious or chronic medical problems, or the containment of extremely dangerous, violent, or escape-prone inmates. Administrative facilities are capable of holding inmates in all security categories.

[a] These minimum security satellite camps are adjacent to the main facilities. A blank indicates no camp facility. Except where noted, the sex of inmates housed in the camp and main facility is the same.

[b] The adjacent facility has an Intensive Confinement Center that houses additional inmates.

[c] The adjacent camp is a minimum security facility for females.

[d] This facility houses low security females and administrative security males.

[e] Located on the New Mexico-Texas border.

[f] This facility houses medium security males and administrative security males and females.

[g] Scheduled to be deactivated in January 2000.

[h] This facility was being activated at the time of data collection. When fully operational, Devens will have a capacity of 986 and the camp will have a capacity of 124.

SOURCE: "Table 1.84: Federal Bureau of Prisons Facilities," *Sourcebook of Criminal Justice Statistics* [Online], Kathleen Maguire and Ann L. Pastore, eds. May 2, 2001 http://www.albany.edu/sourcebook/

The state courts are sentencing more people to prison because more people are being brought to court, not because the courts are becoming more likely to sentence them to prison. From 1988 to 1994 the percentage of felons receiving a state prison sentence remained at about 45 percent, but in 1996 that percentage fell to 38 percent. The drop in prison sentences was accompanied by an increase in the percentage receiving other types of sentences, particularly sentences to local jails. From 1988 to 1994 jail sentences made up about 25 percent of all felony sentences. In 1996 the percentage receiving a jail sentence rose to 31 percent. (See Figure 4.1.) Of all felony offenses burglary had one of the largest decreases in the percentage sentenced to prison between 1988 and 1996. (See Figure 4.4.)

An Increasing Number in Prison for Drug Offenses and Violent Crimes

According to figures reported by the United States Sentencing Commission, in 1999 of 55,408 convicted defendants in federal courts, some 43,536 received prison

TABLE 4.10

Employment characteristics of Federal Bureau of Prisons correctional officers by race, ethnicity, and sex, 1999

	Total		Race and ethnicity							
			White		Black		Hispanic		Other[a]	
	Number	Percent	Number	Percent	Number	Percent	Number	Percent	Number	Percent
Total	13,240	100.0%	8,151	100.0%	3,174	100.0%	1,588	100.0%	327	100.0%
Region										
Male	11,580	87.5	7,404	90.8	2,467	77.7	1,412	88.9	297	90.8
Northeast	2,291	17.3	1,697	20.8	325	10.2	216	13.6	53	16.2
North Central	2,125	16.0	1,724	21.2	209	6.6	153	9.6	39	11.9
Mid-Atlantic	1,801	13.6	1,285	15.8	436	13.7	53	3.3	27	8.3
Southeast	1,985	15.0	838	10.3	769	24.2	325	20.5	53	16.2
South Central	1,986	15.0	1,087	13.3	465	14.7	380	23.9	54	16.5
West	1,392	10.5	773	9.5	263	8.3	285	17.9	71	21.7
Female	1,660	12.5	747	9.2	707	22.3	176	11.1	30	9.2
Northeast	260	2.0	127	1.6	101	3.2	29	1.8	3	0.9
North Central	202	1.5	141	1.7	42	1.3	16	1.0	3	0.9
Mid-Atlantic	231	1.7	132	1.6	87	2.7	8	0.5	4	1.2
Southeast	335	2.5	85	1.0	214	6.7	32	2.0	4	1.2
South Central	391	3.0	149	1.8	191	6.0	46	2.9	5	1.5
West	241	1.8	113	1.4	72	2.3	45	2.8	11	3.4
Length of employment										
Male	11,580	87.5	7,404	90.8	2,467	77.7	1,412	88.9	297	90.8
Less than 1 year	1,076	8.1	605	7.4	279	8.8	160	10.1	32	9.8
1 to 2 years	1,968	14.9	1,201	14.7	468	14.7	253	15.9	46	14.1
3 to 4 years	2,036	15.4	1,277	15.7	445	14.0	252	15.9	62	19.0
5 to 9 years	3,739	28.2	2,370	29.1	768	24.2	517	32.6	84	25.7
10 to 14 years	1,883	14.2	1,325	16.3	345	10.9	157	9.9	56	17.1
15 to 19 years	587	4.4	418	5.1	108	3.4	51	3.2	10	3.1
20 years or more	291	2.2	208	2.6	54	1.7	22	1.4	7	2.1
Female	1,660	12.5	747	9.2	707	22.3	176	11.1	30	9.2
Less than 1 year	287	2.2	103	1.3	143	4.5	37	2.3	4	1.2
1 to 2 years	350	2.6	136	1.7	167	5.3	41	2.6	6	1.8
3 to 4 years	280	2.1	146	1.8	103	3.2	29	1.8	2	0.6
5 to 9 years	441	3.3	209	2.6	168	5.3	51	3.2	13	4.0
10 to 14 years	230	1.7	106	1.3	104	3.3	15	0.9	5	1.5
15 to 19 years	55	0.4	36	0.4	17	0.5	2	0.1	0	X
20 years or more	17	0.1	11	0.1	5	0.2	1	0.1	0	X

[a] Includes Asians and Native Americans as well as non-Hispanic employees in Puerto Rico.

SOURCE: "Table 1.88: Employment characteristics of Federal Bureau of Prisons correctional officers," in *Sourcebook of Criminal Justice Statistics 1999*, Kathleen Maguire and Ann L. Pastore, eds., Bureau of Justice Statistics, Washington, D.C., 2000

sentences. Of those more than 25 percent were sentenced to prison terms exceeding 60 months (5 years). The average federal sentence in 1999 was 56.9 months. The median sentence was 33 months, meaning that, in 1999, half of all federal prison sentences handed down were higher that 33 months and half were lower.

The rise in drug offenders confined to federal prison has contributed dramatically to the overcrowding of those prisons. According to the U.S. Bureau of Prisons, Washington, D.C., of 20,686 total sentenced federal prisoners in 1970, some 3,384 were drug offenders—about 16 percent. (See Table 4.13.) By August 2000 the number of sentenced drug offenders in federal prisons had risen to 63,621 and comprised more than half (about 57 percent) of the 111,885 total sentenced prisoners in the federal correctional system.

In state courts nationwide the rate of prison sentences actually served rose to 45 percent in 1996, up from 38 percent in 1992, and 32 percent in 1988. (See Table 4.14.)

This is mitigated to some extent by a reduction in the average sentence imposed by state courts, from 79 months in 1992 to 62 months in 1996. However, for the crime of murder, the actual imposed sentence rose to 257 months, from 251 months in 1992 and 239 months in 1988. This means that the most serious violent offenders are serving longer prison sentences. Also, for the crime of murder, the approximate likelihood of felony arrest leading to conviction in state court rose to 71 percent in 1996, up from 65 percent in 1992 and 48 percent in 1988. Thus, more and more violent offenders requiring the highest levels of security are flowing from the courts to state prisons.

From 1990 to 1998 the distribution of the four major offense categories—violent, property, drug, and public-order offenses—changed only slightly among state prisoners. (See Table 4.15.) At year-end 1998, some 545,200 state prisoners were incarcerated for violent offenses—159,000 for robbery; 134,600 for murder; 109,500 for assault; and 100,800 for rape and other sexual offenses. Property crimes

TABLE 4.11

Estimated number of felony convictions in state courts, 1996

Most serious conviction offense	Felon convictions in State court	
	Number	Percent
All offenses	**997,970**	**100%**
Violent offenses	**167,824**	**16.8%**
Murder[a]	11,430	1.1
Murder	8,564	0.9
Manslaughter	2,866	0.3
Sexual assault[b]	30,057	3.0
Rape	13,559	1.4
Other sexual assault	16,498	1.7
Robbery	42,831	4.3
Armed	12,041	1.2
Unarmed	12,155	1.2
Unspecified	18,635	1.9
Aggravated assault	69,522	7.0
Other violent[c]	13,984	1.4
Property offenses	**298,631**	**29.9%**
Burglary	93,197	9.3
Residential	10,605	1.1
Nonresidential	18,220	1.8
Unspecified	64,371	6.5
Larceny[d]	123,201	12.3
Motor vehicle theft	17,794	1.8
Other theft	105,406	10.6
Fraud[e]	82,233	8.2
Fraud	41,480	4.2
Forgery	40,753	4.1
Drug offenses	**347,774**	**34.8%**
Possession	135,270	13.6
Trafficking	212,504	21.3
Marijuana	20,618	2.1
Other	68,985	6.9
Unspecified	122,901	12.3
Weapons offenses	**33,337**	**3.3%**
Other offenses[f]	**150,404**	**15.1%**

Note: Detail may not sum to total because of rounding. Data specifying the conviction offense were available for 997,970 cases.
[a] Manslaughter is defined as nonnegligent manslaughter only. A small number of cases were classified as nonnegligent manslaughter when it was unclear if the conviction offense was murder or nonnegligent manslaughter
[b] Includes rape.
[c] Includes offenses such as negligent manslaughter and kidnaping.
[d] Includes a small number of convictions with unspecified offenses.
[e] Includes embezzlement.
[f] Composed on nonviolent offenses such as receiving stolen property and vandalism.

SOURCE: Jodi M. Brown, Patrick A. Langan, and David J. Levin, *Felony Sentences in State Courts, 1996*, Bureau of Justice Statistics, Washington, DC, 1999

TABLE 4.12

Number of felony convictions in state courts, 1988–96

Year	Number of convictions
1988	667,366
1990	829,344
1992	893,630
1994	782,217
1996	997,970

SOURCE: Jodi M. Brown, Patrick A. Langan, and David J. Levin, *Felony Sentences in State Courts, 1996*, Bureau of Justice Statistics, Washington, DC, 1999

FIGURE 4.3

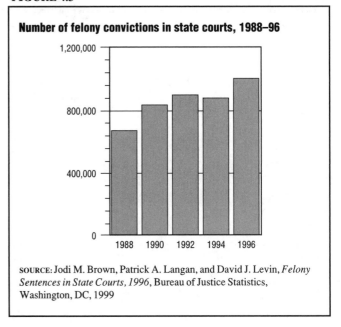

Number of felony convictions in state courts, 1988–96

SOURCE: Jodi M. Brown, Patrick A. Langan, and David J. Levin, *Felony Sentences in State Courts, 1996*, Bureau of Justice Statistics, Washington, DC, 1999

accounted for 242,900 state inmates; drug offenses for 236,800; and public-order offenses for 113,900.

Between 1990 and 1998 the rate of violent male offenders sentenced to state prisons rose by 53 percent while the rate of female prisoners sentenced for violent crimes climbed by 27 percent. (See Table 4.16.) However, the most dramatic rise was seen in the rate of female prisoners sentenced for drug offenses—up 36 percent since 1990. Among sentenced male state prisoners drug offenses accounted for the second-highest rate of increase at 19 percent.

According to the BJS in *Felony Sentences in State Courts, 1996* (Washington, D.C., 1999), inmates released from state prison in 1988 had served an average of one-third of the sentence imposed on them by the court. In 1996 inmates were released after serving approximately half of their court-imposed sentences.

While prisoners are serving a growing percentage of their court-imposed sentence, the average court-imposed sentence has been decreasing. In 1988 the typical felon received a six-year sentence and would normally serve one-third, or two years, of that sentence before being released. (This is assuming a person sentenced in 1988 served the same proportion of the sentence as was typical of those persons released in 1988.) In contrast, in 1996, the typical felon received a five-year sentence (assuming a person sentenced in 1996 served the same proportion of the sentence as was typical of those persons released in 1996), but would serve half of that sentence, or 2.5 years. (See Table 4.17.)

Truth-in-Sentencing Laws

During the 1990s sentencing requirements and release policies became more restrictive, largely in

FIGURE 4.4

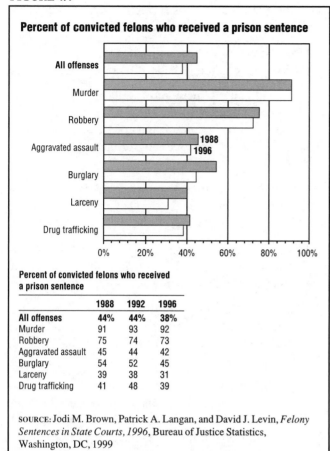

Percent of convicted felons who received a prison sentence

(Chart showing percentages for 1988 and 1996 by offense type)

- All offenses
- Murder
- Robbery
- Aggravated assault
- Burglary
- Larceny
- Drug trafficking

(Scale: 0% to 100%)

Percent of convicted felons who received a prison sentence

	1988	1992	1996
All offenses	44%	44%	38%
Murder	91	93	92
Robbery	75	74	73
Aggravated assault	45	44	42
Burglary	54	52	45
Larceny	39	38	31
Drug trafficking	41	48	39

SOURCE: Jodi M. Brown, Patrick A. Langan, and David J. Levin, *Felony Sentences in State Courts, 1996*, Bureau of Justice Statistics, Washington, DC, 1999

TABLE 4.13

Drug offenders in the federal prison population: 1970–August 2000

Year	Total sentenced and unsentenced population	Total sentenced population	Total sentenced drug offenders	Percentage of sentenced prisoners who are drug offenders
1970	21,266	20,686	3,384	16.3%
1971	20,891	20,529	3,495	17.0%
1972	22,090	20,729	3,523	16.9%
1973	23,336	22,038	5,652	25.6%
1974	23,690	21,769	6,203	28.4%
1975	23,566	20,692	5,540	26.7%
1976	27,033	24,135	6,425	26.6%
1977	29,877	25,673	6,743	26.2%
1978	27,674	23,501	5,981	25.4%
1979	24,810	21,539	5,468	25.3%
1980	24,252	19,023	4,749	24.9%
1981	26,195	19,765	5,076	25.6%
1982	28,133	20,938	5,518	26.3%
1983	30,214	26,027	7,201	27.6%
1984	32,317	27,622	8,152	29.5%
1985	36,042	27,623	9,491	34.3%
1986	37,542	30,104	11,344	37.7%
1987	41,609	33,246	13,897	41.8%
1988	41,342	33,758	15,087	44.7%
1989	47,568	37,758	18,852	49.9%
1990	54,613	46,575	24,297	52.2%
1991	61,026	52,176	29,667	56.9%
1992	67,768	59,516	35,398	59.5%
1993	76,531	68,183	41,393	60.7%
1994	82,269	73,958	45,367	61.3%
1995	85,865	76,947	46,669	60.7%
1996	89,672	80,872	49,096	60.7%
1997	95,513	87,294	52,059	59.6%
1998	104,507	95,323	55,984	58.7%
1999	115,024	104,500	60,399	57.8%
August 2000	122,750	111,885	63,621	56.9%

Note: Data for 1970 to 1976 are for June 30; data for 1977 onward are for September 30. Data are for inmates in Bureau of Prisons facilities only (i.e., do not include inmates in contract facilities).

SOURCE: "Federal prison population over time/drug offenders," U.S. Bureau of Prisons, Washington, D.C., 2000

response to prevailing "get tough on crime" attitudes throughout the country. States enacted truth-in-sentencing laws that require offenders to serve a substantial portion of their prison sentences and reduce the disparity between the sentence imposed and actual time served in prison. Under these laws parole eligibility and good-time credits were restricted or eliminated. The definition of truth-in-sentencing, the percent of sentence required to be served, and the crimes covered vary among states. (See Table 4.18.) Most states have focused on violent offenders under truth-in-sentencing.

Parole Violators

A major contributing factor to the growth in state prison populations between 1990 and 1998 was the 54 percent increase in the number of offenders returning to prison for parole violations. (See Table 4.19.) In 1998 some 206,751 offenders entering state prisons had violated the conditions of their release, an increase from 133,870 in 1990. These offenders had been previously paroled either by a decision of a parole board or by statute. The primary reason for their return to prison was an arrest and/or conviction for a new criminal offense. In 1997 a survey of state prison inmates found that 60 percent were returned to prison as the result of committing a

new offense, 19 percent had failed to report to their parole officer, and 14 percent had a drug-related violation (positive test, possession, or failure to report for treatment).

NATIONAL ASSESSMENT PROGRAM (NAP)

The 1995 National Assessment Program survey of wardens indicates concern about overcrowding. Of the 361 warden responses, 135 (37 percent) reported that their prisons were crowded (they housed more than 100 percent of rated capacity). Thirteen wardens indicated their inmate population was at less than 90 percent of rated capacity, 147 claimed their population was between 90 and 100 percent of rated capacity, and 54 had inmate populations between 101 and 110 percent of rated capacity.

Wardens with crowded conditions gave several reasons for their problems, including drug crime offenders (cited by 88 percent of wardens), violent crime offenders (80 percent), longer sentences for offenders (78 percent),

TABLE 4.14

Percent of imposed prison sentence actually served

	1988	1992	1996
All offenses	32%	38%	45%
Murder	33	44	50
Robbery	33	46	47
Aggravated assault	36	48	54
Burglary	30	35	42
Larceny	29	33	44
Drug trafficking	30	34	42

Average imposed prison sentence length (in months)

	1988	1992	1996
All offenses	76 mo	79 mo	62 mo
Murder	239	251	257
Robbery	114	117	101
Aggravated assault	90	87	69
Burglary	74	76	60
Larceny	50	53	40
Drug trafficking	66	72	55

Estimated actual time to be served in prison (in months)

	1988	1992	1996
All offenses	24 mo	30 mo	28 mo
Murder	79	110	128
Robbery	38	54	48
Aggravated assault	32	42	38
Burglary	22	27	25
Larceny	15	17	17
Drug trafficking	20	24	23

SOURCE: David J. Levin, Patrick A. Langan, Jodi M. Brown, "Trends in the United States: 1988 to 1996" in *State Court Sentencing of Convicted Felons, 1996,* Bureau of Justice Statistics, U.S. Department of Justice, Washington, D.C., 2000

TABLE 4.15

Percent of sentenced state inmates, by offense, 1990 and 1998

	1990	1998
Total	100%	100%
Violent	46	48
Property	25	21
Drug	22	21
Public-order	7	10

SOURCE: Allen J. Beck, Ph.D., *Prisoners in 1999,* Bureau of Justice Statistics, Washington, DC, 2000

parole violators (72 percent), and insufficient alternatives to prisons (71 percent). Observations from wardens supported the following conclusions:

- Drug offenders with heavy sentences fill up about 75 percent of the available cells.

- Approximately 85 percent of female inmates have a history of substance abuse. Whether directly convicted of a drug crime or committing crimes to support drug habits, these offenses account for the highest increase in population.

- Increasing commitments in mandatory drug sentences drive the rapid increase in the growth of female offenders.

- More offenders are being sentenced for violent crimes, and more are given life sentences that are now 40 years or more without parole.

- The increasing number of drug-related offenders has backlogged the system to the point that hundreds of inmates who should be at reduced security facilities end up in prisons.

- The number of violent criminals who are also substance abusers or drug sellers has increased. They are younger and more difficult to control. Consequently they stay in prison longer as parole officials are not inclined to release them.

- Prison crowding especially impacts negatively on classification of inmates for program needs. As the numbers increase the emphasis shifts from treatment and programming to containment. Resources normally allocated to programs are diverted to security. Prison crowding, combined with the states' fiscal austerity, makes for an atmosphere of hard choices, and the first mission becomes confinement.

- Lines for everything are longer—inmate canteen, inmate meals, backlog to get into specialty programs, and backlog for transfers to minimum-security facilities. There is also not enough disciplinary segregation

TABLE 4.16

Partitioning the total growth of sentenced prisoners under state jurisdiction, by offense and gender, 1990–98

	Total		Male		Female	
	Increase 1990-98	Percent of total	Increase 1990-98	Percent of total	Increase 1990-98	Percent of total
Total	452,100	100%	418,600	100%	33,600	100%
Violent	229,300	51	220,300	53	9,000	27
Property	67,900	15	61,200	15	6,800	20
Drug	87,100	19	75,000	18	12,100	36
Public-order	68,100	15	62,600	15	5,600	17

SOURCE: Allen J. Beck, Ph.D., *Prisoners in 1999,* Bureau of Justice Statistics, Washington, DC, 2000

TABLE 4.17

Comparison of imposed prison sentence length with actual time served, 1998–96

	Average imposed prison sentence length (in months)		
	1988	1992	1996
All offenses	**76 mo**	**79 mo**	**62 mo**
Murder	239	251	257
Robbery	114	117	101
Aggravated assault	90	87	69
Burglary	74	76	60
Larceny	50	53	40
Drug trafficking	66	72	55

	Percent of imposed prison sentence actually served		
	1988	1992	1996
All offenses	**32%**	**38%**	**45%**
Murder	33	44	50
Robbery	39	46	47
Aggravated assault	36	48	54
Burglary	30	35	42
Larceny	29	33	44
Drug trafficking	30	34	42

	Estimated actual time to be served in prison (in months)		
	1988	1992	1996
All offenses	**24 mo**	**30 mo**	**28 mo**
Murder	79	110	128
Robbery	38	54	48
Aggravated assault	32	42	38
Burglary	22	27	25
Larceny	15	17	17
Drug trafficking	20	24	23

SOURCE: Jodi M. Brown, Patrick A. Langan, and David J. Levin, *Felony Sentences in State Courts, 1996*, Bureau of Justice Statistics, Washington, DC, 1999

TABLE 4.18

Truth-in-sentencing requirements by state

Meet Federal 85% requirement		50% requirement	100% of minimum requirement	Other requirements
Arizona	Missouri	Indiana	Idaho	Alaska[c]
California	New Jersey	Maryland	Nevada	Arkansas[d]
Connecticut	New York	Nebraska	New Hampshire	Colorado[e]
Delaware	North Carolina	Texas		Kentucky[f]
District of Col.	North Dakota			Massachusetts[g]
Florida	Ohio			Wisconsin[h]
Georgia	Oklahoma[b]			
Illinois[a]	Oregon			
Iowa	Pennsylvania			
Kansas	South Carolina			
Louisiana	Tennessee			
Maine	Utah			
Michigan	Virginia			
Minnesota	Washington			
Mississippi				

[a] Qualified for Federal funding in 1996 only.
[b] Effective July 1, 1999, offenders are required to serve 85% of the sentence.
[c] Two-part sentence structure (2/3 in prison; 1/3 on parole); 100% of prison term required.
[d] Mandatory 70% of sentence for certain violent offenses and manufacture of methamphetamine.
[e] Violent offenders with 2 prior violent convictions serve 75%; 1 prior violent conviction, 56.25%.
[f] Effective July 15, 1998, offenders are required to serve 85% of the sentence.
[g] Requires 75% of a minimum prison sentence.
[h] Effective December 31, 1999, 2-part sentence: offenders serve 100% of the prison term and a sentence of extended supervision at 25% of the prison sentence.

SOURCE: Paula M. Ditton and Doris James Wilson, *Truth in Sentencing in State Prisons*, Bureau of Justice Statistics, Washington, DC, 1999

TABLE 4.19

Number of sentenced inmates admitted to state prisons, by type of admission, 1990–98

Year	All admissions	New court commitments	Parole violators
1990	460,739	323,069	133,870
1991	466,286	317,237	142,100
1992	480,676	334,301	141,961
1993	475,100	318,069	146,366
1994	497,923	322,141	168,383
1995	521,970	337,492	175,726
1996	512,618	326,547	172,633
1997	538,375	334,525	186,659
1998	565,291	347,270	206,751
Percent change 1990-98	22.7%	7.5%	54.4%

Note: Sentenced inmates are those with a sentence of more than 1 year. Admissions exclude returned escapees and AWOL's and transfers from other jurisdictions. Admissions for Alaska were estimated for 1994. Parole violators for Idaho were estimated for 1998.

SOURCE: Allen J. Beck, Ph.D., *Prisoners in 1999*, Bureau of Justice Statistics, Washington, DC, 2000

space. Patience wanes; tempers flare. Staff is more stressed as inmates become more demanding of individual attention and acknowledgment.

PRIVATIZATION OF PRISONS

Many conservatives believe that the government could save money by allowing private businesses to perform some government functions (privatization). This policy has also affected the corrections system, especially as states and the federal government face deteriorating conditions of older public prisons, an increasing number of prisoners, and, as a result, a growing need to build more prisons. Proponents of privatization think that private firms would be more flexible than government bureaucracies in meeting changing needs and that competing firms would both improve the quality of services and reduce costs.

More than 30 types of services are provided to prisons by the private sector. The services most frequently supplied by private enterprise are health services, community treatment centers, facility construction, educational programs, drug treatment, staff training, counseling, and vocational training.

According to *Private Adult Correctional Facility Census* by Charles W. Thomas (Center for Studies in Criminology and Law, 2000) approximately 13 private companies housed a total of 138,726 inmates in 1999, up from 127,262 inmates in 1998 and 103,730 in 1997.

Concerns involving privatization of ownership and management include:

- It is the right of the state to punish. The American Civil Liberties Union commented: "No one but the state should possess the awesome responsibility or power to take away an individual's freedom; freedom should not be contracted to the lowest bidder."

- The profit motive might bring about abuses in the system. The National Association of Criminal Justice Planners commented: "Does the government want to emphasize such a mercenary value as profit in its response to a social problem, as opposed to values such as fairness, equity, and personal accountability?" Proponents of privatization counter that, with government monitoring, the private sector should be able to manage corrections.

- The government is still liable for any suits that are brought against the private company.

- Cost savings and improved quality of services are still not proven.

One of the major corporations in private industry, Corrections Corporation of America based in Nashville, Tennessee, ran 60 correctional institutions in 17 states in 1997. It asserts private prisons can make profits. The company pays the prevailing local wages but is not unionized. It also does not offer pension plans. The wardens assert that keeping prisoners from being troublesome makes the largest gains. While drug rehabilitation and recreational programs cost more at the beginning, they pay for themselves by keeping the prisoners satisfied, thus reducing tension and violence in prison. With less stress on the employees, turnover is less, reducing training costs.

According to one of the wardens, a dissatisfied prisoner in a state prison can destroy his cell, costing the state money in repairs. In privately run facilities better-quality goods are bought up front. For example, a costly $40 hard-to-destroy plastic chair is bought by a private corporation, while a state-run prison might be required to buy a cheaper, more easily destroyed, wooden chair, which has to be replaced.

Do Private Prisons Really Save Money?

A number of studies conducted by the General Accounting Office (GAO) and other research firms have found that trying to determine whether or not using private prisons saves money is difficult because there is little information available that is widely applicable to a broad variety of correctional settings.

However, such findings have not slowed the growth of the private prison industry, which surpassed $1 billion in

revenues in 1997, up sharply from $650 million in 1996. In 1996 the GAO conducted a study of public and private prisons in five states. (*Private and Public Prisons—Studies Comparing Operational Costs and/or Quality of Service*, Washington, D.C.). Of the five states studied in the GAO report (California, New Mexico, Tennessee, Texas, and Washington), the GAO considered the Tennessee study, conducted in 1995, to be the most sound of all the reports. The Tennessee study, conducted in two parts—one for operational costs and one for quality of service—by the Tennessee state legislature compared three multicustody (minimum- to maximum-security) prisons for male inmates over a period of five years. One prison was privately managed and the other two were state-run facilities. That study did not find a significant difference in the cost per inmate per day among the three similar facilities. The prisons run by the government had an average per diem rate per prisoner (adjusted for differences in prison population) of $33.18 compared to $33.78 for the privately run prison.

ON THE OTHER HAND ... A 1997 study prepared by two Louisiana State University professors showed that, in their state, private prisons do save money. The two professors, William G. Archambeault, a criminologist, and Donald R. Deis, a professor of accounting, found that private prisons were better managed and less expensive. The report considered cost savings and performance of three prisons over a five-year period. Two of the institutions were managed by private companies and one by the state. Archambeault and Deis reported that the private facilities averaged $22.93 and $23.49 per diem for each prisoner, while the publicly run prison cost $26.60.

Some officials want to continue experimenting with privatization even though there may be no cost savings by private companies. According to Donald Campbell, Commissioner of the Tennessee Department of Corrections, "as long as it does not cost any more than it costs the state, then we should consider privatization. We should compare and explore the options out there that would save the taxpayers money."

The industry is growing internationally as well as within the United States. Great Britain and Australia have contracts with private companies, and Ontario, Canada, has expressed interest in private prisons. South Africa plans a project that would include the construction of four prisons with a total capacity of 5,300 beds.

Another Option

Many states have moved toward privatization even though studies on the cost of private prisons and their quality of service are mixed. Moreover, some critics claim that the profit motive has no place in corrections.

Some observers have been suggesting another choice—the private, not-for-profit prison. A privately owned and operated not-for-profit institution could be incorporated as a tax-exempt organization, similar to a church or hospital. Such a facility would not necessarily save money but would be exempt from income and property taxes, be eligible for tax-deductible donations, and be free of shareholders to answer to. A private, not-for-profit prison would not be tied to government rules or union and benefits packages.

There are nonprofit organizations that provide treatment and counseling on a contractual basis already involved in the criminal justice system. A few such groups have successfully managed juvenile detention centers. Some supporters of private, nonprofit prisons feel that a nonprofit penitentiary might be able to recruit professionals who are principally committed to penal reform and making changes.

PRISON WORK PROGRAMS AND INDUSTRIES

Work in fields, laundries, and kitchens has always been a part of many inmates' lives; some even participate in work-release programs. According to the 1995 BJS census of correctional facilities more than 94 percent of all prisons operated inmate work programs. About 63 percent of state inmates and 90 percent of federal inmates participated in some type of work program.

According to the CJI (*The Corrections Yearbook— 1998*), among the reporting jurisdictions (including the District of Columbia and the federal government) 76,080 inmates (6.7 percent) worked in prison industries which produced goods or services that could be sold. Almost 29,854 (4.8 percent) worked on prison farms and another 393,275 (44.5 percent) did other work assignments such as laundry, which helped run the prisons. Another 156,888 (16.3 percent) were receiving full-time academic or vocational training.

State and local governments prevent prisoners from working at some jobs generally because they would be in competition with private enterprise or workers. In 1936 Congress barred convicts from working on federal contracts worth more than $10,000. In 1940 Congress made it illegal to transport convict-made goods in interstate commerce. Many states have laws prohibiting the sale of prisoner-made products within their state borders.

Some states allow prisoners to make goods for sale to governmental agencies only. In 1979 Congress allowed prisoners to work in other types of industries if they were paid the prevailing wage and local labor was not affected. Since 1990, 30 states have permitted the contracting out of prison labor to private companies.

According to the ACA the number of inmates employed in prison industries varies from 1 percent in some states to 30 percent in others, with an average of 9 percent. They usually work at producing furniture, license plates, and textiles, and at printing and farming.

Wages

Some private industries pay minimum wage, but many prisons take most of prisoners' wages to pay for room and board, restitution, family support, and taxes. The CJI found that, in 1997, the average daily pay of inmates working for state prison industries ranged from a daily average low of $1.60 to an average high of $7.06. Inmates in Georgia received no wages while Nevada prisoners earned up to $48.75 per day. Private industry generally paid higher wages to the inmates—an average of $24.27 to $38.23 per day. Florida paid inmates the lowest daily wages ($0.20) for private industry work, while Nebraska paid the highest ($67.50). According to the CJI 48 jurisdictions reported annual prison industry gross sales of $1.5 billion for agency-operated industries.

Reasons for Work Programs

Prison administrators generally favor work programs. In a *New York Times* interview, J. Michael Quinlan, former director of the Federal Bureau of Prisons, indicated that work programs are "absolutely the most important ingredient in managing a safe and secure institution to keep the inmates productively occupied, in either work or education or drug treatment or structured recreation." He believes work programs also help prepare prisoners for reentry into the noninstitutionalized world.

A Federal Bureau of Prisons study found that inmates who worked in industry were less likely to cause problems in prison or be rearrested after release than convicts who had not participated. Thomas Townsend, president of the Corrections Industry Association, observed: "It is a matter of public safety: inmates who have worked in prison and gained new skills have a significantly better chance of not returning to crime and prison."

Businesses favor prison industries also. As Bob Tessler, owner of DPAS, a California company, commented: "We don't have to pay health and welfare on top of wages; we don't have to pay vacation or sick pay." However, Jack Henning, executive secretary-treasurer of California's Federation of Labor, asserted that even the paying of minimum hourly wages for some jobs like data entry destabilizes higher-paid labor on the open market. Even though the California law says that industries should consult labor unions before establishing their prison industries, most do not.

Many inmates like the opportunity to work. It gives them relief from boredom and some extra money. When working conditions are substandard, though, convicts cannot protest. They do not have the right to talk to the media, to strike, or to change jobs.

UNICOR

UNICOR is the trade name for Federal Prison Industries, Inc., the government corporation that employs inmates in federal prisons. UNICOR should not be confused with state prison industry programs that are administered by the states. Under UNICOR, established in 1934, federal inmates get job training by producing goods and services for federal agencies. In 1999 items produced by inmates included metal products (lockers, storage cabinets, shelving), clothing and textile products (draperies, canvas goods, military clothing), graphics and services (data entry, text editing, road signs), plastics, electronics (cable assemblies, connectors, power distribution systems), and furniture products and accessories.

UNICOR products and services must be purchased by federal agencies and are not for sale in interstate commerce or to nonfederal entities. UNICOR is not permitted to compete with private industry. If UNICOR cannot make the needed product or provide the required service, federal agencies may buy the product from the private sector through a waiver issued by UNICOR. According to JoAnne O'Bryant and Keith Bea in "Prison Industries: UNICOR," a 1999 Congressional Report for Congress, approximately 18 percent of all inmates incarcerated in federal prisons are employed by UNICOR in 100 factories located in about 25 states.

UNICOR is a self-supporting government corporation that may borrow funds from the U.S. Treasury and use the proceeds to purchase equipment, pay wages to inmates and staff (over 1,600 staffers who are not inmates are employed), and invest in expansion of facilities. No funds are appropriated for UNICOR operations. Inmates earn between $0.25 per hour and $1.15 per hour.

CHAPTER 5

CHARACTERISTICS OF PRISON INMATES

*Prisoners overwhelmingly represent societal "failures,"
young men (and a small percentage of women and older
men) who have had unsuccessful experiences in their families, schools, military services, and labor force. They suffer disproportionately from child abuse, alcohol and drug
abuse, poor self-concept, and deficient social skills. They
tend to be hostile to others, and especially to authority.*

— James B. Jacobs, "Inside Prisons" (Crime File Study
Guide, National Institute of Justice, Washington,
D.C., not dated)

RACE, ETHNICITY, AGE, AND GENDER

About 1.3 million males were incarcerated in federal
or state prisons in 1999, up by 3.3 percent since 1998 and
by 6.4 percent since 1990. (See Table 5.1.) Some 90,668
females were incarcerated under the jurisdiction of federal or state correctional authorities in 1999, up by 4.4 percent since 1998 and by 8.3 percent since 1990.

The Bureau of Justice Statistics (BJS) reported that, at
midyear 2000, an estimated 12 percent of black males in
their twenties and early thirties were in prison or jail. Of the
more than 1.9 million offenders incarcerated, black males
between ages 20 and 39 years accounted for 588,800 prison
and jail inmates. By comparison about 4.1 percent of Hispanic males and 1.7 percent of white males in the same age
group were incarcerated. The BJS also reported that,
although incarceration rates generally decrease with age, as
of midyear 2000 some 3.4 percent of black males ages
45–54 were incarcerated in prison or jails, nearly double
the rate of white males in the younger 30–39 age group.

Women

Similar racial and ethnic disparities are apparent
among female federal and state prisoners. In "Women
Offenders" (*Bureau of Justice Statistics Special Report*,
December 1999, updated October 2000), the BJS estimates that 5 out of 1,000 white women, 36 out of 1,000

TABLE 5.1

**Prisoners under the jurisdiction of state or federal correctional
authorities, by gender, year-end 1990, 1998, and 1999**

	Men	Women
All inmates		
Advance 1999	1,276,053	90,668
Final 1998	1,216,219	84,354
Final 1990	729,840	44,065
Percent change, 1998-99[a]	3.3%	4.4%
Average annual 1990-99	6.4%	8.3%
Sentenced to more than 1 year		
Advance 1999	1,222,799	82,594
Final 1998	1,167,802	77,600
Percent change, 1998-99	3.1%	4.4%
Incarceration rate[b]		
1999	913	59
1990	572	32

[a]For comparisons, percents were based on comparable 1999 counts 1,256,327
males, 88,042 females, 1,204,036 sentenced males, and 81,020 sentenced females.
[b]The number of prisoners with sentences of more than 1 year per 100,000 residents
on December 31.

SOURCE: Allen J. Beck, Ph.D., *Prisoners in 1999*, Bureau of Justice Statistics,
Washington, DC, 2000

black women, and 15 out of 1,000 Hispanic women will be
imprisoned at some time during their life. (See Table 5.2.)

The BJS also reported that, from July 1, 1999, to June
30, 2000, the number of women in state or federal prisons
rose from 89,507 to 92,688, an increase of 3.6 percent. By
comparison the number of men rose by 2.2 percent. California, Texas, and the federal system housed nearly 40
percent of female prisoners as of midyear 2000.

From 1990 to 1999 the number of female prisoners
grew at an annual average rate of 8.3 percent (see Table
5.3) compared to a 6.2 percent growth rate for male

TABLE 5.2

Estimated number of women per 1,000 who will be incarcerated at some point in their lives, by age and race/ethnicity

By age –	Per 1,000 women		
	White	Black	Hispanic
20	—	3	1
25	2	11	4
30	3	20	7
35	4	27	9
40	4	31	12
45	5	33	13
50	5	34	14
55	5	35	15
65	5	36	15
Lifetime	5	36	15

SOURCE: Lawrence A. Greenfeld and Tracy L. Snell, "The prevalence of imprisonment among women" in "Women Offenders," *Bureau of Justice Statistics Special Report,* U.S. Department of Justice, Washington, D.C., 2000

prisoners. During that time the number of female prisoners increased by more than 100 percent compared to about a 75 percent increase among males. As of June 30, 2000, female prisoners comprised 6.7 percent of all prisoners, up from 5.7 percent in 1990.

TYPES OF CRIMES

State Prisoners

The percentage of sentenced prisoners admitted to state prison for violent crimes increased slightly from 1990 to 1997. (See Figure 5.1.) The same held true for drug offenders admitted to state prisons from 1990 to 1997, while property offenders were on a slight decline over that period. As for sentenced prisoners returned to state prisons during the same time period, the rates of recidivism (relapse into criminal behavior) for violent offenders remained fairly constant, from 24.8 percent in 1990 to 24.5 percent in 1997. (See Table 5.4.) The rate of returning property offenders declined during the same period, from 46.1 percent to 34.5 percent. However, drug offenders showed a steady rise in the rate of return to state prison, from 23.1 percent in 1990 to 31.8 percent in 1997.

Federal Prisoners

The percentage of federal prisoners serving time for violent crimes fell from 16.8 percent in 1990 to 11.9 percent in 1997, but the number increased from 9,557 in 1990 to 11,658 in 1997. (See Table 5.5.) In 1997 about 8.4 percent of federal inmates were serving time for property offenses, a decrease from 13.9 percent in 1990. In 1997 more than twice as many prisoners (19,197) were serving public-order offenses (mainly immigration and weapons offenses) as in 1990 (8,585). The percentage of inmates in federal prison for a drug crime rose from 53.5 percent in

TABLE 5.3

Female prisoners under jurisdiction of state and federal correctional authorities by region and jurisdiction, 1990 and 1999

	Female prisoners				
	Number		Percent change 1998 to 1999	Average annual percent change 1990 to 1999	Incarceration rate, 1999[a]
	1990	1999			
United States, total	44,065	90,668	4.4%	8.3%	59
Federal	5,011	9,913	7.9	7.9	6
State	39,054	80,755	3.9	8.4	53
Northeast	6,293	9,754	4.3	5.0	32
Connecticut	683	1,459	7.5	8.8	48
Maine	44	65	-7.1	4.4	9
Massachusetts[b]	582	742	-0.5	2.7	13
New Hampshire	44	117	0.9	11.5	19
New Jersey	1,041	1,862	12.6	6.7	44
New York	2,691	3,644	0.9	3.4	38
Pennsylvania	1,006	1,618	6.7	5.4	26
Rhode Island	166	188	-20.0	1.4	11
Vermont	36	59	13.5	5.6	14
Midwest	7,521	14,143	3.4	7.3	43
Illinois	1,183	2,802	5.9	10.1	45
Indiana[b]	681	1,222	2.0	6.7	40
Iowa	212	539	9.8	10.9	37
Kansas	284	570	9.0	8.0	42
Michigan[b]	1,688	2,027	-1.2	2.1	40
Minnesota	159	355	23.3	9.3	15
Missouri	777	1,891	0.6	10.4	67
Nebraska	145	251	0.8	6.3	28
North Dakota	20	70	1.4	14.9	20
Ohio	1,947	2,841	-2.4	4.3	49
South Dakota	77	189	-6.9	10.5	51
Wisconsin	348	1,386	18.7	(c)	51
South	15,366	37,525	5.6	10.4	67
Alabama	955	1,668	14.2	6.4	70
Arkansas	435	788	13.2	6.8	59
Delaware	226	612	(c)	(c)	56
District of Columbia[b]	606	276	-23.1	-8.4	31
Florida	2,664	3,820	8.3	4.1	49
Georgia	1,243	2,607	5.4	8.6	64
Kentucky	479	1,097	4.9	9.6	54
Louisiana	775	2,268	4.0	12.7	100
Maryland	877	1,113	-2.4	2.7	37
Mississippi	448	1,405	15.8	13.5	89
North Carolina[b]	945	1,880	-3.0	7.9	34
Oklahoma	1,071	2,316	10.8	8.9	134
South Carolina	1,053	1,447	4.6	3.6	65
Tennessee[b,d]	390	1,368	11.7	15.0	48
Texas[d]	2,196	12,502	1.1	(c)	100
Virginia	927	2,119	14.1	10.2	57
West Virginia	76	239	13.3	13.6	26
West	9,874	19,333	1.3	7.8	59
Alaska	128	288	-4.6	9.4	45
Arizona	835	1,855	3.2	9.3	64
California[b]	6,502	11,368	-2.8	6.4	65
Colorado	433	1,213	13.4	12.1	59
Hawaii	171	553	28.6	13.9	80
Idaho	120	399	16.8	14.3	63
Montana	76	262	5.6	14.7	59
Nevada	406	731	-1.6	6.8	81
New Mexico	193	460	2.2	10.1	44
Oregon	362	583	11.3	5.4	35
Utah	125	368	9.6	12.7	33
Washington	435	1,111	9.1	11.0	38
Wyoming[b]	88	142	8.4	5.5	59

[a] The number of female prisoners with sentences of more than 1 year per 100,000 U.S. residents.
[b] Growth from 1990 to 1999 may be slightly overestimated due to a change in reporting from custody to jurisdiction counts.
[c] Not calculated because of changes in reporting procedures.
[d] Excludes an unknown number of female inmates in 1990 who were state inmates held in local jails.

SOURCE: "Figure 6.40: Female prisoners under jurisdiction of State and Federal correctional authorities." in *Sourcebook of Criminal Justice Statistics* [Online], Kathleen Maguire and Ann L. Pastore, eds. May 2, 2001 http://www.albany.edu/sourcebook/

TABLE 5.4

Percent of sentenced prisoners returned to state prisons for a parole revocation by the most serious offense, 1990–97

	Percent of parole violators returned to State prisons[a]							
Most serious offense	1990	1991	1992	1993	1994	1995	1996	1997
Total	100%	100%	100%	100%	100%	100%	100%	100%
Violent offenses	**24.8%**	**24.1%**	**24.0%**	**24.2%**	**24.5%**	**24.0%**	**24.6%**	**24.5%**
Murder[b]	1.7	1.8	1.6	1.5	1.5	1.5	1.4	1.4
Negligent manslaughter	0.5	0.5	0.5	0.5	0.5	0.5	0.4	0.4
Sexual assault[c]	3.0	4.0	4.0	3.0	4.0	3.0	4.0	3.9
Robbery	13.5	11.8	12.2	12.5	11.9	11.1	10.9	10.6
Aggravated assault	5.4	5.6	5.6	5.8	6.1	6.2	6.7	6.9
Other violent	0.7	0.7	0.8	0.8	1.0	1.1	1.1	1.3
Property offenses	**46.1%**	**43.4%**	**40.3%**	**38.6%**	**37.4%**	**36.5%**	**34.7%**	**34.5%**
Burglary	23.4	21.2	20.0	18.8	17.8	17.1	15.1	15.2
Larceny/theft	12.4	11.9	10.8	10.5	10.2	9.9	9.9	9.4
Motor vehicle theft	4.2	4.2	3.6	3.7	3.8	3.8	4.4	3.8
Fraud	4.1	4.2	3.6	3.3	3.1	3.1	2.7	3.0
Other property	2.0	1.9	2.3	2.3	2.5	2.6	2.6	3.1
Drug offenses	**23.1%**	**26.0%**	**26.4%**	**27.7%**	**28.9%**	**30.2%**	**31.1%**	**31.8%**
Public-order offenses	**5.8%**	**6.3%**	**6.8%**	**7.1%**	**7.3%**	**7.6%**	**8.2%**	**8.3%**
Other	**0.2%**	**0.2%**	**2.5%**	**2.4%**	**1.9%**	**1.7%**	**1.4%**	**0.9%**

Note: Data are from the National Corrections Reporting Program and are based on the most serious offense as reported by participating States. Data may not sum to total due to rounding.
[a] Includes only those with sentences of more than 1 year.
[b] Includes nonnegligent manslaughter.
[c] Includes rape and other sexual assault.

SOURCE: *Correctional Populations in the United States, 1997*, Bureau of Justice Statistics, Washington, DC, 2000

1990 to 60 percent in 1997. Nearly twice as many federal inmates were serving a prison sentence for a drug charge in 1997 (58,610) as in 1990 (30,470).

The numbers of drug offenders in federal prisons continued to increase in 1999. As reported by the BJS some 69,047 drug offenders comprised 58 percent of federal prisoners in 1999. This dwarfs the next highest group of offenders in federal prison—the 10,431 inmates convicted of firearms, explosives, or arson crimes, who comprise 8.8 percent of the federal prison population. They are followed by federal prisoners sentenced for robbery (7.6 percent), immigration violations (7.7 percent), and property offenses (5.9 percent).

The Federal Bureau of Prisons reported a slight decline in the number of federal inmates charged with drug offenses from 69,047 in 1999 to 63,448 in August 2000. However, as of August 2000 drug offenders still comprised 58 percent of the federal prison population, the same as in 1999. (See Table 5.6.)

As of August 2000, 72.5 percent of federal prisoners were male and 27.5 percent were female. By ethnicity 65.4 percent were non-Hispanic whites, followed by 20.5 percent African American, 10.6 percent Hispanic, 1.9 percent Asian, and 1.5 percent Native American. The average age of a federal prisoner as of August 2000 was 37 years.

SENTENCES. Women served shorter maximum sentences than men, mainly because of the differences in types

FIGURE 5.1

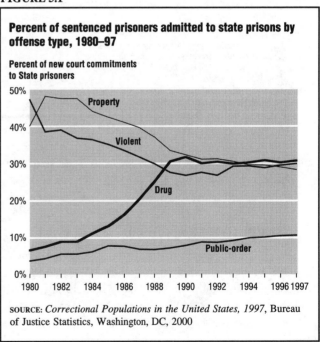

Percent of sentenced prisoners admitted to state prisons by offense type, 1980–97

Percent of new court commitments to State prisoners

SOURCE: *Correctional Populations in the United States, 1997*, Bureau of Justice Statistics, Washington, DC, 2000

of crimes they committed. Women were more likely than men to be imprisoned for drug and property offenses, which generally have shorter average sentences than violent offenses. The median (half were longer, half were shorter) maximum sentence for women was 60 months, while the median for men was 120 months. Excluding life in prison or death sentences, women in prison received

TABLE 5.5

Percent of sentenced inmates in federal prisons by the most serious offense, 1990 and 1995–97

	Percent of inmates in Federal prison[a]			
Most serious offense	1990	1995[b]	1996[b]	1997[b]
Total	**100%**	**100%**	**100%**	**100%**
Violent offenses	**16.8%**	**13.1%**	**12.6%**	**11.9%**
Homicide[c]	2.2	1.1	1.2	1.0
Assault[d]	3.4	3.0	0.7	0.7
Robbery	9.1	7.3	9.1	8.7
Other violent[e]	2.1	1.6	1.6	1.5
Property offenses	**13.9%**	**8.7%**	**8.5%**	**8.4%**
Burglary	0.8	0.2	0.2	0.2
Fraud[f]	9.0	6.5	6.3	6.3
Larceny/theft/other property[g]	4.2	2.0	2.0	1.9
Drug offenses	**53.5%**	**59.9%**	**60.2%**	**60.0%**
Public-order offenses	**15.1%**	**18.3%**	**18.8%**	**19.7%**
Immigration	3.0	4.2	4.9	5.6
Weapons	5.4	8.7	8.4	8.3
Escape/court[h]	0.7	0.4	0.4	0.4
Other public-order[i]	5.9	4.9	5.2	5.4
Other[j]	**0.8%**	**0.0%**	**0.0%**	**0.0%**

Note: All data are from the BJS Federal justice database. Data for 1990 and 1995 are for December 31. Data for 1996 and 1997 are for September 30.
[a] Includes prisoners of any sentence length.
[b] Percents are based on prisoners for whom most serious offense was known.
[c] Includes murder, nonnegligent manslaughter, and negligent manslaughter.
[d] Beginning in 1996 assaults with intent to commit robbery were coded as robbery.
[e] Includes kidnaping, rape, other sexual assault, threats against the President, and other offenses.
[f] Includes embezzlement, counterfeiting, forgery, bankruptcy, and fraud (excluding tax fraud but including securities fraud).
[g] Includes motor vehicle theft, trespassing, destruction of property, and transport of stolen property.
[h] Includes flight to avoid prosecution, escape, parole and probation violation, and other court offenses.
[i] Includes liquor laws, national security laws, income tax, selective service acts, bribery, gambling, traffic offenses, and other public-order offenses.
[j] Includes offenses not classifiable or not a violation of the United States Code.

SOURCE: *Correctional Populations in the United States, 1997*, Bureau of Justice Statistics, Washington, DC, 2000

sentences, on average, 48 months shorter than those of men (mean sentences of 105 and 153 months, respectively).

INMATES WHO WERE ABUSED IN THE PAST

The BJS surveyed prison inmates (*Prior Abuse Reported by Inmates and Probationers,* 1999) and found that 19 percent of state prisoners and 10 percent of federal prisoners claimed that they had been physically or sexually abused prior to committing their current offense. (The survey relied on respondents to define physical and sexual abuse for themselves.)

More than half (57.2 percent) of female state prisoners and 39.9 percent of female federal prisoners reported ever being either physically or sexually abused prior to admission to prison. Far fewer male prisoners (16.1 percent of state prisoners and 7.2 percent of federal prisoners) reported ever being either physically or sexually abused prior to admission to prison. (See Table 5.7.)

An estimated 28 percent of female state inmates and 15.1 percent of female federal inmates reported they had been both sexually and physically abused prior to admittance to prison. Only 3 percent of male state prisoners and 1.1 percent of male federal prisoners reported both physical and sexual abuse before entering prison.

For male inmates physical and sexual abuse tended to abate around the age of 18 years. About 2.5 percent of male state prisoners and 1.3 percent of male federal prisoners reported being abused both before and after the age of 18. On the other hand about one in seven male state prisoners (14.4 percent) and 5.8 percent of male federal prisoners claimed they had been physically or sexually abused before the age of 18. Of these males 11.9 percent of state prison inmates and 5 percent of federal inmates reported that they had been physically abused before the age of 18, while 5 percent of state inmates and 1.9 percent of federal inmates said they had been sexually abused before the age of 18.

The percentages were higher for female prisoners. Some 36.7 percent of female state prisoners and 23 percent of female federal prison inmates reported physical or sexual abuse before the age of 18 years. One-fourth (24.7 percent) of female state inmates and 14.2 percent of female federal inmates reported being abused both before and after the age of 18. About 25.4 percent of female state prisoners and 15 percent of female federal prisoners reported being physically abused before the age of 18, and 25.4 percent of female state prison inmates and 14.7 percent of female federal prisoners reported sexual abuse before the age of 18.

The Abusers

Most of the people who abused state and federal inmates before their incarceration were adults. About 9 of 10 (87.9 percent of men and 93 percent of women) survey participants knew their abuser(s). Men were primarily abused by family members while women mainly suffered at the hands of husbands or boyfriends. (See Table 5.8.)

About half (51.6 percent) of male state and federal prison inmates claimed they were abused by a parent or guardian, while one-fifth (19 percent) were assaulted by another relative. One-fourth of males (23.5 percent) were abused by friends or acquaintances, while about 3 percent identified wives, ex-wives, and girl- or boyfriends.

Family Background

State prisoners who grew up in foster care reported more abuse than those who lived with parents, unless the parents used alcohol or drugs heavily or a family member had been incarcerated. About half (54.7 percent) of female inmates who lived with both parents or one parent (57.3 percent) reported that they had been abused. Meanwhile, 86.7 percent of female prisoners who grew up in a foster family or agency reported abuse. Three-fourths of women inmates whose parents abused alcohol or drugs said they had been

TABLE 5.6

Federal Bureau of Prison Facts, August 2000

Number of institutions: 98

Total inmate population: 144,750

In BOP facilities:	125,861	
In contract facilities:	18,889	

Inmates by security level

Minimum:	28,377	(23.0%)
Low:	44,295	(35.0%)
Medium:	31,462	(25.0%)
High:	12,814	(10.0%)

Inmates by gender

Male:	134,129	(92.6%)
Female:	10,621	(7.4%)

Inmates by race

White:	83,826	(57.9%)
Black:	56,238	(38.8%)
Asian:	2,401	(1.7%)
Native American:	2,285	(1.6%)

Ethnicity

Hispanic:	46,833	(32.3%)

Citizenship

United States:	100,407	(69.4%)
Mexico:	23,240	(16.0%)
Colombia:	4,152	(2.9%)
Cuba:	2,894	(2.0%)
Other:	14,057	(9.7%)

Average inmate age: 37

Sentence imposed (calculated for those with sentencing information available)

Less than 1 year:	1,898	(1.7%)
1-3 years:	14,984	(13.4%)
3-5 years:	16,316	(14.6%)
5-10 years:	33,168	(29.6%)
10-15 years:	21,439	(19.2%)
15-20 years:	10,057	(9.0%)
More than 20 years:	10,731	(9.6%)
Life:	3,285	(2.9%)
Death:	18	(—)

Type of offense (calculated for those with offense-specific information available)

Drug Offenses:	63,448	(58.0%)
Robbery:	8,306	(7.6%)
Firearms, Explosives, Arson:	10,398	(9.5%)
Extortion, Fraud, Bribery:	5,423	(5.0%)
Property Offenses:	6,241	(5.7%)
Homicide, Aggravated Assault, and Kidnapping Offenses:	2,444	(2.2%)
Immigration:	7,695	(7.0%)
Continuing Criminal \ Enterprise:	646	(0.6%)
White Collar:	776	(0.7%)
Courts or Corrections: (e.g., Obstructing Justice)	601	(0.6%)
National security:	66	(0.1%)
D.C. Offenses	1,404	(1.3%)
Sex Offenses	885	(0.8%)
Miscellaneous:	1,069	(1.0%)

Staff by gender

Male:	23,196	(72.5%)
Female:	8,790	(27.5%)

Staff by race/ethnicity

White (Non-Hispanic):	20,912	(65.4%)
African American:	6,596	(20.5%)
Hispanic:	3,375	(10.6%)
Asian:	601	(1.9%)
Native American:	483	(1.5%)
Other:	16	(0.1%)

abused. Of those female prisoners who had a relative (including boyfriend or girlfriend) who had been incarcerated, 63.9 percent reported being abused. (See Table 5.9.)

As with female prisoners there was little difference in abuse among male inmates who grew up with both parents (14 percent) or one parent (16.4 percent), while a much larger percentage of male inmates growing up in a foster home or agency reported abuse (43.6 percent). About 3 of 10 male prisoners (29.4 percent) living with a parent who abused alcohol or drugs reported maltreatment. One-fifth (20.2 percent) of male prisoners who lived with a relative (including boyfriend or girlfriend) who had ever served time reported having been abused.

Associating Violent Crime and Past Abuse of State Prisoners

Abused state prisoners were more likely than prisoners not abused to be serving a sentence for violent crime.

In 1997, 55.7 percent of state prisoners serving a sentence for a violent crime reported that they were abused, while 45.3 percent of prisoners serving a sentence for violent crime reported they had not been abused. About 61 percent of males imprisoned for committing a violent offense claimed they were abused compared to 46.1 percent who reported no past abuse. One-third (33.5 percent) of women who had committed a violent offense reported that they had been abused compared to 20.9 percent who indicated they had not been abused. (See Table 5.10.)

Crimes of sexual assault and homicide, in particular, are often associated with past abuse. A larger proportion of men (16.3 percent) serving sentences for homicide had been abused in the past than were men (12.8 percent) who had not been abused. Furthermore, nearly twice the proportion of women abused in the past (13.9 percent) as women not abused (7.3 percent) were serving time for homicide.

TABLE 5.7

Physical or sexual abuse before admission by gender of inmate or probationer

Before admission	State inmates		Federal inmates	
	Male	Female	Male	Female
Ever abused	**16.1%**	**57.2%**	**7.2%**	**39.9%**
Physically[a]	13.4	46.5	6.0	32.3
Sexually[a]	5.8	39.0	2.2	22.8
Both	3.0	28.0	1.1	15.1
Age of victim at time of abuse				
17 or younger[b]	14.4%	36.7%	5.8%	23.0%
18 or older[b]	4.3	45.0	2.7	31.0
Both	2.5	24.7	1.3	14.2
Age of abuser				
Adult	15.0%	55.8%	6.9%	39.0%
Juvenile only	0.9	1.0	0.2	0.3
Rape before admission	**4.0%**	**37.3%**	**1.4%**	**21.4%**
Completed	3.1	32.8	1.0	17.9
Attempted	0.8	4.3	0.3	3.2

— Not available.
[a] Includes those physically and sexually abused.
[b] Includes those abused in both age categories.

SOURCE: Caroline Wolf Harlow, *Prior Abuse Reported by Inmates and Probationers*, Bureau of Justice Statistics, Washington, DC, 1999

TABLE 5.9

Percent of state inmates reporting abuse by family situation

While growing up –	Percent of State inmates reporting abuse	
	Male	Female
Prisoners lived with		
Both parents	14.0%	54.7%
One parent	16.4	57.3
Foster/agency/other	43.6	86.7
Parent abused alcohol or drugs	29.4%	75.7%
Did not abuse	10.0	45.9
At any time –		
Family* incarcerated	20.2%	63.9%
Not incarcerated	12.3	46.9

* Includes boyfriends or girlfriends with whom the inmate had lived before admission.

SOURCE: Caroline Wolf Harlow, *Prior Abuse Reported by Inmates and Probationers*, Bureau of Justice Statistics, Washington, DC, 1999

Sexual assault was committed by 18.8 percent of previously abused male inmates, but by just 7.1 percent of male inmates who had not been abused. Few female inmates were in prison for crimes of sexual assault but, again, the proportion of abused women who committed a crime of sexual assault was much larger (2 percent) than for women never abused (0.4 percent).

About 76.5 percent of male state prisoners reporting past abuse had been convicted of one or more violent crimes compared to 61.2 percent of males never abused. Abused women (45 percent) were twice as likely as women never abused (29.1 percent) to have committed a violent crime.

TABLE 5.8

Relationship to abuser by the inmate or probationer reporting the abuse

Relationship of victim to abuser	Percent of those persons who reported experiencing physical or sexual abuse before admission			
	State inmates		Federal inmates	
	Male	Female	Male	Female
Knew abuser	**89.5%**	**90.6%**	**86.3%**	**95.4%**
Family	66.6	40.1	56.7	34.8
Parent or guardian	54.1	27.2	49.0	24.3
Other relative	22.9	21.0	15.1	15.4
Intimate	5.8	61.3	6.5	66.3
Spouse/ex-spouse	2.2	36.5	1.9	41.0
Boyfriend/girlfriend	4.4	36.0	4.8	36.0
Friend/acquaintance	22.6	26.2	24.4	17.2
Other	17.4	15.8	18.7	10.5
Knew none of abusers	**10.5%**	**9.4%**	**13.7%**	**4.6%**

Note: Detail does not add to totals because some were abused by more than 1 person.

SOURCE: Caroline Wolf Harlow, *Prior Abuse Reported by Inmates and Probationers*, Bureau of Justice Statistics, Washington, DC, 1999

TABLE 5.10

Current and past violent offenses and past alcohol and drug use by whether abused before admission to state prison, 1997

Offense history and drug and alcohol use	Percent of State prison inmates					
	Reported being abused			Reported being not abused		
	Total	Males	Females	Total	Males	Females
Current or past violent offense	**70.4%**	**76.5%**	**45.0%**	**60.2%**	**61.2%**	**29.1%**
Current violent offense	**55.7%**	**61.0%**	**33.5%**	**45.3%**	**46.1%**	**20.9%**
Homicide	15.9	16.3	13.9	12.7	12.8	7.3
Sexual assault	15.6	18.8	2.0	6.9	7.1	0.4
Robbery	12.5	13.5	7.8	14.5	14.7	6.1
Assault	9.5	9.9	7.6	9.3	9.4	5.7

SOURCE: Caroline Wolf Harlow, *Prior Abuse Reported by Inmates and Probationers*, Bureau of Justice Statistics, Washington, DC, 1999

PRISONERS AND THEIR CHILDREN

In August 2000 the BJS issued a "Special Report on Incarcerated Parents and Their Children." Authored by BJS policy analyst Christopher J. Mumola, the report's findings are somewhat grim in terms of the consequences of incarceration on the American family.

In 1999 an estimated 721,500 state and federal prisoners were parents to some 1.5 million children under the age of 18 years. (See Table 5.11.) Twenty-two percent of all minor children with a parent in state or federal prison were under the age of five years. Since 1991 the number of minor children with one or both parents in state or federal prisons rose by more than 500,000. However, the percentage of state and federal prisoners with minor children changed very little—from 57 percent in 1991 to 56 percent in 1999.

TABLE 5.11

Number of state and federal prisoners with minor children, and number of minor children of state and federal prisoners, by gender of prisoner, 1991 and 1999

	State prisoners			Federal prisoners		
	Total	Male	Female	Total	Male	Female
Number of prisoners with minor children						
1991	413,100	386,500	26,600	39,400	36,500	2,900
1999	642,300	593,800	48,500	79,200	74,100	5,100
Number of minor children						
1991	852,300	794,500	57,800	84,200	78,300	5,900
1999	1,324,900	1,209,400	115,500	173,900	163,300	10,600

Note: These data are estimates based on responses to the 1991 and 1997 Surveys of Inmates in State and Federal Correctional Facilities, and custody counts from the National Prisoners Statistics program. Both data collection programs are sponsored by the U.S. Department of Justice, Bureau of Justice Statistics. "Minor children" are those children under age 18.

SOURCE: Kathleen Maguire and Ann L. Pastore, eds., "State and Federal prisoners with minor children and number of minor children, 1991 and 1999" in *Sourcebook of Criminal Justice Statistics 1999*, Bureau of Justice Statistics, U.S. Department of Justice, Washington, D.C., 2000

TABLE 5.12

Percent of inmate parents in state or federal prison who lived with their minor children at time of admission, by gender of prisoner, 1997

	Percent of inmate parents					
	State			Federal		
	Total	Male	Female	Total	Male	Female
Lived with children at time of admission	45.3%	43.8%	64.3%	57.2%	55.2%	84.0%
Child's current caregiver[a]						
Other parent of child	85.0%	89.6%	28.0%	87.6%	91.7%	30.7%
Grandparent of child	16.3	13.3	52.9	12.2	9.8	44.9
Other relatives	6.4	4.9	25.7	6.2	4.2	33.9
Foster home or agency	2.4	1.8	9.6	1.3	1.1	3.2
Friends, others[b]	5.3	4.9	10.4	6.8	6.4	11.9

[a] Detail may add to more than 100% because some prisoners had multiple children living with multiple caregivers.
[b] Includes cases where parent reported that the child now lived alone.

SOURCE: Christopher J. Mumola, "Percent of inmate parents in State or Federal prison who lived with their minor children at time of admission, by gender, 1997" in "Incarcerated Parents and Their Children," *Bureau of Justice Statistics Special Report*, U.S. Department of Justice, Washington, D.C., 2000

As of 1999 approximately 2.1 percent of all children in the United States had a parent in prison. Broken down by race, 7 percent of all black children had a parent in prison, followed by 2.6 percent of Hispanic children, and slightly less than 1 percent of white children. Approximately 1,372,700 minor children had a father in prison, an increase of 58 percent since 1991, while 126,100 children had a mother in prison—an increase of 98 percent since 1991. Among female prisoners, in 1997 almost two-thirds (64.3 percent) reported living with their children prior to incarceration compared to 43.8 percent of incarcerated males. Children of female prisoners in 1997 were most likely to be living with a grandparent (52.9 percent), while almost 90 percent of children of male prisoners were living with their mothers. (See Table 5.12.)

In 1997 some 47 percent of parents in state and federal prison were black, 25 percent were white, and 24 percent

Hispanic. (See Table 5.13.) Of parents in state prison 15.8 percent were 24 years of age or younger compared to 7.8 percent of parents in federal prison. Most parents in both state and federal prisons were between 25 and 34 years of age, with a median age of 32 years among state prisoners and 35 years among federal inmates. In 1997 parents in federal prison were more likely to be married (35.8 percent) than parents confined to state prison (23 percent).

Male inmate parents in state prison in 1997 were more likely to be violent offenders (45.4 percent) than were female parents (26 percent). (See Table 5.14.) Mothers of minor children were most likely to be in state prison as the result of drug offenses (35.1 percent), followed by property offenses (28.3 percent), violent crimes (26 percent), and public-order offenses (10.4 percent). Mothers were almost twice as likely to have committed their crimes while under the influence of cocaine-based drugs

TABLE 5.13

Selected characteristics of state and federal prisoners with and without minor children, 1997

| | Percent of prisoners | | | |
| | State | | Federal | |
	Parents	Nonparents	Parents	Nonparents
Gender				
Male	92.6%	95.2%	93.2%	91.9%
Female	7.4	4.8	6.8	8.1
Race/Hispanic origin				
White non-Hispanic	28.9%	38.9%	21.9%	43.4%
Black non-Hispanic	49.4	42.8	44.0	27.0
Hispanic	18.9	14.5	30.0	22.9
Other	2.8	3.8	4.0	6.7
Age				
24 or younger	15.8%	25.0%	7.8%	11.3%
25-34	44.9	30.1	41.8	27.9
35-44	32.1	26.0	35.1	23.0
45-54	6.6	13.3	12.8	22.1
55 or older	0.6	5.6	2.5	15.8
Median	32 yr	33 yr	35 yr	40 yr
Marital status				
Married	23.0%	8.7%	35.8%	21.2%
Widowed	1.6	2.2	1.6	1.8
Divorced	20.5	16.1	19.0	22.9
Separated	7.2	3.9	6.0	5.3
Never married	47.7	69.2	37.6	48.8
Education completed				
8th grade or less	12.7%	15.5%	11.5%	11.9%
Some high school	27.1	23.6	16.7	10.7
GED	30.6	32.6	27.0	26.5
High school graduate	16.1	14.9	19.8	20.8
Some college or more	13.4	13.4	25.0	30.1

SOURCE: Christopher J. Mumola, "Selected characteristics of state or federal prisoners, by whether the inmates were parents of minor children, 1997" in "Incarcerated Parents and Their Children," *Bureau of Justice Statistics Special Report,* U.S. Department of Justice, Washington, D.C., 2000

(28 percent) than fathers (15 percent). About 32 percent of mothers in state prison in 1997 reported that they committed their crime to get drugs, or money for drugs, compared to 19 percent of fathers in state prison. Thirty-seven percent of parents in state prison reported being under the influence of alcohol when they committed their offense.

In the federal system drug offenses accounted for the imprisonment of nearly three-fourths (73.9 percent) of mothers with minor children and two-thirds (66.7 percent) of fathers. In 1997, 23 percent of parents in federal prison reported being under the influence of drugs when they committed their offense.

Half of male parents of minor children in state prison in 1997 were serving maximum sentences of 119 months or less compared to almost three-fourths (70.7 percent) of female parents of minor children. (See Table 5.15.) The mean (average) maximum sentence among male parents in state prison was 150 months compared to 94 months for female parents. The average maximum sentence in federal prisons for male parents was 124 months, and 83 months for female prisoners. About 6.3 percent of fathers in state prisons were under a sentence of life imprison-

ment or death compared to 2.8 percent of mothers in state prison. Parents in federal prison fared slightly better, with 3.3 percent of fathers and less than 1 percent of mothers receiving sentences of life in prison or death.

CHARACTERISTICS OF PRISONERS UNDER SENTENCE OF DEATH

Executed Prisoners

In 1999, 20 states executed 98 prisoners, all of whom were men, according to "Capital Punishment 1999" (Bureau of Justice Statistics Bulletin, December 2000). (See Table 5.16.) Of those 61 were white, 33 were black, 2 were American Indian, and 2 were Asian. Ninety-four of the executions were performed by lethal injection, 3 by electrocution, and 1 by lethal gas. From 1930–1999 a total of 4,423 males and 35 females were executed in the United States. Of those 1,971 were white and 2,201 black. When viewed in relation to the proportion of blacks in the population at large, blacks were executed at a much higher rate than whites.

The total number of prisoners executed in 1999 was 30 more than in 1998, and was the largest number since 1951 when 105 were executed. Prisoners put to death in 1999 had been under a death sentence an average of 11 years and 11 months—on average, 13 months longer than inmates executed in 1998.

Of the 98 executions in 1999, 35 were in Texas, followed by 14 in Virginia, 9 in Missouri, and 7 in Arizona. The states of Florida, Illinois, Indiana, Kentucky, Louisiana, Nevada, Idaho, and Utah each executed 1 prisoner in 1999. (See Table 5.17.) From January 1, 1977, to December 31, 1999, 587 executions were carried out in 24 states. Of those 64 percent took place in 5 states—Texas (199), Virginia (73), Florida (44), Missouri (41), and Louisiana (25).

Methods of execution vary by state. As of 1999 lethal injection was the method of execution available in 34 states, followed by electrocution (11 states), lethal gas (4 states), hanging (3 states), and firing squad (3 states). Some states allow for more than one method of execution. The method of execution for federal prisoners is lethal injection.

On July 13, 1999, the U.S. Penitentiary at Terre Haute, Indiana, opened a special unit for the confinement of male prisoners sentenced to death. All federal executions are scheduled to be carried out at this facility. Timothy McVeigh, who was convicted of the April 1995 bombing of the Alfred P. Murrah Federal Building in Oklahoma City, Oklahoma, which killed 168 people and injured more than 500, was executed here by lethal injection in June 2001. Prior to McVeigh's execution the last civilian executed by the federal government was Victor Feguer, who was hanged in 1963 at the Iowa State Penitentiary for the crimes of murder and kidnapping.

TABLE 5.14

Current offense of inmate parents in state or federal prison, by gender, 1997

| | Percent of inmate parents | | | | | |
| | State | | | Federal | | |
Current offense	Total	Male	Female	Total	Male	Female
Violent offenses	43.9%	45.4%	26.0%	11.9%	12.3%	6.5%
Homicide[a]	10.9	11.1	8.6	1.2	1.2	1.3
Sexual assault[b]	8.3	8.8	1.7	0.7	0.8	0.1
Robbery	13.2	13.8	6.4	7.8	8.1	3.4
Assault	9.7	9.9	7.2	1.3	1.3	1.3
Other violent	1.8	1.8	2.1	0.9	0.9	0.4
Property offenses	21.6%	21.1%	28.3%	5.3%	4.9%	10.3%
Burglary	10.2	10.6	5.4	0.3	0.3	0.1
Larceny	4.6	4.3	8.5	0.4	0.4	0.3
Motor vehicle theft	1.5	1.6	1.2	0.2	0.3	0.0
Fraud	2.8	2.1	11.3	3.7	3.3	8.9
Stolen property	1.6	1.7	1.3	0.4	0.4	0.6
Other property	0.9	0.9	0.6	0.3	0.3	0.3
Drug offenses	23.9%	23.0%	35.1%	67.2%	66.7%	73.9%
Possession	10.1	9.7	14.8	12.9	13.1	9.7
Trafficking	13.1	12.7	19.0	48.9	48.0	61.0
Other drug	0.7	0.6	1.3	5.4	5.6	3.2
Public-order offenses	10.3%	10.3%	10.4%	14.6%	15.1%	7.9%
Weapons	2.7	2.8	0.9	6.9	7.3	1.1
Other public-order	7.6	7.5	9.5	7.8	7.9	6.7
Other/unspecified	0.2%	0.2%	0.3%	1.0%	0.9%	1.5%

[a] Includes murder and manslaughter.
[b] Includes rape and other sexual assaults.

SOURCE: Christopher J. Mumola, "Current offense of inmate parents in State or Federal prison, by gender, 1997" in "Incarcerated Parents and Their Children," *Bureau of Justice Statistics Special Report,* U.S. Department of Justice, Washington, D.C., 2000

Prisoners Awaiting Execution

In 1999, of 3,527 prisoners under sentence of death, 99 percent were male and 1 percent were female. (See Table 5.18.) More than half (55.2 percent) were white, 42.9 percent were black, and 10.2 percent Hispanic.

Education

At the end of 1999, of those prisoners under sentence of death for whom information on education was available, three-fourths had either graduated from high school (38.2 percent) or completed ninth, tenth, or eleventh grade (37.7 percent). Almost 14 percent of condemned inmates had not gone beyond eighth grade and just 1 of 10 had attended college. The median level of education for prisoners on death row was the eleventh grade.

Marital Status

In 1999, among inmates under a capital sentence with available information on marital status, more than half (53 percent) had never married, less than one-fourth (22.9) were married, 21.2 percent were divorced or separated, and 2.8 percent were widowed.

Age

Of those inmates on death row in 1999 for whom date of arrest information was available, almost half (49.5 percent) were between the ages of 20 and 29 years at the time of their arrest. About 1 of 8 (13 percent) was under the age of 20 and less than 1 percent was older than 55 years of age. (See Table 5.19.) At the end of 1999, the youngest inmate waiting on death row was 18 years old; the oldest, 84 years of age.

Past Criminal History

At the end of 1999 about two-thirds (64.1 percent) of inmates on death row for whom criminal history information was available had past felony convictions, including 8.4 percent with at least one previous conviction for homicide. Among those awaiting execution 17.9 percent had been on parole and 10 percent had been on probation. More than half (60 percent) had no legal status at the time they committed their capital offense. (See Table 5.20.)

Race/Ethnicity

Criminal history differed by race and Hispanic origin. Blacks (68.3 percent) were somewhat more likely than whites (61.9 percent) or Hispanics (58.3 percent) to have had prior felony convictions. Hispanics (23.8 percent) and blacks (19.2 percent) were slightly more likely than whites (15.5 percent) to be on parole when arrested for their current capital offense. About the same percentage of blacks (8.7 percent) and whites (8.3 percent) had prior homicide convictions, while 6.9 percent of Hispanics had prior homicide convictions.

TABLE 5.15

Maximum sentence length and time to be served until release of state and federal prisoners with minor children, by gender of prisoner, 1997

	Percent of inmate parents					
	State			Federal		
	Total	Male	Female	Total	Male	Female
Maximum sentence length						
Less than 12 months	3.1%	2.8%	7.3%	2.3%	2.1%	5.1%
12-35 months	13.1	12.5	20.3	10.6	9.5	26.3
36-59 months	13.2	12.7	19.9	13.2	13.0	16.2
60-119 months	22.5	22.4	23.2	30.0	30.6	22.4
120-179 months	14.0	14.3	10.7	19.6	19.7	18.1
180-239 months	8.9	9.1	6.3	9.0	9.2	5.2
240+ months	19.1	19.9	9.4	12.2	12.7	5.8
Life/death	6.1	6.3	2.8	3.1	3.3	0.7
Mean[a]	146 mo.	150 mo.	94 mo.	121 mo.	124 mo.	83 mo.
Estimated total time to be served on current sentence[b]						
Less than 24 months	19.3%	17.9%	37.5%	8.5%	7.2%	26.2%
24-47 months	23.1	22.9	24.9	15.0	14.5	22.9
48-71 months	15.7	15.9	14.0	18.1	18.1	17.2
72-119 months	16.6	17.2	8.9	25.1	25.6	17.8
120-179 months	8.7	9.1	3.6	14.9	15.4	8.3
180-239 months	4.0	4.2	1.5	7.1	7.4	3.2
240+ months	5.3	5.6	2.1	6.9	7.3	2.2
No release expected	2.1	2.2	1.0	1.2	1.3	0.5
Do not know	5.1	5.0	6.5	3.2	3.3	1.8
Mean[c]	80 mo.	82 mo.	49 mo.	103 mo.	105 mo.	66 mo.

[a] Excludes sentences to life or death.
[b] Based on time served when interviewed plus time to be served until the expected date of release.
[c] Excludes inmates who do not expect to be released.

SOURCE: Christopher J. Mumola, "Maximum sentence length and time to be served until release of State and Federal prisoners with minor children, by gender, 1997" in "Incarcerated Parents and Their Children," *Bureau of Justice Statistics Special Report,* U.S. Department of Justice, Washington, D.C., 2000

GANG MEMBERSHIP

The BJS defines gangs as groups that commit illegal acts and have five or six of the following characteristics:

- Formal membership with a required initiation or rules for members

- A recognized leader or certain members whom others follow

- Common clothing or group colors, symbols, tattoos, or special language

- A group name

- Members from the same neighborhood, street, or school

- Turf or territory where the group is known and where group activities usually take place

In 1997 about 6 percent of prison inmates had belonged to groups that engaged in illegal activities and that had five or six gang characteristics. Another 6 percent had engaged in illegal activities with groups that had three or four gang characteristics. Among inmates who were gang members half had belonged for 36 months or more and belonged at the time they were arrested for their current offenses. One-third (32 percent) were still members.

PROGRAM PARTICIPATION

Nearly all inmates had participated in work, education, or other programs since their admission to prison. A third of all inmates had participated in a drug treatment program after entering prison.

In a 1995 census of prisons the BJS found that 80 percent of all prisons offered a general equivalency diploma (GED) or other secondary educational program, and almost one-quarter of all prisoners were enrolled. About 70 percent of all facilities offered psychological or psychiatric inmate counseling.

In 1995 the BJS census of prisons also found that fewer convicts than in previous years were involved in prerelease organizations and activities designed to help prisoners return to noninstitutional life. These included classes to improve skills, community programs outside the prison, or ethnic or racial programs such as the National Association for the Advancement of Colored People (NAACP) or the Hispanic Committee.

TABLE 5.16

Prisoners executed under civil authority by sex and race, 1930–99

[Excludes executions by military authorities. The Army (including the Air Force) carried out 160 (148 between 1942 and 1950; 3 each in 1954, 1955, and 1957; and 1 each in 1958, 1959, and 1961). Of the total, 106 were executed for murder (including 21 involving rape), 53 for rape, and 1 for desertion. The Navy carried out no executions during the period.]

Year or period	Total [1]	Male	Female	White	Black	Executed for murder Total [1]	White	Black
All years, 1930-99	**4,458**	**4,423**	**35**	**1,971**	**2,201**	**3,692**	**1,884**	**1,770**
1930 to 1939	1,667	1,656	11	827	816	1,514	803	687
1940 to 1949	1,284	1,272	12	490	781	1,064	458	595
1950 to 1959	717	709	8	336	376	601	316	280
1960 to 1967	191	190	1	98	93	155	87	68
1968 to 1976	-	-	-	-	-	-	-	-
1977 to 1999	598	595	3	-	-	-	-	-
1985	18	-	-	11	7	18	11	7
1986	18	18	-	11	7	18	11	7
1987	25	25	-	13	12	25	13	12
1988	11	11	-	6	5	11	6	5
1989	16	16	-	8	8	16	8	8
1990	23	23	-	16	7	23	16	7
1991	14	14	-	7	7	14	7	7
1992	31	31	-	19	11	31	19	11
1993	38	38	-	23	14	38	23	14
1994	31	31	-	20	11	31	20	11
1995	56	56	-	33	22	56	33	22
1996	45	45	-	31	14	45	31	14
1997	74	74	-	45	27	74	45	27
1998	68	66	2	48	18	68	48	18
1999	98	98	-	61	33	98	61	33

- Represents zero.
[1] Includes races other than White or Black.

SOURCE: "No. 375: Prisoners Executed under Civil Authority by Sex and Race: 1930 to 1999," in *Statistical Abstract of the United States: 2000* U.S. Census Bureau, Washington, D.C., 2001

TABLE 5.17

Prisoners under sentence of death and executed under civil authority by state, 1977–99

[Alaska, District of Columbia, Hawaii, Iowa, Maine, Massachusetts, Michigan, Minnesota, New York, North Dakota, Rhode Island, Vermont, West Virginia, and Wisconsin are jurisdictions without a death penalty]

State	1977 to 1999	1996	1997	1998	1999
U.S	598	45	74	68	98
AL	19	1	3	1	2
AZ	19	2	2	4	7
AR	21	1	4	1	4
CA	7	2	-	1	2
DE	10	3	-	-	2
FL	44	2	1	4	1
GA	23	2	-	1	-
ID	1	-	-	-	-
IL	12	1	2	1	1
IN	7	1	1	1	1
LA	25	1	1	-	1
MD	3	-	1	1	-
MS	4	-	-	-	-
MO	41	6	6	3	9
NE	3	1	1	-	-
NV	8	1	-	1	1
NC	15	-	-	3	4
OK	19	2	1	4	6
SC	24	6	2	7	4
TX	199	3	37	20	35
UT	6	1	-	-	1
VA	73	8	9	13	14
WA	3	-	-	1	-
WY	1	-	-	-	-

- Represents zero.

SOURCE: "No. 376: Prisoners under Sentence of Death and Executed under Civil Authority by State: 1977 to 1999," in *Statistical Abstract of the United States: 2000,* U.S. Census Bureau, Washington, D.C., 2001

TABLE 5.18

Demographic characteristics of prisoners under sentence of death, 1999

Characteristic	Prisoners under sentence of death, 1999		
	Year-end	Admissions	Removals
Total number under sentence of death	3,527	272	210
Gender			
Male	98.6%	98.9%	99.0%
Female	1.4	1.1	1.0
Race			
White	55.2%	57.7%	60.0%
Black	42.9	38.2	37.6
Other*	1.8	4.0	2.4
Hispanic origin			
Hispanic	10.2%	14.9%	11.6%
Non-Hispanic	89.8	85.1	88.4
Education			
8th grade or less	13.9%	14.2%	20.3%
9th-11th grade	37.7	38.6	38.5
High school graduate/GED	38.2	38.6	33.5
Any college	10.1	8.6	7.7
Median	11th	11th	11th
Marital status			
Married	22.9%	16.5%	31.7%
Divorced/separated	21.2	24.5	19.6
Widowed	2.8	3.8	2.6
Never married	53.0	55.3	46.0

Note: Calculations are based on those cases for which data were reported. Missing data by category were as follows:

	Year-end	Admissions	Removals
Hispanic origin	332	51	11
Education	499	39	28
Marital status	341	35	21

*At year-end 1998, "other" consisted of 27 American Indians, 20 Asians, and 12 self-identified Hispanics. During 1999, 4 American Indians, 6 Asians, and 1 self-identified Hispanic were admitted; 3 American Indians and 2 Asians were removed.

SOURCE: Tracy L. Snell, *Capital Punishment 1999,* Bureau of Justice Statistics, Washington, DC, 2000

TABLE 5.19

Age at time of arrest for capital offense and age of prisoners under sentence of death at year-end 1999

| | Prisoners under sentence of death | | | |
| | At time of arrest | | On December 31, 1999 | |
Age	Number*	Percent	Number	Percent
Total number under sentence of death on 12/31/99	3,232	100%	3,527	100%
17 or younger	80	2.5	0	
18-19	343	10.6	16	0.5
20-24	871	26.9	251	7.1
25-29	729	22.6	514	14.6
30-34	534	16.5	594	16.8
35-39	341	10.6	707	20.0
40-44	170	5.3	601	17.0
45-49	101	3.1	370	10.5
50-54	36	1.1	280	7.9
55-59	16	0.5	114	3.2
60 or older	11	0.3	80	2.3
Mean age	28 yrs		38 yrs	
Median age	27 yrs		37 yrs	

Note: The youngest person under sentence of death was a black male in Texas, born in December 1981 and sentenced to death in November 1999. The oldest person under sentence of death was a white male in Arizona, born in September 1915 and sentenced to death in June 1983.
*Excludes 295 inmates for whom the date of arrest for capital offense was not available.

SOURCE: Tracy L. Snell, *Capital Punishment 1999*, Bureau of Justice Statistics, Washington, DC, 2000

TABLE 5.20

Criminal history profile of prisoners under sentence of death, by race and Hispanic origin, 1999

| | Prisoners under sentence of death | | | | | | | |
| | Number | | | | Percent[a] | | | |
	All[b]	White	Black	Hispanic	All[b]	White	Black	Hispanic
U.S. total	3,527	1,651	1,500	325	100%	100%	100%	100%
Prior felony convictions								
Yes	2,085	949	939	172	64.1%	61.9%	68.3%	58.3%
No	1,166	584	436	123	35.9	38.1	31.7	41.7
Not reported	276							
Prior homicide convictions								
Yes	290	134	128	22	8.4%	8.3%	8.7%	6.9%
No	3,166	1,487	1,337	297	91.6	91.7	91.3	93.1
Not reported	71							
Legal status at time of capital offense								
Charges pending	228	127	90	11	7.4%	8.6%	6.9%	4.0%
Probation	311	134	144	27	10.0	9.1	11.1	9.9
Parole	554	229	250	65	17.9	15.5	19.2	23.8
Prison escapee	39	25	10	3	1.3	1.7	0.8	1.1
Incarcerated	86	36	44	5	2.8	2.4	3.4	1.8
Other status	21	11	8	1	0.7	0.7	0.6	0.4
None	1,860	916	755	161	60.0	62.0	58.0	59.0
Not reported	428							

[a] Percentages are based on those offenders for whom data were reported.
  Detail may not add to total because of rounding.
[b] Includes persons of other races.

SOURCE: Tracy L. Snell, *Capital Punishment 1999*, Bureau of Justice Statistics, Washington, DC, 2000

CHAPTER 6

INMATE HEALTH

TABLE 6.1

Estimated number and percent of state and federal inmates with a physical impairment or mental condition, 1997

Physical impairment or mental condition	State inmates		Federal Inmates	
	Number	Percent	Number	Percent
Any	326,256	31.0%	20,734	23.4%
Learning	103,789	9.9	4,477	5.1
Speech	39,166	3.7	1,956	2.2
Hearing	60,054	5.7	4,921	5.6
Vision	87,242	8.3	6,688	7.6
Mental	105,536	10.0	4,256	4.8
Physical	125,257	11.9	9,839	11.1
Condition that limits ability to work	221,198	21.0%	15,821	17.9%

SOURCE: Laura M. Maruschak and Allen J. Beck, "Estimated number and percent of State and Federal inmates with a physical impairment or mental condition, 1997" in "Medical Problems of Inmates, 1997," *Bureau of Justice Statistics Special Report,* U.S. Department of Justice, Washington, D.C., 2001

In January 2001 the Bureau of Justice Statistics (BJS) released "Special Report, Medical Problems of Inmates, 1997." Its findings were based on hour-long personal interviews with inmates in state and federal prisons during 1997. Inmates were asked a series of questions about physical impairments and mental conditions they had, at either the time of their admission to prison or acquired after their imprisonment.

According to the report inmates themselves are the only source for determining the types of physical and mental conditions that exist in prisons because of the somewhat erratic manner in which prison systems keep medical information on inmates. For example, a 1998 inventory of state and federal prison information systems found that only 20 states had electronically available information identifying offenders with physical disabilities at the time of admission. Eighteen states kept the data in paper form only. Just 22 states could identify inmates with mental or emotional

TABLE 6.2

Medical problems reported by state and federal inmates since admission, by selected characteristics, 1997

Characteristics	Percent of inmates who reported since admission		
	Medical problem (excluding injury)		
	Total	Required surgery	Other
State prisoners			
Gender			
Male	21.0%	7.5%	16.3%
Female	27.2	7.9	22.7
Age			
24 or younger	12.1%	3.3%	9.8%
25-34	17.2	5.8	13.2
35-44	25.2	9.0	19.4
45 or older	39.8	15.7	32.0
Federal prisoners			
Gender			
Male	21.0%	9.5%	15.3%
Female	30.1	11.3	24.7
Age			
24 or younger	11.8%	4.1%	9.0%
25-34	14.3	5.7	10.5
35-44	21.0	9.5	14.6
45 or older	37.4	17.7	28.5

SOURCE: Laura M. Maruschak and Allen J. Beck, "Medical problems reported by State and Federal inmates since admission, by selected characteristics, 1997" in "Medical Problems of Inmates, 1997," *Bureau of Justice Statistics Special Report,* U.S. Department of Justice, Washington, D.C., 2001

problems or with specialized medical conditions, and another 10 states reported that they did not collect any data on the current medical condition of their inmates.

THE FINDINGS

In 1997 some 347,000 state and federal prisoners reported having a physical impairment or mental condition, accounting for 31 percent of all state inmates and 23 percent of all federal inmates. The conditions reported by state inmates included impairment in learning (9.9

TABLE 6.3

Physical impairments and mental conditions of state and federal inmates, by selected characteristics, 1997

Characteristic	Percent of inmates who reported a physical impairment or mental condition						
	Any condition	Learning	Speech	Hearing	Vision	Physical	Mental
State prisoners							
Gender							
Male	30.7%	10.0%	3.7%	5.6%	8.2%	11.8%	9.6%
Female	34.4	8.7	3.3	6.5	8.8	13.5	16.1
Age							
24 or younger	23.8%	11.1%	3.3%	2.5%	5.5%	5.0%	7.8%
25-34	26.8	9.8	3.1	4.0	5.5	9.0	9.2
35-44	34.0	9.7	4.5	6.7	8.8	14.6	12.0
45 or older	47.6	8.6	4.3	13.4	19.8	25.2	11.7
Federal prisoners							
Gender							
Male	22.9%	5.0%	2.3%	5.5%	7.5%	10.9%	4.4%
Female	29.9	5.6	1.4	5.8	8.6	13.9	9.7
Age							
24 or younger	13.8%	5.1%	2.7%	2.3%	3.0%	2.1%	4.0%
25-34	16.9	4.6	2.0	2.7	4.5	7.3	3.9
35-44	22.1	5.5	2.1	5.3	6.5	9.9	5.3
45 or older	38.6	5.4	2.5	11.5	15.2	21.9	5.9

SOURCE: Laura M. Maruschak and Allen J. Beck, "Physical impairments and mental conditions of State and Federal inmates, by selected characteristics, 1997" in "Medical Problems of Inmates, 1997," *Bureau of Justice Statistics Special Report,* U.S. Department of Justice, Washington, D.C., 2001

TABLE 6.4

Medical problems among federal inmates: Comparing official prison data with inmate-reported survey data

Medical Problem	Percent of federal inmates	
	Official records, midyear 2000*	1997 survey data
Asthma	4.4%	0.9%
Diabetes	3.6	1.5
Heart	2.6	1.3
High blood pressure	7.8	1.7
HIV/AIDS	1.0	0.5
Mental health	4.8	4.8

*Based on the clinical status on July 29, 2000, except for asthma, which was counted on September 20, 2000. Inmate totals were based on average daily population in each month.

SOURCE: Laura M. Maruschak and Allen J. Beck, "Comparing estimates based on self-reported data to official records" in "Medical Problems of Inmates, 1997," *Bureau of Justice Statistics Special Report,* U.S. Department of Justice, Washington, D.C., 2001

TABLE 6.5

Injuries reported by state and federal inmates since admission, by gender and age, 1997

	Percent of inmates who reported an injury since admission		
	Total	In an accident	In a fight
State prisoners			
Total	28.2%	20.1%	10.1%
Gender			
Male	28.7%	20.3%	10.6%
Female	20.5	17.2	3.3
Age			
24 or younger	29.5%	20.1%	12.8%
25-34	30.1	21.8	10.6
35-44	27.4	19.7	9.3
45 or older	21.9	15.8	6.5
Federal prisoners			
Total	26.2%	22.9%	3.2%
Gender			
Male	26.3%	22.9%	3.4%
Female	24.8	22.9	0.6
Age			
24 or younger	28.7%	25.5%	4.0%
25-34	27.6	24.3	3.9
35-44	25.6	21.8	3.4
45 or older	23.9	21.2	1.6

SOURCE: Laura M. Maruschak and Allen J. Beck, "Percent of State and Federal inmates who reported an injury since admission, by gender and age, 1997" in "Medical Problems of Inmates, 1997," *Bureau of Justice Statistics Special Report,* U.S. Department of Justice, Washington, D.C., 2001

percent), vision (8.3 percent), hearing (5.7 percent), speech (3.7 percent), and other physical impairments (11.9 percent). Ten percent of state and federal inmates reported having mental impairments.

Medical impairments were more prevalent among older inmates. Thirty-nine percent of state prisoners 45 years of age or older reported having a physical impairment or mental condition compared to 23.8 percent of prisoners 24 years of age or younger. Physical impairments or mental conditions were more common among female state inmates (34.4 percent) than male (30.7 per-

cent). Of state inmates 21 percent reported that their mental or physical condition limited their ability to work, slightly more than reported by federal prisoners (17.9 percent). (See Table 6.1.) Of those reporting a medical problem excluding injury since admission to prison, about

FIGURE 6.1

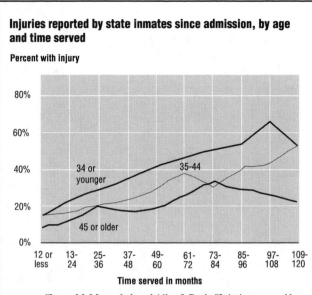

Injuries reported by state inmates since admission, by age and time served

Percent with injury

SOURCE: "Laura M. Maruschak and Allen J. Beck, "Injuries reported by State inmates since admission, by age and time served" in "Medical Problems of Inmates, 1997," *Bureau of Justice Statistics Special Report,* U.S. Department of Justice, Washington, D.C., 2001"

FIGURE 6.2

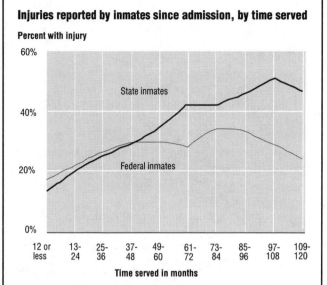

Injuries reported by inmates since admission, by time served

Percent with injury

SOURCE: Laura M. Maruschak and Allen J. Beck, "Injuries reported by inmates since admission, by time served" in "Medical Problems of Inmates, 1997," *Bureau of Justice Statistics Special Report*, U.S. Department of Justice, Washington, D.C., 2001

TABLE 6.6

Injuries reported by state and federal inmates since admission, by time served, 1997

| Time since admission | Percent of inmates who reported an injury since admission | | | | | |
| | Total | | Injured in an accident | | Injured in a fight | |
	State	Federal	State	Federal	State	Federal
Less than 12 mo.	13.2%	17.0%	10.2%	15.6%	2.9%	0.8%
12-23 mo.	19.8	22.0	14.8	20.1	5.3	1.8
24-47 mo.	26.7	26.3	19.0	24.3	9.2	2.1
48-71 mo.	36.8	30.2	26.3	25.3	13.8	5.4
72 mo. or more	45.9	31.6	31.7	26.3	19.7	5.3

SOURCE: Laura M. Maruschak and Allen J. Beck, "Injuries reported by State and Federal inmates since admission, by time served, 1997" in "Medical Problems of Inmates, 1997," *Bureau of Justice Statistics Special Report,* U.S. Department of Justice, Washington, D.C., 2001

15.4 percent of state inmates and 20.8 percent of federal inmates required surgery. (See Table 6.2.)

About 16.1 percent of female state prisoners reported having mental conditions compared to 9.6 percent for male state inmates. Among federal prisoners females were about twice as likely as males to report mental conditions. (See Table 6.3.) As with physical problems, mental problems seemed to increase with age. Twelve percent of state prisoners between the ages of 35 and 44 years, and 11.7 percent of those 45 years of age and older, reported having mental conditions compared to 9.2 percent in the 25–34 age group, and 7.8 percent 24 years of age or younger. The same trend was apparent among federal prisoners, although less pronounced.

About 19 percent of state inmates and 15 percent of federal inmates reported having only one condition, either physical or mental. Seven percent of state inmates said

they had two such conditions, and 5 percent of federal inmates reported three or more.

Using data from the National Center for Health Statistics, comparisons of medical problems among state and federal prisoners to those reported in the general population revealed that:

- Speech disabilities are three times more prevalent among state inmates (3.7 percent) than in the general population (1 percent).

- Vision impairment among inmates (8.3 percent) is more than twice as high as in the population at large (3.1 percent).

- Hearing impairment occurs at a lower rate among prisoners (5.7 percent) than in the general population (8.3 percent).

FIGURE 6.3

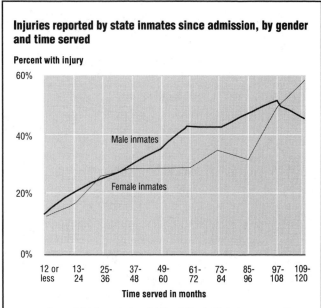

Injuries reported by state inmates since admission, by gender and time served

SOURCE: Laura M. Maruschak and Allen J. Beck, "Injuries reported by State inmates since admission, by gender and time served" in "Medical Problems of Inmates, 1997," *Bureau of Justice Statistics Special Report,* U.S. Department of Justice, Washington, D.C., 2001

FIGURE 6.4

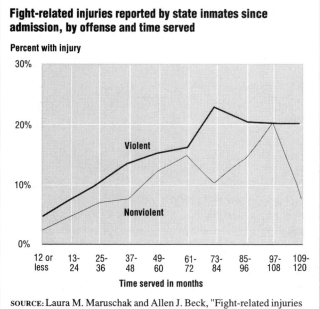

Fight-related injuries reported by state inmates since admission, by offense and time served

SOURCE: Laura M. Maruschak and Allen J. Beck, "Fight-related injuries reported by State inmates since admission, by offense and time served" in "Medical Problems of Inmates, 1997," *Bureau of Justice Statistics Special Report,* U.S. Department of Justice, Washington, D.C., 2001

TABLE 6.7

The risk of injury in state prisons

	Percent of new admissions*	Percent of all inmates	
	Time expected to be served	Any injury	Injury in fight
6 mo or less	22.1%	11.0%	2.2%
7-12	27.4	16.2	3.5
13-24	21.6	19.9	5.7
25-36	8.0	25.4	8.3
37-48	4.8	29.3	10.5
49-60	3.5	34.6	13.7
61-72	2.4	42.0	15.6
73-119	2.7	45.6	18.6
120 mo or more	7.6	46.1	21.3
Weighted average		21.6%	6.8%

*Based on data for inmates admitted in the 6 months prior to the 1997 *Survey of Inmates in State Correctional Facilities.*

SOURCE: Laura M. Maruschak and Allen J. Beck, "Estimating the risk of injury while in State prison" in "Medical Problems of Inmates, 1997," *Bureau of Justice Statistics Special Report,* U.S. Department of Justice, Washington, D.C., 2001

Data from the Federal Bureau of Prisons (FBP) in 2000 shows an increase in medical conditions among inmates from the 1997 survey. (See Table 6.4.) As of midyear 2000, 7.8 percent of federal inmates had high blood pressure (compared to less than 1.7 percent in 1997), 4.4 percent had asthma (compared to less than 1 percent in 1997), and more than twice as many were diabetic. Inmates with mental health conditions comprised about 5 percent of the federal inmate population in both years, although that rate increases significantly when state

prisoners, jail inmates, and those on probation are factored in.

Inmate Injuries

In addition to physical or mental conditions state and federal inmates were also asked if they had been injured in an accident or in a fight since their incarceration. Nearly a quarter of them said that they had. (See Table 6.5.) Of state inmates 29 percent of males and 21 percent of females reported being injured since admission to prison, while 26 percent of males and 25 percent of females in the federal system reported injury since admission. In both systems more males reported being injured in fights than females, although the rate of injury in fights among men was higher in state prison (11 percent) than in federal prison (3 percent).

The younger an inmate the more likely he or she will be engaged in a fight. In state prison 12.8 percent of prisoners 24 years of age or younger reported being injured in a fight compared to about half that number (6.5 percent) among inmates 45 years of age or older. (See Figure 6.1.) The margins between federal prisoners of different age groups injured in fights were narrower than in state prisons.

The likelihood of injury among inmates increased with the length of confinement. (See Table 6.6.) Forty-six percent of state inmates and about one-third of federal inmates who had served at least 72 months reported an injury compared to 13 percent of state inmates and 17 percent of federal prisoners incarcerated less than 12 months. (See Figure

6.2.) Although males in state prison were more likely to report injuries, females surpassed them in the rate of injury after about 108 months of confinement. (See Figure 6.3.)

Violent offenders were more likely to be violent prisoners. Fourteen percent of inmates serving time for violent crimes in state prison reported being in at least one fight since admission compared to 10 percent of other state offenders. (See Figure 6.4.) Among federal violent offenders 9 percent reported an injury by fight since admission compared to 5 percent of other federal offenders.

Assuming that newly admitted inmates will be injured in an accident or fight at the same rate as those inmates who participated in the survey, it is expected that 22 percent of entering state inmates will be injured while in prison. (See Table 6.7.)

HIV AMONG INMATES

The human immunodeficiency virus (HIV) infected some 2.1 percent of all state and federal prisoners at year-end 1997, according to findings released in November 1999 in the BJS bulletin, "HIV in Prisons 1997." The infection rate was slightly lower than the 2.2 percent of infected inmates in 1996. (See Table 6.8.)

In 1997 HIV-positive prisoners comprised 1 percent of the federal inmate population and 2.2 percent of state inmate populations, for a total of 23,548 inmates. Of this number 6,184 were confirmed AIDS cases. In 1997, 538 prisoner deaths were AIDS-related, down from 907 in 1996. (See Table 6.9.) From 1995–1997, among state prisoners, AIDS was second only to natural causes as the leading cause of death. The rate of death per 100,000 inmates due to AIDS in 1997 was 255, down from 308 in 1996 and 311 in 1995. Suicide was the next highest cause of death among state prisoners for those three years.

TABLE 6.8

HIV in state and federal prisons, 1991–97

	HIV-positive State and Federal prison inmates	
Year	Number	Percent of custody population
1991	17,551	2.2%
1992	20,651	2.5
1993	21,475	2.4
1994	22,717	2.4
1995	24,256	2.3
1996	23,881	2.2
1997	23,548	2.1

• Between 1991 and 1997 the number of HIV-positive prisoners grew at a slower rate (34%) than the overall prison population (49%).

• At yearend 1997, 3.5% of all female state prison inmates were HIV positive, compared to 2.2% of male state prisoners.

HIV-positive prison inmates		
Jurisdiction	Number	Percent of custody population
New York	7,500	10.8%
Florida	2,325	3.6
Texas	2,126	1.5
California	1,328	.9
Federal System	1,030	1.0
New Jersey	867	3.4
Georgia	861	2.4
Connecticut	798	5.1
Maryland	766	3.5

Based on jurisdictions with more than 700 HIV-positive inmates.

• New York held about a third of all inmates (7,500 inmates) known to be HIV positive at yearend 1997.

• Of all HIV-positive prison inmates, 26% were confirmed AIDS cases. In state prisons 26% of HIV-positive inmates had AIDS; in federal prisons, 36%.

• The overall rate of confirmed AIDS among the nation's prison population (0.55%) was more than 5 times the rate in the U.S. population (0.10%).

• The number of AIDS-related deaths among prison inmates decreased from 907 in 1996 to 538 in 1997.

• Of all state prison inmates, 2.8% of black inmates and 2.5% of Hispanic inmates, compared to 1.4% of white inmates reported to survey interviewers that they were HIV positive.

	Tested inmates who reported results	
	Number	Percent HIV positive
All inmates	790,128	2.2%
Male	734,327	2.2
Female	55,800	3.4
White	257,919	1.4%
Black	384,870	2.8
Hispanic	123,725	2.5
Age 24 or younger	154,181	.5%
25-34	210,161	2.3
35-44	232,835	3.1
45 or older	92,168	2.7
Ever used drugs	665,977	2.3%
Used in month before offense	460,685	2.7

From the 1997 Survey of Inmates in State Correctional Facilities.

SOURCE: Laura M. Maruschak, "Highlights," in *HIV in Prisons 1997*, U.S. Department of Justice, Bureau of Justice Statistics, Washington, D.C., 1999

TABLE 6.9

Number of inmate deaths in state prisons by cause, 1995–97

	1995		1996		1997	
Cause of death	Number	Rate of death per 100,000 inmates	Number	Rate of death per 100,000 inmates	Number	Rate of death per 100,000 inmates
Total	**3,133**	**311**	**3,095**	**308**	**2,872**	**255**
Natural causes other than AIDS	1,569	156	1,715	170	1,859	165
AIDS	1,010	100	907	90	538	48
Suicide	160	16	154	15	159	14
Accident	48	5	43	4	37	3
Execution	56	6	45	4	74	7
By another person	86	9	65	6	75	7
Other/unspecified	204	20	166	16	130	12

Note: To calculate the rate of death, the number of inmates under State jurisdiction on June 30 of each year was used as an approximation of the average population exposed to the risk of death during the year.

SOURCE: "Laura M. Maruschak, Table 4. Number of inmate deaths in State prisons, by cause, 1995–97," in *HIV in Prisons 1997*, U.S. Department of Justice, Bureau of Justice Statistics, Washington, D.C., 1999

TABLE 6.10

Prison system testing policies for the antibody to HIV by jurisdiction, 1997

	All inmates		At release	High risk group	Upon inmate request	Clinical indication	Involvement in incident	Random sample	Other
	Entering	In custody							
Federal*			X		X	X			
Northeast									
Connecticut				X	X	X	X		
Maine					X				
Massachusetts					X				
New Hampshire	X								
New Jersey					X	X			X
New York				X	X	X	X	X	
Pennsylvania					X				
Rhode Island	X	X			X	X	X		
Vermont					X	X	X		
Midwest									
Illinois				X	X	X	X		
Indiana				X	X	X			
Iowa	X								
Kansas					X	X	X		
Michigan	X				X	X	X		
Minnesota				X	X	X	X		
Missouri	X	X		X	X	X	X		
Nebraska	X					X	X		
North Dakota	X								
Ohio				X	X	X	X		X
South Dakota	X								
Wisconsin					X		X		
South									
Alabama	X		X			X			
Arkansas	X	X		X	X	X	X		
Delaware				X		X	X		
District of Columbia					X				
Florida					X	X	X		
Georgia	X				X	X			
Kentucky				X	X	X	X		
Louisiana					X	X	X		
Maryland					X	X	X		
Mississippi	X								
North Carolina					X	X	X		
Oklahoma	X				X	X	X		
South Carolina				X	X	X	X		
Tennessee				X	X	X	X		X
Texas				X	X	X	X		
Virginia	X	X	X		X	X	X		
West Virginia					X	X			
West									
Alaska									X
Arizona				X	X	X	X		
California					X	X	X		
Colorado	X				X	X	X		X
Hawaii					X	X			
Idaho	X								
Montana				X	X	X	X		
Nevada	X	X			X	X	X		
New Mexico					X				X
Oregon					X				
Utah	X								
Washington					X	X			X
Wyoming						X			

*The Bureau of Prisons tests a random sample of inmates on alternate years.

SOURCE: "Table 6. Prison system testing policies for the antibody to the human immunodeficiency virus, by jurisdiction, 1997," in *HIV in Prisons 1997*, U.S. Department of Justice, Bureau of Justice Statistics, Washington, D.C., 1999

TABLE 6.11

Inmates ever tested or tested since admission for HIV and test results, 1997

Inmate characteristic	Percent of tested inmates who reported results	
	State prisons	Federal prisons
Ever tested	74.6%	79.6%
HIV positive	2.2	0.6
Tested since admission	59.1%	69.7%
HIV positive	2.6	0.7

Note: Data are from the 1997 Surveys of Inmates in State and Federal Correctional Facilities.

SOURCE: Laura M. Maruschak, "Table 7. Inmates ever tested or tested since admission for the human immunodeficiency virus and test results, 1997," in *HIV in Prisons 1997*, U.S. Department of Justice, Bureau of Justice Statistics, Washington, D.C., 1999

TABLE 6.13

Inmates ever tested for HIV and results, by offense and prior drug use, 1997

Characteristic	Tested inmates who reported results			
	State prisons		Federal prisons	
	Number	Percent HIV positive	Number	Percent HIV positive
Current offense				
Violent	360,370	1.9%	10,681	1.0%
Property	178,601	2.4	4,660	1.0
Drug	164,256	2.9	43,815	0.4
Public-order	77,049	1.9	10,029	1.0
Prior drug use				
Never	123,049	1.7%	18,917	0.3%
Ever	665,977	2.3	51,847	0.7
In the month before offense	460,685	2.7	32,113	0.3
Used needle to inject drugs	168,446	4.6	9,443	1.3
Ever shared a needle	74,393	7.7	4,022	2.1

Note: Data are from the 1997 Surveys of Inmates in State and Federal Correctional Facilities.

SOURCE: Laura M. Maruschak, "Table 9. Inmates ever tested for the human immunodeficiency virus and results, by offense and prior drug use, 1997," in *HIV in Prisons 1997*, U.S. Department of Justice, Bureau of Justice Statistics, Washington, D.C., 1999

Since 1991 statistics on HIV and AIDS among prisoners have been provided by the departments of correction in all 50 states, the District of Columbia, and by the FBP. Included in these reports are the testing policies for detecting HIV among state and federal inmates. (See Table 6.10.)

In 1997 the FBP reported testing all federal prisoners at the time of their release. In addition the FBP tested inmates upon inmate request or when there were clinical indications of the possibility of HIV infection.

States vary in their testing polices. Of the 46 reporting states in 1997, 18 states tested all entering inmates for HIV.

TABLE 6.12

Inmates ever tested for HIV and results by selected characteristics, 1997

Characteristic	Tested inmates who reported results			
	State prisons		Federal prisons	
	Number	Percent HIV positive	Number	Percent HIV positive
All inmates	**790,128**	**2.2%**	**70,902**	**0.6%**
Gender				
Male	734,327	2.2%	65,723	0.6%
Female	55,800	3.4	5,179	0.6
Race/Hispanic origin				
White non-Hispanic	257,919	1.4%	21,128	0.3%
Male	239,687	1.4	19,565	0.3
Female	18,232	2.3	1,563	0.3
Black non-Hispanic	384,870	2.8	28,178	0.8
Male	357,736	2.7	26,387	0.8
Female	27,135	3.9	1,791	1.3
Hispanic	123,725	2.5	18,466	0.7
Male	115,344	2.4	16,892	0.7
Female	8,382	4.2	1,573	0
Age				
17–24	154,181	0.5%	5,528	0.1%
25–34	310,161	2.3	26,262	0.5
35–44	232,835	3.1	22,228	0.4
45 or older	92,168	2.7	16,884	1.2
Marital status				
Married	128,834	1.7%	21,545	0.5%
Widowed/divorced	161,468	2.0	16,331	0.4
Separated	45,435	2.9	3,884	0
Never married	453,664	2.4	29,045	0.8
Education				
Less than high school	302,437	2.7%	17,226	0.8%
GED	231,714	1.4	16,389	0.6
High school or more	254,975	2.4	37,237	0.5

Note: Data are from the 1997 Surveys of Inmates in State and Federal Correctional Facilities.

SOURCE: Laura M. Maruschak, "Table 8. Inmates ever tested for the human immunodeficiency virus and results, by selected characteristics, 1997," in *HIV in Prisons 1997*, U.S. Department of Justice, Bureau of Justice Statistics, Washington, D.C., 1999

TABLE 6.14

Estimated number of mentally ill inmates and probationers, 1998

	Estimated number of offenders*			
	State prison	Federal prison	Local jail	Probation
Identified as mentally ill	179,200	7,900	96,700	547,800
Reported a mental or emotional condition	111,300	5,200	62,100	473,000
Admitted overnight to a mental hospital	118,300	5,000	60,500	281,200

*Based on midyear 1998 counts from the *National Prisoner Statistics* and *Annual Survey of Jails* and preliminary year-end 1998 counts from the *Annual Probation Survey.*

SOURCE: Paula M. Ditton, "Highlights" in "Mental Health and Treatment of Inmates and Probationers," *Bureau of Justice Statistics Special Report*, U.S. Department of Justice, Washington, D.C., 1999

TABLE 6.15

Incarceration and the mentally ill

Mentally ill incarcerated in prison or jail

Reported a...	State prison	Federal prison	Jail	Proba-tion
Mental or emotional condition	10.1%	4.8%	10.5%	13.8%
Overnight stay in a mental hospital	10.7	4.7	10.2	8.2
Estimated to be mentally ill*	16.2%	7.4%	16.3%	16.0%

*Reported either a mental or emotional condition or an overnight stay in a mental hospital or program.

Offenses of mentally ill inmates compared to other inmates

	State prisoners	
Offense	Mentally ill inmates	Other inmates
Violent	52.9%	46.1%
Property	24.4	21.5
Drug	12.8	22.2
Public-order	9.9	9.8
Criminal history		
None	18.8%	21.2%
Priors	81.2	78.8

Rates of homelessness, abuse, and substance abuse among mentally ill inmates compared to other inmates

	State prisoners	
Before entering prison	Mentally ill inmates	Other inmates
Homeless in 12 months prior to arrest	20.1%	8.8%
Physical/sexual abuse		
Male	32.8%	13.1%
Female	78.4	50.9
Alcohol/drug use		
At time of offense	58.7%	51.2%
Drug use		
In month before offense	58.8%	56.1%

Mental health treatment since admission	Mentally ill Inmates	
	State prison	Jail
Any treatment	60.5%	40.9%
Medication	50.1	34.1
Counseling	44.1	16.2

SOURCE: Paula M. Ditton, "Highlights" in "Mental Health and Treatment of Inmates and Probationers," *Bureau of Justice Statistics Special Report,* U.S. Department of Justice, Washington, D.C., 1999

TABLE 6.16

Inmates and probationers identified as mentally ill, by gender, race/Hispanic origin, and age

Offender characteristic	Percent identified as mentally ill			
	State inmates	Federal inmates	Jail inmates	Proba-tioners
Gender				
Male	15.8%	7.0%	15.6%	14.7%
Female	23.6	12.5	22.7	21.7
Race/Hispanic origin				
White*	22.6%	11.8%	21.7%	19.6%
Black*	13.5	5.6	13.7	10.4
Hispanic	11.0	4.1	11.1	9.0
Age				
24 or younger	14.4%	6.6%	13.3%	13.8%
25-34	14.8	5.9	15.7	13.8
35-44	18.4	7.5	19.3	19.8
45-54	19.7	10.3	22.7	21.1
55 or older	15.6	8.9	20.4	16.0

*Excludes Hispanics.

SOURCE: Paula M. Ditton, "Inmates and probationers identified as mentally ill, by gender, race/Hispanic origin, and age" in "Mental Health and Treatment of Inmates and Probationers," *Bureau of Justice Statistics Special Report,* U.S. Department of Justice, Washington, D.C., 1999

TABLE 6.17

Victim characteristics and use of weapon, by mental health status of violent state prisoners

	Mentally ill inmates	Other inmates
Gender of victim(s)		
Male	44.3%	51.5%
Female	44.0	37.5
Both males and females	11.7	10.9
Age of youngest victim		
12 or younger	15.4%	10.2%
13-17	11.6	11.0
18-24	17.3	20.7
25-34	25.7	30.9
35-54	23.8	22.8
55 or older	6.2	4.3
Victim-offender relationship		
Knew victim[a]	60.8%	52.1%
Relative	15.6	10.3
Intimate[b]	11.6	8.6
Friend/acquaintance	29.8	27.7
Other[c]	6.5	6.9
Knew none of victims	39.1	47.9
Use of weapon		
Yes	44.0%	41.9%
No	56.0	58.1

[a] More than one victim may have been reported.
[b] Includes spouse, ex-spouse, boyfriend, girlfriend, ex-boyfriend, and ex-girlfriend.
[c] Includes those known by sight only.

SOURCE: Paula M. Ditton, "Victim characteristics and use of weapon, by mental health status of violent State prisoners" in "Mental Health and Treatment of Inmates and Probationers," *Bureau of Justice Statistics Special Report,* U.S. Department of Justice, Washington, D.C., 1999

Forty states provided HIV testing upon inmate request and 37 did so when there was a clinical indication of infection. Testing for HIV infection at the state level also occurred at the time of release if the inmate belonged to a high-risk group (i.e., intravenous drug user), or if there had been involvement in an incident (i.e., an injury or fight where bleeding occurred). Only New York State tested by random sampling. Overall, about 74.6 percent of state prison inmates and 79.6 percent of federal prisoners reported being tested since their admission to prison. (See Table 6.11.)

TABLE 6.18

Fights since admission, and violation of prison/jail rules, by mental health status

Discipline problem reported by inmate	State prison		Federal prison		Local jail	
	Mentally ill inmates	Other inmates	Mentally ill inmates	Other inmates	Mentally inmates	Other inmates
Number of fights since admission						
None	64.3%	75.6%	79.4%	90.9%	80.9%	86.7%
1	1.4	9.6	11.6	5.2	9.4	7.0
2 to 3	12.8	7.8	5.2	2.5	7.0	4.1
4 or more	11.5	7.1	3.8	1.4	2.6	2.3
Charged with breaking prison or jail rules	62.2%	51.9%	41.2%	32.7%	24.5%	16.0%

SOURCE: Paula M. Ditton, "Fights since admission and violation of prison or jail rules, by mental health status" in "Mental Health and Treatment of Inmates and Probationers," *Bureau of Justice Statistics Special Report,* U.S. Department of Justice, Washington, D.C., 1999

TABLE 6.19

Most serious current offense of inmates and probationers, by mental health status

Most serious offense	State prison		Federal prison		Local jail		Probation	
	Mentally ill inmates	Other inmates	Mentally ill inmates	Other inmates	Mentally ill inmates	Other inmates	Mentally ill probationers	Other probationers
All offenses	100.0%	100.0%	100.0%	100.0%	100.0%	100.0%	100.0%	100.0%
Violent offenses	52.9%	46.1%	33.1%	13.3%	29.9%	25.6%	28.4%	18.4%
Murder*	13.2	11.4	1.9	1.4	3.5	2.7	0.5	0.9
Sexual assault	12.4	7.9	1.9	0.7	5.2	2.8	6.8	4.1
Robbery	13.0	14.4	20.8	9.1	4.7	6.9	2.0	1.4
Assault	10.9	9.0	3.8	1.1	14.4	11.0	14.0	10.5
Property offenses	24.4%	21.5%	8.7%	6.7%	31.3%	26.0%	30.4%	28.5%
Burglary	12.1	10.5	1.0	0.3	9.1	7.4	6.4	4.3
Larceny/theft	4.6	4.1	1.3	0.4	8.4	7.9	5.3	8.8
Fraud	3.1	2.6	5.0	4.9	5.2	4.4	11.7	9.2
Drug offenses	12.8%	22.2%	40.4%	64.4%	15.2%	23.3%	16.1%	20.7%
Possession	5.7	9.4	3.9	11.9	7.3	12.3	7.2	11.0
Trafficking	6.6	12.2	35.7	46.6	7.0	9.6	6.7	9.2
Public-order offenses	9.9%	9.8%	17.0%	14.6%	23.2%	24.6%	24.7%	31.6%

Note: Detail does not sum to total because of excluded offense categories.
*Includes nonnegligent manslaughter.

SOURCE: Paula M. Ditton, "Most serious current offense of inmates and probationers, by mental health status" in "Mental Health and Treatment of Inmates and Probationers," *Bureau of Justice Statistics Special Report,* U.S. Department of Justice, Washington, D.C., 1999

In 1997 HIV-positive inmates were concentrated in a small number of states. New York housed the largest number (7,500), followed by Florida (2,325). Combined, these two states housed more than 40 percent of all HIV-infected state prisoners. Although Florida had the second-highest number of HIV-positive inmates, higher rates of infection were reported in Connecticut (5.1 percent) and Massachusetts (3.7 percent).

From 1996 to 1997, 15 states reported a decrease in the number of HIV-positive inmates—the largest being New York, which was down by 1,000 cases. An increase in HIV-infected inmates was reported by 28 states, with Texas reporting the largest increase of 250 cases, followed by California (up by 192), and Florida (up by 173).

In 1997 the rate of confirmed cases of AIDS among state and federal prisoners was over five times higher than in the U.S. population. About 55 prison inmates per 10,000 had confirmed cases of AIDS compared to about 10 per 10,000 people in the general population.

At year-end 1997, 3.4 percent of state female prisoners were HIV-positive compared to 2.2 percent of male inmates. (See Table 6.12.) The rate of HIV-infection rose from 3 percent in 1991 to a peak of 4 percent in 1992 and again in 1995. The 1997 rate among female prisoners was slightly higher than the 3.1 percent rate reported in 1996. Among male prisoners the rate of infection rose from 2.2 percent in 1991 to a high of 2.5 percent in 1993 when it began to decline. HIV infection among female

TABLE 6.20

Criminal history of inmates, by mental health status

	State prison		Federal prison		Local jail	
	Mentally ill inmates	Other inmates	Mentally ill inmates	Other inmates	Mentally ill inmates	Other inmates
Criminal history						
None	18.8%	21.2%	24.3%	38.8%	21.0%	28.4%
Priors	81.2	78.8	75.7	61.2	79.0	71.6
Violent recidivists	53.4	44.9	43.7	21.6	46.0	31.6
Other recidivists	27.8	33.8	32.0	39.6	33.0	40.0
Number of prior probation/ incarceration sentences						
0	18.8%	21.2%	24.3%	38.8%	21.0%	28.4%
1	15.5	19.4	14.0	18.2	14.7	17.9
2	13.8	17.0	12.9	14.7	10.1	11.5
3 to 5	26.3	25.5	23.6	18.9	23.5	19.7
6 to 10	15.6	11.6	15.4	7.3	17.6	14.6
11 or more	10.0	5.3	9.7	2.2	13.2	7.8

SOURCE: Paula M. Ditton, "Criminal history of inmates, by mental health status" in "Mental Health and Treatment of Inmates and Probationers," *Bureau of Justice Statistics Special Report,* U.S. Department of Justice, Washington, D.C., 1999

TABLE 6.21

Prior physical or sexual abuse of inmates and probationers, by mental health status

Reported by offender	State prison		Federal prison		Local jail		Probation	
	Mentally ill inmates	Other inmates	Mentally ill inmates	Other inmates	Mentally ill inmates	Other inmates	Mentally ill probationers	Other probationers
Ever abused before admission	36.9%	15.2%	34.1%	7.6%	36.5%	12.5%	38.8%	12.1%
Male	32.8	13.1	30.0	5.5	30.7	9.6	31.0	6.5
Female	78.4	50.9	64.1	36.1	72.9	40.3	59.4	35.7
Physically abused	31.0%	12.5%	27.5%	6.4%	30.0%	10.1%	28.1%	9.8%
Male	27.4	10.8	24.5	4.7	25.3	8.0	21.0	5.1
Female	67.6	40.2	50.0	29.4	59.8	30.8	46.7	29.7
Sexually abused	19.0%	5.8%	15.6%	2.7%	23.5%	5.9%	21.9%	5.8%
Male	15.0	4.1	11.6	1.5	17.2	3.4	14.2	2.4
Female	58.9	33.1	45.0	19.3	63.4	29.6	42.3	19.9

SOURCE: Paula M. Ditton, "Prior physical or sexual abuse of inmates and probationers, by mental health status" in "Mental Health and Treatment of Inmates and Probationers," *Bureau of Justice Statistics Special Report,* U.S. Department of Justice, Washington, D.C., 1999

prisoners between 1991 and 1997 increased by an annual average of 11.1 percent compared to 3.8 percent for male prisoners during the same time period. Non-Hispanic black females in state prisons showed the highest rate of infection at 3.9 percent.

Inmates of both sexes between the ages of 35 and 44 years were most likely to be HIV-infected of all age groups. By offense type drug offenders in state prison systems had the highest rate of HIV-infection (2.9 percent), while among federal prisoners the highest rate was shared by violent and property offenders (1 percent each). (See Table 6.13.)

MENTAL HEALTH

In the July 1999 *Bureau of Justice Statistics Special Report* entitled "Mental Health and Treatment of Inmates

and Probationers," BJS statistician Paula M. Ditton reported that, as of midyear 1998, some 179,200 state prisoners and 7,900 federal inmates were identified as mentally ill. (See Table 6.14.) Some 16.2 percent of state prisoners and 7.4 percent of federal inmates reported either a mental condition or an overnight stay in a mental hospital, as did 16.3 percent of jail inmates and 16 percent probationers. (See Table 6.15.)

Among state prisoners 23.6 percent of females were identified as mentally ill compared to 15.8 percent of males. The rates of mental illness among federal inmates were 12.5 percent for females and 7 percent for males. (See Table 6.16.) In both state and federal prisons a greater percentage of whites were mentally ill than blacks or Hispanics, and more mentally ill prisoners were between 45 and 54 years of age than in other age

TABLE 6.22

Homelessness, employment, and sources of income among inmates, by mental health status

	State prison		Federal prison		Local jail	
	Mentally ill inmates	Other inmates	Mentally ill inmates	Other inmates	Mentally ill inmates	Other inmates
Homeless						
In year before arrest	20.1%	8.8%	18.6%	3.2%	30.3%	17.3%
At time of arrest	3.9	1.2	3.9	0.3	6.9	2.9
Employed in month before arrest						
Yes	61.2%	69.6%	62.3%	72.5%	52.9%	66.6%
No	38.8	30.4	37.7	27.5	47.1	33.4
Sources of income[a]						
Wages	56.7%	65.6%	54.0%	66.4%	62.9%	77.1%
Family/friends	22.0	17.7	20.1	12.3	19.7	15.4
Illegal sources	23.4	27.0	22.5	28.8	19.4	14.4
Welfare	15.4	7.8	13.7	3.9	21.9	12.3
Pension[b]	17.3	4.1	16.5	3.7	18.4	4.9
Compensation payments	3.1	1.9	4.7	1.8	3.0	2.1

[a] Detail sums to more than 100% because offenders may have reported more than one source of income. For prisoners detail includes any income received in the month prior to arrest. For jail inmates, detail includes any income received in the year prior to arrest.
[b] Includes Supplemental Security Income, Social Security, or other pension.

SOURCE: Paula M. Ditton, "Homelessness, employment, and sources of income among inmates, by mental health status" in "Mental Health and Treatment of Inmates and Probationers," *Bureau of Justice Statistics Special Report,* U.S. Department of Justice, Washington, D.C., 1999

TABLE 6.23

Family background of inmates and probationers, by mental health status

	State prison		Federal prison		Local jail		Probation	
	Mentally ill inmates	Other inmates	Mentally ill inmates	Other inmates	Mentally ill inmates	Other inmates	Mentally ill probationers	Other probationers
Family member ever incarcerated	54.9%	46.5%	41.5%	38.5%	51.5%	45.1%	40.3%	34.0%
Parent	23.4	17.4	13.4	11.1	23.7	18.9	19.6	11.1
Brother/sister	41.8	36.5	29.5	29.9	36.2	32.8	25.7	25.6
While growing up —								
Ever lived in a foster home, agency, or institution	26.1%	12.2%	18.6%	5.8%	24.1%	11.5%	15.9%	6.5%
Parent or guardian abused alcohol or drugs								
Alcohol only	30.6%	22.2%	24.6%	16.0%	29.3%	21.9%	32.4%	19.2%
Drugs only	2.0	1.8	1.2	0.8	1.7	1.2	1.0	0.4
Both	10.9	5.7	8.5	2.8	11.1	6.1	9.0	2.4

SOURCE: Paula M. Ditton, "Family background of inmates and probationers, by mental health status" in "Mental Health and Treatment of Inmates and Probationers," *Bureau of Justice Statistics Special Report,* U.S. Department of Justice, Washington, D.C., 1999

groups. The same also holds true among jail inmates and probationers.

Of those prisoners identified as mentally ill 53 percent were violent offenders compared to 46 percent of other inmates. About a quarter of mentally ill prisoners were incarcerated for property offenses (24.4 percent), followed by drug offenses (12.8 percent) and public-order crimes (9.9 percent).

Violent offenders identified as mentally ill were more likely to report that the victim of the offense was a woman, someone they knew, and under 18 years. (See Table 6.17.) Fifty-one percent of nonmentally ill male prisoners were classified as violent offenders compared to 37.5 percent of nonmentally ill females. However, that gap virtually disappears among mentally ill offenders, with 44.3 percent males and 44 percent females.

Perhaps due to their tendency to be violent offenders, mentally ill inmates reported being involved in more fights while in prison than did other inmates. (See Table 6.18.) Among state prisoners 11.4 percent of mentally ill inmates were involved in at least one fight, and 12.8 percent were involved in two or three fights compared to 9.6 percent and 7.8 percent, respectively, among other state prisoners. In the federal system more than twice the

TABLE 6.24

Maximum sentence length and months served, by offense and mental health status

| Most serious offense | Mean maximum sentence length[a] | | Mean time served | | | |
| | | | To date of interview | | Total time to be served until release[b] | |
	Mentally ill inmates	Other inmates	Mentally ill inmates	Other inmates	Mentally ill inmates	Other inmates
Local jail inmates						
All offenses	20	26	6.5	6.7	8.7	10.7
Violent	30	37	8.8	9.3	14.7	16.0
Property	26	26	5.3	8.0	7.4	11.6
Drug	18	25	8.9	8.4	8.6	13.5
Public-order	8	20	5.0	3.3	7.0	5.7
Other	10	8	8.4	1.6	10.0	5.3
State prison inmates						
All offenses	171	159	54.4	49.3	103.4	88.2
Violent	230	225	71.8	69.7	142.5	130.7
Property	128	118	38.8	36.6	75.0	62.2
Drug	103	111	30.3	28.5	49.8	49.5
Public-order	83	81	29.1	27.8	50.8	47.6
Other	120	104	32.5	47.8	60.1	80.6

Note: Because data on sentence length and time served are restricted to persons in prison and jail, they overstate the average sentence and time to be served by those entering prison or jail. Persons with shorter sentences leave prison and jail more quickly, resulting in a longer average sentence among persons in the inmate samples.

[a] Based on the total maximum sentence for all consecutive sentences.
[b] Based on time served when interviewed plus time to be served until the expected date of release.

SOURCE: Paula M. Ditton, "Maximum sentence length and time served by inmates, by offense and mental health status" in "Mental Health and Treatment of Inmates and Probationers," *Bureau of Justice Statistics Special Report,* U.S. Department of Justice, Washington, D.C., 1999

TABLE 6.25

Treatment for mentally ill inmates and probationers

| | Percent of mentally ill offenders | | | |
	State prison	Federal prison	Local jail	Probation
Since admission, the offender had –				
Been admitted overnight to a mental hospital or treatment program	23.6%	24.0%	9.3%	12.2%
Taken a prescribed medication	50.1	49.1	34.1	36.5
Received counseling or therapy	44.1	45.6	16.2	44.1
Received any mental health service	60.5	59.7	40.9	56.0

SOURCE: Paula M. Ditton, "Mental health treatment in prison or jail or on probation for those identified as mentally ill" in "Mental Health and Treatment of Inmates and Probationers," *Bureau of Justice Statistics Special Report,* U.S. Department of Justice, Washington, D.C., 1999

FIGURE 6.5

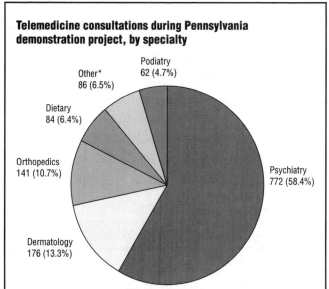

Telemedicine consultations during Pennsylvania demonstration project, by specialty

Other* 86 (6.5%)
Podiatry 62 (4.7%)
Dietary 84 (6.4%)
Orthopedics 141 (10.7%)
Psychiatry 772 (58.4%)
Dermatology 176 (13.3%)

*Includes infectious dieases, cardiology, ENT, pulmonary, gastroenterology, and neurology.

SOURCE: Douglas McDonald, Andrea Hassol, and Kenneth Carlson, "Telemedicine consultations, by specialty" in "Can Telemedicine Reduce Spending and Improve Prisoner Health Care?" *National Institute of Justice Journal,* U.S. Department of Justice, Washington, D.C., April 1999

number of mentally ill inmates reported being in one fight compared to other federal prisoners.

Mentally ill violent offenders were more likely to be incarcerated for murder or sexual assault than other inmates. (See Table 6.19.) The mentally ill were imprisoned for drug offenses at about half the rate of other inmates in state prison. In federal prison 40.4 percent of mentally ill inmates were drug offenders compared to nearly two-thirds of other inmates. Use of a weapon was reported among 44 percent of mentally ill inmates compared to about 42 percent of other inmates.

More than 80 percent of prisoners identified as mentally ill had a criminal history, only slightly higher than the 78.8 percent of other inmates with priors. (See Table 6.20.) Mentally ill federal prisoners were twice as likely to be violent recidivists (repeat offenders) (43.7 percent) compared to other federal inmates (21.6 percent). Of violent recidivists in state prison 53.4 percent were identified as mentally ill compared to 44.9 percent of other state inmates.

Prior to entering prison mentally ill inmates reported significantly higher rates of homelessness and physical and sexual abuse that other inmates. (See Table 6.21.) Levels of prior alcohol and drug use were also higher among mentally ill inmates. Homelessness in the year before arrest occurred at a rate of 20.1 percent among mentally ill state inmates compared to 8.8 percent among other state prisoners. (See Table 6.22.) In federal prison 18.6 percent of mentally ill inmates were homeless in the year before arrest compared to only 3.2 percent of other federal prisoners.

In terms of family backgrounds more than one-quarter of mentally ill state inmates reported living in a foster home, agency, or institution at some time while growing up compared to 12.2 percent of other state prisoners. In federal prison 18.6 percent of mentally ill inmates reported being under foster care or institutionalized during their youth compared to 5.8 percent of other federal inmates. (See Table 6.23.) At both the state and federal levels more mentally ill inmates reported alcohol and/or drug abuse by their parents or guardians than did other inmates.

On average mentally ill inmates received longer prison sentences than other inmates. (See Table 6.24.) In 1998, for all offenses, mentally ill state inmates received sentences of 171 months compared to 159 months for other state inmates, a difference of one year. In terms of average time served, at the time of their interview mentally ill inmates on average reported being in state prison longer (54.4 months) than other state inmates (49.3 months).

As for mental health treatment during their incarceration, 60.5 percent of state prisoners and 59.7 percent of federal inmates identified as mentally ill reported receiving some type of mental health services while in prison. (See Table 6.25.) About half of state and federal mentally ill inmates said they were taking prescribed medication for their mental illness. Mentally ill inmates in local jails were least likely to have received any mental health treatment while incarcerated.

REDUCING THE COST AND IMPROVING THE AVAILABILITY OF TREATMENT

Telecommunication links now make it possible for physicians and other health care specialists to evaluate and treat patients who are hundreds or thousands of miles away. This technology, called telemedicine, offers the prospect of providing prisoners with cost-effective health care. For example, telemedicine makes it possible for physicians to examine prisoners without the inconve-

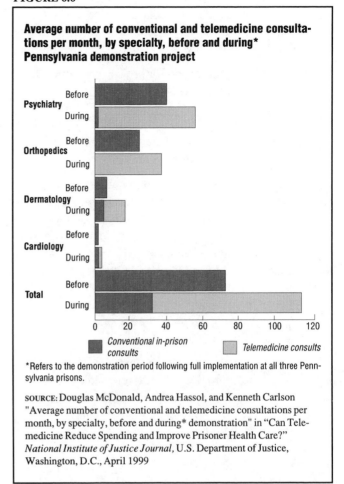

FIGURE 6.6

Average number of conventional and telemedicine consultations per month, by specialty, before and during* Pennsylvania demonstration project

*Refers to the demonstration period following full implementation at all three Pennsylvania prisons.

SOURCE: Douglas McDonald, Andrea Hassol, and Kenneth Carlson "Average number of conventional and telemedicine consultations per month, by specialty, before and during* demonstration" in "Can Telemedicine Reduce Spending and Improve Prisoner Health Care?" *National Institute of Justice Journal,* U.S. Department of Justice, Washington, D.C., April 1999

nience of traveling to prison facilities, often located in remote or isolated areas. Likewise, the cost and security concerns of transporting prisoners to physicians are also eliminated.

In their article, "Can Telemedicine Reduce Spending and Improve Health Care?" (*National Institute of Justice Journal,* April 1999, U.S. Department of Justice, Washington, D.C.), authors Douglas McDonald, Andrea Hassol, and Kenneth Carlson reported on a demonstration program to evaluate a telemedicine system in prison. The pilot project was conducted jointly at four federal prisons:

- U.S. Penitentiary, Lewisburg, Pa. Maximum security. Houses an average of 1,300 male prisoners

- U.S. Penitentiary, Allenwood, Pa. Maximum security. Houses an average of 1,000 male prisoners

- Federal Correctional Institution, Allenwood, Pa. Low and medium security. Houses an average of 1,100 male prisoners

- Federal Medical Center, Lexington, Ky. Medium and minimum security. Houses an average of 1,450 mostly male prisoners with chronic illnesses

The pilot program was conducted from September 1996 to December 1997. It did not replace routine medical care provided by prison staff. As reported the goal of the telemedicine test program was to reduce three types of care:

- Consultations with specialty physicians who would normally visit the prison

- Prisoner trips to hospitals or off-site physicians

- Transfers of prisoners to federal medical centers for intensive or long-term treatment

At each prison a dedicated telemedicine room was equipped with interactive video-conferencing equipment, specialized medical cameras, an electronic stethoscope, and a computer workstation with appropriate software. For most examinations a medical staff member from the prison (usually a physician's assistant) presented the inmate patient to an off-site specialist linked via video-conferencing and equipped with remote controls that enabled the specialist to manipulate cameras located in the patient examination room.

During the 15 months of the demonstration project physicians made approximately 100 telemedicine consultations each month, for a total of 1,321 consultations. About 58 percent of the telemedicine "visits" were for psychiatric consultations, followed by dermatology (13.3 percent), orthopedics (10.7 percent), dietary (6.4 percent), and podiatry (4.7 percent). (See Figure 6.5.) The remaining 6.5 percent of telemedicine consultations were with specialists from other disciplines, including infectious diseases, cardiology, and neurology.

Four specialties were selected for purposes of comparing conventional medical care in prisons with telemedicine consultations—psychiatry, orthopedics, dermatology, and cardiology. Specialists in these four fields were among the most frequently consulted prior to the pilot project, and that frequency increased with the implementation of telemedicine. (See Figure 6.6.)

During the pilot program the cost of in-prison consultations decreased from approximately $108 per conventional consultation to $71 per telemedicine consultation, a savings of $37 per consultation. However, because there was not a one-for-one substitution of regular consultations and telemedicine consultations, the total number of consultations increased with the addition of telemedicine.

Some 35 trips for inmates to visit specialists outside of prison were eliminated through telemedicine for a total savings of about $27,500. Some trips were unavoidable when inmates required invasive tests, surgery, or intensive trauma care. The Bureau of Prisons estimated that it saved an additional $59,134 because, in certain cases, telemedicine eliminated the need for air transfers of inmates to federal medical centers. Most of the averted air transfers were for psychiatric patients who required intensive monitoring that was made possible through telemedicine consultations.

There were other nonfinancial benefits to the implementation of telemedicine consultations. Waiting time to see specialists decreased and new services became available, including more specialized HIV/AIDS care. Also, inmate patients reported feeling that the quality of care improved with telemedicine.

As a result of the success of this pilot program, the National Institute of Justice began studies using telemedicine in jails.

CHAPTER 7
JUVENILE CONFINEMENT

The children detained in our correctional facilities represent a significant challenge to our Nation. As a result of acts of crime and violence that contradict our ideals of childhood and adolescence, these youth require strong intervention that serves public order and safety. However, while we must protect society from their misconduct, we must also enable these young offenders to adopt more conventional attitudes and behaviors.

—Shay Bilchik, Administrator, Office of Juvenile Justice and Delinquency, 1993

WHO IS A JUVENILE?

In most states offenders charged with a crime who are below the age of 18 years are considered juveniles and under the jurisdiction of juvenile court, as opposed to adult criminal court. More states are sending more offenders under the age of 18 to adult court due to changes in state laws that support a so-called "get tough" policy on crime.

In *Juvenile Offenders and Victims: 1999 National Report* (Office of Juvenile Justice and Delinquency Prevention, U.S. Department of Justice), Howard N. Snyder and Melissa Sickmund reported that, as of 1997, most states retained juvenile court jurisdiction for offenders 17 years of age and younger. In some states the age was 16 years and younger; and in Connecticut, New York, and North Carolina, the age was 15 years and younger. (See Table 7.1.)

In 1997 the oldest age at which juvenile court could retain jurisdiction was 24 years (California, Montana, Oregon, and Wisconsin). In most states the oldest age was 20. In Arizona and North Carolina, the oldest age for juvenile court jurisdiction in 1997 was 17 years. (See Table 7.2.)

JUVENILE CUSTODY

The Office of Juvenile Justice and Delinquency Prevention (OJJDP) was established in 1974. It is part of the

TABLE 7.1

Oldest age for original juvenile court jurisdiction in delinquency matters

Age	State
15	Connecticut, New York, North Carolina
16	Georgia, Illinois, Louisiana, Massachusetts, Michigan, Missouri, New Hampshire, South Carolina, Texas, Wisconsin
17	Alabama, Alaska, Arizona, Arkansas, California, Colorado, Delaware, District of Columbia, Florida, Hawaii, Idaho, Indiana, Iowa, Kansas, Kentucky, Maine, Maryland, Minnesota, Mississippi, Montana, Nebraska, Nevada, New Jersey, New Mexico, North Dakota, Ohio, Oklahoma, Oregon, Pennsylvania, Rhode Island, South Dakota, Tennessee, Utah, Vermont, Virginia, Washington, West Virginia, Wyoming

SOURCE: Howard N. Snyder and Melissa Sickmund, *Juvenile Offenders and Victims: 1999 National Report*, Office of Juvenile Justice and Delinquency Prevention, Washington, DC, 1999

TABLE 7.2

Oldest age over which the juvenile court may retain jurisdiction for disposition purposes in delinquency matters

Age	State
17	Arizona*, North Carolina
18	Alaska, Iowa, Kentucky, Nebraska, Oklahoma, Tennessee
19	Mississippi, North Dakota
20	Alabama, Arkansas, Connecticut, Delaware, District of Columbia, Florida, Georgia, Idaho, Illinois, Indiana, Louisiana, Maine, Maryland, Massachusetts, Michigan, Minnesota, Missouri, Nevada, New Hampshire, New Mexico, New York, Ohio, Pennsylvania, Rhode Island, South Carolina, South Dakota, Texas, Utah, Vermont, Virginia, Washington, West Virginia, Wyoming
22	Kansas
24	California, Montana, Oregon, Wisconsin
**	Colorado, Hawaii, New Jersey

* Arizona statute extends jurisdiction through age 20, but a 1979 State Supreme Court decision held that juvenile court jurisdiction terminates at age 18.
**Until the full term of the disposition order.
Note: Extended jurisdiction may be restricted to certain offenses or juveniles.

SOURCE: Howard N. Snyder and Melissa Sickmund, *Juvenile Offenders and Victims: 1999 National Report*, Office of Juvenile Justice and Delinquency Prevention, Washington, DC, 1999

TABLE 7.3

Percent of juvenile offenders in residential placement on October 29, 1997

Most serious offense	All facilities	Public facilities			Private facilities		
		Total	Committed	Detained	Total	Committed	Detained
Delinquency	**98,913**	**74,552**	**50,163**	**23,819**	**24,361**	**21,515**	**2,450**
	100%	100%	100%	100%	100%	100%	100%
Person	36	37	39	31	33	33	31
Criminal homicide	2	2	3	2	0	0	1
Sexual assault	6	5	6	3	7	7	5
Robbery	10	11	12	8	6	6	4
Aggravated assault	10	10	11	9	8	8	7
Simple assault	7	6	5	6	10	10	12
Other person	9	2	2	9	12	12	13
Property	32	31	33	26	37	37	36
Burglary	13	13	14	11	13	13	11
Larceny-theft	7	7	8	5	9	9	8
Auto theft	7	6	6	6	9	9	7
Arson	1	1	1	1	1	1	1
Other property	5	4	5	4	6	5	8
Drug	9	9	9	9	11	11	9
Trafficking	3	3	3	3	3	3	2
Other drug	6	6	5	6	8	8	7
Public order	10	10	10	10	11	10	12
Weapons	4	4	5	4	4	3	4
Alcohol	0	0	0	0	0	0	1
Other public order	5	5	5	5	7	6	7
Technical violation[†]	13	14	9	24	9	8	13
Violent Crime Index*	27	29	32	23	20	21	17
Property Crime Index**	28	26	28	22	31	32	28
Status offense	**6,877**	**1,783**	**973**	**695**	**5,094**	**3,852**	**716**
	100%	100%	100%	100%	100%	100%	100%
Running away	22	27	15	40	20	18	29
Truancy	19	23	32	9	18	19	18
Incorrigibility	41	26	29	22	47	47	45
Curfew violation	3	4	3	6	2	2	1
Underage drinking	5	6	6	8	4	4	3
Other status offense	10	14	14	15	9	10	5

- ■ Juveniles charged with crimes against persons made up a greater share of the delinquent population in public facilities (37%) than in private facilities (33%).
- ■ Juveniles held for Violent Crime Index offenses (a subset of crimes against persons) made up 27% of the overall delinquency population in residential facilities—32% of delinquents committed to public facilities and 21% of delinquents committed to private facilities.

[†]Includes violations of probation, parole, and valid court order.
*Includes criminal homicide, sexual assault, robbery, and aggravated assault.
**Includes burglary, larceny-theft, auto theft, and arson.

SOURCE: Howard N. Snyder and Melissa Sickmund, *Juvenile Offenders and Victims: 1999 National Report*, Office of Juvenile Justice and Delinquency Prevention, Washington, DC, 1999

TABLE 7.4

Number of persons under age 18 held in juvenile or adult correctional facilities, 1997

Year	Total number of persons under 18 in custody	State prison	Local jails[a]	Juvenile facilities[b]		Incarceration rate[c]
				Public	Private	
1997	100,510	5,400	9,100	63,670	22,340	509

[a] Jail estimates are midyear counts from the Annual Survey of Jails.
[b] Data on persons held in juvenile facilities are from the Census of Juveniles in Residential Placement (1997). These data include only persons under age 18 committed or detained in juvenile facilities and exclude status offenders and nonoffenders. In the Federal system, persons under 18 sentenced to prison are confined in contract juvenile correctional f facilities.
[c] Rates are based on the number of persons under age 18 in custody per 100,000 U.S. residents ages 13 to 17 on July 1, 1997, and have been adjusted for Census undercount.

SOURCE: Kevin J. Strom, "Number of persons under age 18 held in juvenile or adult correctional facilities, 1997" in "Profile of State Prisoners under Age 18, 1985–97," *Bureau of Justice Statistics Special Report*, U.S. Department of Justice, Washington, D.C., 2000

TABLE 7.5

Juvenile offenders by state, type of offense, and type of facility, 1997

	Upper Age of Juvenile Court Jurisdiction	Number of Offenders Oct. 29, 1997	Custody Rate							
			All Offenders		Delinquent Offenders				Status Offenders	
					Public		Private		Public	Private
			Rate	Rank	Rate	Rank	Rate	Rank	Rate	Rate
Total United States		105,790	368		260		85		6	18
Alabama	17	1,685	349	23	178	32	129	9	9	33
Alaska	17	352	419	10	314	12	82	23	0	21
Arizona	17	1,868	345	24	292	16	39	39	4	9
Arkansas	17	603	198	44	115	42	68	28	2	13
California	17	19,899	549	4	498	1	44	32	2	6
Colorado	17	1,748	380	17	179	31	189	3	1	10
Connecticut	15	1,326	508	6	361	8	123	13	17	7
Delaware	17	311	403	12	272	18	128	11	0	0
District of Columbia	17	265	662	1	412	4	232	1	15	0
Florida	17	5,975	394	14	198	27	193	2	1	2
Georgia	16	3,622	480	7	397	5	68	27	10	4
Hawaii	17	134	106	50	83	49	14	48	5	5
Idaho	17	242	146	49	101	47	43	33	0	0
Illinois	16	3,425	286	33	266	19	18	45	1	1
Indiana	17	2,485	366	19	209	26	94	18	34	29
Iowa	17	1,064	308	31	112	44	156	7	4	36
Kansas	17	1,242	387	16	256	20	59	31	4	67
Kentucky	17	1,079	244	40	180	29	40	38	2	22
Louisiana	16	2,776	583	2	368	7	186	4	1	28
Maine	17	318	220	41	162	35	42	36	15	4
Maryland	17	1,498	273	34	139	39	128	10	1	4
Massachusetts	16	1,065	194	47	69	50	124	12	0	1
Michigan	16	3,710	375	18	186	28	148	8	11	29
Minnesota	17	1,522	258	37	147	37	84	22	3	25
Mississippi	17	756	219	42	214	25	2	51	1	1
Missouri	16	1,401	248	38	180	30	29	40	20	18
Montana	17	302	267	35	146	38	85	20	5	29
Nebraska	17	741	354	22	236	24	86	19	6	24
Nevada	17	857	460	8	446	2	13	49	0	2
New Hampshire	16	186	154	48	97	48	42	35	2	12
New Jersey	17	2,251	266	36	255	21	4	50	4	4
New Mexico	17	778	343	25	325	10	15	47	1	3
New York	15	4,661	323	30	176	33	84	21	4	60
North Carolina	15	1,204	196	45	174	34	16	46	2	5
North Dakota	17	272	338	26	115	43	101	15	4	115
Ohio	17	4,318	333	28	297	15	22	41	7	6
Oklahoma	17	808	196	46	125	40	60	30	4	8
Oregon	17	1,462	390	15	310	14	73	25	2	6
Pennsylvania	17	3,962	302	32	107	46	164	5	4	27
Rhode Island	17	426	412	11	325	11	78	24	3	6
South Carolina	16	1,583	427	9	368	6	43	34	8	8
South Dakota	17	528	559	3	416	3	70	26	44	25
Tennessee	17	2,118	358	21	156	36	103	14	47	53
Texas	16	6,898	327	29	279	17	41	37	4	3
Utah	17	768	248	39	123	41	99	16	6	20
Vermont	17	49	70	51	34	51	22	43	4	9
Virginia	17	2,879	400	13	358	9	22	42	12	7
Washington	17	2,216	335	27	310	13	20	44	4	0
West Virginia	17	398	201	43	107	45	65	29	0	29
Wisconsin	16	2,013	359	20	241	23	97	17	10	11
Wyoming	17	340	513	5	244	22	163	6	9	95

Note: State is where the offense occurred. The total for the United States includes 3,401 juveniles in private facilities for whom state of offense was not reported. Rates are per 100,000 juveniles age 10 through upper age of jurisdiction. State ranks are based on unrounded rates.

SOURCE: Melissa Sickmund, "Most delinquents are in public facilities; most stats offenders are in private facilities" in "State Custody Rates, 1997," *Juvenile Justice Bulletin, Office of Juvenile Justice and Delinquency Prevention*, U.S. Department of Justice, Washington, D.C., December 2000

TABLE 7.6

Percentage of juvenile offenders held in public facilities, in-state private facilities, and out-of-state private facilities, 1997

State	Public Facilities	In-State	Out-of-State
Total United States	74%	23%	2%
Alabama	54	46	0
Alaska	75	25	0
Arizona	86	13	1
Arkansas	59	41	0
California	91	8	1
Colorado	48	41	12
Connecticut	74	24	2
Delaware	68	5	28
District of Columbia	65	32	3
Florida	47	52	2
Georgia	85	15	0
Hawaii	83	9	7
Idaho	69	14	16
Illinois	93	5	2
Indiana	65	33	2
Iowa	38	60	3
Kansas	67	32	0
Kentucky	71	29	0
Louisiana	63	36	0
Maine	80	16	4
Maryland	51	48	1
Massachusetts	34	66	0
Michigan	53	42	5
Minnesota	58	34	8
Mississippi	99	0	1
Missouri	81	19	0
Montana	57	14	29
Nebraska	69	22	10
Nevada	97	3	0
New Hampshire	65	29	5
New Jersey	97	3	0
New Mexico	95	4	0
New York	56	44	1
North Carolina	89	10	0
North Dakota	35	58	7
Ohio	91	8	0
Oklahoma	65	35	0
Oregon	78	22	0
Pennsylvania	37	58	5
Rhode Island	80	20	0
South Carolina	88	12	0
South Dakota	82	16	1
Tennessee	57	43	0
Texas	87	13	0
Utah	52	42	6
Vermont	44	36	20
Virginia	93	7	0
Washington	94	6	0
West Virginia	54	29	18
Wisconsin	69	31	0
Wyoming	50	49	2

Note: State is where the offense occurred. Throughout the United States, there were 3,401 juveniles in private facilities (12%) for whom state of offense was not reported. All but 91 juveniles in public facilities were held in-state.

SOURCE: Melissa Sickmund, "The proportion of juvenile offenders held in public facilities ranges from 34% to 99%" in "State Custody Rates, 1997," *Juvenile Justice Bulletin, Office of Juvenile Justice and Delinquency Prevention,* U.S. Department of Justice, Washington, D.C., December 2000

TABLE 7.7

Public and private juvenile custody residential facilities operating above their design capacity, February 1995

	Facilities		Residents	
Design capacity	Total	Percent operating above design capacity	Total	Percent held in facilities operating above design capacity
All public facilities	**1,080**	**40%**	**69,929**	**69%**
Fewer than 31 residents	595	21	8,543	29
31–110 residents	324	58	18,506	59
111–200 residents	90	63	13,141	66
201–350 residents	39	82	10,075	82
More than 350 residents	32	88	19,664	91
All private facilities	**1,989**	**8%**	**39,706**	**15%**
Fewer than 31 residents	1,694	7	17,377	10
31–110 residents	259	14	14,078	16
111–200 residents	25	20	3,672	17
201–350 residents	5	20	1,345	19
More than 350 residents	6	33	3,234	32

Note: Design capacity is the number of residents a facility is constructed to hold without double bunking in single rooms and without using areas not designed as sleeping quarters to house residents.

SOURCE: Howard N. Snyder and Melissa Sickmund, *Juvenile Offenders and Victims: 1999 National Report,* Office of Juvenile Justice and Delinquency Prevention, Washington, DC, 1999

U.S. Department of Justice and its goal is to provide national leadership in addressing the issues of juvenile delinquency and improving juvenile justice.

According to the OJJDP, a juvenile may be taken into custody for:

- Violating or allegedly violating a federal, state, or local delinquency or criminal statute or local ordinance regarding noncriminal misbehavior

- Violating a judicial order, decree, or condition of supervision (either probation or aftercare)

- Being the subject of dependency, neglect, or child abuse allegations, investigation, or petition

The purpose for custody may include providing care, protection, treatment, supervision, control, or punishment. The OJJDP defines a custody facility as one that admits juveniles into custody for at least six hours, during which time the juvenile is under the supervision of facility staff. The facilities may be operated by governmental or private agencies.

Snyder and Sickmund also reported that, by a rate of 14-to-1, juveniles confined for delinquency (criminal offenses) in 1997 outnumbered minors in custody for status offenses (such as running away, truancy, and incorrigibility). (See Table 7.3.) Most juveniles were "committed" (permanently placed in the facility), as opposed to "detained" (awaiting adjudication or permanent placement). The same held true for status-offending juveniles in residential placement.

TABLE 7.8

Delinquency cases involving detention, 1988–97

Case Type	Percent of all cases involving detention			Percent change in number of cases, 1988–1997		Change in number of cases detained, 1988–1997
	1988	1993	1997	All Cases	Detained Cases	Additional Cases
Total	**20%**	**21%**	**19%**	**48%**	**35%**	**85,100**
Person	24	24	22	97	82	39,200
Property	17	17	15	19	6	7,000
Drugs	32	31	22	125	51	13,500
Public order	25	25	22	67	51	25,500
Male	**21%**	**22%**	**20%**	**39%**	**30%**	**61,400**
Person	26	26	24	82	68	27,700
Property	18	18	16	11	3	2,600
Drugs	34	32	23	124	52	12,200
Public order	25	25	23	60	48	18,900
Female	**16%**	**16%**	**15%**	**83%**	**65%**	**23,700**
Person	18	17	18	155	156	11,500
Property	12	13	10	54	28	4,300
Drugs	26	23	16	132	44	1,300
Public order	25	23	21	93	63	6,500
White	**17%**	**17%**	**15%**	**43%**	**25%**	**34,600**
Person	20	20	19	111	100	22,200
Property	14	14	12	16	−4	−3,200
Drugs	21	20	14	144	67	7,000
Public order	23	21	19	50	26	8,700
Black	**28%**	**29%**	**27%**	**57%**	**52%**	**49,300**
Person	29	29	28	76	65	15,700
Property	23	24	23	25	27	10,900
Drugs	51	45	38	93	42	6,400
Public order	30	32	29	112	104	16,300

Note: Detail may not total 100% because of rounding.

SOURCE: Gillian Porter, "Delinquency cases involving detention, 1988–1997" in "Detention in Delinquency Cases, 1988–1997," *Office of Juvenile Justice and Delinquency Prevention Fact Sheet,* #17, U.S. Department of Justice, Washington, D.C., November 2000

FIGURE 7.1

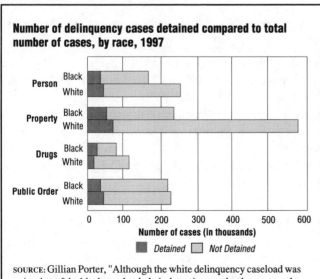

Number of delinquency cases detained compared to total number of cases, by race, 1997

SOURCE: Gillian Porter, "Although the white delinquency caseload was twice that of the black caseload, their detention caseloads were nearly equal in 1997" in "Detention in Delinquency Cases, 1988–1997," *Office of Juvenile Justice and Delinquency Prevention Fact Sheet,* #17, U.S. Department of Justice, Washington, D.C., November 2000

The Bureau of Justice Statistics (BJS) reported that, as of July 1997, the incarceration rate for all persons under the age of 18 years was 509 per 100,000 juveniles in the general population. (See Table 7.4.)

Public and Private Confinement

According to "State Custody Rates, 1997" (*Juvenile Justice Bulletin, Office of Juvenile Justice and Delinquency Prevention*, December 2000), most delinquent juveniles were confined in public facilities while status offenders were more often placed in private facilities. (See Table 7.5.)

Of the total number of juveniles confined for delinquency as of October 1997, the confinement rate in public facilities was 260 per 100,000 juveniles in the general population compared to a confinement rate of 85 in public facilities. Three times as many status offenders were confined in private facilities (at a rate of 18) than in public facilities (a rate of 6).

Among all offenders in all juvenile facilities the highest rate of confinement occurred in the District of Columbia (662 per 100,000), followed by Louisiana (583),

FIGURE 7.2

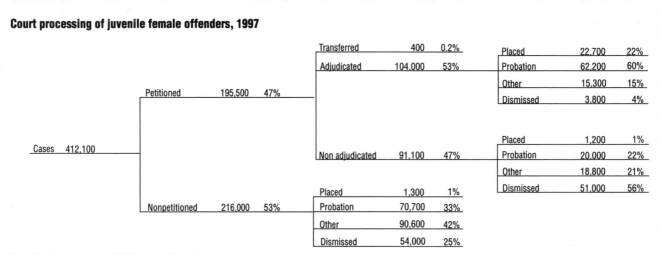

Court processing of juvenile female offenders, 1997

					Transferred	400	0.2%		Placed	22,700	22%
					Adjudicated	104,000	53%		Probation	62,200	60%
									Other	15,300	15%
		Petitioned	195,500	47%					Dismissed	3,800	4%
									Placed	1,200	1%
Cases	412,100				Non adjudicated	91,100	47%		Probation	20,000	22%
									Other	18,800	21%
									Dismissed	51,000	56%
					Placed	1,300	1%				
		Nonpetitioned	216,000	53%	Probation	70,700	33%				
					Other	90,600	42%				
					Dismissed	54,000	25%				

Note: Detail may not add to 100% because of rounding.

SOURCE: Meghan C. Scahill, "Court processing of juvenile female offenders, 1997" in "Female Delinquency Cases, 1997," *Office of Juvenile Justice and Delinquency Prevention Fact Sheet*, #16, U.S. Department of Justice, Washington, D.C., November 2000

TABLE 7.9

Percent change in detained delinquency cases, 1988–97

Most Serious Offense	Number of Cases			Percent Change	
	1988	1993	1997	1988–97	1993–97
Delinquency	241,700	307,500	326,800	35%	6%
Person	47,900	76,400	87,000	82	14
Property	117,400	139,000	124,300	6	−11
Drugs	26,300	27,400	39,800	51	45
Public Order	50,200	64,700	75,700	51	17

Note: Detail may not add to totals because of rounding. Percent change calculations are based on unrounded numbers.

SOURCE: "Table 6. Percent Change in Detained Delinquency Cases, 1988–1997" in *Juvenile Court Statistics 1997,* National Center for Juvenile Justice, Office of Juvenile Justice and Delinquency Prevention, U.S. Department of Justice, Washington, D.C., 2000

South Dakota (559), California (549), and Wyoming (513). The lowest confinement rate for all juvenile offenders was in Hawaii (106), followed by Idaho (146) and New Hampshire (154).

The rate of juvenile offenders confined in public facilities varied from state to state by a wide margin—from 34 percent in Massachusetts to 99 percent in Mississippi. (See Table 7.6.) When averaged nationally 74 percent of juveniles were confined to public facilities; of those some 23 percent were housed in-state and 2 percent out-of-state. The highest rate of in-state juvenile confinement occurred in Massachusetts, at 66 percent, with no juveniles placed out-of-state. Conversely, Montana placed 29 percent of confined juveniles out-of-state, closely followed by Delaware (28 percent) where only 5 percent were placed in-state.

Of public juvenile facilities more than two-thirds (69 percent) were operating at or above design capacity as of

February 1995 compared to only 15 percent of all private juvenile facilities. (See Table 7.7.) Among public juvenile facilities the higher the design capacity, the more likely it was for overcrowded conditions to exist. Eighty-eight percent of juvenile facilities with design capacities of more than 350 residents were operating above capacity in February 1995 compared to 33 percent of private facilities with the same design capacity.

Institutional Facilities

Institutional facilities, such as training schools, house juvenile inmates for long-term placement. In 1991 and 1995 the proportion of institutional facilities that were operating above their capacity remained the same (about 45 percent), but the number of residents held in crowded facilities increased. There were 10,000 more residents in over-capacity training schools and other public long-term institutional facilities in 1995 than in 1991—an increase of 55 percent. Over-capacity public long-term institutional facilities held more than 70 percent of public long-term institutional residents in 1995 compared to 62 percent in 1991.

FIGURE 7.3

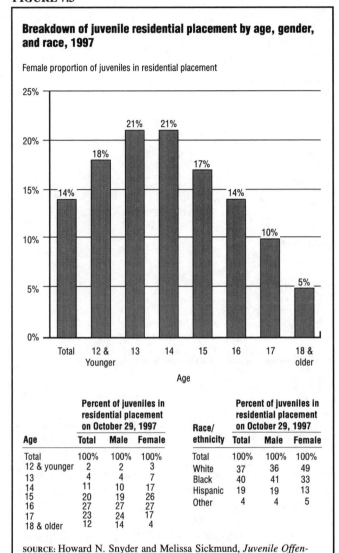

Breakdown of juvenile residential placement by age, gender, and race, 1997

Female proportion of juveniles in residential placement

Age	Percent of juveniles in residential placement on October 29, 1997			Race/ethnicity	Percent of juveniles in residential placement on October 29, 1997		
	Total	Male	Female		Total	Male	Female
Total	100%	100%	100%	Total	100%	100%	100%
12 & younger	2	2	3	White	37	36	49
13	4	4	7	Black	40	41	33
14	11	10	17	Hispanic	19	19	13
15	20	19	26	Other	4	4	5
16	27	27	27				
17	23	24	17				
18 & older	12	14	4				

SOURCE: Howard N. Snyder and Melissa Sickmund, *Juvenile Offenders and Victims: 1999 National Report*, Office of Juvenile Justice and Delinquency Prevention, Washington, DC, 1999

In 1995 public facilities were more crowded than private facilities. An average public facility that held more than 350 residents was operating 88 percent over capacity, while an average private facility holding more than 350 residents was operating at 33 percent over capacity. A public facility designed to hold fewer than 31 residents was 21 percent over capacity in 1995 compared to a small private facility holding 31 or fewer residents at 7 percent over capacity in 1995.

Nine of 10 residents (91 percent) held in large public facilities (more than 350 residents) were held in overcrowded facilities compared to 32 percent of residents held in large private facilities. While 29 percent of inmates in small (fewer than 31 residents) public facilities lived in overcrowded conditions, only 10 percent of inmates in small private facilities lived that way.

CHARACTERISTICS OF JUVENILES IN RESIDENTIAL PLACEMENT

Race and Ethnicity

In "Detention in Delinquency Cases, 1988–1997" (*Office of Juvenile Justice and Delinquency Prevention*

TABLE 7.10

Profile of detained delinquency cases, 1988, 1993, and 1997

Most Serious Offense	1988	1993	1997
Person	20%	25%	27%
Property	49	45	38
Drugs	11	9	12
Public Order	21	21	23
Total	100%	100%	100%
Number of Cases Involving Detention:	241,700	307,500	326,800

Note: Detail may not total 100% because of rounding.

SOURCE: "Table 7. Offense Profile of Detained Delinquency Cases, 1988, 1993, 1997" in *Juvenile Court Statistics 1997*, National Center for Juvenile Justice, Office of Juvenile Justice and Delinquency Prevention, U.S. Department of Justice, Washington, D.C., 2000

TABLE 7.11

Percent change in adjudicated delinquency cases that resulted in formal probation, 1988–97

Most Serious Offense	Number of Cases			Percent Change	
	1988	1993	1997	1988–97	1993–97
Delinquency	190,900	248,400	318,700	67%	28%
Person	31,400	52,300	70,800	125	35
Property	113,200	135,100	149,800	32	11
Drugs	15,600	17,100	37,400	141	119
Public Order	30,700	43,900	60,800	98	38

Note: Detail may not add to totals because of rounding. Percent change calculations are based on unrounded numbers.

SOURCE: "Table 19. Percent change in adjudicated delinquency cases that resulted in formal probation, 1988–97" in *Juvenile Court Statistics 1997*, National Center for Juvenile Justice, Office of Juvenile Justice and Delinquency Prevention, U.S. Department of Justice, Washington, D.C., 2000

TABLE 7.12

Number of juveniles incarcerated, 1997

Type of Facility	Number	Percentage*
Total	107,169	100%
Juvenile Facility	92,664†	86
Jail	9,105	8
Prison	5,400	5

*Discrepancy in total is due to rounding.

†This number reflects juveniles in public or private detention and correctional facilities, including status offenders, and is limited to persons under age 18.

SOURCE: James Austin, Kelly Dedel Johnson, Maria Gregoriou, "Table 1: Number of Juveniles Incarcerated, 1997," in *Juveniles in Adult Prisons and Jails: A National Assessment*, U.S. Department of Justice, Bureau of Justice Assistance, Washington, D.C., 2000

TABLE 7.14

State prison inmates under and over age 18, by selected characteristics, 1997

	State prison inmates	
Characteristic	Under 18	Age 18 or older
Gender		
Male	92%	94%
Female	8	6
Race/Hispanic origin		
White*	19%	34%
Black*	60	46
Hispanic	13	17
Other	8	3
Most serious offense		
Violent offenses	69%	47%
Murder/nonnegligent manslaughter	13	13
Rape/sexual assault	2	9
Robbery	37	14
Assault	13	9
Property offenses	15%	22%
Burglary	8	11
Larceny	5	4
Drug offenses	11%	21%
Public-order offenses	5%	10%

*Excludes Hispanics.

SOURCE: Kevin J. Strom, "Nearly three-fourths of inmates under 18 were black or Hispanic" in "Profile of State Prisoners under Age 18, 1985–97," *Bureau of Justice Statistics Special Report*, U.S. Department of Justice, Washington, D.C., 2000

TABLE 7.13

Attributes of juveniles admitted to state prisons, 1985 and 1997*

Attribute	1985 Prison Admissions	1997 Prison Admissions
Total Admissions	**3,400**	**7,400**
Offense Type		
Violent	52%	61%
Property	42	22
Drug	2	11
Public Order	4	5
Race/Ethnicity		
White	32%	25%
Black	53	58
Hispanic	14	15
Other	1	2
Gender		
Male	97%	97%
Female	3	3
Age at Admission		
17	80%	74%
16	18	21
15	2	4
14 and Younger	0	1
Average Sentence		
Maximum	86 months	82 months
Minimum	35 months	44 months

*Discrepancies in totals are due to rounding.

SOURCE: James Austin, Kelly Dedel Johnson, Maria Gregoriou, "Table 3: Attributes of Juveniles Admitted to State Prisons, 1985 and 1997," in *Juveniles in Adult Prisons and Jails: A National Assessment*, U.S. Department of Justice, Bureau of Justice Assistance, Washington, D.C., 2000

Gender

From 1988 to 1997 the number of detained female juveniles rose by 65 percent compared to a rise of 30 percent for males. During this period the number of juvenile females confined for person offenses increased by 156 percent compared to 68 percent for male juveniles confined for person offenses.

In 1997, 23 percent of delinquency cases involved a female offender, as reported in "Female Delinquency Cases, 1997" (*Office of Juvenile Justice and Delinquency Prevention Fact Sheet*, November 2000). Of all juvenile delinquency cases in 1997 involving a female, 49 percent were property offenses (down by 9 percent from 1988), 25 percent were person offenses (up by 7 percent), public order offenses remained about the same (20 percent in 1997 compared to 19 percent in 1988), while drug offenses were up slightly (from 5 percent in 1988 to 7 percent in 1997).

For every juvenile arrest for delinquency a decision is made to dismiss, divert, or refer the case for formal court action. Cases forwarded for court action are called "petitioned" cases, because a petition alleging the juvenile's offense(s) is filed with the juvenile court. Those cases that are not brought to court for adjudication (trial) are called "nonpetitioned" cases. (See Figure 7.2.)

In 1997 nearly half (47 percent) of all delinquency cases involving females were petitioned cases referred for

Fact Sheet, November 2000), Gillian Porter reported that, although the rate of detained delinquency cases remained fairly stable, the profile of detained juveniles changed over the period 1988–1997. (See Table 7.8.) During that period the rate of detention among black youths (52) percent) grew at twice the rate as that for white youths (25 percent). In each year between 1988 and 1997 black youths were more likely to be detained that white youths. In 1997 far more white than black juveniles were charged with delinquency; however, the rate of detention among white and black youths was roughly the same. (See Figure 7.1.)

TABLE 7.15

Number of persons under 18 admitted to state prison by most serious offense, 1985–97

Most serious offense	New court commitments of persons under age 18 to State prisons					
	1985		1990		1997	
	Number	Percent	Number	Percent	Number	Percent
All offenses	3,400	100%	5,100	100%	7,400	100%
Violent offenses	1,730	52%	2,270	45%	4,510	61%
Murder[a]	230	7	310	6	500	7
Sexual assault[b]	230	7	180	4	300	4
Robbery	930	28	1,020	20	2,360	32
Aggravated assault	230	7	570	11	1,060	14
Property offenses	1,410	42%	1,780	35%	1,590	22%
Burglary	930	28	940	19	950	13
Larceny/theft	230	7	300	6	230	3
Motor vehicle theft	110	3	320	6	160	2
Drug offenses	70	2%	820	16%	840	11%
Public-order offenses	140	4%	200	4%	360	5%

Note: All data are estimated. Includes only those with a sentence of more than 1 year. In 1997, 1% of offenders under 18 were admitted for "other" offense types. Other offense types are not shown in detail.
[a] Includes nonnegligent manslaughter.
[b] Includes forcible rape and other sexual assaults.

SOURCE: Kevin J. Strom, "Table 2. Number of persons under 18 admitted to State prison by most serious offense, 1985–97" in "Profile of State Prisoners under Age 18, 1985–97," *Bureau of Justice Statistics Special Report,* U.S. Department of Justice, Washington, D.C., 2000

TABLE 7.16

Number of persons under age 18 admitted to state prison, per 1,000 arrests of persons under age 18, 1985–97

Most serious offense	Number of new court commitments per 1,000 arrests				
	1985	1990	1992	1994	1997
Violent offenses[a]	18	17	21	23	33
Murder[b]	153	98	136	150	200
Sexual assault[c]	12	9	9	11	15
Robbery	29	27	33	34	63
Aggravated assault	6	10	12	12	16
Property offenses[d]	2	3	3	2	2
Burglary	6	8	8	7	8
Larceny/theft	1	1	1	1	1
Motor vehicle theft	2	4	4	3	2
Drug offenses	1	10	10	6	4

Note: All data are estimated. Arrests reflect the proportion of persons age 13 to 17 for a given offense by the total estimated number of persons arrested by offense (UCR).
[a] Includes only murder, sexual assault, robbery, and aggravated assault.
[b] Includes nonnegligent manslaughter.
[c] Includes forcible rape and other sexual assault.
[d] Includes only burglary, larceny/theft, and motor vehicle theft.

SOURCE: Kevin J. Strom, "Table 4. Number of persons under age 18 admitted to state prison, per 1,000 arrests of persons under age 18, 1985–97" in "Profile of State Prisoners under Age 18, 1985–97," *Bureau of Justice Statistics Special Report,* U.S. Department of Justice, Washington, D.C., 2000

formal court action, either for adjudication in juvenile court or for transfer to adult criminal court. Of female offenders who were adjudicated in 1997, 60 percent were placed on probation—an increase of 129 percent since 1988. Twenty-two percent of delinquent female offenders were confined in a public or private facility—an increase of 105 percent since 1988.

Female juvenile offenders confined in public and private facilities tended to be younger than their male counterparts. (See Figure 7.3.) As of October 1997 17 percent of confined female juveniles were 14 years of age com-

pared to 10 percent of male juveniles. Twenty-six percent of all confined female juveniles were 15 years old compared to 19 percent of males.

About half of juvenile females in residential placement were white (compared to 36 percent for males), 33 percent were black (compared to 41 percent males), and 13 percent were Hispanic (compared to 19 percent males).

Types of Offenses

From 1988 to 1997 the total number of detained delinquency cases increased from 241,700 to 326,800—a

TABLE 7.17

Persons under age 25 admitted to state prison, by selected characteristics, 1997

An estimated 111,100 offenders under age 25 were admitted to state prison as new court commitments in 1997. At the time of admission, 51% were ages 21 to 24, 42% were 18 to 20, and 7% were under 18.

	Under 18	18-20	21-24
Total	100%	100%	100%
Gender			
Male	97%	96%	94%
Female	3	4	6

Persons admitted under 18 were more likely to be black males sentenced to prison for a violent offense, especially robbery and aggravated assault (not shown in table).

Race/Hispanic origin			
White*	25%	31%	30%
Black*	58	50	47
Hispanic	15	17	21
Other	2	2	2

Nearly 30% of offenders admitted under 18 in 1997 were black males convicted of robbery or aggravated assault, compared to 16% of those ages 18 to 20 and 11% of persons 21 to 24.

Most serious offense			
Violent	61%	39%	32%
Property	21	30	28
Drug	11	22	31
Public-order	5	7	8

Note: Includes only offenders with a sentence of more than 1 year. Detail may not add to total due to rounding.
*Excludes Hispanics.

SOURCE: Kevin J. Strom, "Nearly two-thirds of offenders admitted to State prison under age 18 were sentenced for a violent offense compared to a third of those aged 18–24" in "Profile of State Prisoners under Age 18, 1985–97," *Bureau of Justice Statistics Special Report*, U.S. Department of Justice, Washington, D.C., 2000

TABLE 7.18

Persons under 18 admitted to facilities under contract to the Federal Bureau of Prisons, by selected characteristics, 1997

Characteristic	Percent admitted under 18
Gender	
Male	95%
Female	5
Race	
White	18%
Black	7
American Indian	72
Asian	3
Hispanic origin	
Hispanic	11%
Non-Hispanic	89
Offense type	
Violent	52%
Property	31
Drug	6
Public-order	11
Country of origin	
United States	95%
Mexico	4
Other	1
Number of admissions	189

SOURCE: Kevin J. Strom, "Persons under 18 admitted to facilities under contract to the Federal Bureau of Prisons" in "Profile of State Prisoners under Age 18, 1985–97," *Bureau of Justice Statistics Special Report*, U.S. Department of Justice, Washington, D.C., 2000

rise of 35 percent. (See Table 7.9.) During that period the number of delinquency cases involving person offenses increased by 82 percent, followed by drug offenses (51 percent), public order offenses (51 percent), and property offenses (6 percent). Measured by the number of delinquency cases per 1,000 juveniles, the rate of cases involving drug offenses increased by 99 percent, followed by person offenses (74 percent), public order offenses (48 percent), and property offenses (5 percent).

Of delinquency cases that resulted in the detention of the juvenile offender, cases involving person offenses occurred at a rate of 20 percent in 1988, increasing to 25 percent by 1993, and increasing again to 27 percent in 1997. Property offenses that resulted in detention decreased during the same time period, from 49 percent in 1988, to 45 percent in 1993, to 38 percent in 1997. Drug offense cases resulting in detention dropped from 11 percent in 1988 to 9 percent in 1993, but rose to 12 percent in 1997. (See Table 7.10.)

Delinquency cases that resulted in placing the juvenile offender on formal probation rose from a total of 190,900 in 1988 to 318,700 in 1997—an increase of 67 percent. (See Table 7.11.) The greatest increase in delin-

quency cases resulting in probation occurred for drug offenses (up by 141 percent from 1988 to 1997), followed by person offenses (up 125 percent), public order offenses (up 98 percent), and property offenses (up 32 percent).

JUVENILES SENTENCED TO ADULT PRISONS AND JAILS

The Bureau of Justice Assistance reported that, in 1997, a total of 107,169 juveniles were incarcerated. Eighty-six percent were held in juvenile facilities, while an additional 13 percent of were confined to adult prisons and jails. (See Table 7.12.)

In 1983 some 221,815 adult offenders and 1,736 juveniles were admitted to adult jails in the United States. By 1998 the number of adults admitted to jail had risen to 584,372, an increase of 163 percent. However, the 8,090 juveniles admitted in 1993 constituted an even larger increase at 366 percent. (See Table 3.9, Chapter 3.)

Juvenile admissions to state prison increased from 3,400 in 1985 to 7,400 in 1997. (See Table 7.13.) Seventy-four percent of juveniles admitted to state prison in 1997 were 17 years of age, down from 80 percent in 1985. However, the percentage of 16-year-olds admitted to state prison rose from 18 percent in 1985 to 21 percent in 1997. Fifteen-year-olds admitted to state prisons doubled from 1985 (2 percent) to 1997 (4 percent).

TABLE 7.19

State prison populations, youth and adult, 1998

State	Youth	Adult	State	Youth	Adult
Alabama	104	20,488	Montana	81	2,714
Alaska	24	2,897	Nebraska	29	3,532
Arizona	140	25,154	Nevada	36	9,164
Arkansas	89	10,677	New Jersey	35	23,989
California	163	161,466	New Mexico	9	5,031
Colorado	23	13,773	New York	316	69,499
Connecticut	505	15,778	North Carolina	369	32,118
Delaware	20	3,211	Ohio	158	48,972
D.C.	26	6,719	Oklahoma	46	14,603
Florida	572	66,117	Oregon	25	8,253
Georgia	152	39,347	Pennsylvania	98	35,765
Hawaii	2	4,009	Rhode Island	0	3,657
Idaho	10	3,545	South Carolina	200	20,916
Illinois	162	42,292	South Dakota	N/R*	2,359
Indiana	89	18,830	Tennessee	37	15,554
Iowa	9	7,394	Texas	272	129,661
Louisiana	87	33,572	Utah	21	5,084
Maryland	76	22,566	Vermont	15	1,198
Massachusetts	13	11,224	Virginia	84	26,578
Michigan	208	38,927	Washington	104	13,866
Minnesota	32	5,562	Wisconsin	22	166
Mississippi	164	16,291	Wyoming	37	1,233
Missouri	111	25,493	**Total**	**4,775**	**1,069,244**

*Not reported.

SOURCE: James Austin, Kelly Dedel Johnson, Maria Gregoriou, "Table 5: State Prison Populations, Youth and Adult, 1998," in *Juveniles in Adult Prisons and Jails: A National Assessment*, U.S. Department of Justice, Bureau of Justice Assistance, Washington, D.C., 2000

TABLE 7.20

Characteristics of state prison inmates, 1998*

Offense/Crime	Youth Number	Youth Percentage	Adult Number	Adult Percentage	Total
Persons	2,722	57%	473,821	44%	476,544
Property	974	21%	216,756	20%	217,730
Alcohol Related	135	3%	20,457	2%	20,592
Drug Related	467	10%	210,975	20%	211,442
Public Order	185	4%	40,468	4%	40,653
Parole/Probation	79	2%	90,260	8%	90,339
Unknown	92	2%	5,676	1%	5,768
Other	85	2%	13,327	1%	13,412
Total	**4,739**	**100%**	**1,071,740**	**100%**	**1,076,479**
Race/Ethnicity					
Asian	65	1%	11,056	1%	11,121
Black	2,706	55%	497,343	48%	500,050
White	1,309	26%	355,960	35%	357,269
Hispanic	689	14%	156,782	15%	157,471
Native American	176	4%	9,421	1%	9,597
Total	**4,945**	**100%**	**1,030,562**	**100%**	**1,035,507**
Housing Type†					
Single Cell	1,019	30%	120,221	22%	121,240
Double Cell	670	19%	193,754	35%	194,424
Dormitory	1,757	51%	237,801	43%	239,559
Total	**3,446**	**100%**	**551,776**	**100%**	**555,222**

*Discrepancies in totals are due to rounding.
†Housing type statistics are reported for 21 states that house juveniles in adult correctional facilities.

SOURCE: James Austin, Kelly Dedel Johnson, Maria Gregoriou, "Table 7: Characteristics of State Prison Inmates, 1998," in *Juveniles in Adult Prisons and Jails: A National Assessment*, U.S. Department of Justice, Bureau of Justice Assistance, Washington, D.C., 2000

TABLE 7.21

Minimum age authorized for capital punishment, 1999

Age 16 or less	Age 17	Age 18	None specified
Alabama (16)	Georgia	California	Arizona
Arkansas (14)	New Hampshire	Colorado	Idaho
Delaware (16)	North Carolinaᵃ	Connecticut	Louisiana
Florida (16)	Texas	Federal system	Montanaᵇ
Indiana (16)		Illinois	Pennsylvania
Kentucky (16)		Kansas	South Carolina
Mississippi (16)ᶜ		Maryland	South Dakotaᵈ
Missouri (16)		Nebraska	
Nevada (16)		New Jersey	
Oklahoma (16)		New Mexico	
Utah (14)		New York	
Virginia (14)ᵉ		Ohio	
Wyoming (16)		Oregon	
		Tennessee	
		Washington	

Note: Reporting by States reflects interpretations by offices of State attorneys general and may differ from previously reported ages.
ᵃ Age required is 17 unless the murderer was incarcerated for murder when a subsequent murder occurred; then the age may be 14.
ᵇMontana law specifies that offenders tried under the capital sexual assault statute be 18 or older. Age may be a mitigating factor for other capital crimes.
ᶜThe minimum age defined by statute is 13, but the effective age is 16 based on interpretation of U.S. Supreme Court decisions by the Mississippi Supreme Court.
ᵈJuveniles may be transferred to adult court. Age can be a mitigating factor.
ᵉThe minimum age for transfer to adult court by statute is 14, but the effective age is 16 based on interpretation of U.S. Supreme Court decisions by the State attorney general's office.

SOURCE: Tracy L. Snell, *Capital Punishment 1999*, Bureau of Justice Statistics, Washington, DC, 2000

In 1997 some 8 percent of juveniles offenders in state prison were females and 92 percent were males. (See Table 7.14.) Sixty percent of juvenile state prisoners in 1997 were black, 19 percent white, and 13 percent Hispanic. Together, blacks and Hispanics comprised almost three-fourths of the state prison population under the age of 18 years.

Of juveniles confined to state prison in 1997, 69 percent were violent offenders. By comparison, in 1985, 52 percent of juveniles admitted to state prison were violent offenders, and by 1990 that rate had dropped to 45 percent. (See Table 7.15.) Juvenile property offenders admitted to state prison declined from 42 percent in 1985 to 22 percent in 1997. Juvenile drug offenders admitted to state prison rose from 2 percent in 1985 to 16 percent in 1990, then declined to 11 percent in 1997.

The number of juveniles sent to state prison for violent offenses per 1,000 juvenile arrests increased from a rate of 18 in 1985 to 33 in 1997. (See Table 7.16.) The rate for murder increased from 153 in 1985 to 200 in 1997. The rate for drug offenses increased from 1 in 1985 to 10 in 1990 and 1992, then decreased to 6 in 1994 and 4 in 1997. Of juveniles admitted to state prison in 1997 some 61 percent were convicted of violent offenses. By comparison 39 percent of adults ages

18–24 years admitted to state prison in 1997 were violent offenders, as were 32 percent of adults ages 21–24 years. (See Table 7.17.)

TABLE 7.22

Offenders sentenced to death for crimes committed before age 18, 1973–October 31, 1998

State	Total Offenders
	164
Texas	42
Florida	23
Alabama	15
Mississippi	10
Louisiana	9
Georgia	7
South Carolina	7
North Carolina	6
Ohio	6
Oklahoma	6
Pennsylvania	5
Arizona	5
Missouri	4
Virginia	4
Indiana	3
Arkansas	2
Kentucky	2
Maryland	2
Nevada	2
Nebraska	1
New Jersey	1
Washington	1

SOURCE: Howard N. Snyder and Melissa Sickmund, *Juvenile Offenders and Victims: 1999 National Report*, Office of Juvenile Justice and Delinquency Prevention, Washington, DC, 1999. Based on data from: *The Juvenile Death Penalty Today: Death Sentences and Executions for Juvenile Crimes, January 1, 1973 – December 31, 2000*, Ohio Northern University College of Law, 2001. Available on-line at: http://www.law.onu.edu/faculty/streib/juvdeath.pdf

In 1997 some 189 offenders under the age of 18 years were confined to juvenile facilities under contract to the Federal Bureau of Prisons (which does not operate any of its own juvenile facilities). Of the 189 juvenile offenders in federally contracted facilities in 1997, 72 percent were Native American, followed by 11 percent Hispanic, 18 percent white, 7 percent black, and 3 percent Asian. (See Table 7.18.)

By 1998 a total of 4,775 juveniles were confined in state prisons. (See Table 7.19.) Florida had the largest number of juveniles in state prison (572), followed by Connecticut (505), North Carolina (369), and New York (316). Hawaii had the fewest number of juveniles confined to state prison, (2). Juveniles in state prisons in 1998 were most likely to be incarcerated for person offenses (57 percent), followed by property offenses (21 percent), and drug offenses (10 percent). (See Table 7.20.)

More than one-half of juveniles in adult prison in 1998 were black (55 percent), followed by white (26 percent), Hispanic (14 percent), and Native American (4 percent). These figures roughly mirror the rates among adult prisoners in state prisons in 1998.

Programs

Another issue related to the incarceration of juveniles is ensuring that young inmates are able to participate in the educational and physical programs they require and receive the nutrition they need. Young inmates may be subject to state mandatory education laws as well as federal mandates for special education. In addition they have dietary needs different from those of adult inmates; yet

TABLE 7.23

Juvenile offenders executed, January 1973 through December 2000

Name	Date of Execution	Place of Execution	Race	Age at Crime	Age at Execution
Charles Rumbaugh	9/11/1985	Texas	White	17	28
J. Terry Roach	1/10/1986	S.Carolina	White	17	25
Jay Pinkerton	5/15/1986	Texas	White	17	24
Dalton Prejean	5/18/1990	Louisiana	Black	17	30
Johnny Garrett	2/11/1992	Texas	White	17	28
Curtis Harris	7/1/1993	Texas	Black	17	31
Frederick Lashley	7/28/1993	Missouri	Black	17	29
Ruben Cantu	8/24/1993	Texas	Latino	17	26
Chris Burger	12/7/1993	Georgia	White	17	33
Joseph John Cannon	4/22/1998	Texas	White	17	38
Robert A. Carter	5/18/1998	Texas	Black	17	34
Dwayne A. Wright	10/14/1998	Virginia	Black	17	26
Sean R. Sellars	2/4/1999	Oklahoma	White	16	29
Christopher Thomas	1/10/2000	Virginia	White	17	26
Steve E. Roach	1/19/2000	Virginia	White	17	23
Glen C. McGinnis	1/25/2000	Texas	Black	17	27
Gary L. Graham	6/22/2000	Texas	Black	17	36

SOURCE: "Table 1. Executions of Juvenile Offenders, January 1 1973, through June 30, 2000" in *Juveniles and the Death Penalty, Coordinating Council on Juvenile Justice and Delinquency Prevention*, U.S. Department of Justice, Washington, D.C., 2000. Based on data from: V. L. Streib, *The Juvenile Death Penalty Today: Death Sentences and Executions for Juvenile Crimes, January 1, 1973–December 31, 2000*, Ohio Northern University College of Law, 2001. Available on-line at: http://www.law.onu.edu/faculty/streib/juvdeath.pdf

their food allowance (in caloric value and type of food) is likely to be the same as that of adult inmates. Misconduct by young inmates is, to some extent, linked to their development as adolescents. Staff responses based on adult patterns of misconduct is likely to be less effective in managing juveniles.

Programs offered to juveniles offenders in state prisons in 1998 varied. All reporting state prisons offered GED preparation and counseling programs. However, little more than one-half of state prisons provided juveniles with family counseling (53 percent) or drug/alcohol treatment (56 percent). (See Table 4.11.) As discussed earlier, most juvenile offenders in state prisons are violent offenders, yet only 40 percent of state prisons offered youth violent offender programs.

JUVENILES AND THE DEATH PENALTY

It is rare for the death penalty to be imposed on juveniles 17 years of age or younger. The Supreme Court, reversing the death sentence of a 16-year-old in *Eddings v. Oklahoma* (455 U.S. 104, 1982), noted that adolescents are not mature, responsible, or self-disciplined enough to consider the long-range implications of their actions. The court also held that a defendant's young age and mental and emotional development should be considered an important mitigating factor when deciding whether to apply the death penalty. Nonetheless, the High Court failed to indicate the age at which a defendant would be mature enough to receive the death penalty, indicating only that it was not 16 years.

In most states allowing the death penalty in 1999 the minimum age authorized for capital punishment was 18 years. However, four states—Georgia, New Hampshire, North Carolina, and Texas—authorized the death penalty at age 17 years. The minimum age for capital punishment was 16 years or less in 13 other states. (See Table 7.21.) Seven states had no minimum age for the death penalty in 1999.

In 1998 Texas and Florida accounted for some 40 percent of the 164 offenders under a sentence of death for crimes committed before the age of 18 years. (See Table 7.22.) Alabama had 15 such offenders, followed by Mississippi (10) and Louisiana (9).

From 1973 to midyear 2000, 17 offenders were executed for crimes committed when they were under the age of 18 years. All were 17 years of age at the time of their offense—except Sean R. Sellars, executed in Oklahoma on February 4, 1999, for a crime committed when he was 16 years old. (See Table 7.23.) Of the 17 offenders executed for crimes committed before their eighteenth birthday, 9 were put to death in Texas. Nine were white, 7 were black, and 1 was Latino.

TABLE 7.24

Blended sentencing options create a "middle ground" between traditional juvenile sanctions and adult sanctions

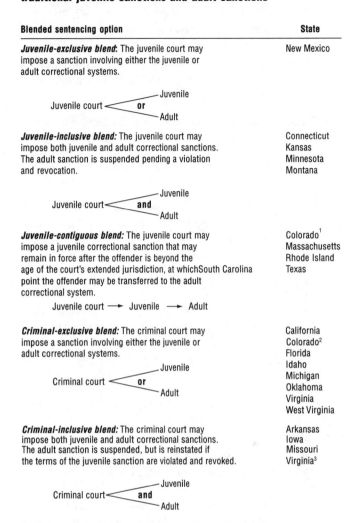

Note: Blends apply to a subset of juveniles specified by State statute.
[1] Applies to those designated as "aggravated juvenile offenders."
[2] Applies to those designated as "youthful offenders."
[3] Applies to those designated as "violent juvenile felony offenders."

SOURCE: Howard N. Snyder and Melissa Sickmund, *Juvenile Offenders and Victims: 1999 National Report,* Office of Juvenile Justice and Delinquency Prevention, Washington, DC, 1999

ADULT SENTENCING OF JUVENILE OFFENDERS

With the passage of Proposition 21 in March 2000, Californians joined the nationwide trend to "get tough" on violent juvenile offenders. The provisions of Proposition 21 contain significant changes in the way in which juvenile offenders are dealt with in California in a number of key areas. Under Proposition 21:

• Juveniles 14 years of age or older charged with committing certain types of murder or serious sex crimes are no longer eligible for juvenile court and must be tried as adults. Also, under certain circumstances, prosecutors may directly file charges against a juvenile offender in adult court without any type of hearing or judicial review.

- Probation departments no longer have the discretion to determine if juveniles arrested for certain offenses should be released or detained. Detention is required for those offenses. In addition juveniles 16 years of age or older who are convicted in adult criminal court must be sentenced to the California Department of Corrections and not the California Youth Authority.

- The confidentiality protections for juveniles are reduced.

- Prison terms are automatically increased for crimes that are gang-related. Juveniles convicted of gang-related murder are eligible for the death penalty.

In 2000 the California Supreme Court was reviewing Proposition 21 to determine its constitutionality. Even if deemed constitutional in California, Proposition 21 could face challenges in federal court.

Blended Sentencing

As of 1997, 22 states were using blended sentencing, which combines juvenile and adult sentences. Blended sentences permit courts to impose juvenile and/or adult correctional sanctions on certain young offenders. (See Table 7.24.)

In April 1999 Arkansas governor, Mike Huckabee, signed The Extended Juvenile Jurisdiction Act (Act 1192 of 1999), which is an example of blended sentencing. The law allows for extended juvenile jurisdiction (also known as blended sentencing), in which juvenile offenders first could be sent to the Division of Youth Services. Then, before they turn 18 years of age, a second hearing could be held and a judge would decide whether or not to trans-fer them to adult prison. The new law could keep children of any age, who have committed crimes of capital or first-degree murder, imprisoned for life. The law does not allow the death penalty for those children, but it does permit youths serving life sentences for murder to be eligible for parole. The bill was passed in response to the 1998 Jonesboro school shootings in which two young boys murdered five people and wounded another 10.

BOOT CAMPS

Boot camps for juvenile offenders are a relatively recent phenomenon. The oldest program, in Orleans Parish, Louisiana, began in 1985. Boot camps for juveniles are typically intended for "midrange" offenders—those who have failed with lesser sanctions like probation but are not yet hardened criminals. Juvenile programs typically exclude some types of offenders, such as sex offenders, armed robbers, and youths with a record of serious violence. Definitions of terms like "nonviolent" vary from program to program.

Most juvenile boot camps share the 90–120 day duration typical of military boot camps. They employ military customs and have uniformed drill instructors, use a platoon sergeant, and subject participants to verbal harassment, summary punishment, and group punishment under some circumstances.

Besides military discipline most juvenile boot camps include some type of work detail. Because of state-mandated education rules, all programs spend a minimum of three hours daily on academic education. Most programs also include some vocational education, work-skills training, or job preparation.

CHAPTER 8

PROBATION AND PAROLE

Any society that depends on only two sentencing options—confinement or nothing at all—is unsafe and unjust. We need a full array of effective sentencing tools that actually suit our various sentencing purposes.

— Michael Smith, Vera Institute of Justice

During 1999 the number of adults on probation was 3,773,600, while 712,700 adults were on parole, according to the Bureau of Justice Statistics (BJS). (See Table 8.1.) About one-quarter of all probationers and parolees were in two states—Texas (556,410) and California (446,460). States with the largest percent increase in probationers were Idaho (17.7 percent), Vermont (17.1 percent), and Arizona (11.2 percent). States with the lowest rates of probationers per 100,000 adult residents were West Virginia (427), North Dakota (576), and Virginia (576). (See Table 8.2.) As for parolees the largest increases during 1999 occurred in Ohio (39.6), South Dakota (20.9), and West Virginia (18.8). States with the lowest rates of parolees per 100,000 adult residents were Maine (3), Washington (5), and North Dakota (33).

PROBATION

Probation is the suspension of a sentence of a person convicted, but not yet imprisoned, on condition of continued good behavior and regular reporting to a probation officer. The whole sentence might be served under probation, or probation might be combined with a short sentence in a prison or jail.

Rates and Numbers

In 1999 almost 1,864 adults per 100,000 adult U.S. residents were on state or federal probation. (See Table 8.3.) Of adult state probationers in 1999 the rate was highest in the South (1,503,679), followed by the Midwest (849,703), the West (710,987), and the Northeast (572,832).

Adult offenders placed on federal probation rose from 64,261 in 1957 to 97,190 in 1999—an increase of about

TABLE 8.1

Adults under community supervision or in jail or prison, 1990–99

Year	Total estimated correctional population[a]	Probation[b]	Parole	Jail	Prison
1990	4,348,000	2,670,234	531,407	403,019	743,382
1995	5,335,100	3,077,861	679,421	499,300	1,078,542
1996	5,482,700	3,164,996	679,733	510,400	1,127,528
1997	5,725,800	3,296,513	694,787	557,974	1,176,564
1998	6,124,200	3,670,591	696,385	584,372	1,222,436
1999	6,288,600	3,773,624	712,713	596,485	1,254,577
Percent change[c]					
1998-99	2.7%	2.8%	2.3%	2.1%	3.7%
1990-99	44.6	41.3	34.1	48.0	68.8
Average annual percent change					
1990-99	4.2%	3.9%	3.3%	4.5%	6.4%

Note: The probation and parole counts may vary from previously reported estimates. Counts are for December 31, except for jail counts and the 1999 prison count, which are for June 30. All jail and prison counts are for inmates in custody.

[a] A small number of individuals has multiple correctional statuses; consequently, the total of persons under correctional supervision is an overestimate, and is rounded to the nearest 100.

[b] Totals in 1999 exclude 23,907 probationers in jail, 22,758 probationers in prison, and 2,163 probationers in an Immigration and Naturalization Service holding facility.

[c] Percent change in the prison population was calculated for 6/30/98 to 6/30/99 and for 12/31/90 to 6/30/99.

SOURCE: *U.S. Correctional Population Reaches 6.3 Million Men and Women: Represents 3.1 Percent of the Adult U.S. Population*, Bureau of Justice Statistics, Washington, DC, 2000

66 percent. During that same time period the number of federal probation officers increased from 1,377 to 3,913, up by almost 300 percent. (See Table 8.4.)

Characteristics

Women made up about 22 percent of the nation's probationers in 1999. Approximately 63 percent of the adults on probation were white, 35 percent were black, 16 percent Hispanics. (See Table 8.5.)

TABLE 8.2

Community corrections among the states, year-end 1999

10 States with the largest community corrections population	Number supervised	10 States with the largest percent increase, 1998-99	Percent increase	10 States with the highest rates of supervision, 1999	Persons supervised per 100,000 adult residents*	10 States with the lowest rates of supervision, 1999	Persons supervised per 100,000 adult residents*
Probation							
Texas	447,100	Idaho	17.7%	Georgia	5,368	West Virginia	427
California	332,414	Vermont	17.1	Idaho	4,073	North Dakota	576
Georgia	307,653	Arizona	11.2	Washington	3,705	Virginia	616
Florida	292,399	Montana	10.2	Delaware	3,673	Mississippi	618
Ohio	184,867	New Mexico	8.6	Texas	3,121	Kentucky	634
New York	183,686	Maine	8.2	Minnesota	2,986	South Dakota	647
Michigan	170,978	Mississippi	8.0	Rhode Island	2,902	Utah	663
Washington	158,213	Kentucky	7.9	Florida	2,533	Maine	782
Illinois	134,270	Iowa	6.7	Indiana	2,399	Nevada	894
New Jersey	128,634	Louisiana	6.3	Michigan	2,341	Montana	896
Parole							
California	114,046	Ohio	39.6%	Pennsylvania	916	Maine	3
Texas	109,310	South Dakota	20.9	Texas	763	Washington	5
Pennsylvania	83,702	West Virginia	18.8	Oregon	718	North Dakota	33
New York	57,956	Louisiana	16.8	Louisiana	688	Nebraska	50
Illinois	30,484	Iowa	14.6	California	471	Rhode Island	55
Georgia	22,003	Hawaii	12.1	New York	421	Florida	56
Louisiana	21,904	Delaware	10.8	Arkansas	404	Oklahoma	62
Oregon	17,874	Missouri	10.4	Maryland	389	Connecticut	62
Ohio	15,776	Arkansas	9.5	Georgia	384	Mississippi	67
Michigan	15,541	Connecticut	9.3	Illinois	341	North Carolina	77

Note: The District of Columbia as a wholly urban jurisdiction is excluded.
*Rates are computed using the adult resident population in each State on July 1, 1999.

SOURCE: *U.S. Correctional Population Reaches 6.3 Million Men and Women: Represents 3.1 Percent of the Adult U.S. Population*, Bureau of Justice Statistics, Washington, DC, 2000

More than half (51 percent) of all offenders on probation in 1999 were on probation for a felony. Forty-eight percent were on probation for a misdemeanor. Of adults entering probation in 1999, 79 percent did so without incarceration. Of those leaving probation in 1999 less than two-thirds (61 percent) had successfully completed the terms of their probation, and some 14 percent were returned to incarceration.

According to the CJI (*The Corrections Yearbook, 1998*, Middletown, Connecticut, 1998), the caseload for a regular probation officer averaged 175 probationers (93 for combination probation and parole agencies). For intensive supervision, the caseload was 34 people per probation officer (25 for combination). Other caseloads were 20 for electronic supervision (24 for combination) and 62 for special caseloads (37 for combination).

Conditions Imposed

Felons released on probation to the community are required, as a condition of their freedom, to comply with the orders of the court. These orders frequently include having the probationer meet with the probation officer on a periodic basis, maintain steady employment, remain in school, or avoid certain places or people. Judges may also impose special conditions—often tailored to specific offender characteristics—such as drug treatment, community service, restitution, or mental health counseling.

In *Characteristics of Adults on Probation, 1995* (1997), the BJS reported that 82 percent of probationers were given three or more conditions on their sentences. Nearly all probationers (98.6 percent) had one or more conditions, 17 percent had one or two conditions, 36 percent had three or four conditions, and 46 percent had five or more. Almost all (98.4 percent) felony probationers had at least one special condition imposed.

A monetary requirement was the most common condition, affecting 84.3 percent of all probationers. Types of financial penalties included victim restitution (30.3 percent), court costs (54.5 percent), fines (55.8 percent), and supervision fees (61 percent). Performing community service as a condition was required for 25.7 percent of probationers, and 40.3 percent had to have jobs or enroll in an education or training program.

One-tenth of all probationers were monitored or had their movements restricted. This means that they might have been required to stay away from certain places (bars or particular businesses) or might have been subject to electronic monitoring, house arrest, or curfew. Another 10.4 percent were restricted from contacting their victim or victims.

TABLE 8.3

Adults on probation, 1999

Region and jurisdicition	Probation population				Percent change during 1999	Number on probation on 12/31/99 per 100,000 adult residents
	1/1/99	1999		12/31/99		
		Entries	Exits			
U.S. total	3,670,591	1,819,403	1,714,630	3,773,624	2.8%	1,864
Federal	33,390	14,571	14,793	32,816	-1.7%	16
State	3,637,201	1,804,832	1,699,837	3,740,808	2.8	1,848
Northeast	572,832	195,038	187,977	575,270	0.4%	1,465
Connecticut	55,000	30,000	29,930	55,070	0.1	2,244
Maine	6,953	5,379	4,808	7,524	8.2	782
Massachusetts[a]	46,567	40,676	40,976	46,267	-0.6	983
New Hampshire	5,175	:	:	3,160	...	...
New Jersey[a]	129,377	58,500	59,543	128,634	-0.6	2,095
New York[a]	178,612	45,618	40,544	183,686	2.8	1,335
Pennsylvania[a,b]	121,094	1,072	623	118,635	-2.0	1,298
Rhode Island	21,049	7,972	7,268	21,753	3.3	2,902
Vermont	9,005	5,821	4,285	10,541	17.1	2,320
Midwest	849,703	458,923	436,681	871,319	2.5%	1,858
Illinois	131,850	58,695	56,275	134,270	1.8	1,501
Indiana[a]	104,624	87,517	86,270	105,871	1.2	2,399
Iowa[a]	18,447	18,863	17,635	19,675	6.7	915
Kansas	17,219	21,090	20,542	17,767	3.2	909
Michigan[a]	170,997	69,124	69,210	170,978	**	2,341
Minnesota	100,818	60,872	58,164	104,615	3.8	2,986
Missouri	49,992	26,037	23,536	52,493	5.0	1,290
Nebraska	16,527	19,095	15,160	20,462	...	1,674
North Dakota	2,726	1,620	1,617	2,729	0.1	576
Ohio[a,c]	178,830	68,480	60,661	184,867	5.2	2,198
South Dakota	3,441	3,064	3,044	3,461	0.6	647
Wisconsin	54,232	24,466	24,567	54,131	-0.2	1,387
South	1,503,679	837,091	783,397	1,556,507	3.5%	2,170
Alabama	40,379	15,835	14,457	41,757	3.4	1,264
Arkansas	28,698	8,537	6,755	30,480	6.2	1,612
Delaware	20,030	11,015	10,069	20,976	4.7	3,673
District of Columbia	11,234	10,877	9,265	12,129	8.0	2,863
Florida[a]	283,965	194,529	189,140	292,399	3.0	2,533
Georgia[a]	278,669	183,322	154,944	307,653	...	5,368
Kentucky[a]	17,594	16,848	12,311	18,988	7.9	634
Louisiana	33,028	14,425	12,335	35,118	6.3	1,104
Maryland	78,051	41,117	37,882	81,286	4.1	2,105
Mississippi[a]	11,530	5,748	4,830	12,448	8.0	618
North Carolina	105,227	59,195	59,327	105,095	-0.1	1,841
Oklahoma	29,093	12,257	13,213	27,997	-3.8	1,131
South Carolina	46,482	15,244	16,797	44,929	-3.3	1,534
Tennessee[a,d]	38,924	23,289	22,153	40,060	2.9	967
Texas	443,688	198,573	195,161	447,100	0.8	3,121
Virginia	30,576	26,280	24,758	32,098	5.0	616
West Virginia	6,511	:	:	5,994	-7.9	427

PROBATIONERS PAY FOR THEIR OWN SUPERVISION. With correctional costs skyrocketing, many government officials have decided that offenders should help pay for their supervision and rehabilitation. Most jail and prison work programs require inmates to contribute a portion of their earnings to their own upkeep. Another approach to recouping taxpayers' dollars is to require offenders on probation and who are capable of working to pay for at least some of the cost of their supervision. More than half the states allow local probation departments to charge fees to probationers. The amount of fees states collect varies widely. In 1997, according to the CJI, the jurisdictions responding to its survey charged an average monthly fee of $29.62.

The increasing use of probation fees has prompted heated debate among correctional professionals. Some critics argue that correctional fees are not an efficient way to generate revenue because many correctional clients are indigent and the cost of collecting fees may exceed the amount of money earned. Others assert that it is unethical or even illegal to force convicted offenders to pay for services they are required to receive.

Opponents of the idea allege that creating incentives to accumulate probation fees may cause probation officers to neglect their supervisory responsibilities. Finally, they warn that collecting fees may cause government officials to lose control over local probation departments if these departments achieve significant fiscal independence from the states and counties.

Disciplinary Action

According to the *Characteristics of Adults on Probation* survey, nearly one of five (18.4 percent) of all

TABLE 8.3

Adults on probation, 1999 [CONTINUED]

Region and jurisdicition	Probation population					Number on probation on 12/31/99 per 100,000 adult residents
	1/1/99	1999		12/31/99	Percent change during 1999	
		Entries	Exits			
West	710,987	313,780	291,782	737,712	3.8%	1,653
Alaska[a]	4,274	1,795	1,552	4,517	5.7	1,069
Arizona	51,329	32,611	26,864	57,076	11.2	1,657
California	324,427	162,543	152,604	332,414	2.5	1,372
Colorado[a]	45,502	26,601	26,613	45,339	-0.4	1,516
Hawaii	15,711	7,228	7,232	15,707	**	1,753
Idaho	31,172	2,970	3,033	36,705	17.7	4,073
Montana[a]	5,358	1,102	634	5,906	10.2	896
Nevada	12,561	:	:	11,787	-6.2	894
New Mexico[a]	10,397	8,850	7,956	11,291	8.6	907
Oregon	44,809	17,140	16,459	45,490	1.5	1,828
Utah	9,482	3,843	3,899	9,426	-0.6	663
Washington[a]	152,140	47,213	43,088	158,213	4.0	3,705
Wyoming	3,825	1,884	1,848	3,841	0.4	1,089

Note: Because of nonresponse or incomplete data, the probation population for some jurisdictions on December 31, 1999, does not equal the population on January 1, 1999, plus entries, minus exits. During 1999 an estimated 2,042,500 persons entered probation supervision, and 1,927,700 exited, based on imputations for agencies which did not provide data.

: Not known.

. . . Comparable percentage or rate could not be calculated.

** Between -0.05% and 0.05%.

[a] Data do not include cases in one or more of the following categories: absconder, out of State, inactive, intensive supervision, or electronic monitoring.

[b] Entries and exits do not include county data.

[c] Percent change in probation population during 1999 excludes 134 local probation agencies for which a single population estimate was obtained for 12/31/99.

[d] Data are for the period beginning May 1, 1999, and ending April 30, 2000.

SOURCE: *U.S. Correctional Population Reaches 6.3 Million Men and Women: Represents 3.1 Percent of the Adult U.S. Population*, Bureau of Justice Statistics, Washington, DC, 2000

---

probationers faced one or more disciplinary hearings while on probation. Probationers may face such a hearing if they violate a condition of their probation or are arrested for a new offense. A disciplinary hearing might result in an arrest warrant being issued for the probationer (if he or she has disappeared), the probationer being sent back to prison, or probation being reinstated with or without new conditions.

The longer a probationer was on probation, the more likely it was that he or she had experienced at least one disciplinary hearing. More than one-third (37.6 percent) of probationers who had been on probation for 36 months or more had faced a disciplinary hearing compared to 4.8 percent who had served less than six months. The survey did not include those probationers who were incarcerated at the time of the survey.

Probationers who were employed were less apt to face a disciplinary hearing than those who were not working (15.9 percent and 22.9 percent, respectively). Probationers who had no prior sentence were less likely to have a disciplinary hearing than those who had a prior sentence (14.9 percent and 23.2 percent, respectively).

REASONS FOR FACING A HEARING. The most common reason for a probationer having to face a disciplinary hearing was failure to contact the probation officer (41.1 percent). This was followed by arrest or conviction for a new crime (38.4 percent), failure to pay fines or restitu-

tion (37.9 percent), failure to attend or complete an alcohol or drug treatment program (22.5 percent), a positive drug test (11.2 percent), and failure to complete a community service requirement (8.5 percent.)

Overall, felons were more likely than misdemeanants to fail to maintain contact with the probation officer (43.3 and 37.6 percent, respectively) and to be arrested or convicted for a new offense. On the other hand, misdemeanants (43 percent) were more apt than felons (34.1 percent) to fail to pay fines or restitution and to fail to complete drug or alcohol treatment programs (33 percent and 17.5 percent, respectively).

RESULTS OF THE HEARINGS. Of those probationers who had faced one or more disciplinary hearings, 42 percent were permitted to continue their probation, but with additional conditions. One of three (29 percent) were incarcerated in jail or prison, another 29 percent had their probation reinstated without any new conditions, and 4 percent had charges that were not sustained. (The percentages for hearing outcomes total more than 100 percent because some probationers faced more than one hearing or outcome.)

Types of Crimes

In 1995, 17.3 percent of probationers had been convicted of violent offenses and 21.4 percent for drug offenses. Almost equal proportions had been sentenced

TABLE 8.4

Persons under the supervision of the Federal Probation System and authorized probation officers, 1975–99

	Number of persons under supervision	Number of probation officers
1975	64,261	1,377
1976	64,246	1,452
1977	64,427	1,578
1978	66,681	1,604
1979	66,087	1,604
1980	64,450	1,604
1981	59,016	1,534
1982	58,373	1,637
1983	60,180	1,574
1984	63,092	1,690
1985	65,999	1,758
1986	69,656	1,847
1987	73,432	1,879
1988	76,366	2,046
1989	77,284	2,146
1990	80,592	2,361
1991	83,012	2,802
1992	85,920	3,316
1993	86,823	3,516[a]
1994	89,103	NA
1995	85,822	NA
1996	88,966	3,473
1997	91,434	3,603
1998	93,737	3,842
1999	97,190	3,913

Note: The "number of probationers" data for 1975-87 are reported for the 12-month period ending June 30. Beginning in 1988, these data are reported for the Federal fiscal year, which is the 12-month period ending September 30. The "number of probation officers" data for 1975-90 are reported as of June 30. Beginning in 1991, these data are reported as of September 30.
[a] Approximate.

SOURCE: "Table 6.11: Persons under supervision of the Federal Probation System and authorized probation officers," in *Sourcebook of Criminal Justice Statistics 1999*, Kathleen Maguire and Ann L. Pastore, eds., Bureau of Justice Statistics, Washington, D.C., 2000

TABLE 8.5

Characteristics of adults on probation, 1990 and 1999

Characteristic	1990	1999
Total	100%	100%
Gender	100%	100%
Male	82	78
Female	18	22
Race	100%	100%
White	68	63
Black	31	35
Other	1	2
Hispanic 2origin	100%	100%
Hispanic	18	16
Non-Hispanic	82	84
Status of supervision	100%	100%
Active	83	77
Inactive	9	10
Absconded	6	9
Supervised out of State	2	2
Other	—	2
Adults entering probation	100%	100%
Without incarceration	87	79
With incarceration	8	16
Other	5	5
Adults leaving probation	100%	100%
Successful completion	69	61
Returned to incarceration	14	14
With new sentence	3	4
With the same sentence	11	7
Type of return unknown	0	3
Absconder	7	3
Other unsuccessful	2	11
Death	**	1
Other	7	9
Severity of offense		100%
Felony	—	51
Misdemeanor	—	48
Other infractions	—	1
Status of probation	100%	100%
Direct imposition	38	58
Split sentence	6	10
Sentence suspended	41	22
Imposition suspended	14	8
Other	1	3

Note: For every characteristic there were persons of unknown status or type. Detail may not sum to total because of rounding.
—Not available.
**Less than 0.5%.

SOURCE: *U.S. Correctional Population Reaches 6.3 Million Men and Women: Represents 3.1 Percent of the Adult U.S. Population*, Bureau of Justice Statistics, Washington, DC, 2000

for property offenses (28.9 percent) and for public-order offenses (31.1 percent). Driving while intoxicated (DWI; 16.7 percent) was the most frequent single offense among those on probation, followed by larceny/theft (9.9 percent), drug possession (9.8 percent), drug trafficking (9.7 percent), and assault (9.2 percent).

In 1995, 58 percent of all adults on probation had been convicted of a felony. Half of those had been convicted of a violent (19.5 percent) or drug (30.7 percent) offense. Drug trafficking (15.4 percent) was the most frequent offense among felons on probation, followed by drug possession (13.1 percent), larceny/theft (11.1 percent), and burglary (9.7 percent.)

Most misdemeanants on probation (59.6 percent) had been convicted of a public-order offense. In fact, one-third (35.2 percent) of all misdemeanor probationers were convicted of DWI, 10.2 percent for other traffic offenses, and 4.5 percent for drunkenness or morals offenses. Approximately 14 percent of probationers convicted of a misdemeanor had also committed a violent offense (most often,

assault). Nearly one of five (18.2 percent) had been convicted of a property offense and 7.6 percent of a drug offense.

Among federal probationers in 1998, 88.4 percent had been convicted of felonies. (See Table 8.6.) Federal probationers in 1998 were most likely to have been convicted of drug offenses (38.3 percent), followed by property offenses (29.7 percent) and public order offenses (14.1 percent). Misdemeanants accounted for about 12 percent of federal probationers in 1998.

Also in 1998 more than 80 percent of federal probationers terminating probation successfully completed the terms of their probation with no violations. (See Table 8.7.)

TABLE 8.6

Federal offenders under community supervision by offense, 1998

	Total offenders under supervision		Type of supervision					
			Probation		Supervised release[b]		Parole	
Most serious conviction offense	Number	Percent[a]	Number	Percent[a]	Number	Percent[a]	Number	Percent[a]
All offenses	92,768	100%	32,119	100%	54,822	100%	5,827	100%
Felonies	81,784	88.4	21,685	67.9	54,285	99.2	5,814	99.8
Violent offenses	5,577	6.0	797	2.5	3,231	5.9	1,549	26.6
Murder, nonnegligent manslaughter	259	0.3	41	0.1	96	0.2	122	2.1
Negligent manslaughter	135	0.1	5	(c)	8	(c)	122	2.1
Assault	474	0.5	155	0.5	272	0.5	47	0.8
Robbery	3,805	4.1	330	1.0	2,258	4.1	1,217	20.9
Rape	347	0.4	98	0.3	207	0.4	42	0.7
Other sex offenses[d]	463	0.5	150	0.5	290	0.5	23	0.4
Kidnaping	166	0.2	8	(c)	61	0.1	97	1.7
Threats against the President	50	0.1	10	(c)	39	0.1	1	(c)
Property offenses	27,493	29.7	12,072	37.8	14,799	27.0	622	10.7
Fraudulent	22,655	24.5	9,735	30.5	12,535	22.9	385	6.6
Embezzlement	3,529	3.8	1,197	3.7	2,302	4.2	30	0.5
Fraud[e]	16,834	18.2	7,374	23.1	9,165	16.7	295	5.1
Forgery	617	0.7	311	1.0	272	0.5	34	0.6
Counterfeiting	1,675	1.8	853	2.7	796	1.5	26	0.4
Other	4,838	5.2	2,337	7.3	2,264	4.1	237	4.1
Burglary	268	0.3	78	0.2	137	0.3	53	0.9
Larceny[f]	3,296	3.6	1,815	5.7	1,378	2.5	103	1.8
Motor vehicle theft	407	0.4	137	0.4	248	0.5	22	0.4
Arson and explosives	317	0.3	85	0.3	199	0.4	33	0.6
Transportation of stolen property	468	0.5	182	0.6	261	0.5	25	0.4
Other property offenses[g]	82	0.1	40	0.1	41	0.1	1	(c)
Drug offenses	35,401	38.3	3,586	11.2	28,766	52.6	3,049	52.4
Trafficking	31,415	34.0	3,152	9.9	25,477	46.5	2,786	47.8
Other drug offenses[h]	3,986	4.3	434	1.4	3,289	6.0	263	4.5
Public-order offenses	13,049	14.1	5,055	15.8	7,403	13.5	591	10.1
Regulatory	2,182	2.4	1,299	4.1	845	1.5	38	0.7
Agriculture	84	0.1	60	0.2	23	(c)	1	(c)
Antitrust	18	(c)	13	(c)	4	(c)	1	(c)
Food and drug	66	0.1	51	0.2	14	(c)	1	(c)
Transportation	92	0.1	56	0.2	31	0.1	5	0.1
Civil rights	140	0.2	35	0.1	100	0.2	5	0.1
Communications	114	0.1	76	0.2	37	0.1	1	(c)
Customs laws	126	0.1	74	0.2	51	0.1	1	(c)
Postal laws	134	0.1	85	0.3	47	0.1	2	(c)
Other regulatory offenses	1,410	1.5	849	2.7	538	1.0	23	0.4

Characteristics of Probationers

In 1995 women made up 20.9 percent of probationers. Non-Hispanic whites accounted for 58.3 percent of all probationers, 55.4 percent of felons, and 61.8 percent of misdemeanants. Non-Hispanic blacks made up 27.9 percent of all probationers, 30.8 percent of felons, and 24.5 percent of misdemeanants. Hispanics, who may be of any race, made up 11 percent of both felons and misdemeanants. About 51.4 percent of probationers were never married, and a great proportion (42.4 percent) had not completed high school.

Substance Abuse and Treatment of Adults on Probation

According to *Substance Abuse and Treatment of Adults on Probation, 1995* (Bureau of Justice Statistics, 1998), nearly 70 percent of adult probationers admitted to using drugs in the past, and half of probationers who used alcohol or drugs had received treatment during their current probation sentence. This was the first survey ever conducted to collect data on drug abuse and treatment in the probation population. Personal interviews were conducted with more than 2,000 adult probationers under active supervision in 1995.

DRUGS AND ALCOHOL. More than two-thirds (67.3 percent) of all probationers claimed to have been involved with drugs or alcohol. Male probationers (70.9 percent) were more likely than female probationers (53.7 percent) to have used drugs or alcohol. A somewhat higher proportion of non-Hispanic white probationers (70.6 percent) than non-Hispanic black probationers (64 percent) or Hispanic probationers (58.8 percent) reported using alcohol or drugs. A greater percentage (73 percent) of those between the ages of 25 and 44 years used alcohol or drugs than those of any other ages.

The BJS analyzed probationers' use of drugs or alcohol based on whether they had been under the influence of

TABLE 8.6

Federal offenders under community supervision by offense, 1998 [CONTINUED]

Most serious conviction offense	Total offenders under supervision		Type of supervision					
			Probation		Supervised release[b]		Parole	
	Number	Percent[a]	Number	Percent[a]	Number	Percent[a]	Number	Percent[a]
Other	10,867	11.7	3,756	11.8	6,558	12.0	553	9.5
Weapons	4,038	4.4	608	1.9	3,243	5.9	187	3.2
Immigration offenses	1,272	1.4	639	2.0	623	1.1	10	0.2
Tax law violations including tax fraud	1,857	2.0	1,166	3.7	646	1.2	45	0.8
Bribery	394	0.4	226	0.7	163	0.3	5	0.1
Perjury, contempt, intimidation	344	0.4	136	0.4	193	0.4	15	0.3
National defense	47	0.1	23	0.1	18	(c)	6	0.1
Escape	305	0.3	52	0.2	222	0.4	31	0.5
Racketeering and extortion	1,885	2.0	502	1.6	1,145	2.1	238	4.1
Gambling offenses	289	0.3	178	0.6	108	0.2	3	0.1
Mail or transport of obscene material	72	0.1	36	0.1	34	0.1	2	(c)
Migratory birds	16	(c)	10	(c)	4	(c)	2	(c)
All other offenses	350	0.4	180	0.6	159	0.3	11	0.2
Misdemeanors[i]	10,984	11.9	10,434	32.7	537	1.0	13	0.2

Note: These data are from the U.S. Department of Justice, Bureau of Justice Statistics' Federal Justice Statistics Program database. Sources of information include the Executive Office for U.S. Attorneys, the Administrative Office of the United States Courts (AOUSC), the U.S. Sentencing Commission, the Federal Bureau of Prisons, the Federal pretrial services agencies, and the Federal probation and supervision service. These data are from the probation, parole, and supervision data files of the Federal Probation Supervision Information System maintained by the AOUSC. Only records with offenders under active supervision as of the end of fiscal year 1998 were selected. Corporate defendants were excluded. Total includes 264 felony offenders whose offense category could not be determined.

[a] Percents may not add to 100 because of rounding.
[b] Under the Federal Sentencing Reform Act, supervised release replaces parole for Federal offenders sentenced on or after Nov. 1, 1987.
[c] Less than 0.05%.
[d] May include some nonviolent offenses.
[e] Excludes tax fraud.
[f] Excludes transportation of stolen property.
[g] Excludes fraudulent property offenses; includes destruction of property and trespass.
[h] Includes drug misdemeanors.
[i] Includes misdemeanors, petty offenses, and unknown offense level.

SOURCE: "Table 6.8: Federal offenders under community supervision," in *Sourcebook of Criminal Justice Statistics 1999,* Kathleen Maguire and Ann L. Pastore, eds., Bureau of Justice Statistics, Washington, D.C., 2000

drugs or alcohol ever in the past, in the month before committing the offense, or at the time of the offense. More than 69 percent said they had ever used drugs in the past, 31.8 percent said they had used drugs in the month prior to the offense, and 13.5 percent admitted using drugs at the time the offense was committed. About 4 of 10 probationers (39.9 percent) said they were under the influence of alcohol at the time they committed the offense.

DRUG TESTING AND TREATMENT. Probationers were also asked if they had ever received drug treatment in the past. Nearly half (49 percent) had been tested for drug use while on their current probation sentence, but only 17.4 percent received treatment while on probation. The longer a person was on probation the more likely he or she was to be tested and to receive treatment.

Probationers who had received treatment for drugs took part in different types of programs. Moreover, some probationers who had received drug treatment more than once may not have participated in the same type of treatment program each time. The most common types of drug treatment programs were outpatient care (used by 16.5 percent of those being treated) followed by self-help programs (used by 13.7 percent). More probationers (51.2 percent) who had used drugs in the month prior to committing the offense received treatment than those who used drugs regularly (45.9 percent) or those who had ever used drugs in the past (31.6 percent.)

ALCOHOL TESTING AND TREATMENT. A significantly larger proportion (40.6 percent) of probationers with a history of alcohol use had received treatment than those who had used drugs (22.1 percent). Nearly three-fourths (72.5 percent) of probationers under the influence of alcohol at the time of the offense sought treatment, as did 62.9 percent of those who had binged on alcohol and 65.3 percent of those who had gotten into a physical fight because of their drinking. It is important to remember when using these statistics that alcohol and drug abusers tend to underestimate the amount of alcohol and/or drugs they use.

Nearly 8 of 10 (78.1 percent) of those who had had three or more positive CAGE responses had received some kind of treatment. A CAGE questionnaire is a diagnostic device used to detect a person's history of alcohol

TABLE 8.7

Federal probationers terminating supervision by outcome and offense, fiscal year 1996

Most serious conviction offense	Number of probationers terminating probation	Percent of probationers terminating supervision with:					
		Technical violations[a]				New crime[b]	Administrative case closure
		No violation	Drug use	Fugitive status	Other		
All offenses	16,011	81.3%	3.5%	2.1%	5.8%	5.4%	1.9%
Felonies	8,192	83.9	3.0	1.9	4.6	4.5	2.1
Violent offenses	244	66.7	4.9	3.7	11.9	9.1	3.7
Murder, nonnegligent manslaughter	15	66.7	0.0	0.0	13.3	13.3	6.7
Negligent manslaughter	4	B	B	B	B	B	B
Assault	67	66.7	6.1	6.1	9.1	10.6	1.5
Robbery	78	67.9	7.7	5.1	9.0	7.7	2.6
Rape	37	48.6	2.7	0.0	29.7	13.5	5.4
Other sex offenses[c]	38	81.6	0.0	2.6	2.6	5.3	7.9
Kidnaping	2	B	B	B	B	B	B
Threats against the President	3	B	B	B	B	B	B
Property offenses	4,615	84.4	2.8	1.9	5.0	4.1	1.9
Fraudulent offenses	3,669	85.8	2.6	1.7	4.3	3.7	1.9
Embezzlement	455	89.7	1.3	1.1	4.4	2.6	0.9
Fraud[d]	2,821	86.5	2.5	1.8	3.9	3.5	1.8
Forgery	129	81.3	4.7	1.6	3.9	5.5	3.1
Counterfeiting	264	74.2	4.2	1.9	8.3	7.2	4.2
Other offenses	946	78.7	3.6	2.4	7.6	5.7	1.9
Burglary	29	58.6	6.9	3.4	13.8	13.8	3.4
Larceny[e]	728	78.1	4.0	2.6	8.0	5.2	2.1
Motor vehicle theft	53	81.1	0.0	1.9	5.7	9.4	1.9
Arson and explosives	33	84.8	0.0	3.0	12.1	0.0	0.0
Transportation of stolen property	91	89.0	1.1	1.1	2.2	5.5	1.1
Other property offenses[f]	12	58.3	16.7	0.0	8.3	16.7	0.0
Drug offenses	1,322	81.5	4.0	26	4.0	4.8	3.0
Trafficking	1,163	81.6	4.0	2.5	3.8	5.1	3.1
Possession and other[g]	159	81.0	4.4	3.2	5.7	3.2	2.5

abuse or dependence. CAGE is an acronym for the four questions asked on the questionnaire—attempts to (C)ut back on drinking, (A)nnoyance at others' criticism of one's drinking, feelings of (G)uilt about drinking, and needing a drink first thing in the morning as an (E)ye opener to steady the nerves. The number of positive responses to these four questions determines a person's likelihood of alcohol abuse.

One-third (31.5 percent) of probationers received alcohol treatment through self-help groups while one-fourth (25.5 percent) received help through outpatient care. Fewer participated in counseling (12.4 percent), crisis/emergency care (12 percent), and inpatient care (8.1 percent.)

PAROLE

Parole is the release of a prisoner before his or her sentence has expired, on condition of future good behavior. The sentence is not set aside, and the parolee remains under the supervision of a parole board. There are three kinds of releases from prisons:

- Supervised mandatory release is most common in jurisdictions with determinate (set) sentencing, conditionally releasing inmates at the end of their sentence (with time off for good behavior) into a parole portion of their sentence.

- Discretionary parole release is a decision made by a parole board based on statutory (state law) or administrative (parole board rules) determination of eligibility.

- An unconditional prison release is given when the offender's obligation to serve a sentence has been fully satisfied—the prisoner has served his or her time.

Because of prison overcrowding parole boards routinely release prisoners to make room for new prisoners. At the same time, because of the public's fear of violent crime, many states are imposing sentences without parole. For example, North Carolina has prison room for 21,500 inmates but has 30,000 annual admissions to prison. The state spent $550 million from 1985 into the mid-1990s to add 16,600 new beds and more than doubled its prison budget from $195 million in 1985 to $472 million in 1993.

At the same time the state wanted to end the "revolving door" for felons. Starting in January 1995 parole was abolished and a sentencing system was set up to establish sentences based on the type of crime, the mitigating circumstances, and available room in the prisons. Offenders who fell into certain levels of less serious crimes would be put under probation or house arrest, placed in boot camp or a drug treatment program, or made to pay restitution. Such sentences for low-level offenders would allow for more prison space for offenders convicted of more serious crimes.

TABLE 8.7

Federal probationers terminating supervision by outcome and offense, fiscal year 1996 [CONTINUED]

Most serious conviction offense	Number of probationers terminating probation	Percent of probationers terminating supervision with:					
		Technical violations[a]				New crime[b]	Administrative case closure
		No violation	Drug use	Fugitive status	Other		
Public-order offenses	1,960	87.4	2.4	1.4	3.0	4.1	1.7
Regulatory offenses	495	89.1	2.4	1.2	2.4	3.6	1.2
Agriculture	26	92.3	3.8	0.0	0.0	3.8	0.0
Antitrust	10	B	B	B	B	B	B
Food and drug	12	100	X	X	X	X	X
Transportation	16	87.5	0.0	0.0	6.3	6.3	0.0
Civil rights	13	100	X	X	X	X	X
Communications	31	96.8	0.0	0.0	3.2	0.0	0.0
Customs laws	32	96.9	0.0	0.0	0.0	3.1	0.0
Postal laws	56	73.2	10.7	7.1	1.8	5.4	1.8
Other regulatory offenses	299	89.0	1.7	0.7	3.0	4.0	1.7
Other offenses	1,465	86.8	2.4	1.5	3.2	4.2	1.8
Weapons	236	80.5	5.5	1.3	3.8	7.6	1.3
Immigration offenses	233	70.8	2.6	5.6	6.9	9.9	4.3
Tax law violations including tax fraud	486	94.4	0.8	0.0	1.4	2.1	1.2
Bribery	90	87.8	2.2	2.2	3.3	1.1	3.3
Perjury, contempt, intimidation	55	92.7	1.8	0.0	1.8	3.6	0.0
National defense	7	B	B	B	B	B	B
Escape	36	69.4	11.1	2.8	8.3	5.6	2.8
Racketeering and extortion	163	92.0	0.6	1.2	3.1	1.2	1.8
Gambling offenses	87	97.7	1.1	0.0	0.0	1.1	0.0
Mail or transport of obscene material	14	100	X	X	X	X	X
Migratory birds	7	B	B	B	B	B	B
Other felonies	51	82.4	3.9	2.0	3.9	5.9	2.0
Misdemeanors[h]	7,819	78.6	4.0	2.3	7.0	6.3	1.7

Note: Only records with one or more terminations of active supervision during fiscal year 1998 were selected. Each termination was counted separately. Technical violations and terminations for new crimes are shown only if supervision terminated with incarceration or removal from active supervision for reason of a violation. The data exclude corporate offenders. Total includes 51 felony offenders whose offense category could not be determined.

[a] Supervision terminated with incarceration or removal to inactive status for violation of supervision conditions other than charges for new offenses.
[b] Supervision terminated with incarceration or removal to inactive status after arrest for a "major" or "minor" offense.
[c] May include some nonviolent offenses.
[d] Excludes tax fraud.
[e] Excludes transportation of stolen property.
[f] Excludes fraudulent property offenses; includes destruction of property and trespass.
[g] Includes drug misdemeanors.
[h] Includes misdemeanors, petty offenses, and unknown offense level.

SOURCE: "Table 6.13: Federal probationers terminating supervision," in *Sourcebook of Criminal Justice Statistics 1999,* Kathleen Maguire and Ann L. Pastore, eds., Bureau of Justice Statistics, Washington, D.C., 2000

In 1999 the Midwest had the lowest ratio of parolees to adult residents (213 per 100,000 adults), while the Northeast had the highest ratio (415 per 100,000). Among individual jurisdictions the District of Columbia had the highest ratio (1,204 per 100,000), while Pennsylvania reported the second highest ratio (916 per 100,000). At the end of 1999 Texas maintained the largest parole population of any reporting jurisdiction, with 109,820 adults, barely edging out California which had 108,424. (See Table 8.8.)

In 1999, 88 percent of individuals on parole were male, 12 percent female, 55 percent white, 44 percent black, and 21 percent Hispanic. (See Table 8.9.) Of those entering parole in 1999 one-half did so because of mandatory parole requirements set forth in the law. One way this is done is so-called "good time" provisions that allow an offender to reduce his or her stay in prison for good behavior. Most states have "good time" provisions but they vary in terms of how much a sentence can be reduced for good behavior. (See Table 8.10.) For instance, in Alaska and Washington it is possible for an offender to eliminate one-third of his or her sentence for good behavior. Delaware allows 90 days per year maximum, or about one-fourth of the overall sentence.

Abolishing Parole

Abolishing Parole: Why the Emperor Has No Clothes (Lexington, Kentucky, 1995), a report commissioned by the American Probation and Parole Association and the Association of Parole Authorities, International, concluded that states that abolished parole have less control over violent offenders who have been released. The report

TABLE 8.8

Adults on parole, 1999

Region and jurisdiction	Parole population 1/1/99	Parole population 1999 Entries	Parole population 1999 Exits	Parole population 12/31/99	Percent change during 1999	Number on parole on 12/31/99 per 100,000 adult residents
U.S. total	696,385	429,172	412,167	712,713	2.3%	352
Federal	67,169	26,653	22,575	71,020	5.7%	35
State	629,216	402,519	389,592	641,693	2.0	317
Northeast	162,006	49,962	51,023	162,840	0.5%	415
Connecticut	1,396	1,338	1,208	1,526	9.3	62
Maine	33	0	2	31	-6.1	3
Massachusetts*	4,489	4,033	3,689	4,304	-4.1	91
New Hampshire	1,141	:	:	1,146	0.4	128
New Jersey	13,218	10,394	10,644	12,968	-1.9	211
New York	59,548	25,200	26,792	57,956	-2.7	421
Pennsylvania	81,001	8,199	7,917	83,702	3.3	916
Rhode Island	432	515	534	413	-4.4	55
Vermont*	748	283	237	794	6.1	175
Midwest	94,110	77,648	71,737	100,021	6.3%	213
Illinois	30,432	25,422	25,370	30,484	0.2	341
Indiana*	4,258	4,898	4,617	4,539	6.6	103
Iowa*	2,194	2,805	2,485	2,514	14.6	117
Kansas	6,025	5,352	5,468	5,909	-1.9	302
Michigan	15,331	9,681	9,471	15,541	1.4	213
Minnesota	2,995	3,464	3,308	3,151	5.2	90
Missouri	10,366	8,501	7,419	11,448	10.4	281
Nebraska*	624	687	699	612	-1.9	50
North Dakota	174	370	387	157	-9.8	33
Ohio˙	11,304	11,237	6,765	15,776	39.6	188
South Dakota*	1,125	964	729	1,360	20.9	254
Wisconsin	9,282	4,267	5,019	8,530	-8.1	219
South	223,922	96,430	94,250	223,469	-0.2%	312
Alabama*	5,221	1,861	2,170	5,005	-4.1	151
Arkansas	6,979	5,519	4,853	7,645	9.5	404
Delaware*	572	268	206	634	10.8	111
District of Columbia	7,055	:	:	5,103	. . .	1,204
Florida*	6,487	4,780	4,413	6,418	-1.1	56
Georgia	20,482	12,149	10,290	22,003	7.4	384
Kentucky*	4,508	3,117	2,757	4,868	8.0	163
Louisiana	18,759	14,185	11,040	21,904	16.8	688
Maryland*	15,528	8,059	8,580	15,007	-3.4	389
Mississippi	1,489	688	821	1,356	-8.9	67
North Carolina	5,806	5,603	7,020	4,389	-24.4	77
Oklahoma	1,532	610	615	1,527	-0.3	62
South Carolina	4,404	786	1,246	3,944	-10.4	135
Tennessee	7,605	3,288	3,555	7,338	-3.5	177
Texas	109,820	30,316	30,826	109,310	-0.5	763
Virginia	6,700	4,357	5,197	5,860	-12.5	113
West Virginia	975	844	661	1,158	18.8	83

claimed that "public confidence in the system has plummeted, costs have skyrocketed, prison populations have grown out of control, and violent and dangerous offenders have been routinely released without any judgement or accountability." In other words, claimed the report, parole apparently provides community supervision for less violent prisoners and allows room in the prisons to maintain the more violent prisoners.

Eleven states (California, Delaware, Illinois, Indiana, Maine, Minnesota, New Mexico, North Carolina, Oregon, Virginia, and Washington) have abolished parole. Colorado, Connecticut, and Florida had abolished the system but reinstated it. Most states without parole use systems that grant prisoners early release by earning good behavior credits. In these states parole boards do not review whether a convict is a safe risk to be released into the community.

Florida reinstated parole hearings after an inmate released under a credit system murdered a police officer.

COST OF PROBATION AND PAROLE

The CJI estimated that the total administrative budgets for probation and parole for fiscal year 1998 were $1.2 billion for probation agencies, $1 billion for parole agencies, and $1.2 billion for those that combined their probation and parole agencies.

REASONS FOR THE INCREASING NUMBERS OF VIOLATORS AND ABSCONDERS

Given the growth in the probation and parole population, an increase in the number of violators would be expected, but not necessarily the violation rates. However,

TABLE 8.8

Adults on parole, 1999 [CONTINUED]

Region and jurisdiction	1/1/99	Parole population 1999		12/31/99	Percent change during 1999	Number on parole on 12/31/99 per 100,000 adult residents
		Entries	Exits			
West	149,178	178,479	172,582	155,363	4.1%	348
Alaska*	478	321	306	493	3.1	117
Arizona*	3,742	6,490	6,517	3,715	-0.7	108
California*	108,424	153,571	148,303	114,046	5.2	471
Colorado*	5,204	3,979	3,920	5,263	1.1	176
Hawaii*	2,009	1,058	911	2,252	12.1	251
Idaho*	1,309	873	872	1,310	0.1	145
Montana*	667	500	618	549	-17.7	83
Nevada	4,055	:	:	3,893	-4.0	295
New Mexico	1,773	1,710	1,561	1,922	8.4	154
Oregon	17,270	7,485	6,881	17,874	3.5	718
Utah	3,424	2,249	2,285	3,388	-1.1	238
Washington	375	15	190	200	-46.7	5
Wyoming	448	228	218	458	2.2	130

Note: Because of nonresponse or incomplete data, the probation population for some jurisdictions on December 31, 1999, does not equal the population on January 1, 1999, plus entries, minus exits. During 1999 an estimated 451,600 persons entered parole supervision, and 434,300 exited, based on imputations for agencies that did not provide data.
. . .Comparable percentage could not be calculated.
: Not known.
*Data do not include parolees in one or more of the following categories: absconder, out of State, inactive, intensive supervision, or electronic monitoring.

SOURCE: *U.S. Correctional Population Reaches 6.3 Million Men and Women: Represents 3.1 Percent of the Adult U.S. Population*, Bureau of Justice Statistics, Washington, DC, 2000

according to the National Institute of Justice, in *Responding to Probation and Parole Violations* (Washington, D.C., 1994), about one-third of the states said their rates of violation also had risen. They cited several reasons believed to have caused this increase, including:

• A shift in the purposes of community supervision—In the 1970s and 1980s, the idea of community supervision as a treatment to rehabilitate offenders declined, and the idea of sentencing alternatives, such as "community-based punishments" that could be applied in increments to match the seriousness of the offenders' crimes or their blameworthiness, took hold. If control and surveillance were objects of supervision, then detected violations and revocations were indicators of success. As one probation officer put it, his job was to "trail 'em, nail 'em, and jail 'em."

• An increase in probation and parole caseloads—As the parole and probation populations grew, the number of cases each officer supervised increased, and the time the officer had for each case decreased. Rising caseloads, it is argued, cause officers to focus their attention on rule enforcement generally and on individual offenders who have the most trouble following rules. As revocations increase probation and parole officers spend more and more time on the procedures and paperwork linked to revocation and thus have even less time available to supervise offenders.

• An increase in the number of conditions probationers and parolees are expected to obey—Instead of facing a year of standard probation an offender might now have to perform 200 hours of community service, participate in an outpatient drug-treatment program, and pay $500 restitution during the year of supervision. As the number of conditions grows offenders have more chances to violate.

• The use of improved technology to detect violations—As emphasis on control increases new technologies such as drug-use testing and electronic monitoring have made it easier to detect some violations.

• Changes in the types of offenders supervised on probation and parole—Many believe that more hardened, dangerous offenders are being placed on community supervision to avoid or reduce prison and jail crowding. Others argue that offenders now are more likely to be involved with drugs and to resort to violence than offenders were in the past. Not all those involved in law enforcement agree with this view. Some believe that the officers' emphasis on control and their use of tools like improved criminal-history information systems, risk assessment, and drug testing, merely make today's offenders seem tougher than in the past.

TABLE 8.9

Characteristics of adults on parole, 1990 and 1999

Characteristic	1990	1999
Total	100%	100%
Gender	100%	100%
Male	92	88
Female	8	12
Race	100%	100%
White	52	55
Black	47	44
Other	1	1
Hispanic origin	100%	100%
Hispanic	18	21
Non-Hispanic	82	79
Status of supervision	100%	100%
Active	82	83
Inactive	6	5
Absconded	6	7
Supervised out of State	6	5
Other	—	**
Adults entering parole	100%	100%
Discretionary parole	59	42
Mandatory parole	41	50
Reinstatement	—	6
Other	—	2
Adults leaving parole	100%	100%
Successful completion	50	43
Returned to incarceration	46	42
With new sentence	17	11
Other	29	31
Absconder	1	10
Other unsuccessful	1	2
Transferred	1	1
Death	1	1
Other	—	2
Length of sentence	100%	100%
Less than 1 year	5	3
One year or more	95	97

Note: For every characteristic there were persons of unknown status or type. Detail may not sum to total because of rounding.
—Not available.
**Less than 0.5%.

SOURCE: *U.S. Correctional Population Reaches 6.3 Million Men and Women: Represents 3.1 Percent of the Adult U.S. Population,* Bureau of Justice Statistics, Washington, DC, 2000

TABLE 8.10

Good time accumulation and parole

	Is there a parole board with discretionary release authority?	Do incarcerated felons accumulate "good time"?	What rate does "good time" accrue?
Alabama[1]	■	■	Up to 75 days for 30 served
Alaska	■	■	1/3 of term reduced
Arizona[3]	■	■	Varies, usually 1 for 2 days served
Arkansas	■	■	Day for day
California	■[4]	■	Varies from 15% to 50%[5]
Colorado	■	■	15 days per month[6]
Connecticut	■	■	~[7]
Delaware	Limited (advisory)	■	90 day/year max
District of Columbia	■	[8]	~
Florida	■	■	~[9]
Georgia	■		~
Hawaii	■	■	~[10]
Idaho	■	[11]	~
Illinois	■	■	Depends on offense[12]
Indiana	■	■	Day for day/one for two[13]
Iowa	■	■	Day for day
Kansas	■	■	Max 15% of sentence
Kentucky	■	■	10 days/month
Louisiana	~[14]	■	Day for day
Maine	~[14]		Up to 10 days/month
Maryland	■	■	~[15]
Massachusetts	■	■[15]	2½ to 12½ days/month
Michigan	■	■[16]	5 to 15 days/month[16]
Minnesota			1 day for 2 days served
Mississippi	■[17]	■	4.5 days/month
Missouri	■	■	~[18]
Montana	■		~
Nebraska	■	■	7 days for 14 days
Nevada	■	■	10 days/month[19]
New Hampshire	■	■	12.5 days/month
New Jersey	■	■	~[20]
New Mexico	■	■	30 days/month
New York	■[21]	■[22]	1 for 3 days served indeterminate, 1 for 7 days determinate
North Carolina	■	■	~[23]
North Dakota	■	■	5 days/month
Ohio	■		~
Oklahoma	[24]	■	~[25]
Oregon	~[26]	■[27]	~[28]
Pennsylvania	■		~
Puerto Rico	■	■	~[29]
Rhode Island[30]	■	■	Varies[31]
South Carolina[32]	■	■	~[33]
South Dakota	■	■	~[34]
Tennessee	■	■	~[35]
Texas	■	■	~[36]
Utah	■	■[37]	~[38]
Vermont[39]	■	■	Day for day[40]
Virginia	■	■	~[41]
Washington		■	1 day for 3 days served
West Virginia	■	■	Day for day
Wisconsin	■	■	¼ of term
Wyoming	■	■	Day for day
Federal Courts	■		~

Legend: ■ = Yes, ~ = Not applicable, LWOP = Life without parole

TABLE 8.10

Good time accumulation and parole [CONTINUED]

FOOTNOTES:

Alabama:
[1] Governor has power to commute a LWOP sentence to a term of years.
[2] Not applicable to prisoners convicted of Class A felony, sentenced to life or death or who have received a sentence in excess of fifteen years. Defendant's convicted of drug trafficking are prohibited from earning good time.

Arizona:
[3] Governor does not have power to commute a LWOP sentence to a term of years.

California:
[4] For "life" sentences only.
[5] "Good time" accrual depends upon factors such as offense and/or prior record.

Colorado:
[6] Earned time is also available up to 30 days every 6 months.

Connecticut:
[7] For offenses committed after 7/1/83, 10 days/month for first 5 years, and 12 days/month for each month thereafter.

District of Columbia:
[8] Before June 20, 1994, felon received good time based on sentence structure. After June 20, 1994 no good time.

Florida:
[9] Basic good time accrues 10 days/month. Meritorious good time can be awarded up to 60 days.

Hawaii:
[10] Varies by paroling authority.

Idaho:
[11] Meritorious time only, for prisoners sentenced after 1986.

Illinois:
[12] First degree murder—no good time credit; other serious offenses (e.g., attempt to commit first degree murder, aggravated kidnapping)—no more than 4-5 days per month; other offenses that resulted in great bodily harm to victim (e.g., aggravated vehicular hijacking)—no more than 4-5 days per month; remaining offenses—day for day.

Indiana:
[13] Various meritorious times for education.

Maine:
[14] Parole was abolished in 1976, but the Parole Board still exists for pre-1976 cases.

Maryland:
[15] Up to 10 days good time, plus 5 days work time, plus 5 days education good time accrual possible in one month.

Michigan:
[16] Unless the offense was committed prior to April of 1987, the concept of "good time" is irrelevant to prison sentences. Most prisoners sentenced for offenses committed between April 1987 and December 15, 1998, are eligible to earn "disciplinary credits" of up to 84 days per year. For certain enumerated offenses committed on or after December 15, 1998, prisoners who are convicted of these offenses cannot earn disciplinary credit, are subject to "disciplinary time," and will not be eligible for parole until service of the entire minimum sentence imposed by the court. Effective for all felony offenses committed on or after December 15, 2000, prisoners will not earn disciplinary credit, are subject to disciplinary time, and will not be eligible for parole until service of the entire minimum sentence imposed by the court is completed. This concept is also known as Truth in Sentencing.

Mississippi:
[17] On July 1, 2000 the Department of Corrections was scheduled to assume all powers of the parole board (§47-7-53).

Missouri:
[18] Policy of good time credit determined by Department of Corrections.

Nevada:
[19] For terms over 270 days; slower accumulation rates for shorter sentences.

New Jersey:
[20] Custody credits are applied by a formula which takes into account the length of the original sentence, jail credits prior to sentence imposition, and work credits.

New York:
[21] Expires and repealed effective 9/1/99.
[22] Repeated effective 9/30/2005.

North Carolina:
[23] At discretion of Department of Corrections or Prison custodian, may reduce up to minimum term of imprisonment.

Oklahoma:
[24] Parole Board makes recommendation to Governor, who has discretionary release authority. Governor not bound by Board.
[25] Scale depending on class of inmate: 4 classes. 1 credit = 1 day. Class 1: if crime committed before 7/1/98 = 0 credits; on/after 7/1/98 = 0 credits; Class 2: if crime committed before 7/1/98 = 22 credits/month; on/after 7/1/98 = 3 credits/month; Class 3: if crime committed before 7/1/98 = 33 credits/month; on/after 7/1/98 = 5 credits/month; Class 4: if crime committed before 7/1/98 = 44 credits/month; on/after 7/1/98 = 4 credits/month.

Oregon:
[26] Yes/no (pre-sentence guidelines yes; post-sentence guidelines no).
[27] If confined to county facility.
[28] Scale depending on length of sentence: 10-30 days = 1 day for 10 served; 30-90 days = 3 days for 30 served; 90-180 days = 4 days for 30 served; 180-270 days = 5 days for 30 served; 270 + days = 6 days for 30 served.

Puerto Rico:
[29] For good behavior (1) for a sentence not in excess of 15 years, 12 days per month; (2) for 15 years or more, 13 days per month.

Rhode Island:
[30] Governor does not have power to commute a LWOP sentence to a term of years.
[31] Number of days of good time earned each month is equal to the number of years of sentence. Can earn 2 additional days per month for participation in institutional industries program.

South Carolina:
[32] Governor does not have power to commute a LWOP sentence to a term of years.
[33] Twenty days for 30 days served, in addition: 1 day for 2 days work credits; 1 day for 2 days education credit.

South Dakota:
[34] Has a graduated scale of reductions from sentence for good conduct. 4 months per year served for years 1-10; 6 months per year after 10 years. Pro-rated.

Tennessee:
[35] Not more than 8 days per month for good behavior, and not more than 8 days per month for program performance.

TABLE 8.10

Good time accumulation and parole [CONTINUED]

FOOTNOTES:

Texas:

[36] Depends on inmate classification: 1) 20 days for 30 served with possibility of 10 more days if trusty; 2) 20 days for 30 served if Class I; 3) 10 days for 30 served if Class II; 4) none if Class IV. All earn 15 more days per month if participants diligently in programs.

Utah:

[37] For misdemeanors only.

[38] Five days for 30 days served; if less than 30 days, 2 days for every 10 days served.

Vermont:

[39] Governor does not have power to commute a LWOP sentence to a term of years.

[40] 5 days/month; plus may earn 10 more days reduction if inmate participates in educational, vocational, or treatment programs. Serves to reduce number of days of minimum and maximum term.

Virginia:

[41] For crimes committed after July 1981; Level I: day for day; Level II: 20 days good time/30 days served; Level III: 20 days good time/30 days served; Level IV: no good time.

SOURCE: "Good Time Accumulation and Parole" in *State Court Organization 1998*, Bureau of Justice Statistics, U.S. Department of Justice, Washington, D.C., 2000

CHAPTER 9
SENTENCING

Congress decided to hit the problem of drugs, as they saw it, with a sledgehammer, making no allowance for the circumstances of any particular case.... Under the statutory minimum, it can make no difference whether he is a lifetime criminal or a first-time offender. Indeed, under this sledgehammer approach, it could make no difference if the day before making this one slip in an otherwise unblemished life, defendant had rescued fifteen children from a burning building, or had won the Congressional Medal of Honor while defending his country.

—U.S. District Judge J. Spencer Letts, on having to impose a ten-year sentence on a situational offender.

Of federal offenders from October 1997 to September 1998, the average sentence imposed was 58.8 months. On average, the longest sentences were imposed for violent offenses (84.2 months), followed by drug offenses (78.8 months) and nonregulatory public order offenses (48.1 months). When measured in terms of median sentences (50 percent are higher, and 50 percent are lower), violent offenders and drug offenders each received 57 months, followed by nonregulatory public order offenses (26 months) and nonfraudulent property offenses (18.5 months).

On average, males in federal court were sentenced to longer terms (61.8 months) than females (36.2 months). Blacks received higher average sentences than whites for all offenses. Black violent offenders were sentenced nearly twice as severely (90.2 months) than white violent offenders (46.7 months). Similarly, black drug offenders received, on average, about 110 months, versus 61.8 months for white drug offenders. This disparity is just as pronounced when measured by medium sentences, with blacks receiving 60 months versus 27 months for white for violent offenses, and 78 months versus 41 months for whites for drug offenses.

Sentences were the harshest for violent offenders 16 to 18 years old, who received an average of 107.1 months and a median sentence of 60 months. Federal offenders

aged 40 years or older received the harshest average sentences for drug offenses, at 79.8 months.

Those with prior adult convictions received significantly longer sentences for all offenses. High school graduates were sentenced more severely than offenders with either less or more education.

SENTENCING GUIDELINES

Legislatively created commissions develop presumptive sentencing guidelines. These guidelines lay out the sentence structure within which a judge must operate. They also contain enforcement mechanisms. If judges want to depart from the sentences recommended in the guidelines for a particular offender, they must hold a hearing to determine whether the facts warrant such a decision.

The main goal of presumptive sentencing guidelines is to impose just punishment on convicted offenders. For punishment to be just it must be proportionate, uniform, and neutral. To be proportionate serious crimes should be punished more severely than minor crimes, and repeat offenders should be punished more severely than first-time offenders. To be uniform punishment for similar offenders must be similar, and variations should be allowed only for very relevant reasons. To be neutral punishments should not vary because of such factors as race, gender, and/or ethnicity.

IMPACT OF GUIDELINES ON SENTENCING PRACTICES

According to *The Impact of Sentencing Guidelines* (Dale Parent et al., National Institute of Justice, 1996), most evaluations of presumptive guidelines have had a mixed, but generally positive, record in the following areas:

- Achieving adherence to the guidelines by judges and other justice system officials—Studies show that judges, even those who publicly criticize the guidelines, adhere to them at a high rate.

• Improving sentencing neutrality—Virtually all studies of presumptive guidelines report sentencing uniformity and proportionality. However, it is difficult to compare sentencing patterns before and after guidelines took effect because general sentencing practices have become harsher. In addition, to avoid having to impose the sentencing guidelines in some cases, many officials reduced the charges to lesser offenses.

• Improving sentencing neutrality—In Minnesota, the first state to implement presumptive guidelines, racial, ethnic, and gender differences declined, even though minority defendants were still more likely to be imprisoned due to departures from the guidelines. Also, men were still more likely to receive longer sentences than similarly situated women. An analysis of the U.S. Sentencing Commission guidelines found no compelling evidence of racial or ethnic bias in sentencing at the federal level. However, blacks received longer sentences because of the differences in the mandatory minimums imposed for crack cocaine and powder cocaine.

• Altering sentencing patterns in intended ways—Commissions in Minnesota, Oregon, and Washington intended to reduce imprisonment sentences for property offenders and increase them for violent offenders. In all three states these outcomes were achieved. At the federal level the sentencing commission sought to increase use of imprisonment and decrease the use of probation and succeeded in meeting these goals. However, Minnesota's experience suggests that, when judicial departures from the guidelines are allowed, reversions to previous practices occur.

State legislators want to respond to voters' fear of crime and demands for tougher punishments while recognizing the need to limit spiraling correctional costs. Given these concerns elected officials are interested in sentencing guidelines. When properly developed presumptive sentencing guidelines can link the severity of punishment more rationally to the seriousness of crimes. They can modify the use of punishment so that available prison capacity is used for more serious and habitual offenders. They can ensure that punishments are applied more uniformly and more equitably.

TRUTH-IN-SENTENCING LAWS

Truth in sentencing supposedly lets offenders and the public know exactly how many years an inmate will be serving. For example, in states such as Connecticut, Florida, Illinois, Louisiana, Mississippi, New York, North Dakota, South Carolina, and Tennessee, laws require 85 percent of a sentence to be served. These laws usually apply to serious violent criminals; however, all prison inmates in Florida, Mississippi, and Ohio fall under mandatory sentencing requirements. In Arkansas offend-

ers serve 70 percent of the sentence given. South Carolina has "no parole offenses" for which the offenders must serve 95 percent of their sentences and at least 80 percent before qualifying for work-release programs.

According to *Truth in Sentencing in State Prisons* (Bureau of Justice Statistics, 1999), four states—Indiana, Maryland, Nebraska, and Texas—have a 50 percent requirement, and three states—Idaho, Nevada, and New Hampshire—have a 100 percent requirement, on the minimum sentence. (See Table 4.18.)

SENTENCE LENGTH AS A FACTOR OF DEFENSE COUNSEL

In *Defense Counsel in Criminal Cases* (Bureau of Justice Statistics Special Report, November 2000), Caroline Wolf Harlow, Ph.D., reports that, from 1996 to 1998, most individuals charged with felony criminal offenses in state or federal courts were represented by counsel. Of those conviction rates were approximately the same for defendants represented by publicly financed attorneys and those represented by private lawyers. About 90 percent of federal defendants and 75 percent of state defendants in the 75 largest counties were found guilty, regardless of type of counsel.

The report found that more guilty defendants with publicly financed attorneys were sentenced to incarceration. In federal courts 88 percent of defendants with publicly financed counsel went to prison or jail while the rate for private attorneys was 77 percent. State court defendants with publicly financed lawyers were incarcerated at a rate of 72 percent compared to 54 percent for those with private attorneys. (See Table 9.1.)

Of defendants who went to prison in 1997, 73.4 state inmates were represented by court-appointed (publicly financed) attorneys, down slightly from 73.8 percent in 1991. (See Table 9.2.) Almost 23 percent of state prisoners in 1997 had private lawyers, a slight increase from 21.2 percent in 1991. Of federal inmates about two-thirds had publicly-financed counsel in 1997, up from 53.7 percent in 1991.

In 1996, although a greater share of guilty defendants with publicly financed attorneys were sent to state prison, they tended to serve shorter sentences than state inmates with private counsel. Overall, of 11,089 state inmates with publicly financed lawyers, the average mean sentence in was 31.2 months compared to 38.3 months for those with private attorneys. Similarly, the median state prison sentence for inmates with publicly financed attorneys was 16 months compared to 17 months for those with private counsel. Violent offenders in state prison who had publicly-financed counsel were sentenced to an average of 55.2 months in 1996 compared to 59.4 months for those with private attorneys.

Drug offenders with court-appointed lawyers were sentenced to an average of 25.3 months compared to 38.8 months for those with private attorneys.

In 1997 the same held true for both state and federal inmates. Overall, those with publicly financed attorneys served less time on average than those with private attorneys. (See Table 9.3.) The margins tended to be narrower for federal inmates in 1997, and violent offenders in federal prison in 1997 actually fared somewhat better on average with a private attorney (162 months) than with a publicly appointed attorney (164 months).

MANDATORY SENTENCING

By 1994 all 50 states had at least one mandatory sentencing law. These most often required prison terms for certain offenses and a minimum number of years the offenders must serve. Judges could not offer parole or other alternative sentencing for these crimes despite any mitigating (moderating) circumstance. In Alabama a person convicted of selling a small amount of drugs was

TABLE 9.1

Sentences for convicted defendants in the 75 largest counties of the United States by type of counsel, 1996

	Type of counsel	
Sentences	Public	Private
Incarcerated	71.3%	53.9%
Prison	31.0	23.6
Jail	40.2	30.3
Not incarcerated	28.7%	46.1%
Probation	27.8	43.3
Fine	1.0	2.9
Number of defendants	20,131	4,666

Note: Data were missing for 36.4% of cases and excluded for an additional 17.8% that were acquitted, dismissed, or not yet adjudicated.

SOURCE: Caroline Wolf Harlow, Ph.D., "Table 11. Sentences for convicted defendants in the Nation's 75 largest counties, by type of counsel, 1996" in "Defense Counsel in Criminal Cases," *Bureau of Justice Statistics Special Report,* U.S. Department of Justice, Washington, D.C., 2000

TABLE 9.2

Type of counsel for state and federal prison inmates, 1997 and 1991

	Percent of inmates in —			
	State prison		Federal prison	
Type of counsel	1997	1991	1997	1991
Court appointed	73.4%	73.8%	60.3%	53.7%
Inmate hired	22.7	21.2	36.4	42.1
Both appointed and hired	1.6	2.1	2.1	3.2
No counsel	2.2	2.9	1.3	1.0
Number of prison inmates	1,048,236	702,116	88,483	53,342

SOURCE: Caroline Wolf Harlow, Ph.D., "Table 16. Type of counsel for state and federal prison inmates, 1997 and 1991" in "Defense Counsel in Criminal Cases," *Bureau of Justice Statistics Special Report,* U.S. Department of Justice, Washington, D.C., 2000

TABLE 9.3

Sentence length and total time to expected release, by offense and type of counsel, for state and federal inmates, 1997

	State inmates			Federal inmates		
	Maximum sentence[a]		Mean time to expected release[b]	Maximum sentence[a]		Mean time to expected release[b]
Offense and type of counsel	Median	Mean		Median	Mean	
Total						
Private	120 mo	179 mo	96 mo	96 mo	126 mo	104 mo
Public	114	155	89	96	126	106
Violent offenses						
Private	180 mo	231 mo	131 mo	156 mo	162 mo	150 mo
Public	180	223	133	120	164	134
Property offenses						
Private	84 mo	128 mo	68 mo	36 mo	59 mo	43 mo
Public	72	118	64	36	59	52
Drug offenses						
Private	84 mo	140 mo	58 mo	114 mo	132 mo	111 mo
Public	60	97	46	108	126	107
Public-order offenses						
Private	54 mo	98 mo	50 mo	70 mo	119 mo	84 mo
Public	48	80	48	70	103	85

Note: Because data are restricted to persons in prison, they may overstate the average sentence and time to be served by those entering prison. Persons with shorter sentences leave prison more quickly, resulting in a longer average sentence among persons in the inmate sample.

[a] Based on the total maximum for all consecutive sentences. Means exclude prisoners sentenced to life or death.
[b] Based on time served when interviewed plus time to be served until the expected date of release. Excludes prisoners sentenced to life without expected release or to death.

SOURCE: Caroline Wolf Harlow, Ph.D., "Table 18. Sentence length and total time to expected release, by offense and type of counsel, for state and federal inmates, 1997" in "Defense Counsel in Criminal Cases," *Bureau of Justice Statistics Special Report,* U.S. Department of Justice, Washington, D.C., 2000

sentenced to two years, with an additional five years if the sale was made within three miles of a school or housing project and another five years if the sale was within three miles of both.

Federal mandatory minimum drug sentences for first-time offenders included five years with no parole for one gram of LSD, 100 plants or 100 kilos of marijuana, 5 grams of crack cocaine, and 100 grams of heroin. Five years were added to a drug sentence if the offender carried a gun during a drug offense. Michigan gave a life sentence to offenders convicted of delivering more than 650 grams of cocaine or heroin. Although aimed at kingpins (heads of narcotics rings), the law often hit youthful first-time offenders. Kingpins were often prosecuted under laws with lesser penalties as they plea bargained by turning in other dealers. Low-level dealers or addicts caught with them usually had very few names to "deal" (exchange names of other offenders for a reduction in charges).

Judge Stanley Sporkin, U.S. District Judge, upon sentencing a single homeless mother, Renee Jackson, whose sole remuneration was to be leftover drugs, remarked that he did not know if the government had made any efforts to bring to justice any of the drug kingpins who were ultimately responsible for Jackson's possession of drugs. Judge Sporkin further summarized that, too frequently, "this Court and other district courts find themselves sentencing underlings to substantial sentences while the drug overlords remain at large. In this case, and unfortunately too many others, the government seeks to justify a severe and disproportionate sentence by pointing to the need to fight the drug war. I will not treat the Renee Jacksons of the nation as stand-ins for drug kingpins simply because those genuinely deserving of harsh sentences are not before me. The drug war simply cannot be won on the backs of Renee Jackson and others like her."

IMPACT OF MANDATORY SENTENCING

Opponents of mandatory sentencing argue that judges can no longer take into account mitigating circumstances, reduce sentences, use alternative sentences, or assign the offender to parole. They argue that mandatory sentencing does not have a deterrent effect. A 1992 Delaware study showed that, despite mandatory drug-sentencing laws, there was no reduction in drug arrests, sales, or use, but there was an increase in the prison population. States sometimes may not realize that mandatory sentencing laws add significant costs to the corrections system. In Louisiana an impact statement had to accompany any mandatory sentencing bills on how the law would affect trials, budgets, and prisons.

Federal Findings on Mandatory Sentencing

Mandatory sentencing exists side by side with sentencing guidelines. The Sentencing Reform Act of 1984

(PL 98-473) created the United States Sentencing Commission, an independent, expert commission designed to set criminal penalties (sentencing guidelines). Because Congress enacted mandatory minimums to show it was tough on crime before the first set of sentencing guidelines was issued, the commission automatically incorporated many of the mandatory minimum sentences into its guidelines. Chief Justice William Rehnquist (National Symposium on Drugs and Violence in America, 1993) commented:

> Mandatory minimums ... are frequently the result of floor amendments to demonstrate that legislators want to "get tough on crime." Just as frequently they do not involve any careful consideration of the effect they might have on the Sentencing Guidelines as a whole. Indeed, it seems to me that one of the best arguments against any more mandatory minimums, and perhaps against some of those that we already have, is that they frustrate the careful calibration of sentences, from one end of the spectrum to the other, which the Sentencing Guidelines were intended to accomplish.

NOT EFFECTIVE. According to the Federal Judicial Center (Barbara S. Vincent and Paul J. Hofer, *The Consequences of Mandatory Minimum Prison Terms: a Summary of Recent Findings*, Washington, D.C., 1994), federal mandatory minimum-sentence statutes have not helped reduce crime or drug availability, but have helped to incapacitate the most dangerous offenders. In New York the mandatory minimum drug laws increased both the probability of incarceration upon conviction and the severity of the sentences imposed.

Not wanting to send small-time offenders away for long prison terms, many police, prosecutors, and judges have not always arrested, indicted, or convicted as many as they might have if the sentences had not been so strict. The result has been that the overall probability of imprisonment after the law's enactment is lower than before the law. Nonetheless, the number arrested, indicted, and convicted is still rising.

In addition, conventional assumptions of deterrence theory may not apply to high-level drug traffickers. To be deterred offenders must stop to weigh the costs and benefits, be aware of the penalties, find those penalties intolerable, and have other more attractive options. Very few of the offenders convicted under the federal mandatory minimum-standards statutes are organizers or leaders of an extensive drug operation.

Most drug offenders do not manage or supervise trafficking activity. In the profitable drug business there are always replacements for the low-level drug dealers when they are arrested. These low-level offenders are the types who are easily replaced in a drug ring and whose removal by arrest does not disrupt drug distribution. The arrests do not act as a deterrent for those who control the drug trade.

Chief Justice William Rehnquist stated (June 18, 1993) that these laws were "perhaps a good example of the law of unintended consequences." Researchers maintain that every year there is evidence that mandatory minimums result in the lengthy incarceration of thousands of low-level offenders. These offenders could be effectively sentenced to shorter periods at an annual savings of several hundred million dollars.

In addition, researchers argue that the mandatory minimums do not narrowly target violent criminals or major drug traffickers. Proponents of mandatory sentences believe that the negative side effects are exaggerated and that mandatory minimums serve an important symbolic function and have a broad deterrent effect.

Mandatory Minimum Sentences for Drug Offenses

RAND Corporation is a nonprofit institute in Santa Monica, California, that "helps improve public policy through research and analysis." In its 1997 publication *Mandatory Minimum Drug Sentences—Throwing Away the Key or the Taxpayers' Money?*, Jonathan Caulkins, C. Peter Rydell, William Schwabe, and James Chiesa evaluated the "cost-effectiveness of mandatory minimum sentences" in relationship to crimes connected to cocaine distribution.

The analysis concluded that "mandatory minimum sentences are not justifiable on the basis of cost-effectiveness at reducing cocaine consumption, cocaine expenditure, or drug-related crime." As projected from the research, at first, prices of cocaine would go up as drug dealers would want to be compensated for their increased risk because of potential longer sentencing. As prices went up consumption immediately would go down. Benefits from reduced consumption would be immediate, while the costs for more prison cells would be in the future. If more users were treated the immediate price of treatment would be higher, and the savings from reduced consumption would be in the future. At two years out treatment and longer mandatory sentences would reduce consumption at equal levels for the same amount of money; at three years out conventional sentencing and longer sentences would reduce consumption at the same level. At 15 years, per million dollars spent, treatment would reduce consumption by over 100 kilograms, longer sentences would reduce consumption by almost 13 kilograms, and conventional enforcement would reduce consumption by more than 27 kilograms.

When the same analysis was applied to higher-level dealers, those who run the drug distribution system, there were similar results. Mandatory minimum sentences for higher-level dealers (federal mandatory sentences) lessened consumption more than longer sentences for all drug dealers. However, longer mandatory sentences at all levels of government were less cost-effective than conventional methods.

The researchers found that mandatory minimums were cost-effective only if arrest costs were more than $30,000 and dealers valued their time at more than $250,000 annually. For dealers making less and costing less to arrest, taxpayers' money would be better spent on conventional methods of corrections; for dealers at the lower end, the money would be better spent on treatment.

Mandatory Minimums Are Not Applied Uniformly

Mandatory minimum penalties, combined with a power to grant exceptions, create a prospect of inverted sentencing. The more serious the defendant's crimes, the lower the sentence—because the greater his wrongs, the more information and assistance he has to offer to a prosecutor. Discounts for the top dogs have the virtue of necessity, because what makes the post-discount sentencing structure topsy-turvy is the mandatory minimum, binding only for the hangers on. What is to be said for such terms, which can visit draconian penalties on the small fry without increasing prosecutors' ability to wring information from their bosses? Our case illustrates a sentencing inversion. Such an outcome is neither illegal nor unconstitutional, because offenders have no right to be sentenced in proportion to their wrongs.... Still, meting out the harshest penalties to those least culpable is troubling because it accords with no one's theory of appropriate punishments.

— Judge Frank J. Easterbook, U.S. Court of Appeals for the Seventh Circuit

A major goal of federal sentencing reform was to reduce disparity in sentencing; however, the federal mandatory minimums have been applied inconsistently. Charges carrying mandatory minimum sentences are often not pursued. Charges may be dropped after indictment, usually through a process of plea-bargaining in which a defendant agrees to plead guilty to a lesser charge or to cooperate with the government and assist in prosecuting another offender.

The sentences applied may be fair sentences; however, the discretion is no longer in the hands of the judge but in those of the prosecutor, who may use mandatory sentencing as a tool to intimidate the accused or force plea bargaining.

Disparate Impact on Non-White Offenders

Studies by both the Sentencing Commission and the Federal Judicial Center have found that, among offenders who engaged in conduct warranting a mandatory minimum, white offenders were less likely than blacks or Hispanics to receive the mandatory minimum term. Statutes having a disparate impact on blacks include those that make offenses involving five or more grams of crack cocaine (a weekend's supply to a serious abuser) subject to the same mandatory minimum term of 56 years in prison, as offenses involving 100 times that amount of powder cocaine.

Because blacks are more likely to be prosecuted for crack offenses and whites for powder cocaine offenses, the longer sentence lengths for smaller amounts of crack lead to longer prison terms for blacks. Two other factors have the unintended consequence of reducing sentences for whites more than blacks: the discount afforded defendants who plead guilty and the discount for defendants who cooperate and provide substantial assistance. Whites tend to plead guilty and receive motions for reduction for cooperation more frequently than do blacks.

The Department of Justice, however, found no significant differences in sentence lengths for black defendants and white defendants who plead guilty. Questions that need to be asked are

- Is crack cocaine sufficiently more dangerous than powder cocaine to justify harsher treatment?

- Should defendants who exercise their right to trial get longer sentences than those who plead guilty?

- Could ways be found to minimize the adverse impact of current policies on cooperation, for example, by taking into account the willingness of small-time drug defendants to cooperate and tell all they know, even though they are too low-level to have any useful information? All too often kingpins who possess a lot of information are willing to talk to get reduced sentences, while low-level pushers get long mandatory terms because they have no information with which to bargain.

Weight of Drugs

An offender who sells 10 grams of heroin mixed with 89 grams of sugar has no required mandatory minimum term; the minimum for an offender who sells 10 grams of heroin mixed with 90 grams of sugar is five years. The courts struggle with cases in which the weight of suitcases in which drugs are hidden, wash-water used to clean drug laboratory equipment, or paper wrapping that weighs hundreds of times as much as the drugs, are added to the weight of the drugs in order to increase the sentence. Using the weight of mixtures penalizes persons lower in the distribution chain who typically dilute the drug. Atmospheric humidity and the type of paper used to carry the drug can dramatically affect the sentences.

Recommendations

In an April 1997 report to Congress the United States Sentencing Commission concluded that the five-gram trigger should be increased to better target serious dealers. For powder cocaine the commission suggested that the trigger for the five-year mandatory sentence should be less than 500 grams. The commission stated:

Because nearly all cocaine is initially distributed in powder form until some later time in the distribution chain when some is then converted to crack, the Com-

mission believes that it is appropriate to increase penalty levels for trafficking in powder cocaine to partially reflect the greater harms associated with crack and to reduce unwarranted sentencing disparity between powder and crack cocaine traffickers. In addition, the ease with which powder cocaine is converted to crack cocaine also suggests that some increase in powder cocaine penalties may be appropriate....

The Commission reiterated its 1995 conclusion that, when applicable, guideline enhancements should be used to account for harms related to crack and powder cocaine offenses with less reliance put on drug quantity. For example, any cocaine trafficker who possesses or uses a firearm or other dangerous weapon during a drug crime ought to receive a substantially enhanced sentence. Other factors, such as the use of juveniles in a drug-trafficking offense, a defendant's prior drug-trafficking convictions, or a defendant's role in the offense, all are important in determining an appropriate drug sentence.

Vice Chairman Michael S. Gelacak, in a concurring opinion of the Commission's report, said that, while he supported "severe sentences for serious criminal conduct," he opposed "a penalty structure that results in unfair sentences." He continued:

During the year 1993, of those sentenced for crack cocaine, 88.3 percent were black and 95.4 percent were nonwhite. Even although the commission has conceded that there was no intent by the legislature that penalties fall disproportionately on one segment of the population, the impact of these penalties nonetheless remains. It is a little like punishing vehicular homicide while under the influence of alcohol more severely if the defendant had become intoxicated by ingesting cheap wine rather than Scotch whiskey. That suggestion is absurd on its face and ought to be no less so when the abused substance is cocaine.... The current policy focuses law enforcement efforts on the lowest level of the distribution line—the street dealer. Unless we ignore all evidence to the contrary, the current policy has little or no impact upon the drug abuse problem. The jails are full....

OPINIONS ON MANDATORY SENTENCING AND SENTENCING GUIDELINES

According to a 1995 survey (Survey Research Program, College of Criminal Justice, Sam Houston University), more than one-half of the respondents thought that mandatory sentences were a good idea, while just over one-third believed judges should decide the sentences. Blacks, younger people, those with less than a high-school education, and those earning less than $15,000 annually were more likely to want a judge to decide the case.

Federal Judicial Center's Survey

In 1996 the Federal Judicial Center surveyed federal district and circuit judges and chief probation officers for their opinions on the federal sentencing guidelines. In general the study found that respondents disliked that the prosecutors had so much discretion in determining charges. Narrative responses to open-ended questions reflected frustration with the power and discretion held by prosecutors under the guidelines in determining the charges. The second guideline in which the district judges wanted substantive change was the use of quantity in drug cases.

Some respondents commented:

The excessive power granted prosecutors by the guidelines scheme has resulted in a situation where the Court is viewed as a rubber stamp for the prosecutors' determination.... As a practical matter, prosecutors, by charging or not charging, by bargaining or not bargaining, and by making facts known—or failing to make facts known, control the ultimate sentence. Any system that permits such a result is wrong.

The respondents preferred advisory guidelines (52 percent of circuit judges, 67 percent of district judges, and 68 percent of probation officers) to mandatory penalties (0.2 percent of district judges and none of the others). Other choices (7 percent to 27 percent of the respondents) were "discretion-based sentencing with or without parole" and "other."

Responding to the question: "To what classes of offenders do you think alternatives to incarceration should be made available?" (the respondents could check more than one answer), most district judges (63.5 percent) and chief probation officers (56.1 percent) thought first-time offenders should be eligible. They were not in favor of fines being used instead of prison terms, but were agreeable to community confinement, boot camps, and home detention.

CHAPTER 10
"THREE STRIKES" LAWS

"THREE STRIKES AND YOU'RE OUT"

Public concern with the increase in violent crime has led state and federal lawmakers to pass legislation increasing penalties for criminal offenses, particularly violent crimes. Many states have adopted policies to lock up three-time felons for life without parole. These policies are referred to as the "three strikes and you're out" laws. (The baseball term "three strikes and you're out" was used during the campaign in Washington State in 1993, in which voters approved a Persistent Offender Act requiring life sentences with no parole for three-time serious felony offenders.) The purpose of these laws is to remove from society for long periods of time, and in many cases, for life, offenders convicted repeatedly of serious offenses. Washington State and California were the first states to implement the "three strikes" laws in 1993 and 1994 respectively. In Washington all three strikes must be for felonies specifically listed in the legislation. Under the California law only the first two convictions need to be from the state's list of "strikeable" offenses. Any subsequent felony can count as the third strike.

In 1997 John Clark, James Austin, and D. Alan Henry, in "'Three Strikes and You're Out': A Review of State Legislation" (National Institute of Justice, September 1997), studied variations in the "three strikes" laws in the 24 states that had legalized this legislation. They found that, although statutes may have the same title, "three strikes and you're out" can have different meanings in different states. For example, Georgia (and a number of other states) has a "two strikes" law, and California's "three strikes" law has a twist: it provides for doubling of sentences on a second felony conviction.

Strike Zone

A strike zone refers to the crimes that constitute a strike and under what conditions those crimes become a strike. A strike generally is a serious offense, such as a vio-lent felony, including murder, rape, robbery, arson, aggravated assault, and carjacking. Offenders convicted repeatedly of such crimes, usually violent and career criminals, may be incarcerated for many years or, in some cases, for life. These crimes apply in all 24 states that have enacted strikes laws. However, some states have included other offenses, such as the sale of drugs to minors (California), any drug offense punishable by imprisonment for more than five years (Louisiana), treason (Washington state), and embezzlement and bribery (South Carolina).

Number of Strikes Needed to Be "Out"

There are variations in the number of strikes required to be "out." In South Carolina a person convicted a second time for any of a list of "most serious offenses" is sentenced to life without parole. In North Dakota two convictions of a felony can bring about an extended sentence. There is no third strike. Three strikes are required to be "out" in 20 states. However, seven states—Arkansas, California, Connecticut, Kansas, Montana, Pennsylvania, and Tennessee—also have increased sentences for two strikes, depending upon the offense.

What It Means to Be "Out"

States also vary in the punishments meted out when enough strikes have accumulated. Twelve states—Georgia, Indiana, Louisiana, Maryland, Montana, New Jersey, North Carolina, South Carolina, Tennessee, Virginia, Washington, and Wisconsin—impose mandatory life sentences with no possibility of parole. (Virginia law provides for the release of prisoners 65 years of age and older who have served a specified length of time. In North Carolina a law separate from the three-strikes statute allows those sentenced to life without parole to a review of their sentences after serving 25 years.)

In three states—California, Colorado, and New Mexico—parole is possible after an offender has struck out, but only after an offender has been incarcerated for a long period of time. In California a minimum of 25 years must be served; in Colorado, 40 years; and in New Mexico, 30 years.

Some States Have Increased Penalties

While most three-strikes laws demand mandatory minimum sentences, Arkansas, Connecticut, Kansas, and Nevada passed laws increasing the possible penalties for multiple convictions for particular serious felonies, but leave the actual sentence to the discretion of the court.

A judge in Connecticut can sentence an offender to 40 years in prison for a second conviction for certain serious felonies, and to life imprisonment for a third such conviction. In Arkansas judges may select either a mandatory sentence short of life imprisonment or a life sentence for a second or third strikeable offense.

The Kansas legislature passed sentencing guidelines that provide judges with a sentencing range based on the offense and the offender's prior record. An amendment permits judges to double guideline sentences for offenders convicted of certain listed violent felonies for a second time, and triple them for a third conviction. Nevada law allows judges the option on a third-strike conviction of imposing a life sentence with parole possible after 10 years, or a 25-year sentence with parole possible after 10 years. Five states—Florida, North Dakota, Pennsylvania, Utah, and Vermont—permit sentences ranging up to life, depending upon the state, when certain violent offenses are committed by repeat offenders.

Opinions of the "Three Strikes" Laws

The "three-strikes" law is popular with politicians because it makes them appear tough on crime. The public seems to favor the laws, too. People in California and Washington voted for the laws at the polls. However, Brandon Applegate et al., in "Assessing Public Support for Three Strikes and You're Out Laws: Global versus Specific Attitudes" (*Crime and Delinquency,*. 42, no. 4, October 1996), found that, when questioned more closely, people supported the broad idea of the "three-strikes" concept but when presented with individual cases they often did not think sentencing the offender to life in prison was necessary.

Given individual scenarios only 7 percent thought life imprisonment was the appropriate punishment. Most supported 5–15 years in prison (24 percent for five years; 18 percent for 10 years, and 12 percent for 15 years). One scenario was a man who had been convicted of attempted aggravated burglary. While carrying a gun he had attempted to burglarize $400 worth of property from an occupied home. His previous crimes had been a similar burglary and rape. The respondents took into account various circumstances, such as the nature of the offenses, length of time between crimes, characteristics of offender (mentally retarded; an older person), and the effect on the institutions (overcrowding of prisons).

Supporters of a "three-strikes law" think that it will protect the public by imprisoning habitual dangerous offenders and at the same time deter repeat offenders. They believe such legislation will save money because it will decrease the number of times certain offenders go through the system. In addition proponents of the laws believe that justice is served when habitual offenders are locked up for life.

Opponents of the law argue that increasing the time served has not affected the violent crime rates. The penalty for the "third strike" is too harsh for criminals convicted of certain felonies, such as nonviolent crimes like drug possession. In addition murderers are often set free to make room for more prisoners, while the "three-strikes" laws lock up for life those who have perhaps committed three robberies in their life, netting only hundreds of dollars. Critics believe the costs to the criminal justice system would be better spent on other alternatives and that the present habitual offender laws should incarcerate the truly dangerous offenders.

Also, older offenders who are beyond the peak ages of criminal activity would take up prison space. The Sentencing Project, a group that supports alternatives to prison sentences, holds that the new laws will not have much effect on violent crime because most violent crime is committed by young first offenders. As they become older, criminals usually do not commit acts of violence.

Marc Mauer of the Sentencing Project claims that prosecutors often do not plea bargain for lesser charges with two-time felons who have minor roles in drug operations because they have no useful information. These low-level offenders get mandatory life sentences, while the high-level dealers who bargain for a lesser charge in exchange for information get a reduced charge and avoid the sentencing impact of the "three-strike" laws.

IMPACT OF "THREE STRIKES AND YOU'RE OUT"

According to Walter Dickey and Pam Stiebs Hollenhorst, in "Three-Strikes Laws: Massive Impact in California and Georgia, Little Elsewhere" (*Overcrowded Times,*. 9, no. 6, December 1998), three-strikes laws are used most often in California and Georgia. (California has made more use of the law than other states, either due to the broad nature of the law or because other states already have harsh penalties in place with habitual offender laws.) In California and Georgia three-strikes laws have had important effects on prison populations, racial disparities, system crowding, plea bargaining, and other aspects of the justice system.

Besides these two states 15 states reported six or fewer convictions under their three-strikes laws, and three (Montana, Utah, and Virginia) reported no convictions in

TABLE 10.1

Use of "Three-Strikes" types of laws

Jurisdiction	Year Law Enacted	Data Current as of:	Number of convictions	Comments
Alaska	1996	8/98	1	Although adopted following following the wave of get-tough-on-crime legislation, Alaska faces prison overcrowding issues, and the law was narrowly tailored—all strikes must be for serious felonies, and a third strike earns a 40 to 99 year sentence.
Arkansas	1995	8/98	12	Two-strike provision allows 40 year sentence without parole; three strikes allows life sentence without parole. More frequently used is a habitual offender law that permits both graduated increases in length of sentences and reductions in parole eligibility.
California	1994	7/30/98	40,511	Second-strike convictions; 36,043 Third-strike convictions: 4,468
Colorado	1994	8/98	2	Used more often are Colorado's "big" and "little" habitual offender laws, under which 36 persons were sentenced in 1997.
Connecticut	1994	8/98	1	Connecticut does not have a mandatory-life type of law; instead its law permits enhanced sentences for persistent offenders by upgrading the felony one higher grade, e.g., a class B felony (10-20 years) becomes a class A (life sentence). There is one known person sentenced but may be others; an exact number is not extractable from the DOC database.
Florida	1995	6/98	116	In contrast, under Florida's 1988 habitual offender law, 23,000 persons have been sentenced (about 20 percent of the state prison population). The 1988 law allows for an imposition of a sentence double the statutory minimum for crimes committed.
Georgia	1994 One Strike and Two Strikes	3/31/98	57 serving life without parole for 2nd strike; 885 serving 20 years or more for a first strike.	Georgia's law covers "seven deadly sins" for which a first strike earns a minimum of 10 years without parole, and a second strike earns life without parole. Of the 1,833 persons serving various terms for a first strike, 617 were sentenced to life (with parole eligibility after 14 years), 7 were sentenced to 50 years or more, and 261 were sentenced to 20 years or more.
Indiana	1994 Life without parole	7/1/98	38	Indiana's habitual offender law is used more often; estimated at least 1,000 times over 20 years. It allows a sentencing enhancement for a person with two prior felonies, increasing the sentence up to three times the presumptive sentence for the underlying offense, not to exceed 30 years.
Louisiana	1994			DOC officials did not respond to request for information.
Maryland	1994 Four Strikes	12/97	1995: 3 1996: 1 1997: 1	Before 1994, about 250 people were sentenced under Maryland's 1975 law which provided for 25 years without parole for a third felony conviction. Amended in 1994, the law now provides for life without parole for a fourth strike when prison terms have been served for the first three strikes.
Montana	1995	8/98	0	Montana has a persistent offender statute that allows a sentence enhancement of 5-100 years to be served consecutively for certain repeat felons.
Nevada	1995	8/98	164 greater, 140 lesser, with parole options—see comment	Nevada has several life-sentence options under its "greater" and "lesser" habitual offender statutes which, depending on the nature of the crime, include life with no parole, life with parole possible after 10 years served, and 25 years with parole possible after serving 10.
New Jersey	1995	8/17/98	6	Another statute provides for a life sentence with parole eligibility after serving 30 years; as of 1/1/98, 1,029 persons were serving such sentences (this number may also include some persons sentenced before 1980 who may have been eligible for parole after 14 years under a prior version of the law).
New Mexico	1994	8/98	1	The offense and conditions that qualify for life with parole eligibility after 30 years are very restrictive. Pre-existing law provided for sentencing enhancements of 1, 4, and 8 years on second, third, and fourth convictions.
North Carolina	1994	12/97	5 in fiscal year 96-97	During this time, although only 5 persons were sentenced to life without parole as violent habitual felons under Three Strikes and You're In, 15 death sentences and 47 life without parole sentences were imposed. In addition, 248 were sentenced as habitual felons on a fourth felony conviction. Of these, the most frequently occurring serious crimes are Felony Breaking and/or Entering (48), Possession of Stolen Goods (18), and Felony Possession of Cocaine (19). It is believed that the law is used as a bargaining chip to elicit guilty pleas, and that there may be others who qualify for a three-strikes conviction.
Pennsylvania	1995	8/98	3 through 1996	Data set is currently being compiled; numbers not yet available for 1997 or 1998.
South Carolina	1995	10/97	2 Strikes: 13 3 Strikes: 1 "No Parole" offenses: 811	South Carolina's 1995 Crime Bill contained three provisions relevant to "Non-Parolable" Inmates: Life without parole for repeat violent offenders under the two/three strikes provisions, and a new category of "no parole" offense for crimes committed after 1/1/96 which includes felonies punishable by 20 years or more, irrespective of criminal history, a group that includes proportionally more younger offenders (205 or 15 percent of the 1,349 currently serving nonparolable offenses are 21 or younger; 396 or 30 percent of this group show no prior criminal history).

TABLE 10.1

Use of "Three-Strikes" types of laws [CONTINUED]

Jurisdiction	Year Law Enacted	Data Current as of:	Number of convictions	Comments
Tennessee	1994	7/13/98	5	Tennessee has both a second- and third-strike provision, both of which can mandate life without parole depending on the offense. The state also has a 1989 habitual offender statute under which 156 persons have been sentenced.
Utah	1995	8/98	0	Utah's flexible sentencing structure allows for three possible sentences: 1-5 years, 1-15 years, and 5 years to life, and most serious crimes earn a lengthy indeterminate sentence. The Board of Pardons and Parole determines the release date and virtually never grants pardons. Because of this scheme, there has also been little use of a sentencing enhancement law for repeat offenders which ratchets a second degree felony (1-15) up to a first degree felony (5-life), under which just 16 persons have been sentenced since 1990. Prosecutors know that they can bargain away a three-strike enhancement in exchange for a guilty plea because a dangerous person is unlikely to be released yearly.
Vermont	1995	8/98	4	Considered a "habitual offender law," it provides for up to life for certain third strikes and for any fourth felony conviction.
Virginia	1994	8/98	0	Shortly after the law was passed, Virginia eliminated parole for all sentences, effectively negating the need for a three-strikes law.
Washington	1993	8/21/98	121	Washington has also sentenced 3 persons under its Two Strike Sex Offender law.
Wisconsin	1994	8/98	3	Reported by DOC analyst though could not be confirmed by DOC databases. In contrast, Wisconsin's habitual offender statute which permits increased penalities for persistent repeaters was applied to over 300 offenders per year in the past 3 years.
Federal Law	1994	10/97	35	By September 30, 1996 (the end of FY 1996), there were a total of 35 convictions under three strikes. Figures for FY 1997 are not yet available.

SOURCE: Walter Dickey and Pam Stiebs Hollenhorst, "Data on Use of 'Three-Strikes' Type Laws" in "Three-Strikes Laws: Massive Impact in California and Georgia, Little Elsewhere," *Overcrowded Times,* Vol. 9, No. 6, December 1998

1998. Alaska, Connecticut, New Mexico, and South Carolina had implemented it only once. Only Florida, Nevada, and Washington reported more than 100 convictions. (See Table 10.1)

The federal three-strikes law resulted in only 35 convictions by 1996. According to a spokesperson for the Office of Public Affairs, U.S. Department of Justice, by October 1997 there were 59 federal three-strikes provision requests resulting in 35 convictions, 14 cases pending trial or sentencing, one acquittal, and nine cases withdrawn.

California

The most dramatic impact of the "three strikes and you're out" program has been in California, where by July 1998, there were 36,043 "second-strike" and 4,468 "third-strike" convictions. Since California treats any felony as a third-strike crime, the law is applied to many nonviolent, repeat felons. As an example, one resident of Redondo Beach, California, was convicted of a third strike for stealing a slice of pizza. Because the 27-year-old man had two prior robbery convictions, he was sentenced to 25 years to life under the three-strikes law.

As of March 1996 twice as many people had been sentenced for second- and third-strike marijuana possession (192) than the total combined number (89) of those sentenced for murder (40), rape (25), and kidnapping

(24). In all, 85 percent of those sentenced under the law were convicted of nonviolent offenses as their final strike. As of June 1998 the offenses that triggered the third strike continued to be mostly property and drug crimes. Among second-strike cases 37 percent were property crimes, 31 percent were drug crimes, and 19 percent were crimes against persons. Among third-strike cases, 39 percent were crimes against persons, 32 percent were property crimes, and 19 percent were drug crimes.

PRISON POPULATION AND SYSTEM CROWDING. The crime rate in California has been declining since the late 1900s, as it has for the nation. California's governor, secretary of state, and attorney general claim that three strikes is responsible for the decline. However, a 1997 statistical analysis by Lisa Stolzenberg and Steward J. D'Alessio, in "'Three Strikes and You're Out': The Impact of California's New Mandatory Sentencing Law on Serious Crime Rates" (*Crime and Delinquency,*. 43, no. 4, October 1997), found no indication in nine of the state's 10 largest cities that three strikes had reduced either serious crime or petty theft rates below levels that would be expected based on the downward trends.

Because of the downward trends prison projections have been revised downward, but much more prison space will be needed even to meet the revised estimates. Based on 1997 projections the prison system will experience a shortage of more than 70,000 beds by 2006. To keep capacity at its 1998 level, California will have to build 15 new prisons by 2002, at a cost of $4.5 billion, when, according to the Department of Corrections, one of four prisoners will be a second- or third-striker.

GOING TO TRIAL AND PLEA BARGAINING. The "Three Strikes and You're Out" law seems to have encouraged felony offenders to go to trial rather than plead guilty. In June 1997 the State Judicial Council reported that jury trials were up by 13 percent in the first fiscal year following passage of three strikes, and another 4 percent in the second full year. Because there is much less plea bargaining, more county jails are overcrowded as three-strike defendants awaiting trial are occupying limited jail space. Other consequences of fewer plea bargains are that court resources, such as judges, intended for civil cases must now be transferred to criminal cases, and space needed for trials of three-strikes cases overflow to civil court space. Some counties have been forced to temporarily stop hearing civil lawsuits because their civil-case courtrooms are not available.

More trials mean increased costs and more backlogs. In March 1997 Fresno County (Fresno) attempted to deal with its three-strikes backlog by transferring some cases to a mock courtroom at the San Joaquin College of Law in Clovis, California. Ventura County (Ventura) experienced a 50 percent increase in felony trials due to three-strikes legislation, resulting in nearly $1 million in budget overruns for the offices of the district attorney and the public defender. In 1998 Los Angeles County officials estimated the added costs for the first full year after the three-strikes law at more than $64 million. By 1998 one official estimated the cumulative cost to be $200 million.

Georgia

Georgia, while nowhere near California in terms of the number of people convicted under three-strikes legislation, has significantly increased its use of "one-strike" and "two-strikes" laws. The 1994 law covers "seven deadly sins" (murder or felony murder, armed robbery, kidnapping, rape, aggravated child molestation, aggravated sodomy, and aggravated sexual battery). For these crimes a first strike results in a minimum of 10 years without parole and a second strike brings life without parole. As of April 1998, 1,833 persons had been sentenced under the law and accounted for 4.4 percent of Georgia's 42,000 state prisoners. There has been no significant change in the Georgia prison population, as these inmates would be serving prison sentences anyway.

Most of the prisoners were serving time on a first strike for which they received sentences ranging from 10 years without parole to life with parole eligibility after 14 years. The average time to be served by first strikers is 16 years, and 21 percent will serve 20 years or more. The 57

persons who have been convicted a second time (and not convicted of capital murder) will serve life without parole.

Compared to Other Programs

The RAND Corporation (Peter Greenwood et al., *Diverting Children from a Life of Crime: What Are the Costs and Benefits?*, 1996) compared the cost-effectiveness of "three strikes and you're out" with long-term prevention programs designed to deter at-risk children from criminal activities. The study concluded that spending $1 million on constructing and operating prisons for repeat offenders would prevent 60 crimes annually.

Spending the same amount of money on parent-training programs could deter 157 crimes per year (parent-training programs cost an average of $3,000 per child), and investing $1 million in graduation-incentive programs could prevent 258 crimes annually (incentive programs typically cost about $12,500 per student). In addition, spending $1 million on programs to monitor the behavior of 12- and 13-year-old delinquents could avert 72 crimes annually.

Most researchers admit that the impact of the laws will not be known for many years as there are not yet enough statistics to prove the deterrence effect. Certainly, the costs of incarcerating more prisoners will increase. For many proponents of the law the deterrent effects will balance the costs. If there is no significant deterrent effect the building and operating of more prisons might not be worth the cost; however, if there is a significant deterrent effect, these costs might be worthwhile.

A CONSEQUENCE: ELDER CARE

In 1996, 24,641 prisoners were over 55 years of age, a 7 percent increase from 1992. While only 915 prisoners were older than 75 years of age, that number represented a 56 percent increase from 1992. As of 1996 about 2.5 percent of those in federal prisons were at least 60 years old. By 1997, in Florida, the oldest prisoner was 89 years of age, and more than 300 prisoners were in wheelchairs.

Prison officials fear that, with more mandatory determinate sentencing, more crimes requiring life terms, and the "three strikes and you're out" rule, prisons will be housing an ever-increasing number of elderly inmates. Jenni Gainsborough of the National Prison Project of the American Civil Liberties Union believes "it's all very foolish. Violent crime is a young man's game. We pay all this money to keep people in prison who could easily be safely living on the outside."

Prisons do not have the health-care facilities to provide the long-term care the elderly often require. One study found that 80 percent of those 63–80 years old claimed to have at least one medical problem, and 60 percent asserted that they had at least three. Prison administrators will have to deal with more patients with cancer, heart disease, mental incompetence, and Alzheimer's disease as prisoners age. Prisoners are not eligible for Medicare or Medicaid so the states will have to pay for the costs of health care for elderly prisoners, which are estimated to be three times the costs for younger prisoners.

Administrators wonder where the money and staff will come from to handle inmates with these special needs. Facilities will have to be modified or new sections built to house the elderly population. Access ramps, dormitories, or special cellblocks will have to be constructed not only to care for elderly inmates, but also to protect them from younger, more violent prisoners. More programs for those who cannot work or who have physical limitations will have to be implemented. Staff will also have to care for elderly inmates who are not ill, but who require care for their basic needs. Janet Thompson, attorney for Faye Copeland, the oldest woman on death row in 1996, commented that "the state's going to end up running a nursing home."

The question also arises as to what to do when elderly patients have served their sentences. After decades in prison, where do they go? Who will take care of them? Does the state have a right or responsibility to keep them in prison, or do the prisoners have a right to their freedom no matter what their physical or mental condition?

CHAPTER 11
ALTERNATIVE SENTENCING

Lawmakers increasingly are looking to corrections to develop and demonstrate safe, cost-effective alternatives to prison as a step toward getting corrections spending under control.

—Donna Hunzeker, Program Manager for Criminal Justice, National Conference of State Legislatures

If we recognize gradations in the seriousness of criminal behavior, then we should have gradations in sanctions as well. That's why we need a portfolio of intermediate punishments.... Intermediate punishments can provide the means by which we can hold offenders accountable for their illegal actions and achieve our goal of increasing public safety.

— Richard Thornburgh, former U.S. Attorney General, 1990

INCARCERATION VERSUS COMMUNITY SANCTIONS

Sentencing practices in the United States suggest that offenses can be divided into two categories. When the crime is relatively serious offenders are put behind bars; when it is less so they are put on probation—often with very little supervision. This twofold division disregards the range of severity in crime. As a result sentencing can often be either too harsh, incarcerating people whose crimes might not be serious enough to warrant imprisonment, or too lenient, putting people on probation whose crimes might call for more severe punishments.

Many penal reformers have called for a "continuum of punishments with probation at one end, more severe community-based sanctions in the middle, and incarceration at the most restrictive end" (*Americans Behind Bars,* The Edna McConnell Clark Foundation, New York City, New York, 1993). During the 1990s many states experimented with intermediate sanctions (alternative sentencing or community sanctions) such as intensive supervision, as well as probation and parole techniques, to put nonviolent inmates back into the community. The community corrections authorities can provide punishment and rehabilitation while keeping an offender

out of prison. They can restrict an offender's movements, impose treatment programs, and/or require restitution.

Proponents believe that many offenders will not commit other crimes and deserve alternative sanctions so they will not become "hardened" and "embittered." They also hope that alternative sentencing will rehabilitate the criminal. Some believe alternative sanctions can reduce prison and jail costs and relieve overcrowding. In January 1995, for example, George Pataki, governor of New York, proposed using alternative sentencing for nonviolent criminals to make room in prison for violent offenders. Opponents, on the other hand, see prison sentencing as the only "real punishment" for criminals.

In 1998 all 50 State Departments of Correction, the District of Columbia, and the Federal Bureau of Prisons offered a range of alternative sentencing options for criminal offenders. (See Table 11.1.) Among those options shock incarceration (sometimes called boot camp) was offered by the fewest number of states, and was not available in the District of Columbia or in the federal correctional system. Intensive probation, work release, house arrest, and electronic monitoring programs were available in most correctional systems. There was more variation in the availability of other types of alternative sentencing options, such as restitution, weekend sentencing, community service, day reporting centers, and treatment programs.

Client-Specific Planning

In 1980 the National Center on Institutions and Alternatives proposed the idea of client-specific planning. In these programs independent sentencing specialists provide judges background information on offenders and assess their potential for meeting the requirements of a community-based punishment plan. Based on this information the specialist recommends penalties that can include probation, treatments, payment of restitution, or other conditions. The judge may use the plan, change it, or reject it.

TABLE 11.1

The availability of intermediate sanctions

	Intensive Probation	Work Release	House Arrest	Electronic Monitoring Program	Shock Incarceration*	Other
Alabama	■	■	■	■	■	Supervised Intensive Restitution
Alaska	■					Community service, day fine, periodic imprisonment
Arizona	■	■	■	■		Day Reporting Center, Day Fines (Phoenix), Community Service Program (Local option), weekend sentencing and diversionary treatment
		local option	local option	local option		
Arkansas	■	■	■	■	■	Community Punishment Programs
California	■	■	■	■		Weekend Sentencing, day reporting, community service, diversion treatment for specific first offenders
			prob. condition	prob. condition		
Colorado	■	■	■	■	■	Day reporting, community corrections, specialized restitution
Connecticut	■	■	■	■		Community Service, Day Reporting Center, Day Fines
Delaware	■	■	■	■	■	Community Service
Dist. Of Columbia				■		Community Service, Community Management Resource Program for youthful offenders ages 18-26
Florida	■	■	■	■	■	Nonsecure, residential and secure drug treatment; workcamps, probation and restitution centers
Georgia	■	■	■	■	■	Restitution, Community Service, Weekend Sentences
Hawaii	■	■	■	■	■	Restitution
Idaho	N/S	■	N/S			None
Illinois	■	■	■	■		Community Service, periodic imprisonment
Indiana	■	■	■	■		Community Corrections Programs, day reporting
Iowa	■	■	■	■	■	Residential Community Corrections
Kansas	■	■	■	■		Residential Community Corrections
Kentucky	■	■	■	■		Community Correction Program
Louisiana	■	■	■	■[1]	■	Community Rehabilitation Center; Community Service
Maine	■	■	■	■		Community Service, Residential Community Correction
Maryland		■	■	■		Weekend Sentencing, Community Service Program, Community Rehabilitation Center
Massachusetts	■	■	■	N/S	■	Day Reporting Center; Community Service
Michigan	■	■	■	■	■	Community Service, Community Corrections
Minnesota	■	■	■	■	■	Day Reporting Center, Diversionary Treatment Program operated privately by court referral
Mississippi	■[2]		■[2]	■[2]		None
Missouri	■	■	■	■	■	Day Reporting Centers, Diversionary Treatment Programs, Community Service, Residential Community Corrections
Montana	■	■	■	■	■	Residential community Corrections
Nebraska	■	■	■	■		Residential Community Corrections, Community Service
Nevada	■	■	■	■	■	Community Service, Residential Centers, Restitution
New Hampshire	■	■	■	■		Community Service, Restitution, Weekend Sentencing
New Jersey	■	■	■	■		Diversionary Treatment, Super. Community Service, Juvenile Residential Center (County), SLAP, Restitution, Weekend Sentencing
			(in one county only)			
New Mexico	■	■	■	■		Restitution, Community Service
New York	■	■	■	■	■	Restitution, Ignition Interlock, alcohol and substance abuse treatments, community service, day reporting
North Carolina	■	■	■	■		Community Service, Diversionary Treatment, Residential Community Corrections, Weekend Sentencing, Curfew
North Dakota	■	■	■	■		Restitution, Treatment Programs, Residential Community Corrections, Curfew
Ohio	■	■	■	■	■	Community-based Corrections, Community Service Treat., Restitution, Curfew, VictOff Mediations, Ignition Interlock
Oklahoma	■	■	■	■	■	Treat. Programs; Residential Community Corrections; Weekend Sent, Restitution, Vic. Imp. Panels, Ignition Interlock
Oregon	■	■	■	N/S		Day Fines (Portland), Community Service
Pennsylvania	■	■	■	■	■	Community Service
Puerto Rico	■	■	N/S			Restitution fine, Residential Community Corrections
Rhode Island	■	■	■	■	■	Community Confinement
South Carolina			■	■	■	Community Control Centers
South Dakota	■	■	N/S			Community Service, Community Corrections

Alternatives to Confinement in Jail

In 1998, 11 percent of the 664,847 persons under jail supervision were supervised outside of a jail facility. Among persons under community supervision, about half (48 percent) were required to perform community service or to participate in a weekend reporting program (24 percent each). Another 15 percent were under home detention with electronic monitoring. An estimated 10 percent were in an alternative work program, and about 8 percent were supervised outside of a jail facility in a drug, alcohol, mental health, or other medical treatment program.

Felons Sentenced to Prison with Additional Penalties

Besides being sentenced to incarceration or probation, some convicted felons were also ordered to pay a fine, pay victim restitution, receive treatment, perform community service, or comply with some other additional

TABLE 11.1

The availability of intermediate sanctions [CONTINUED]

	Intensive Probation	Work Release	House Arrest	Electronic Monitoring Program	Shock Incarceration*	Other
Tennessee	■■■■					Community Service
Texas	■■■■					Residential Community Corrections, Community Service
Utah	■	■	■	■	N/S	Community Service
Vermont	■	■	N/S	N/S		Supervised Community Sentencing
Virginia	■■■■					Community-based corrections systems, Diversion Centers
Washington						Community service, diversionary treatment, restitution, work ethic camp
West Virginia		■ if 1 yr. or less	■	■	■	Weekend jail, Community Service Work Programs
Wisconsin	■■■■				3	Alcohol/drug abuse/mental health treatment community service, restitution, residential community corrections.
Wyoming	■■■■					Community Corrections
Federal[4]	■	■	■	■ Curfew Parole		Drug Treatment Program, Community Service Program[5] Restitution[6]

Legend: *=Shock Incarceration (Applicable to adult only, not juvenile) N/S=Not Stated, ■ =Yes

DEFINITIONS:

Community Service Program:
An exception to unconstitutional servitude, requires offenders to pay for their crimes while helping others by working "pro bono" for nonprofit or tax-supported agencies.

Day Fines:
Court determines the monetary penalties under a formula that multiplies a set number of days by an amount of money determined on the basis of an offender's ability to pay. Unlike restitution, fines do not compensate the victim, but are paid to treasury.

Day Reporting Centers:
Offender resides in community but there continues to be a high degree of control through daily reporting, intensive surveillance, and strict enforcement of program conditions.

Diversionary Treatment Programs:
Programs respond to need for treatment of drug and alcohol abuse, and sex offenders. Mostly limited to non-violent crimes, includes group therapy, probation, and supervised professional treatment.

Electronic Monitoring Program (EMP):
Requires offender to wear an electronic bracelet around wrist or ankle, location is verified either by telephone or by continuous radio signal.

House Arrest:
Offenders legally ordered to remain in their residences for the duration of their sentences. Usually, they may leave for medical reasons, employment or approved treatment.

Intensive Probation Supervision (IPS):
Offenders are closely supervised on small caseloads; in most programs they must pay victims restitution and perform community service, hold a job, submit to random urine and alcohol testing, and pay a probation supervision fee.

Residential Community Corrections:
Also known as "halfway houses," prerelease programs that serve to facilitate prisoners' successful reintegration into communities. Many include job counseling. Many states use to relieve overcrowding.

Shock Incarceration:
Young, first offenders sentenced to "boot camp" correctional facilities where they are confined for short periods under rigid standards and strict military discipline.

Weekend Sentencing:
A type of "intermittent incarceration," judge orders an offender to serve an incarceration term inside the institution on certain days of the week, generally weekends.

Work Release:
Also known as "intermittent incarceration," offenders leave institution in morning, work, and return in evening for counseling, social activities, and sleep. Usually not imposed in violent, sex or drug offenses.

FOOTNOTES:
Louisiana:
1 R.S. 15:571.32, provides for pilot programs for alternatives to imprisonment, including the use of electronic monitoring devices.

Mississippi:
2 §47-5-1001 through §47-5-1015 of Mississippi code authorizing these sanctions expires June 30, 1999.

Wisconsin:
3 Wisconsin has one "boot camp" environment for non-violent, alcohol and other drug abuse offenders who are not dealers, operated by the Department of Corrections.

Federal:
4 There are two federal systems since the Sentencing Commission Guidelines became effective in 1987. Prisoners sentenced under the Guidelines may not be eligible for the same alternatives as those sentenced under Parole Commission authority.
5 Federal Community Service Program: Subject to budgetary constraints. Parole date advanced by 60 days for 400 hours of community service.
6 Restitution: Federal law presumes the appropriateness of restitution orders, judges must provide reasons when not doing so. The first $100,000,000 in federal fines collected each year is paid to Victims Compensation Fund.

SOURCE: "The Availability of Intermediate Sanctions" in *State Court Organization 1998*, Bureau of Justice Statistics, U.S. Department of Justice, Washington, D.C., 2000

penalty (for example, undergo house arrest or appear periodically for drug testing). A fine was imposed on at least 20 percent of convicted felons. Conservative estimates for other penalties were 14 percent restitution, 6 percent some form of treatment, and 6 percent community service. (See Table 11.2.)

MEDIATION AND RESTITUTION

Mediation began in Canada in 1974 and spread to the United States, where more than 20 states were using mediation by the beginning of the twenty-first century. In mediation the victim and the offender meet under the auspices of a community worker and work out a "reconciliation"

TABLE 11.2

Felons sentenced to an additional penalty by state courts by offense, 1996

Most serious conviction offense	Percent of felons with an additional penalty of –				
	Fine	Restitution	Treatment	Community service	Other
All offenses	**20%**	**14%**	**6%**	**6%**	**3%**
Violent offenses	**14%**	**12%**	**5%**	**4%**	**3%**
Murder[a]	8	9	1	1	2
Sexual assault[b]	13	9	8	3	4
Robbery	8	11	3	2	2
Aggravated assault	19	14	5	6	4
Other violent[c]	18	13	6	6	4
Property offenses	**20%**	**25%**	**4%**	**7%**	**4%**
Burglary	17	21	4	6	3
Larceny[d]	20	22	5	6	5
Fraud[e]	24	32	4	10	3
Drug offenses	**22%**	**7%**	**7%**	**6%**	**2%**
Possession	19	7	10	6	3
Trafficking	23	6	5	6	2
Weapons offenses	**16%**	**6%**	**3%**	**4%**	**2%**
Other offenses[f]	**25%**	**12%**	**7%**	**6%**	**4%**

Note: Where the data indicated affirmatively that a particular additional penalty was imposed, the case was coded accordingly. Where the data did not indicate affirmatively or negatively, the case was treated as not having an additional penalty. These procedures provide a conservative estimate of the prevalence of additional penalties. A felon receiving more than one kind of additional penalty appears under more than one table heading. Data on additional penalties were available for 997,970 cases.
[a] Includes nonnegligent manslaughter.
[b] Includes rape.
[c] Includes offenses such as negligent manslaughter and kidnaping.
[d] Includes motor vehicle theft.
[e] Includes forgery and embezzlement.
[f] Composed of nonviolent offenses such as receiving stolen property and vandalism.

SOURCE: Jodi M. Brown, Patrick A. Langan, and David J. Levin, *Felony Sentences in State Courts, 1996*, Bureau of Justice Statistics, Washington, DC, 1999

between them, usually involving some type of restitution and requiring offenders to take responsibility for their actions. This technique is used mainly for minor crimes and often involves private organizations; therefore, the judiciary does not always accept its resolution. Most often restitution is not considered the complete punishment but part of a wider punishment, such as probation or working off the restitution dollar amount while in prison.

HALFWAY HOUSES AND RESIDENTIAL PROGRAMS

Halfway houses, also called community treatment centers, provide an intermediate place for offenders at the end of their prison sentence to ease themselves back into the life of a community. In 1997, according to the Criminal Justice Institute, the Federal Bureau of Prisons had the largest number of inmates (5,070) in the largest number of halfway houses (260). Twenty-five states had inmates in 272 community treatment centers operated by contractors. In 1997, 21,117 inmates were in halfway houses in 30 agencies. Alaska had the highest percentage of its inmates

in halfway houses (16.9 percent), and Iowa operated the largest number of halfway houses (20).

In 1997 monitoring an offender in a halfway house cost $49.03 a day in a facility run by the Department of Corrections (up from $47.28 in 1990), compared to $42.97 to house an offender in a halfway house operated by a contractor (up from $36.66 in 1990). Offenders in federal halfway houses must pay 25 percent of their gross income to the government.

Residential programs house offenders in a structured setting. Offenders work full time, maintain the residence center, perform community service, and can attend educational or counseling programs. They may leave the centers only for work or approved programs such as substance-abuse treatment. One type of residential program, called the restitution center, allows the offender to work to pay restitution and child-support payments. Centers also regularly test the residents for drugs.

Brooklyn, New York, established a program in which those arrested for drug sales who had no prior felonies could have their charges held in abeyance or deferred if they entered residential treatment for 15–24 months. If they completed treatment the government dropped the charges and helped them find jobs and housing.

DAY REPORTING CENTERS

Developed in Great Britain, day reporting centers (DRCs) first appeared in the United States in the mid-1980s. A 1990 study by the National Institute of Justice (NIJ) found only 13 day reporting centers in the United States. By 1994 an updated study by the NIJ identified 114 DRCs operating in 22 states.

These programs require persons on pretrial release, probation, or parole to appear at day reporting centers on a frequent and regular basis in order to participate in services or activities provided by the center or other community agencies. Failure to report or participate could cause revocation of conditional release or community supervision. Many DRCs operate in distinct phases in which offenders move from higher to lower levels of control based on their progress in treatment and compliance with supervisory guidelines. Most DRC programs last five to six months.

The primary goal of most DRCs is to provide offenders with access to treatment service, although older DRCs (those that opened before 1992) give greater emphasis to providing treatment and services than do newer programs. Most provide a wide array of on-site treatment and services. Their secondary goal is to reduce jail or prison crowding.

The average daily cost per offender of a DRC is $35.04. DRCs that provide few services cost less than those that provide many. The cost of operating DRCs grows with increasingly stringent surveillance practices. Day reporting appears to be less expensive than imprisonment, but is often more expensive than other community sanctions. As a rule DRCs pay for 8 of the 10 most common categories of services. If DRCs cannot fund services themselves other agencies usually finance the treatment provided. Seldom do offenders pay for services themselves. The average daily population of DRCs is 85.

DRCs do not generally exclude serious offenders, although many programs appear to be selecting nonserious drug- and alcohol-using offenders who do not require residential treatment. Two-thirds of the responding DRCs require offenders to perform community service, but the level and type of community service performed differs greatly from jurisdiction to jurisdiction. DRCs terminate a high rate of participants when they are charged with a new crime, fail to participate in treatment, or violate other DRC rules . An average of 50 percent of participants are terminated but the number varies widely (from 14 percent to 86 percent). Privately run DRCs are more likely than public ones to terminate enrolled offenders. No systematic research has been completed to answer important questions on cost effectiveness and recidivism (repeat offender or rearrest) reduction.

Chicago Day Reporting Center Study

The Department of Community Supervision and Intervention (DCSI), part of the Cook County (Chicago, Illinois) Sheriff's Office, established the Cook County Day Reporting Center (CCDRC) in 1993. CCDRC's social services are contracted to Treatment Alternatives for Safe Communities (TASC). Day reporting clients (nonviolent pretrial detainees) receive services on site.

In 1993 the Cook County Jail was operating at more than 150 percent of capacity. The major goal of establishing the CCDRC was to reduce the need for prison beds. Additional goals included providing clients with drug treatment and educational and vocational services, trying to make sure that program participants did not commit further crimes while awaiting trial and trying to make sure they appeared at scheduled court dates. Between 1993 (when the program began) and 1998, 7,200 participants—all male—went through CCDRC. Clients must have stable residences and phone services and are required to be in DSCI's electronic monitoring program prior to becoming eligible for the program. The DSCI staff chooses program participants who have nonviolent criminal records, no psychiatric histories, and bonds of less than $150,000.

The center is open five days per week and participants' schedules vary from three to eight hours each day. Every program participant receives three weeks of program orientation, including 90 hours of educational programming in the areas of drug and alcohol abuse, violence interruption, HIV/AIDS prevention, drug treatment readi-

ness, and life skills management. TASC coordinates social services including class scheduling, counseling sessions and other types of interventions, and oversees on-site drug treatment services. Program participants must submit urine samples regularly for drug and alcohol tests.

In "Chicago Day Reporting Center Reduces Pretrial Detention, Drug Use, and Absconding" (*Overcrowded Times,* vol. 9, no. 3 June 1998), Arthur J. Lurigio, David E. Olson, and James A. Swartz reported on an unpublished study of the Cook County (Chicago) Day Reporting Center (CCDRC). The study (D. C. McBride and C. J. Vander-Waal, "An Assessment of the Cook County Day Reporting Center," Andrews University, Berrien Springs, Michigan, 1996) looked at case results of 2,253 clients discharged between October 1, 1996, and August 12, 1997. Most of those discharged were relatively young single males (average age 27 years). Nearly 90 percent were black, and more than 80 percent had never married. Less than one-third had completed high school or had a GED, 95 percent were unemployed, and 91 percent lived with family members.

The average (mean) number of prior arrests for program participants was 4.2, and the average number of previous convictions was 1.4. Most of the offenses involved drugs or were property offenses. Nearly three-fourths (71 percent) were charged with possession or delivery of a controlled substance.

According to TASC tests most program participants were dependent on illicit drugs. Of those who were discharged fewer than 2 percent had no symptoms of substance abuse or dependency upon entrance to the program or when they were discharged. Of those who tested positive for substance abuse 42.5 percent abused marijuana, 27.8 percent used heroin, and 9.4 percent abused cocaine. Forty percent abused more than one drug. More than 42 percent of those who were abusing or dependent upon drugs said they used drugs at least once daily, and 24.3 reported that they used drugs several times per week. Two-thirds (66.6 percent) used drugs a minimum of several times per week. Most of the participants claimed that CCDRC had given them their first opportunity to face their substance abuse problems; fewer than 10 percent had ever been in substance abuse treatment programs prior to being placed in CCDRC.

Nearly two-thirds of program participants were successfully discharged during the period of the study. Of those who were unsuccessfully discharged, most were terminated for program violations such as being absent without leave or violating administrative rules. Those with severe drug problems were more likely to be unsuccessfully terminated from the program. Prior criminal history was not a factor in a client being successfully or unsuccessfully discharged.

Less than 5 percent were rearrested for new crimes while enrolled in the program compared to more than one-third in traditional programs who were rearrested for new crimes prior to settlement of their court cases.

One of CCDRC's goals is to reduce clients' drug use. During the study period the percentage testing positive for any drug decreased for those who had participated in the program for at least 12 weeks—from 74 percent at the first week, to 47 percent at the sixth week, and to 39 percent at the twelfth week.

CCDRC also met its goal to reduce failure-to-appear court rates. Since the program's beginning, including the study period, CCDRC's failure-to-appear rate was just 2 percent compared to 30 percent in other large jurisdictions throughout the United States.

CCDRC seems to have met its major goals with two-thirds of participants successfully completing the program. Participation in the program decreased drug use among the detainees and ensured court appearances. However, it should be noted that CCDRC's clients were carefully screened before they were admitted to the program, making comparisons between CCDRC participants and other pretrial populations difficult.

DAY FINES

Most judges assess fixed, flat-fee fines sparingly. The fees are tied to the seriousness of the crimes and the criminal records of the offenders, and they bear no relationship to the wealth of the offender. As a result judges often think the fixed fines are too lenient on wealthy offenders and too harsh on poor ones. Using the day fine alternative, however, permits judges to first determine how much punishment an offender deserves, which is defined in some unit other than money.

For example, a judge decides that the gravity of the offense is worth 15, 60, or 120 punishment units, without regard to income. Then the value of each unit is set at a percentage of the offender's daily income, and the total fine amount is determined by simple multiplication. European countries use day fines much more frequently than the courts in the United States.

COMMUNITY SERVICE

Begun in the United States in Alameda County, California (Alameda being the major city in that county) in 1966 as a penalty for traffic offenses, community service has spread throughout the United States. The penalty is most often a supplement to other penalties and mainly given to "white-collar" criminals, juvenile delinquents, and those who commit nonserious crimes. Offenders are usually required to work for government or private nonprofit agencies cleaning parks, collecting roadside trash, setting up chairs for community events, and helping out at nursing homes.

The Vera Institute of Justice's Community Service Sentencing Project in New York has been the most evalu-

ated program of this type. Offenders who could have had sentences of up to six months in jail usually work 70 hours of community service over a two-week period. In Stark County, (Canton) Ohio, because of jail overcrowding, municipal judges began using community service as a way to relieve the jail conditions. In the early 1990s average per-judge sentences totaled 350 hours of community service. By 1995 the average per-judge sentence increased to a total of 35,000 hours.

TREATMENT PROGRAMS

Some jurisdictions have substance-abuse treatment programs but many lack the necessary resources. Attending a drug-treatment program is often a condition of probation. In a 1997 survey by the Bureau of Justice Statistics (BJS), 37 percent of felony probationers were required to be in alcohol or drug treatment programs. A treatment program was required for 6 percent of felons convicted in 1996.

INTENSIVE SUPERVISION PROBATION

Increasingly, more of the probation population consists of people convicted of felonies rather than misdemeanors. Routine probation, however, was neither intended nor structured to handle this type of offender. Therefore, Intensive Supervision Probation/Parole (ISP) was developed as an alternative to prison or routine probation. Between 1980 and 1990 every state implemented some form of ISP.

Many states use ISP to alleviate prison overcrowding and provide rigorous supervision of high-risk probationers, with the aim of reducing the risk to public safety posed by such offenders. In 1996, according to BJS, 92,559 adults on probation and 24,885 adults on parole were under intensive supervision.

The caseloads of supervising officers normally range from 30 to 50 ISP probationers, compared to traditional probation caseloads of 150–200 where supervision sometimes amounts to the probationer mailing a card to the supervisor monthly. ISP requires some combination of multiple weekly contacts with a supervising officer, random and unannounced drug testing, stringent enforcement of probation/parole conditions, and participation in relevant treatment, employment, and perhaps community service.

An Example of an ISP

An example of an ISP is described by the Oregon Department of Corrections:

> ... the offender will be visited by a probation officer two or three times per week, who will phone on the other days. The offender will be subject to unannounced searches of his home for drugs and have his urine tested regularly for alcohol and drugs. He must strictly abide by other conditions set by the court—not carrying a

weapon, not socializing with certain persons—and he will have to perform community service and be employed or participate in training or education. In addition, he will be strongly encouraged to attend counseling and/or other treatment, particularly if he is a drug offender.

—Joan Petersilia, "When Probation Becomes More Dreaded Than Prison," *Federal Probation,* Washington, D.C., 1990

Joan Petersilia has evaluated ISP programs for the National Institute of Justice and the RAND Corporation, a nonprofit public policy research institute. She observed that an ISP is in the conflicting position of having to appear punitive enough to be acceptable to the "get-tough" public while appearing not too punitive to prisoners. When given the choice of serving time or taking ISP, one-third of nonviolent offenders in New Jersey chose prison. Petersilia points out that prison is not always the deterrent it is meant to be. Sanctions are most effective if social standing is injured and the offender feels that he or she may be excluded from his or her group. For some people, however, having a prison record is not the stigma it once was. In some social milieus it is common for peers and family members to have served time.

Such a high proportion of black men is incarcerated that, for some, prison is accepted as a part of life rather than a terrible dishonor. In gangs imprisonment can even confer status. Petersilia adds that, "the grim fact—and national shame—is that for most people who go to prison, the conditions inside are not all that different from the conditions outside." For some it is even an improvement, providing regular food, shelter, medical care, and a community.

Ironically, social programs and job training are often more available inside prisons than outside. "Prisons are becoming the place where we provide services to our poor people," claims Robert Gangi, executive director of the Correctional Association of New York, a nonpartisan prison watchdog agency. Moreover, the offender often finds a large social network on "the inside." As the warden of a penitentiary described it, "When a new guy comes up here it's almost a homecoming—undoubtedly there are people from his neighborhood and people who know him." On the other hand an ISP does change one's social standing. To be isolated and restricted within your own community can be harder to handle than prison. The intrusions, lack of privacy, and curfews are more stressful to the offender within his normal community than within a prison, where such limitations are considered normal.

How Successful Are ISPs?

In "Key Legislative Issues in Criminal Justice: Intermediate Sanctions" (*Research in Action,* National Institute of Justice, January 1997), Dale Parent, Terence Dunworth, Douglas McDonald, and William Rhodes found that intermediate sanctions, such as ISPs, have not

achieved the expected results. Appraising these programs nationally is difficult because they have developed independently in many different jurisdictions, and only a few programs in scattered jurisdictions have been evaluated. Nonetheless, it appears that ISPs and community service have not rehabilitated or kept program participants from committing more crimes any better than the traditional sentencing choices they replaced.

The costs of running ISPs have been found to be higher than expected, mostly because the costs to adjudicate the many technical violations that occur with intermediate sanction program participants and to reincarcerate such offenders can quickly use up any potential savings.

Parent, et al, concluded that, despite mixed results in achieving hoped-for benefits of intermediate sanctions, ISPs should be continued since they offer more alternatives than just confinement or probation.

HOUSE ARREST AND ELECTRONIC MONITORING

Some nonviolent offenders are sentenced to house arrest in which they are legally ordered to remain confined in their own homes. They are allowed to leave only for medical purposes or to go to work, although some curfew programs permit offenders to work during the day and have a few hours of free time before returning home at a specified time.

The most severe type of house arrest is home incarceration, where the offender's home is actually a prison that he or she cannot leave except for very special reasons, such as medical emergencies. Home-detention programs require the offender to be at home when he or she is not working. Some offenders are required to perform a certain number of hours of community service and, if they are employed, to repay the cost of probation and/or restitution.

Electronic monitoring is a fast-growing addition to the house-arrest concept. In 1984 just three house-arrest programs existed in the United States; experts now estimate that agencies in all 50 states use electronic monitoring for more than 45,000 people. In 1998 electronic monitoring accounted for 15 percent of persons supervised outside a jail facility.

Electronic monitoring consists of a small radio transmitter attached to the offender in a nonremovable bracelet or anklet. Some systems send a signal to a small monitoring box, which is programmed to phone a Department of Corrections computer if the signal is broken; other systems randomly call probationers, and the computer makes a voice verification of the prisoner. In some cases, a special device in the electronic monitor sends a confirmation to the computer.

Electronic monitoring costs states much less than building a new prison cell or housing another inmate. In

1995 Florida corrections reported monitoring costs were $6.41 a day versus $38.14 to house, feed, and guard a prisoner. Florida requires monitored convicts to be employed to help keep their families off welfare and to pay taxes, restitution to victims, court costs, and $40 a month for the monitoring. Electronic monitoring cost New Jersey about $4,700 annually per detainee compared to $26,000 per inmate in prison.

WORK RELEASE

Work-release programs permit selected prisoners nearing the end of their terms to work in the community, returning to prison facilities or community residential facilities in nonworking hours. Such programs are designed to prepare inmates to return to the community in a relatively controlled environment while they are learning how to work productively. Work release also allows inmates to earn income, reimburse the state for part of their confinement costs, build up savings for their eventual full release, and acquire more positive living habits.

During the 1970s prison work-release programs expanded considerably but have since declined. Although 43 states have existing statutes authorizing work release, only about one-third of U.S. prisons report operating such programs and fewer than 3 percent of U.S. inmates participate in them.

Washington State Evaluations

The NIJ sponsored two evaluations of Washington State's work release program conducted between 1991 and 1994 (Susan Turner and Joan Petersilia, *Work Release: Recidivism and Corrections Costs in Washington State,* Washington, D.C., 1996). The first study analyzed a group of 2,452 males released from Washington prisons in 1990, nearly 40 percent of whom spent a part of their sentences on work release. The second compared the recidivism of 218 offenders; approximately half participated in work release, and half completed their sentences in prison.

In contrast to the national decline of work release as a means of preparing imprisoned offenders for rejoining the community, Washington allocated more than one-third of its community corrections budget to work release. Those on release obtained daytime jobs, lived in community facilities, and contributed to their room and board costs.

Overall the studies found that the program achieved its most important goal, preparing inmates for final release and facilitating their adjustment to the community. The program did not cost the state more than keeping the inmates in prison. The public safety risks were nearly nonexistent because almost no work release inmate committed new crimes, and when they committed rule violations they were quickly returned to prison. The results of the evaluation were mostly positive:

- Nearly one-quarter of all prisoners released in Washington made a successful transition to the community through work release.

- Less than 5 percent of the work release inmates committed new crimes while on work release, 99 percent of which were less serious property offenses such as forgery or theft. No one committed a violent felony. However, with heightened supervision under strict conditions, many work release inmates incurred infractions (most for rule violations and drug possession).

- Middle-aged offenders and those convicted of property crimes were most likely to participate in work release. Hispanic offenders were less likely to go to work release than white or black offenders.

- Fifty-six percent of the 965 work release inmates in the group studies were termed "successful"; they incurred no program infractions or arrests. Another 13.5 percent were "moderately successful"; their infractions were not serious enough to return them to prison. Almost 30 percent were "unsuccessful"; they returned to prison. Most were returned for program rule violations (58 percent) or drug possession (35 percent).

- Older offenders were more successful than younger ones, and whites were more successful than either Hispanics or blacks. Success was also associated with having no prior criminal record.

- About 4 percent of both the nonwork release inmates (control group) and the work release inmates (experimental group) were returned to prison for a new crime during the year.

- An offender serving part of his or her sentence in prison and then participating in a work-release program cost the state the same ($25,883 average) as the inmate who served his or her entire sentence in prison ($25,949 average).

CONCLUSION OF STUDIES. While in the program inmates kept a job, reconnected with their local communities, and paid for their room and board; most remained drug-free. However, the work release program did not reduce offender recidivism or corrections costs. Critics of community corrections often argue that such programs should deliver all of the above (jobs, drug-free inmates, etc.), while showing a reduction in recidivism and costs.

Turner and Petersilia think that those expectations are unrealistic. Realistic measures of correction programs' effectiveness should account for what was accomplished and the constraints under which the programs operated. Realism, however, does not mean easy to achieve. Most participants in Washington's work-release program had lengthy criminal histories, serious substance abuse problems, and limited education and job skills. Yet, when supervised in this work-release program, they found jobs, paid rent, and refrained from crime.

According to Turner and Petersilia, although most corrections evaluations adopt recidivism as their primary outcome measure, few corrections officials believe that what they do chiefly determines recidivism rates. As John J. DiIulio observed in "Rethinking the Criminal Justice System: Toward a New Paradigm," (*Performance Measures for the Criminal Justice System,* Bureau of Justice Statistics, Washington, D.C., 1993), most justice practitioners understand that they can rarely do for their clients what parents, teachers, friends, neighbors, clergy, or economic opportunities may have failed to do.

Adopting more realistic outcome measures may make it possible to better bridge the wide gap between public expectations for the justice system and what most practitioners recognize as the system's actual capacity to control crime. By documenting what corrections programs can accomplish, the systems can move toward integrating programs like work release into a more balanced corrections strategy. Such a strategy would successfully return low-risk inmates to the community, thereby making room to incarcerate the truly violent offenders.

BOOT CAMPS

Shock incarceration, a term often used for boot camps, is one of the most controversial alternatives to prison. The idea is not new. For example, Elmira Reformatory had a military regimen in the 1800s. After World War II the British set up quasi-military detention centers for adolescents in England and Wales. These centers, which emphasized tough discipline, were intended to give teenagers the "short, sharp, shock that would end their criminal careers." The programs continued into the 1960s and 1970s despite research that showed their recidivism outcomes were no better than other institutional programs.

First Camps

In the United States the first modern correctional boot camp opened in Georgia in 1983. Faced with unprecedented overcrowding in its prisons and jails, Georgia was looking for alternatives to incarceration for adult offenders. Oklahoma began its program in 1984 and, by the end of 1988, 15 programs were operating in nine states. The majority of programs have been started since 1990.

As of January 1, 1998, according to the Criminal Justice Institute (*The Corrections Yearbook—1998*), 33 correctional agencies (state and federal) operated 49 camps for adult inmates. This is the fewest number of adult boot camps in operation in the United States since 1993 when there were 46 camps. In 1995, 75 adult boot camps were in operation. The 49 camps housed 6,857 inmates: 6,349 males and 508 females. The average length of stay for the

inmates was five months at an average daily cost per inmate of $59.76. Costs ranged from $32.00 per inmate per day in South Carolina to $113.98 in Minnesota.

Nine jail systems operated a total of 15 boot camps for 1,015 prisoners. The length of the programs averaged three months, and the average cost was $69.54 a day.

In addition, 7 probation agencies operated 10 boot camps, and three parole agencies operated 3 boot camp programs. The average stay at a probation boot camp was six months and at a parole boot camp five months. The average daily cost was $59.65 per probationer and $49.00 per parolee. (Of the three states that ran probation and parole boot camps—Maryland, New York, and Ohio—only Ohio reported a cost per day figure.)

According to "Prisons: Policy Options for Congress" (*Congressional Issue Brief,* JoAnne O'Bryant, September 1998), the Federal Bureau of Prisons operated one Intensive Confinement Center (prison boot camp) for males (209 inmates) and one for females (112 inmates). In 1996, 500 male and female inmates completed this program.

Public, Politicians, and Criminal Justice Administration

Boot camps are generally popular with politicians and the public and usually get positive media attention. They are intended to be both punitive in their rigid discipline and rehabilitative in the self-esteem they claim to confer upon successful completion of the program. Shock incarceration is intended to motivate prisoners, teach respect for oneself and others, and break the destructive cycles of behavior. Virtually all work on the assumption that a military regimen is beneficial.

The major selling points for boot camps have been saving money and reducing prison crowding. However, the major factor contributing to reduced costs and less overcrowding is that the boot camp programs are shorter in duration than traditional sentences, and thus participants are released earlier.

Despite positive publicity, the few studies of boot camps have found that the camps have not had a major effect on recidivism. In *National Assessment Program: 1994 Survey Results* (Washington, D.C., 1995), the NIJ reported the responses of more than 2,500 directors of criminal justice agencies. About 42 percent of the directors of probation and parole agencies indicated that they did not have boot camp programs and did not want or need them. Judges and trial court administrators expressed stronger support for boot camps. Eighty-two percent of the judges and 63 percent of trial court administrators indicated that boot camps were an available option in their states or jurisdictions, with about half of each group indicating a need for improvement in the boot camps. Less than 10 percent of the judges and trial court administrators stated they did not want boot camps as an option.

Directors of probation and parole agencies expressed concern about the effectiveness of boot camps and about the staff time required to monitor them. One director called boot camps a "silly idea and a throwback to the '50s and '60s with no demonstrated value in positively impacting our population of offenders." This director believed that day treatment programs with structured learning offered the best potential for success.

Another director wrote that "boot camp aftercare [community supervision] has taken up half of the intensive probation slots and is not very effective." Other comments illustrated that workload concerns prevailed over the value of boot camp aftercare. According to one director, "The programs cause significant workload problems when agents assigned to them must be granted reduced caseload allowances, placing a burden on the other agents."

Many judges also commented on boot camps. One judge expressed his unhappiness: "Boot camp has proved a disappointment because a lack of follow-up skill training and supervision has resulted in graduates committing additional crimes." Another judge wrote, "I think boot camps are a good idea, but our present emphasis tends to be on offenders who have already been through probation and jail. A better plan might be to use boot camp on first-time offenders who are 'just drifting.'"

Several respondents believed that boot camps might be beneficial but that more follow-up was needed for participants in terms of aftercare services. One prosecutor noted, "Our concern with 'boot camp' programs is that there is little evidence that they result in long-term behavior modification and they currently have insufficient fol-low-up." A public defender stated, "Shock incarceration has had poor success because of the lack of options and structure upon release."

Boot Camp Goals and Aims

The Center for the Study of Crime, Delinquency and Corrections (Southern Illinois University at Carbondale) studied federal, state, and boot camp programs and reported its findings in *"Boot Camp" Drug Treatment and Aftercare Interventions: An Evaluation Review* (National Institute of Justice, Washington, D.C., 1995). Although shock incarceration's acceptance by the public is based mostly upon the appeal generated by "tough" media images of drill instructors, most adult boot camps surveyed were positively oriented towards developing programs aimed at offender rehabilitation.

Typically, the boot camp programs include physical training and regular drill-type exercise, housekeeping and maintenance of the facility, and often hard labor. Some states include vocational, educational, or treatment programs. Drug and alcohol counseling, reality therapy, relaxation therapy, individual counseling, and recreation therapy are often incorporated into shock incarceration programs. Many offenders in boot camps have drug problems—95 percent of the participants in Mississippi, for example.

Virtually all programs give at least several hours of drug treatment weekly. All the programs closely regulate dress, talking, movement, eating, hygiene, etc. Obedience to rules reinforces submission to authority and forces the prisoners to handle a challenge that is both tedious and demanding.

CHAPTER 12

PRISONERS, DRUGS, ALCOHOL, AND TREATMENT

What we're doing is simply a holding action. We've arrested more people than the prosecutors can prosecute, than the judges can convict, than the jails can hold. Until there's a demand reduction—and that means education and treatment—you're not going to see any change.

—Captain Harvey Ferguson, former chief of narcotics enforcement, Seattle

Loading our prisons with nonviolent drug criminals means that, today, we are committing more nonviolent offenders to hard time than we are violent criminals, and there's little room left for the violent offenders who should be put away to make our streets safer.

— Senator Paul Simon, 1994

INCREASING NUMBER OF PRISON INMATES FOR DRUG OFFENSES

In 1998 drug offenders accounted for 236,800 inmates in state prison and 63,011 federal prisoners. Of jail inmates in 1998 an estimated 417,000—about 70 percent—had either committed a drug offense or used drugs regularly prior to arrest.

State Prisons

The number of state prison inmates in custody for drug offenses increased from 148,600 in 1990 to 222,100 in 1997. In 1990, 313,600 inmates were in prison for violent offenses; by 1997 that number had increased to 507,800. (See Table 12.1.) In 1990 drug offenders accounted for 21.7 percent of the prisoners in custody of state correctional authorities, in 1995 for 21.5 percent, and in 1997 for 20.7 percent. Violent offenders made up 45.8 percent of those in custody in 1990, 46.5 percent in 1995, and 47.2 percent in 1997. (See Figure 12.1.)

Of new court commitments to state prisons, in 1990 drug offenders accounted for 31.7 percent, with 30.8 percent in 1995 and 30.7 percent in 1997. Violent offenders comprised 26.8 percent of new court commitments to

state prisons in 1990, 28.8 percent in 1995, and 29.9 percent in 1997. (See Table 12.2.)

Federal Prisons

Almost all of the increase in the population of federal prisons is attributable to a growth in the number of drug convictions. Prisoners sentenced for drug offenses grew from 30,470 in 1990 to 51,737 in 1995 and to 63,011 in 1998, a total increase of 106.8 percent.

DRUG USE HISTORY

State Prisoners

In 1997 more than four out of five (83 percent) state prisoners reported that they had used drugs at some time during the past, up slightly from 1991 when 79.4 declared they had used drugs in the past. In 1997 marijuana or hashish (77 percent) and cocaine or crack (49.2 percent) were the most commonly used drugs, followed by hallucinogens and stimulants (over 28 percent each), heroin or opiates (24.5 percent), depressants (23.7 percent), and inhalants (14.4 percent). (See Table 12.3.)

In 1997, 56.5 percent of state prisoners reported that they had used drugs in the month prior to committing their current offense, up from 49.9 percent in 1991. Marijuana or hashish use rose from 32.2 percent in 1991 to 39.2 percent in 1997, while use of most other drugs remained about the same.

Federal Prisoners

In 1997 nearly three-fourths (72.9 percent) of federal prisoners claimed to have used drugs in the past, up from 60.1 percent in 1991. As with state prisoners, marijuana or hashish (65.2 percent) and cocaine or crack (44.8 percent) were the most common choices. One of five federal prisoners reported past use of stimulants (20.9 percent) and hallucinogens (19 percent), while about 16.1 percent used

TABLE 12.1

Estimated number of prisoners in custody of state correctional authorities by the most serious offense, 1990–97

Most serious offense	Number of inmates in State prison							
	1990	1991	1992	1993	1994	1995	1996	1997
Total	684,544	728,605	778,245	828,400	904,647	989,005	1,032,676	1,075,167
Violent offenses	313,600	339,500	369,100	393,500	425,700	459,600	484,800	507,800
Murder[a]	72,000	77,200	85,900	92,800	100,700	110,600	118,200	125,800
Manslaughter	13,200	13,100	14,000	14,600	15,200	16,300	16,800	17,000
Rape	24,500	25,500	27,300	27,100	27,700	28,500	28,200	27,500
Other sexual assault	39,100	43,000	46,200	49,000	53,300	57,000	60,700	64,200
Robbery	99,200	107,800	113,600	122,100	131,700	139,600	146,100	152,000
Assault	53,300	59,000	67,600	72,200	80,100	89,000	95,200	100,500
Other violent[b]	12,400	13,100	14,500	15,600	17,000	18,600	19,600	20,700
Property offenses	173,700	180,700	181,600	189,600	207,000	226,600	231,700	236,400
Burglary	87,200	90,300	90,500	94,300	101,800	108,900	111,700	114,900
Larceny	34,800	35,700	33,500	35,300	39,600	44,500	45,000	45,100
Motor vehicle theft	14,400	16,000	18,100	18,900	19,700	21,300	20,200	19,800
Fraud	20,200	20,400	20,200	21,300	23,600	26,300	27,600	28,900
Other property[c]	17,100	18,200	19,400	19,800	22,300	25,600	27,200	27,700
Drug offenses	148,600	155,200	168,100	177,000	193,500	212,800	216,900	222,100
Public-order offenses[d]	45,500	49,500	56,300	64,000	74,400	86,500	96,000	106,200
Other/unspecified[e]	3,100	2,900	3,200	4,300	3,900	3,500	3,200	2,700

Note: Previously published estimates for 1992-96 have been revised based on data from the 1997 Survey of Inmates in State Correctional Facilities. The offense distributions for year-end 1991 and 1997 are based on survey data.

The offense distributions for other years are estimated using forward and backward stock-flow methods. See *Explanatory notes* for further details on the estimations. All estimates are based on the total number of prisoners in physical custody, including those with sentences of 1 year or less and those who were unsentenced. See definitions for the distinction between custody and jurisdiction counts. Due to rounding, detail may not sum to total.

[a] Includes nonnegligent manslaughter.
[b] Includes extortion, intimidation, criminal endangerment, and other violent offenses.
[c] Includes possession and selling of stolen property, destruction of property, trespassing, vandalism, criminal tampering, and other property offenses.
[d] Includes weapons, drunk driving, escape, court offenses, obstruction, commercialized vice, morals and decency charges, liquor law violations, and other public-order offenses.
[e] Includes juvenile offenses and unspecified felonies.

SOURCE: *Correctional Populations in the United States, 1997*, Bureau of Justice Statistics, Washington, DC, 2000

FIGURE 12.1

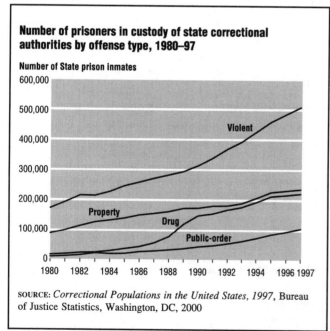

Number of prisoners in custody of state correctional authorities by offense type, 1980–97

SOURCE: *Correctional Populations in the United States, 1997*, Bureau of Justice Statistics, Washington, DC, 2000

ting their current offense was considerably higher than it had been in 1991 (31.8 percent). The use of marijuana or hashish (30.4 percent) during the month before the offense in 1997 increased significantly from 19.2 percent in 1991. The month-prior use of cocaine or crack also increased, rising from 15.4 percent in 1991 to 20 percent in 1997. Similarly, the use of depressants and stimulants in the month before committing the crime also rose between 1991 and 1997.

DRUG USE AT THE TIME OF THE MOST RECENT OFFENSE

One-third (32.6 percent) of state prisoners reported that they were under the influence of drugs when they committed their current offense. Prisoners incarcerated for drug offenses (41.9 percent) and property offenses (36.6 percent) reported the highest incidence of drug use at the time of the crime. Nearly one of three (29 percent) violent offenders and 23.1 percent of public-order offenders were under the influence of drugs at the time of their current offense. The crimes most closely tied to drug influence were drug possession (42.6 percent), drug trafficking (41 percent), and robbery (39.9 percent). Prisoners who had committed manslaughter (17.4 percent) or sexual assault (21.5 percent) were least

heroin or opiates, 16.5 percent used depressants, and 7.7 percent used inhalants. (See Table 12.4.)

In 1997 the percentage (44.8 percent) of federal inmates reporting drug use in the month prior to commit-

TABLE 12.2

Percent of sentenced prisoners admitted to state prisons by the most serious offense, 1990–97

Most serious offense	Percent of new court commitments to State prisons[a]							
	1990	1991	1992	1993	1994	1995	1996	1997
Total	100%	100%	100%	100%	100%	100%	100%	100%
Violent offenses	**26.8%**	**28.9%**	**28.6%**	**29.2%**	**29.3%**	**28.8%**	**29.5%**	**29.9%**
Murder[b]	2.7	3.0	2.9	3.0	3.1	2.9	2.8	2.7
Negligent manslaughter	1.2	1.3	1.2	1.3	1.2	1.2	1.1	1.0
Sexual assault[c]	5.5	5.6	5.7	6.0	6.1	5.9	6.0	6.2
Robbery	9.2	10.1	9.9	9.8	9.5	9.0	9.1	9.2
Aggravated assault	7.0	7.6	7.5	7.7	8.0	8.2	8.7	8.9
Other violent	1.3	1.4	1.3	1.4	1.6	1.6	1.8	1.9
Property offenses	**32.3%**	**31.1%**	**31.2%**	**30.5%**	**29.6%**	**29.5%**	**29.0%**	**28.3%**
Burglary	14.5	13.5	13.3	12.9	12.4	11.9	12.0	11.7
Larceny/theft	8.1	8.0	8.1	8.0	7.7	7.8	7.5	7.0
Motor vehicle theft	2.6	2.4	2.5	2.4	2.4	2.4	2.1	2.0
Fraud	3.9	3.8	3.8	3.8	3.9	4.1	4.1	4.0
Other property	3.2	3.4	3.6	3.4	3.2	3.3	3.3	3.5
Drug offenses	**31.7%**	**30.0%**	**30.4%**	**29.9%**	**30.2%**	**30.8%**	**30.2%**	**30.7%**
Public-order offenses	**8.0%**	**8.9%**	**8.8%**	**9.3%**	**10.0%**	**10.2%**	**10.6%**	**10.7%**
Other	**1.1%**	**1.1%**	**1.1%**	**1.1%**	**0.9%**	**0.7%**	**0.7%**	**0.4%**

Note: Data are from the National Corrections Reporting Program and are based on the most serious offense as reported by participating states. Data may not sum to total due to rounding.
[a] Includes only those with sentences of more than 1 year.
[b] Includes nonnegligent manslaughter.
[c] Includes rape and other sexual assault.

SOURCE: *Correctional Populations in the United States, 1997*, Bureau of Justice Statistics, Washington, DC, 2000

TABLE 12.3

Drug use of state prisoners, 1991 and 1997

Type of drug	Percent of State prisoners who reported –							
	Ever using drugs		Ever using drugs regularly[a]		Using drugs in the month before offense		Using drugs at the time of offense	
	1997	1991	1997	1991	1997	1991	1997	1991
Any drug[b]	83.0%	79.4%	69.6%	62.2%	56.5%	49.9%	32.6%	31.0%
Marijuana/hashish	77.0	73.8	58.3	51.9	39.2	32.2	15.1	11.4
Cocaine/crack	49.2	49.4	33.6	31.9	25.0	25.2	14.8	14.5
Heroin/opiates	24.5	25.2	15.0	15.3	9.2	9.6	5.6	5.8
Depressants[c]	23.7	24.0	11.3	10.8	5.1	3.8	1.8	1.0
Stimulants[d]	28.3	29.7	16.3	16.6	9.0	7.4	4.2	2.9
Hallucinogens[e]	28.7	26.9	11.3	11.5	4.0	3.7	1.8	1.6
Inhalants	14.4	—	5.4	—	1.0	—	—	—

Note: Detail adds to more than total because prisoners may have used more than one type of drug.
— Not reported.
[a] Used drugs at least once a week for at least a month.
[b] Other unspecified drugs are included in the totals.
[c] Includes barbiturates, tranquilizers, and Quaalude.
[d] Includes amphetamine and methamphetamine.
[e] Includes LSD and PCP.

SOURCE: Christopher J. Mumola, *Substance Abuse and Treatment, State and Federal Prisoners, 1997*, Bureau of Justice Statistics, Washington, DC, 1999

likely to be under the influence of drugs during the offense. (See Table 12.5.)

More than one-fifth (22.4 percent) of federal prisoners committed offenses while under the influence of drugs in 1997. One-fourth of drug offenders (25 percent) and violent offenders (24.5 percent) used drugs when committing the offense, as did 10.8 percent of property offenders.

Those federal inmates imprisoned for murder (29.4 percent) and robbery (27.8 percent) were most likely to be under the influence of drugs when committing their current offense.

Approximately one-third of jail inmates said they were under the influence of drugs at the time of their arrest. (See Table 12.6.)

TABLE 12.4

Drug use of federal prisoners, 1991 and 1997

	Percent of Federal prisoners who reported –							
	Ever using drugs		Ever using drugs regularly[a]		Using drugs in the month before offense		Using drugs at the time of offense	
Type of drug	1997	1991	1997	1991	1997	1991	1997	1991
Any drug[b]	72.9%	60.1%	57.3%	42.1%	44.8%	31.8%	22.4%	16.8%
Marijuana/hashish	65.2	52.8	46.6	32.2	30.4	19.2	10.8	5.9
Cocaine/crack	44.8	37.3	28.2	20.6	20.0	15.4	9.3	7.7
Heroin/opiates	16.1	14.1	8.9	9.3	5.4	5.5	3.0	3.7
Depressants[c]	16.5	13.1	8.0	5.3	3.2	1.4	1.0	0.3
Stimulants[d]	20.9	16.8	12.9	8.3	7.6	3.9	4.1	1.8
Hallucinogens[e]	19.0	14.8	6.4	4.8	1.7	1.2	0.8	0.5
Inhalants	7.7	—	2.6	—	0.5	—	—	—

Note: Detail adds to more than total because prisoners may have used more than one type of drug.
— Not reported.
[a] Used drugs at least once a week for at least a month.
[b] Other unspecified drugs are included in the totals.
[c] Includes barbiturates, tranquilizers, and Quaalude.
[d] Includes amphetamine and methamphetamine.
[e] Includes LSD and PCP.

SOURCE: Christopher J. Mumola, *Substance Abuse and Treatment, State and Federal Prisoners, 1997*, Bureau of Justice Statistics, Washington, DC, 1999

TABLE 12.5

Alcohol or drug use at time of offense of state and federal prisoners by type of offense, 1997

	Estimated number of prisoners[a]		Percent of prisoners who reported being under the influence at time of offense					
			Alcohol		Drugs		Alcohol or drugs	
Type of offense	State	Federal	State	Federal	State	Federal	State	Federal
Total	1,046,705	88,018	37.2%	20.4%	32.6%	22.4%	52.5%	34.0%
Violent offenses	494,349	13,021	41.7%	24.5%	29.0%	24.5%	51.9%	39.8%
Murder	122,435	1,288	44.6	38.7	26.8	29.4	52.4	52.4
Negligent manslaughter	16,592	53	52.0	...	17.4	...	56.0	...
Sexual assault[b]	89,328	713	40.0	32.3	21.5	7.9	45.2	32.3
Robbery	148,001	8,770	37.4	18.0	39.9	27.8	55.6	37.6
Assault	97,897	1,151	45.1	46.0	24.2	13.8	51.8	50.5
Other violent	20,096	1,046	39.6	32.2	29.0	15.9	48.2	37.2
Property offenses	230,177	5,964	34.5%	15.6%	36.6%	10.8%	53.2%	22.6%
Burglary	111,884	294	37.2	...	38.4	...	55.7	...
Larceny/theft	43,936	414	33.7	...	38.4	...	54.2	...
Motor vehicle theft	19,279	216	32.2	...	39.0	...	51.2	...
Fraud	28,102	4,283	25.2	10.4	30.5	6.5	42.8	14.5
Other property	26,976	757	36.0	22.8	30.6	16.4	53.2	34.6
Drug offenses	216,254	55,069	27.4%	19.8%	41.9%	25.0%	52.4%	34.6%
Possession	92,373	10,094	29.6	21.3	42.6	25.1	53.9	36.0
Trafficking	117,926	40,053	25.5	19.4	41.0	25.9	50.9	35.0
Other drug	5,955	4,922	29.9	19.7	47.1	17.1	59.2	29.0
Public-order offenses	103,344	13,026	43.2%	20.6%	23.1%	15.6%	56.2%	30.2%
Weapons	25,642	6,025	28.3	23.0	22.4	24.4	41.8	37.1
Other public-order	77,702	7,001	48.1	18.5	23.3	8.1	60.9	24.1

... Too few cases in the sample to permit calculation.
[a] Based on cases with valid offense data.
[b] Includes rape and other sexual assault.

SOURCE: Christopher J. Mumola, *Substance Abuse and Treatment, State and Federal Prisoners, 1997*, Bureau of Justice Statistics, Washington, DC, 1999

Committing Crimes to Get Drug Money

In 1997, 19 percent of all state prison inmates and 16 percent of all federal prisoners claimed that they committed their current offense to get money for drugs. In 1991, 17 percent of state prisoners and 10 percent of federal prisoners cited drug money as the reason they committed their current offense.

TABLE 12.6

Drug use, testing, and treatment in jails: Highlights

Drug use among local jail inmates, 1998

	Percent of inmates[a]	Estimated 1998
• An estimated 61,000 (16%) convicted jail inmates committed their offense to get money for drugs.		
All inmates		
Drug offense/regular use	70.3%	417,000
Any drug offense	25.6	152,000
Convicted inmates		
Under the influence		
at the time of offense	35.6%	138,000
Use in month before	55.0	213,000
• Overall, 71% of local jail jurisdictions reported that they had a policy to test inmates or staff for drug use in 1998. In June, a fourth of the jails tested samples from inmates.		
Drugs used at time of offense		
Marijuana or hashish	18.5%	72,000
Cocaine/crack	15.2	59,000
Heroin	5.6	22,000
Active drug involvement[b]	65.5%	253,000

[a] Based on personal interviews, 1996
[b] See below for definition.

Samples for drug tests collected from inmates during June 1998*

	Number	Percent positive
Total	36,215	10.5%
Random only	3,776	7.6
Indication of use only	2,904	13.6
Random/indication of use	9,190	12.7
Combined methods	20,344	9.6

*Multiple samples may have been collected from one inmate.

CHARACTERISTICS OF DRUG USERS IN PRISON

Gender

In 1997 more than 8 of 10 (83 percent) of the nearly 1.15 million prisoners in state and federal prisons reported having ever used drugs. Nearly equal percentages of men (82.9 percent) and women (84 percent) in state prisons had ever used drugs. Women in state prisons were somewhat more likely to have been regular drug users than were men (73.6 and 69.3 percent respectively). Women (62.4 percent) were also more likely than men (56.1 percent) to have used drugs in the month prior to the most recent offense. A higher proportion of women (40.4 percent) than men (32.1 percent) claimed to have been under the influence of drugs while committing their current offense. (See Table 12.7.)

On the other hand, among federal prisoners, higher percentages of men reported drug use. More men (73.7 percent) than women (62.8 percent) ever used drugs in the past, and more men (58.1 percent) than women (47.2 percent) said they used drugs regularly. About 45.4 percent of the men and 36.7 percent of the women used drugs in the month prior to the offense. A higher percentage of men (22.7 per-

TABLE 12.6

Drug use, testing, and treatment in jails: Highlights [CONTINUED]

Drug involvement of jail inmates, 1996

	Percent of jail inmates		
	All	Convicted	Unconvicted
Current drug offenses[a]	25.6%	28.4%	22.1%
Possession	14.6	16.6	11.9
Trafficking	9.3	9.7	9.0
Prior sentence for drug offenses[b]	26.6%	29.6%	21.4%
Prior drug use			
Ever used drugs	82.4%	84.5%	79.0%
Ever used regularly[c]	64.2	67.2	59.8
Intravenous drug use	17.0	18.3	14.5
Used in the month before the offense	/	55.0	/
Used at time of the offense	/	35.6	/
Committed offense to get money for drugs	/	15.8%	/

Note: Based on the Survey of Inmates in Local Jails, 1996. Of the estimated 507,026 jail inmates in 1996, 62.7% were convicted on their current offense or serving a sentence for a prior offense; 33.4% were unconvicted, awaiting trial, on trial, or not yet arraigned; and 3.9% had an unknown conviction status.
/ Not reported.
[a] Excludes inmates for whom the offense was unknown.
[b] Excludes inmates for whom the offense of a prior probation or incarceration was unknown.
[c] Used drugs at least once a week for a least a month.

Drug use of jail inmates, 1996	Percent of inmates
Past drug involvement of all inmates	73.7%
Includes persons who –	
–regularly used drugs in the past	
–received drug treatment in the past	
–may not currently use drugs regularly	
–used intravenous drugs	
–were sentenced for past drug offenses	
Active drug involvement prior to current admission of convicted inmates	65.5%
Includes persons who –	
–used drugs in month before the offense	
–used drugs at the time of the offense	
–committed the offense for money for drugs	
–were sentenced for a current drug offense	
–had received treatment since admission	

cent) than women (19.3 percent) were under the influence of drugs when they committed their current offense.

In U.S. jails in 1998 males comprised almost 90 percent of actively drug-involved inmates compared to 11 percent of female jail inmates.

Race/Ethnicity

Among state prisoners there was little variance in drug use patterns across racial or ethnic groups. Similar percentages of non-Hispanic whites (83.6 percent) and non-Hispanic blacks (83.7 percent) reported past drug use, while 80.7 percent of Hispanics reported using drugs in the past. Slightly more blacks (58.3 percent) than whites (55.2 percent) and Hispanics (55 percent) used drugs in the month prior to the offense. About one-third of each group claimed to have been under the influence of drugs at the time the offense was committed.

In federal prisons higher proportions of non-Hispanic whites (77.2 percent) and non-Hispanic blacks (77.5

TABLE 12.6

Drug use, testing, and treatment in jails: Highlights [CONTINUED]

Types of drugs used by convicted jail inmates, 1996

	Used drugs –	
	In month before offense	At time of the offense
Any	55.0%	35.6%
Marijuana or hashish	36.8%	18.5%
Cocaine or crack	24.1	15.2
Heroin or opiates	8.8	5.6
Depressants[a]	5.9	2.4
Stimulants[b]	10.4	6.1
Hallucinogens[c]	4.6	1.6
Inhalants	1.0	0.3

Note: Details may add to more than total because inmates may have used more than one drug.

[a] Depressants include barbiturates, tranquilizers, and Quaalude.
[b] Stimulants include amphetamine and methamphetamine.
[c] Hallucinogens include LSD and PCP.

Selected characteristics of convicted jail inmates, 1996

	Percent of convicted jail inmates	
	Active drug involvement	Other
Gender		
Male	89.0%	91.3%
Female	11.0	8.7
Race/Hispanic origin		
White non-Hispanic	38.2%	42.3%
Black non-Hispanic	41.2	34.5
Hispanic	17.9	19.2
Other*	2.7	4.0
Age		
17 or younger	1.3%	1.4%
18-24	29.0	25.9
25-29	20.3	18.2
30-34	20.2	17.4
35-44	24.6	24.4
45-54	4.2	9.2
55 or older	0.4	3.4

*Other includes Asians, Native Hawaiian or other Pacific Islanders, American Indians, and Alaska Natives.

SOURCE: Doris James Wilson, "Highlights" in "Drug Use, Testing and Treatment in Jails," *Bureau of Justice Statistics Special Report,* U.S. Department of Justice, Washington, D.C., 2000

TABLE 12.7

Levels of prior drug abuse by selected characteristics of state and federal prisoners, 1997

		Percent of prisoners reporting use of drugs –			
Characteristic	Estimated number of prisoners[a]	Ever in the past	Used regularly[b]	In the month prior to offense	At the time of offense
All State prisoners	**1,059,607**	**83.0%**	**69.6%**	**56.5%**	**32.6%**
Sex					
Male	993,365	82.9%	69.3%	56.1%	32.1%
Female	66,242	84.0	73.6	62.4	40.4
Race/Hispanic origin					
White non-Hispanic	352,864	83.6%	70.5%	55.2%	33.9%
Black non-Hispanic	492,676	83.7	70.5	58.3	31.9
Hispanic	179,998	80.7	65.6	55.0	33.0
Other	34,069	79.0	66.7	52.7	27.8
Age					
24 or younger	209,343	84.1%	71.1%	63.2%	33.3%
25–34	404,034	86.4	72.9	60.0	35.0
35–44	311,999	86.3	73.4	56.5	34.5
45–54	103,470	70.5	55.2	40.4	22.7
55 or older	30,761	39.0	24.3	18.4	9.7
All Federal prisoners	**89,072**	**72.9%**	**57.3%**	**44.8%**	**22.4%**
Sex					
Male	82,646	73.7%	58.1%	45.4%	22.7%
Female	6,426	62.8	47.2	36.7	19.3
Race/Hispanic origin					
White non-Hispanic	26,616	77.2%	63.5%	49.4%	28.6%
Black non-Hispanic	33,697	77.5	61.9	47.2	22.2
Hispanic	24,349	63.5	45.5	37.5	16.9
Other	4,411	64.2	50.0	38.5	18.1
Age					
24 or younger	7,933	80.4%	65.4%	57.2%	28.1%
25–34	32,634	76.0	60.6	48.5	23.0
35–44	27,259	77.2	60.6	46.8	24.7
45–54	14,501	67.6	52.5	35.2	18.8
55 or older	6,746	43.6	28.6	24.3	11.8

[a] Based on probability of selection in the sample and adjusted to June 30, 1997, custody counts.
[b] Regular use is defined as once a week or more for at least a month.

SOURCE: Christopher J. Mumola, *Substance Abuse and Treatment, State and Federal Prisoners, 1997,* Bureau of Justice Statistics, Washington, DC, 1999

percent) reported ever using drugs in the past than did Hispanics (63.5 percent). Similarly, more non-Hispanic whites (63.5 percent) and non-Hispanic blacks (61.9 percent) used drugs regularly than did Hispanics (45.5 percent). A higher percentage of non-Hispanic whites (28.6 percent) were under the influence of drugs when committing their current offense than were non-Hispanic blacks (22.2 percent) and Hispanics (16.9 percent).

Of drug offenders incarcerated in U.S. jails in 1998, 41.2 percent were black or African American, 38.2 percent were white, and 17.9 percent were Hispanic.

Age

Inmates who were younger than 45 years of age in state (87 percent) and federal (76 percent) prisons reported simi-

lar levels of drug use, and their incidence of drug use was higher than that of older prisoners. More than 80 percent of state prisoners under the age of 45 years reported some prior drug use compared to about 55 percent of those ages 45 years and older. About one-third of state prisoners under the age of 45 years claimed they committed their offense while on drugs compared to one-fifth of those 45 years of age and older. In federal prisons about half of inmates under the age of 45 years had used drugs in the month prior to their offense compared to about one-third of older prisoners. Approximately 95 percent of jail inmates 44 years of age or younger reported active drug involvement in 1998.

ALCOHOL

The Bureau of Justice Statistics (BJS), in *Substance Abuse and Treatment, State and Federal Prisoners, 1997*

(Washington, D.C., 1999) found that assault, murder, and sexual assault were the offenses most closely tied to alcohol use at the time of the offense. In 1997 one-third (37.2 percent) of state and one-fifth (20.4 percent) of federal inmates claimed to have been under the influence of alcohol at the time they committed their current offense. Among state inmates 43.2 percent of public-order offenders and 41.7 percent of violent offenders were drinking at the time of the offense, followed by 34.5 percent of property offenders and 27.4 percent of drug offenders. More than half (52 percent) of negligent manslaughter crimes were committed while under the influence of alcohol (generally driving while intoxicated that resulted in a death), as were 48.1 percent of "other public-order" offenses. Fewer fraud (25.2 percent) and drug trafficking (25.5 percent) offenses were committed while the offender was inebriated.

Among federal prisoners 24.5 percent of violent offenses were committed while under the influence of alcohol, as were 20.6 percent of public-order offenses, 19.8 percent of drug offenses, and 15.6 percent of property offenses. Nearly half (46 percent) of assault offenses were committed while the perpetrator was drinking, as were 38.7 percent of murders. However, only 10.4 percent of fraud offenses and 18 percent of robbery offenses were committed while the perpetrator was drinking.

According to the CAGE diagnostic questionnaire, 24.4 percent of state prisoners reported experiences consistent with a history of alcohol abuse or dependence (at least three positive responses). (A CAGE questionnaire is a diagnostic device used to detect a person's history of alcohol abuse or dependence. CAGE is an acronym for the four questions asked on the questionnaire—attempts to (C)ut back on drinking, (A)nnoyance at others' criticism of one's drinking, feelings of (G)uilt about drinking, and needing a drink first thing in the morning as an (E)ye opener to steady the nerves. The number of positive responses to these four questions determines a person's likelihood of alcohol abuse.) The incidence of alcohol abuse among state prisoners varied somewhat by offense type. A larger proportion of public-order offenders (31 percent) responded positively to the CAGE questionnaire, followed by property offenders (27.3 percent), and violent offenders (24.2 percent). Drug offenders (19.1 percent) were the least likely to have a positive response to the CAGE questionnaire. It is important to remember when reading these statistics that alcoholics and drug abusers tend to lie about (underestimate) their drinking and drug use.

CHARACTERISTICS OF ALCOHOL USE AMONG PRISONERS

Gender

Previous alcohol abuse was most common among white male prisoners. Among state prisoners males

TABLE 12.8

Levels of prior alcohol abuse by selected characteristics of state and federal prisoners, 1997

Characteristic	Estimated number of prisoners*	Percent of prisoners reporting prior alcohol abuse		
		Ever had a "binge drinking" experience	Under the influence of alcohol at the time of offense	3 or more positive CAGE responses
All State prisoners	**1,059,607**	**41.0%**	**37.2%**	**24.4%**
Sex				
Male	993,365	41.8%	37.7%	24.5%
Female	66,242	29.9	29.1	23.4
Race/Hispanic origin				
White non-Hispanic	352,864	53.5%	42.7%	33.5%
Black non-Hispanic	492,676	31.9	33.0	18.6%
Hispanic	179,998	39.9	36.7	22.0
Other	34,069	49.6	41.7	27.7
Age				
24 or younger	209,343	40.2%	30.7%	15.8%
25–34	404,034	42.3	37.7	24.8
35–44	311,999	42.3	41.3	28.6
45–54	103,470	37.4	37.7	28.5
55 or older	30,761	29.3	30.2	22.5
All Federal prisoners	**89,072**	**30.3%**	**20.4%**	**16.2%**
Sex				
Male	82,646	31.2%	20.9%	16.6%
Female	6,426	18.8	15.1	11.6
Race/Hispanic origin				
White non-Hispanic	26,616	38.3%	22.1%	19.3%
Black non-Hispanic	33,697	25.0	21.1	12.5
Hispanic	24,349	28.2	16.8	17.8
Other	4,411	34.9	26.0	17.6
Age				
24 or younger	7,933	31.8%	18.4%	12.0%
25–34	32,634	32.1	22.5	15.3
35–44	27,259	30.8	20.5	17.2
45–54	14,501	29.1	20.2	19.7
55 or older	6,746	20.8	13.4	14.5

* Based on probability of selection in the sample and adjusted to June 30, 1997, custody counts.

SOURCE: Christopher J. Mumola, *Substance Abuse and Treatment, State and Federal Prisoners, 1997*, Bureau of Justice Statistics, Washington, DC, 1999

(41.8 percent) were more likely than females (29.9 percent) to report binge drinking. In addition males (37.7 percent) were more likely than females (29.1 percent) to claim to have been under the influence of alcohol at the time of their current offense. However, similar proportions of males (24.5 percent) and females (23.4 percent) fit the CAGE profile of alcohol dependence. (See Table 12.8.)

Similarly, among federal prisoners, a higher percentage of men (31.2 percent) than women (18.8 percent) said they had experienced binge drinking, and a higher percentage of men (20.9 percent) than women (15.1 percent) admitted being under the influence of alcohol when committing their current offense. However, men (16.6 percent) in federal prison were more likely than women (11.6 percent) to have met the CAGE criteria for alcohol dependence.

TABLE 12.9

Substance abuse treatment history of state and federal prisoners by reported prior substance abuse, 1997

	Total		Alcohol- or drug-involved prisoners		Under the influence of alcohol or drugs at the time of offense	
Type of treatment	State	Federal	State	Federal	State	Federal
Ever in any treatment or programs	**56.4%**	**46.4%**	**64.8%**	**51.4%**	**69.3%**	**66.1%**
Any treatment	34.5	24.6	41.5	27.7	46.3	40.6
Other alcohol/drug programs	43.1	35.4	49.4	39.2	52.5	50.8
Participated while under correctional supervision	**47.8%**	**39.2%**	**55.2%**	**43.5%**	**59.2%**	**55.8%**
Any treatment	26.2	18.9	31.7	21.3	35.5	30.4
In prison/jail	19.7	15.0	23.9	16.9	27.0	24.6
On probation/parole	15.0	8.4	18.3	9.6	20.6	14.6
Other alcohol/drug programs	37.5	30.9	43.2	34.4	46.2	44.9
In prison/jail	33.3	27.4	38.3	30.5	41.0	40.6
On probation/parole	17.2	10.1	20.5	11.4	22.6	16.1
Participated since admission	**32.5%**	**28.2%**	**37.7%**	**31.6%**	**41.1%**	**42.7%**
Any treatment	12.0	10.4	14.6	11.7	16.7	17.4
Residential facility or unit	6.9	7.3	8.5	8.2	10.1	12.4
Counseling by a professional	5.1	3.8	6.2	4.3	6.9	6.3
Detoxification unit	0.8	0.2	1.0	0.2	1.3	0.3
Maintenance drug	0.2	0.2	0.3	0.2	0.3	0.2
Other alcohol/drug programs	27.5	23.1	31.9	26.0	34.6	35.2
Self-help group/peer counseling	22.7	11.2	26.7	12.8	29.3	20.5
Education program	12.6	16.8	14.8	18.8	16.2	24.2
Estimated number of prisoners	1,047,933	87,839	806,758	73,103	543,869	29,468

Note: Detail adds to more than total because prisoners may have participated in more than one type of treatment program.

SOURCE: Christopher J. Mumola, *Substance Abuse and Treatment, State and Federal Prisoners, 1997*, Bureau of Justice Statistics, Washington, DC, 1999

TABLE 12.10

Substance abuse treatment or programs in local jails, by size of jurisdiction, 1998

	Percent of jurisdictions with treatment or programs by size of jurisdiction*						
Type of treatment	Total	Fewer than 50 inmates	50-99	100-249	250-499	500-999	1,000 or more
Any treatment or program	**72.8%**	**63.2%**	**75.0%**	**83.9%**	**91.0%**	**91.9%**	**90.2%**
Substance abuse treatment[a]	**42.8%**	**33.5%**	**38.7%**	**53.3%**	**62.2%**	**70.2%**	**73.8%**
Detoxification	32.1	26.0	26.2	39.7	48.1	51.2	56.6
Other programs[b]	**67.5%**	**57.3%**	**70.1%**	**77.0%**	**87.8%**	**88.0%**	**89.4%**
Education or awareness	29.6	20.2	30.0	32.0	46.8	61.8	72.1
Self-help programs	63.7	52.1	67.8	73.5	86.2	87.8	88.5

Note: Jurisdictions may have more than one program.
*Based on the average daily population between July 1, 1997, and June 30, 1998.
[a] Includes residential facilities, detoxification units, professional group or individual counseling, rehabilitation, and maintenance drug programs.
[b] Includes drug or alcohol education or awareness programs, self-help groups, such as Alcoholics Anonymous and Narcotics Anonymous, and other peer counseling groups.

SOURCE: Doris James Wilson, "Table 7. Substance abuse treatment or programs in local jails, by size of jurisdiction, 1998" in "Drug Use, Testing and Treatment in Jails," *Bureau of Justice Statistics Special Report*, U.S. Department of Justice, Washington, D.C., 2000

Race/Ethnicity

Non-Hispanic whites reported the highest levels of alcohol abuse among state prisoners. More non-Hispanic whites (53.5 percent) than non-Hispanic blacks (31.9 percent) or Hispanics (39.9 percent) reported ever having had a binge drinking experience. A higher percentage of non-Hispanic whites (42.7 percent) than non-Hispanic blacks (33 percent) or Hispanics (36.7 percent) claimed to have been under the influence of alcohol when they committed their current offense. One-third (33.5 percent) of non-Hispanic whites reported positive responses on the CAGE questionnaire compared to 18.6 percent of non-Hispanic blacks and 22 percent of Hispanics.

TABLE 12.11

Drug treatment of state and federal prisoners since admission by levels of prior drug use, 1991 and 1997

	Estimated number of prisoners, 1997		Percent of prisoners reporting participation							
			Drug treatment since admission				Other drug abuse program since admission			
			State		Federal		State		Federal	
Level of prior drug use	State	Federal	1997	1991	1997	1991	1997	1991	1997	1991
All prisoners	1,048,752	87,720	9.7%	24.5%	9.2%	15.7%	20.3%	15.5%	20.0%	10.1%
Prisoners who used drugs										
Ever	870,558	63,979	11.5%	31.1%	12.4%	26.3%	24.0%	19.6%	26.0%	16.9%
Regularly*	729,578	50,244	13.1	33.9	14.5	30.9	26.4	22.2	29.6	20.1
In the month before offense	592,611	39,275	14.6	36.5	15.4	33.7	28.3	23.7	31.7	22.0
At the time of the offense	338,481	19,507	18.0	41.0	18.9	39.4	32.2	27.2	38.0	25.4

*Regular use is defined as once a week for at least a month.

SOURCE: Christopher J. Mumola, *Substance Abuse and Treatment, State and Federal Prisoners, 1997*, Bureau of Justice Statistics, Washington, DC, 1999

Non-Hispanic white federal inmates reported the highest percentage of binge drinking (38.3 percent), followed by Hispanics (28.2 percent) and non-Hispanic blacks (25 percent). However, there was little variance by race or ethnicity among federal prisoners who reported being intoxicated when committing their offense.

Age

Age differences played a very small role in prior alcohol abuse or dependence for either state or federal inmates. Among state prisoners similar percentages of those between the ages of 25 and 54 years reported comparable incidences of binge drinking, being under the influence of alcohol when committing the current crime, and fitting the CAGE profile. The same held true for federal prisoners.

DRUG AND ALCOHOL TREATMENT

State Prisoners

Only one-third (34.5 percent) of state inmates reported that they had participated in any alcohol or drug abuse treatment in the past (including time spent in a residential facility, professional counseling, detoxification, or use of a maintenance drug). Since being admitted to prison, 12 percent of state prisoners had participated in the same types of drug or alcohol treatment. Two-fifths (43.1 percent) of state detainees reported past participation in other alcohol or drug abuse programs, including self-help groups, peer counseling, and education/awareness programs. One-fourth (27.5 percent) of state inmates had participated in these programs since their most recent admittance to prison. A little more than half (56.4 percent) of state inmates had taken part in either substance abuse treatment or other alcohol and drug programs in the past. One-third (32.5 percent) of state prisoners began treatment after admission to prison. (See Table 12.9.)

Federal Prisoners

Among federal prisoners one-fourth (24.6 percent) reported that they had participated in any alcohol or drug abuse treatment in the past (including time spent in a residential facility, professional counseling, detoxification, or use of a maintenance drug). Since being admitted to prison, 10.4 percent of federal prisoners had participated in the same types of drug or alcohol treatment. One-third (35.4 percent) of federal inmates reported past participation in other alcohol or drug abuse programs, including self-help groups, peer counseling, and education/awareness programs. One-fourth (23.1 percent) of federal inmates had participated in such programs since their most recent admittance to prison. Slightly less than half (46.4 percent) of federal prisoners had taken part in either substance abuse treatment or other alcohol and drug programs in the past. More than one-fourth (28.2 percent) of federal detainees began treatment after admission to prison. (See Table 12.9.)

JAIL INMATES. In 1998 about three-fourths (72.8 percent) of jails nationwide reported having some type of substance abuse treatment or other type of drug program. (See Table 12.10.) Of dedicated substance abuse treatment programs about one-third (32.1 percent) were detoxification programs. About 30 percent of jail systems offered education or awareness programs, and some 63.7 percent offered self-help programs.

Less Participation in Drug Treatment Since 1991

Between 1991 and 1997 the percentage of both state and federal inmates who reported being treated for drug abuse after admission to prison dropped. In 1991, 24.5 percent of state prisoners received drug treatment after being admitted to prison; in 1997 only 9.7 percent reported receiving drug treatment. Of federal prisoners in 1991, 15.7 percent reported treatment since being admitted to prison; in 1997, 9.2 percent reported receiving treatment. (See Table 12.11.)

TABLE 12.12

Types of alcohol treatment received by state prisoners since admission by prior alcohol use, 1997

Type of alcohol treatment or program since admission	Committed offense under the influence of alcohol
Any treatment or program	**38.8%**
Treatment	14.4%
Residential facility or unit	8.7
Professional counseling	6.3
Detoxification unit	1.0
Maintenance drug	0.1
Other programs	33.7%
Self-help group/peer counseling	28.8
Education	15.6
Estimated number of State prisoners	387,137

SOURCE: Christopher J. Mumola, *Substance Abuse and Treatment, State and Federal Prisoners, 1997*, Bureau of Justice Statistics, Washington, DC, 1999

TABLE 12.13

Types of alcohol treatment received by federal prisoners since admission by prior alcohol use, 1997

Type of alcohol treatment or program since admission	Committed offense under the influence of alcohol
Any treatment or program	**36.0%**
Treatment	13.8%
Residential facility or unit	9.6
Professional counseling	4.9
Detoxification unit	0.4
Maintenance drug	0.1
Other programs	30.5%
Self-help group/peer counseling	17.8
Education	19.3
Estimated number of Federal prisoners	17,829

SOURCE: Christopher J. Mumola, *Substance Abuse and Treatment, State and Federal Prisoners, 1997*, Bureau of Justice Statistics, Washington, DC, 1999

Since 1991 fewer prisoners using drugs in the past reported treatment after admission to prison. In 1991, of those prisoners using drugs in the month before the current offense, 36.5 percent of state prisoners and 33.7 percent of federal prisoners reported receiving treatment. By 1997 only 14.6 percent of state prisoners and 15.4 percent of federal prisoners reported receiving help. In 1991, 41 percent of state prisoners and 39.4 percent of federal prisoners using drugs at the time they committed their current offense reported receiving drug treatment while in prison. By 1997 only 18 percent of state and 18.9 percent of federal prisoners who had used drugs when they committed their current offense were receiving treatment.

Increased Participation in Other Programs Since 1991

On the other hand, enrollment in other drug abuse programs, such as self-help or peer groups and drug education classes, rose between 1991 and 1997. These are cheaper programs for the authorities because they do not require professionals to run them. In 1997, 20.3 percent of state inmates and 20 percent of federal inmates reported taking part in drug abuse programs during their current prison term, up from 1991 when 15.5 percent of state prisoners and 10.1 percent of federal prisoners had participated in such programs.

In 1997, of those using drugs in the month prior to committing their current offense, 28.3 percent of state and 31.7 percent of federal prisoners were enrolled in substance abuse programs compared to the 1991 figures of 23.7 percent of state prisoners and 22 percent of federal prisoners. In 1997, 32.2 percent of state prisoners and 38 percent of federal prisoners who were using drugs at the time of their current offense were taking part in drug abuse programs. The proportions of prisoners enrolled in those programs in 1991 were lower, with 27.2 percent of state and 25.4 percent of federal prisoners participating.

PARTICIPATION OF JAIL INMATES. As of June 30, 1998, some 92,000 jail inmates had participated in substance abuse treatment or drug programs. Of those 42,100 had gone to Alcoholics Anonymous, Narc-Anon, or other self-help groups. Another 27,000 had participated in drug or alcohol education—some 24,400 in substance abuse treatment and 2,100 in detoxification.

Participation in Alcohol Abuse Programs

State prisoners who had abused alcohol were less apt to report participation in alcohol treatment than in other abuse programs. More state prisoners who committed their offense while under the influence of alcohol enrolled in self-help or peer groups (28.8 percent) and education classes (15.6 percent) after admission to prison. Fewer state prisoners participated in residential treatment (8.7 percent) or professional counseling programs (6.3 percent). (See Table 12.12.)

Federal prisoners who had histories of alcohol abuse also reported greater enrollment in alcohol abuse programs than in treatment. About one-fifth (19.3 percent) of federal prisoners who had committed their current offense while drinking enrolled in alcohol education classes and self-help or peer groups (17.8 percent) after incarceration, while 9.6 percent participated in residential treatment and 4.9 percent sought professional counseling. (See Table 12.13.)

Both types of programs are available to prisoners. The data do not specify whether the prisoners choose the type of help they get or whether they take whatever is available to them at the time they enroll.

CHARACTERISTICS OF PRISONERS RECEIVING TREATMENT

Gender

Among state prisoners involved with drugs or alcohol, women (55.6 percent) were more likely than men

TABLE 12.14

TABLE 12.15

Alcohol- or drug-involved state prisoners treated for substance abuse by selected characteristics, 1997

| Characteristic | Estimated number of State prisoners | Percent of alcohol- or drug-involved State prisoners reporting – | | | |
| | | Treatment for substance abuse | | Participation in other substance abuse programs | |
		Ever	Since admission	Ever	Since admission
Total	806,758	41.5%	14.6%	49.4%	31.9%
Sex					
Male	754,418	40.5%	14.2%	49.4%	31.9%
Female	52,340	55.6	19.6	49.3	31.9
Race/Hispanic origin					
White non-Hispanic	271,345	51.8%	17.0%	58.0%	36.3%
Black non-Hispanic	367,331	36.6	13.5	46.7	31.6
Hispanic	142,610	33.8	12.5	39.2	23.9
Other	25,472	46.2	16.2	54.2	34.8
Age					
24 or younger	158,705	29.3%	10.2%	37.9%	22.6%
25–34	316,744	43.1	15.2	50.2	33.1
35–44	242,579	47.4	16.8	54.4	35.5
45–54	71,936	42.4	14.9	53.9	35.5
55 or older	16,794	36.7	10.1	52.4	31.8

SOURCE: Christopher J. Mumola, *Substance Abuse and Treatment, State and Federal Prisoners, 1997*, Bureau of Justice Statistics, Washington, DC, 1999

Alcohol- or drug-involved federal prisoners treated for substance abuse by selected characteristics, 1997

| Characteristic | Estimated number of Federal prisoners | Percent of alcohol- or drug-involved Federal prisoners reporting – | | | |
| | | Treatment for substance abuse | | Participation in other substance abuse programs | |
		Ever	Since admission	Ever	Since admission
Total	73,103	27.7%	11.7%	39.2%	26.0%
Sex					
Male	67,856	27.6%	11.6%	39.6%	26.1%
Female	5,247	28.8	13.3	34.2	25.2
Race/Hispanic origin					
White non-Hispanic	20,178	39.5%	16.0%	51.6%	34.9%
Black non-Hispanic	28,514	25.7	11.9	39.0	25.0
Hispanic	21,185	19.0	8.2	28.1	18.5
Other	3,225	29.1	7.3	38.5	29.1
Age					
24 or younger	6,736	21.8%	8.1%	35.2%	24.0%
25–34	27,500	27.3	12.5	39.2	26.4
35–44	22,634	30.2	12.6	41.9	27.6
45–54	11,074	32.8	13.7	40.8	26.8
55 or older	5,159	15.0	4.5	29.5	17.7

SOURCE: Christopher J. Mumola, *Substance Abuse and Treatment, State and Federal Prisoners, 1997*, Bureau of Justice Statistics, Washington, DC, 1999

(40.5 percent) to have ever been treated for substance abuse. In addition women (19.6 percent) were more likely than men (14.2 percent) to have been treated since being admitted to prison. However, equal proportions of men (49.4 percent) and women (49.3 percent) reported ever participating in a substance abuse program in the past, and 31.9 percent of each reported participation since being admitted to prison. (See Table 12.14.)

Percentages were much closer for federal prisoners involved with drugs or alcohol. Better than one of four women (28.8 percent) and men (27.6 percent) reported ever being treated for substance abuse, and approximately one of eight women (13.3 percent) and men (11.6 percent) reported being treated since being admitted to prison. Approximately one-fourth of women (25.2 percent) and men (26.1 percent) participated in other substance abuse programs since their admission to prison, but women (34.2 percent) were less likely than men (39.6 percent) to have ever participated in a substance abuse program in the past. (See Table 12.15.)

Race/Ethnicity

In state prisons non-Hispanic white inmates (51.8 percent) were more likely than non-Hispanic black (36.6 percent) or Hispanic (33.8 percent) inmates to have ever received treatment for substance abuse. Non-Hispanic white detainees (17 percent) were somewhat more likely than non-Hispanic black (13.5 percent) or Hispanic (12.5 percent) prisoners to have been treated for substance

abuse since being incarcerated. Similarly, non-Hispanic white inmates (58 percent) were more likely than non-Hispanic black (46.7 percent) or Hispanic (39.2 percent) inmates in state prisons to have ever participated in other substance abuse programs. In addition non-Hispanic white prisoners (36.3 percent) were more likely than non-Hispanic black (31.6 percent) or Hispanic (23.9 percent) prisoners to have taken part in other substance abuse programs since admission to prison.

As with state prisoners non-Hispanic white inmates (39.5 percent) in federal prison were more likely to have received treatment for substance abuse than non-Hispanic black (25.7 percent) or Hispanic (19 percent) inmates. A larger proportion of non-Hispanic whites (16 percent) also reported receiving treatment since being admitted to federal prison than non-Hispanic blacks (11.9 percent) or Hispanics (8.2 percent). Similarly, non-Hispanic whites (51.6 percent) were more likely than non-Hispanic blacks (39 percent) or Hispanics (28.1 percent) to have ever taken part in other substance abuse programs. Non-Hispanic whites (34.9 percent) were more likely than non-Hispanic blacks (25 percent) or Hispanics (18.5 percent) to have participated in other substance abuse programs after being admitted to prison.

Age

Age did not seem to matter. About two of five state prisoners between the ages of 25 and 54 years reported ever receiving treatment for substance abuse. Approximately one of six had received treatment since admittance. About one-half of state prisoners between the ages of 25 and 54 years reported ever taking part in other substance abuse programs, and one-third said they had participated in other substance abuse programs since entering prison. (State inmates older than 54 years and younger than 25 years reported lower incidences of participation in substance abuse treatment or other programs.)

As with state prisoners the rate of treatment for federal inmates varied little by age. About three of ten prisoners between the ages of 25 and 54 years reported ever receiving treatment for substance abuse, and approximately one of eight in each age group had received treatment since being admitted to prison. About two-fifths of federal prisoners between the ages of 25 and 54 years said they had taken part in other substance abuse programs, and one-fourth reported participating in other substance abuse programs since being admitted to prison. (As with state inmates federal prisoners older than 54 years or younger than 25 years reported lower rates of participation in substance abuse treatment or other substance abuse programs.)

TREATMENT PROGRAMS

Drug treatment programs in prisons began in the 1930s at federal institutions in Lexington, Kentucky and Fort Worth, Texas. Many have been ineffective and poorly run. In 1997, according to the Criminal Justice Institute, only about 14 percent of inmates participated in drug programs. The *New York Times* reported that, although one of six inmates receives some kind of treatment, only about 2 percent have the kind of serious rehabilitation that changes the inmates' behavior for a lifetime. Most are "just say no" types of treatment programs that last for several weeks. The majority of participants are rearrested after release.

The most effective programs take many months but reduce the rearrest rate considerably. A study in California (*Controlling Cocaine: Supply Versus Demand Programs,* Peter Rydell and Susan Everingham, RAND Corporation, Santa Monica, California, 1994) showed that, for every $1.00 spent on effective drug treatment, the state saved $7.00 in costs of crime and imprisonment. States that had established serious drug treatment programs, such as New York and Texas, began cutting back their programs by the late 1990s due to budget constraints.

Drug treatment advocates say that drug treatment programs have fallen victim to prison expansion. According to Richard Rosenfeld, a professor of criminology at the University of Missouri at St. Louis, "What is particularly tragic is that drug treatment in prison has proven to be effective as an anti-crime program . . . . This is an unintended consequence of prison expansion. Each time we spend a dollar on building a new prison or expanding an existing one, it is one less dollar for drug treatment." In January 1999 President Bill Clinton announced that he would propose $215 million in his next budget for testing and treating prisoners for drug use. Approximately $115 million was, at the time, budgeted for fighting drug use by prisoners, parolees, and probationers.

In 1995 Joseph Califano, head of the National Center on Addiction and Substance Abuse (CASA) at Columbia University, commented that average Americans think that prisoners are like those represented by famous actors such as Humphrey Bogart and James Cagney in 1930s movies. The reality, however, is that prisons are full of drug and alcohol abusers, as well as the mentally ill. He further noted that prisoners are "not hardened criminals; they're people who can change. But they can't change without help."

Not all inmates participate in the programs offered. Inmates may refuse to participate or may have already completed the program. Inmates may not qualify—they may be too new to the institution or not close enough to the end of their sentence, or they may be rule breakers, under administrative segregation, or in the wrong custody level. Facilities may also keep some slots open to gain flexibility to deal with unexpected situations.

California's Proposition 36

With the passage of Proposition 36 in November 2000, California virtually abolished jail and prison sentences for nonviolent drug offenders. Effective July 1, 2001, the new law requires that:

- Offenders convicted of nonviolent drug possession be sentenced to probation and drug treatment instead of prison, jail, or probation without treatment

- Parole violators who commit nonviolent drug possession offenses or who violate drug-related conditions of parole complete drug treatment in the community rather than being returned to state prison

- Eligible offenders receive up to one year of drug treatment in the community and up to six months of additional follow-up care

The terms of Proposition 36 allow courts (for probationers) and a prison board (for parole violators) to require offenders to participate in training, counseling, literacy programs, or community service, and stipulate that all treatment be paid for by the offender unless it creates a financial hardship.

Therapeutic Community

The most effective treatment for inmates is provided in a therapeutic community (TC). TCs typically house clients in residential settings that offer opportunities for intensive intervention and support that may not be available in outpatient care. As applied to corrections, clients live isolated from the rest of the prison population and receive treatment to change negative patterns of behavior, thinking, and feeling that predispose them to drug use. Participation generally lasts for an extended period. The time and isolation are primary resources; the isolation shields clients from competing demands of the street, work, friends, and family.

TCs offer other features including the use of ex-offenders and ex-addicts as staff, use of confrontations and support groups, and a set of rules and sanctions to govern behavior. In prisons TCs also focus on criminal behavior, sex abuse, and other issues. It may be this multiple focus that explains why TCs are more likely to be successful in the long run than programs aimed mainly at drug abuse. Treatment for drug abusers in jails is more limited than in prisons, in part because inmates stay there for less time.

EVALUATIONS OF TC PROGRAMS. The Stay'n Out prison-based TC program was begun in New York in 1977 by recovered addicts who were also ex-offenders. The program successfully reduced recidivism (repeat offenses or rearrests) for both men and women. Program participants had a significantly lower rearrest rate than those receiving no treatment and those receiving all other types of treatment.

The main conclusion of the evaluation was that hardcore drug abusers who remained in the prison-based TC longer were much more likely to succeed than those who left earlier. As time participating in TC treatment increased, recidivism declined. Male and female clients did significantly better on parole if they remained in the program 9 to 12 months rather than terminating earlier or later.

Two evaluation studies produced similar results. A three-year follow up evaluation of an Oregon program (Cornerstone) found that 71 percent of the graduates stayed out of prison, while only 26 percent of the dropouts of the program did. A second evaluation also showed that a much higher percentage of graduates (75 percent) stayed out of prison than did dropouts (37 percent). The longer the time in treatment the less likely the inmate was to be rearrested.

The Amity Prison TC program (California), established in 1989, lasts 12 months and provides an aftercare (any community program aimed at helping those released from prisons or residential care) in a community-based TC. A study of the California program found that, while 63 percent of a control group was reincarcerated within a year after parole, only 26 percent of those who completed the program plus the aftercare were reincarcerated.

Key-Crest (Delaware) also showed success in keeping participants drug-free and arrest-free. The program has a primary stage of 12-month intensive residential treatment (Key). The second phase consists of inmates nearing release working outside the institution while spending nonwork time in the setting of the TC (Crest). Inmates who participated in both phases tended to be more successful than others in staying drug- and arrest-free.

A SOUND INVESTMENT. According to the National Institute of Justice (NIJ), these programs are cost effective. Programs such as Stay'n Out cost about $3,000–$4,000 more than the standard correctional cost per inmate per year, and programs such as Cornerstone cost a little over twice as much because they have a higher number of professional staff members and lighter caseloads. However, the savings in crime-related and drug use-associated costs pay for the treatment in about two to three years. NIJ concludes that treatment lowers crime and health costs, as well as related social and criminal justice costs.

The greater the investment in rehabilitating the most severe offender-addicts, the greater the probable impact. These studies have shown that chronic heroin and cocaine users (about 3–10 percent of all offenders) who commit a large percentage of crimes are responsive to TC treatment if it continues long enough. The studies also showed TCs are effective in diverse locales and populations.

AMOUNT OF DRUG TRAFFICKING IN PRISON

Many inmates claim that drugs are easily attainable in prison, while prison administrators maintain that the inmates are exaggerating. James Flateau, a spokesperson for the New York State Department of Correctional Services, in a *New York Times* interview, denied the "widespread availability" of drugs. However, he continued, "unless you searched everyone going in and out, kept all packages out, and locked all inmates in their cells for 24 hours a day, you're going to have contraband."

Indeed, the price of drugs in the barter economy of prisons is the equivalent of 3–10 times the street price, indicating a smaller supply. Bobby Lewis, a senior security specialist with the Federal Bureau of Prisons, declared in a *New York Times* interview that denial of the drug trade in prison is a "public relations gimmick. If a warden acknowledges he has a drug problem, he's going to pay a terrible price," so most present their prisons as places where drugs are kept out.

Probably the only prison without heavy drug trafficking is the federal maximum security prison at Marion, Illinois, where inmates are locked in their cells most of the day and visitors are separated by a glass window. A normal visitation day in a Washington, D.C., prison has 80 prisoners sitting in the room with two or three visitors each. Prolonged hugging and kissing can cover up exchanges of drugs. Even with searches of both the inmates and the visitors the presence of drugs can go undetected.

According to some prisoners mandatory sentencing that sends more nonviolent people to prison for longer periods of time causes inmates to take up drugs. Drugs help deaden them to the boredom and discouragement they face and to the often hostile, violent environment. In addition, with more and more inmates in prison for possessing and trading in drugs, there is a ready market.

Drug Sweeps

According to the National Criminal Justice Association (*Justice Bulletin,* vol. 16, no. 4, April 1996), more states are staging surprise lockdowns and raids to stem the amount of drugs in their prisons. For example, on October 24, 1995, more than 600 corrections officers conducted a cell-by-cell raid and strip search at the prison in Graterford, Pennsylvania, the nation's fifth largest state prison. The search turned up more than 200 weapons and several hundred dollars in cash, but only a very small amount of drugs. Officials assumed that once the raid began, the inmates either flushed drugs down the toilets or swallowed them.

A similar raid at the Muskegon Correctional Facility in Michigan was conducted after the inmates at the facility tested at a rate of 6 percent for positive use of drugs, compared to the statewide average of 3.8 percent. The search found two alcohol stills, two to three ounces of cocaine and heroin, and about one ounce of marijuana, as well as basic prison-made weapons.

SMOKING

More and more correctional institutions have banned smoking within the facilities. For example, more than 13 of 62 New York counties have prohibited, or announced their intention to prohibit, smoking in their jails. In neighboring Connecticut, 14 of the state's 27 prisons ban smoking; the rest operate at least one nonsmoking housing unit. In New Jersey's 12 adult prisons inmates cannot smoke if their cellmates are nonsmokers.

Death row inmates in California and Texas are not allowed to smoke, even before their executions. Larry Todd, a spokesperson for the Department of Criminal Justice in Texas, in a *New York Times* interview, maintained that nicotine was just another drug. "We wouldn't give them a shot of whisky or cocaine, so I doubt we'd give them a cigarette," he declared.

Many inmates and guards oppose the smoking bans, asserting that cigarettes soothe their nerves in a highly stressful atmosphere. Meanwhile, the black-market price of cigarettes has soared, with individual cigarettes selling for as much as $3.00 and a single puff for $1.00. Some inmates have requested smoking and nonsmoking facilities.

While corrections departments know that it is difficult to curtail the smoking habit among inmates, many have enacted no-smoking policies because of a growing number of complaints and fears of lawsuits from nonsmoking prisoners and guards who worry about the health risks of secondhand smoke. In 1993, in *Helling v. McKinney* (509 U.S. 25), the Supreme Court held that inmates have a constitutional right under the Eighth Amendment's protection against cruel and unusual punishment not to be exposed to cellmates' tobacco smoke if the exposure creates an extreme health hazard.

At the end of 1996 the Third Court of Appeals in Texas rejected a prisoner's arguments that prisoners' rights were violated when Texas banned smoking in prisons in 1995. According to the opinion, in order to assert a claim under either constitution (federal or state), the complainant was required to establish that the alleged wrongful action interfered with a protected right. "Neither the state nor the federal constitution protects a citizen's interest in smoking."

In a similar case in 1994 a federal judge issued an injunction to limit smoking in the District of Columbia's Lorton Correctional Complex in Lorton, Virginia, as the staff had failed to enforce the policy of only allowing smoking in certain areas. The judge ruled that "the effect of this lack of enforcement is particularly harsh on those prisoners with pre-existing medical conditions," and that "deliberate indifference exists where a prison official 'knows of and disregards an excessive risk to inmate health and safety'" (*Farmer v. Brennan,* 1511 U.S. 825, 1994).

Jails and prisons also come under many new ordinances prohibiting smoking in public buildings. In Westchester County, New York, for example, the county jail bans smoking to comply with a county order prohibiting smoking in county buildings.

CHAPTER 13
PRISONERS' RIGHTS—COURT DECISIONS AND RELATED LAWS

He is for the time being the slave of the state.

— *Ruffin v. Commonwealth,* 1871

Simply because prison inmates retain certain constitutional rights does not mean that these rights are not subject to restrictions and limitations.

— *Bell v. Wolfish,* 1979

Prisoners do not shed all constitutional rights at the prison gate.

— *Sandin v. Conner,* 1995

NO RIGHTS

Until the 1960s the courts took little notice of prisoners' rights. Prisoners fell under the jurisdiction of the executive departments of federal, state, and local governments. In 1871 a Virginia court, in *Ruffin v. Commonwealth* (62, Va. 790, 1871), commented that a prisoner "has, as a consequence of his crime, not only forfeited his liberty, but all his personal rights except those which the law in its humanity accords to him. He is for the time being the slave of the state."

Eighty years later, in *Stroud v. Swope* (187 F. 2d. 850, 9th Circuit, 1951), a federal circuit judge asserted that "we think it well settled that it is not the function of the courts to superintend the treatment and discipline of persons in penitentiaries, but only to deliver from imprisonment those who are illegally confined." Correctional administrators considered that prisoners lost all constitutional rights after conviction, that the prison staff knew what should be done for the prisoner, and that prisoners had privileges, not rights, that could be taken away arbitrarily. (William C. Collins, *Legal Responsibility and Authority of Correctional Officers,* American Correctional Association, Laurel, Maryland, 1982.)

PRISONERS HAVE RIGHTS

In the 1960s, not only did women and minorities demand civil rights and protesters march against the Viet-

nam War, prisoners insisted that they, too, needed the protection of the courts. Indeed, in 1964 the Supreme Court changed its position of noninterference in the prison system to one of involvement. In *Cooper v. Pate* (378 U.S. 546) the Supreme Court ruled that the Civil Rights Act of 1871 (42 United States Code 1983) granted protection to prisoners. The law states that:

> Every person who, under color of any statute, ordinance, regulation, custom, or usage, of any State or Territory or the District of Columbia, subjects, or causes to be subjected, any citizen of the United States or other person within the jurisdiction thereof to the deprivation of any rights, privileges, or immunities secured by the Constitution and laws, shall be liable to the party injured in an action at law, suit in equity, or other proper proceeding for redress.

With the *Cooper* decision the Supreme Court announced that prisoners had rights guaranteed by the Constitution and could ask the judicial system for help in challenging the conditions of their imprisonment. (Cases brought under this law are called Section 1983 lawsuits. One in every 10 civil lawsuits in U.S. District Courts is a Section 1983 lawsuit.) Between 1966 and 1992 prisoners' suits in federal courts skyrocketed from 218 to 26,824. Since then laws have been passed making it harder for prisoners to sue.

Observers differ about the nature of the lawsuits, how the federal courts process them, and the manner in which they are resolved. Many consider some of the lawsuits frivolous and not warranting the scarce resources of federal courts. Others think that some lawsuits have merit, but that the federal courts tend to treat all Section 1983 lawsuits in an assembly line fashion with little or no individual attention.

Nonetheless, despite different opinions about this substantial body of litigation, there is very little systematic data on which to draw conclusions and to inform Congress

ACCESS TO THE COURTS

In *Johnson v. Avery* (393 U.S. 483, 1969) the Supreme Court emphasized the basic purpose of the writ of *habeas corpus* (petitions) in enabling those unlawfully imprisoned to obtain their freedom. The justices asserted that "it is fundamental that access of prisoners to the courts for the purpose of presenting their complaints may not be denied or obstructed." In this case the High (Supreme) Court ruled that, until the state provides some reasonable alternative to assist inmates in the preparation of petitions for postconviction relief, it "may not validly enforce a regulation which absolutely bars inmates from furnishing such assistance to other prisoners."

The state interest in preserving discipline did not outweigh the rights of prisoners to be able to file petitions. The High Court had already ruled that states could not deny a writ of *habeas corpus* to prisoners who could not pay a filing fee (*Smith v. Bennett,* 365 U.S. 708, 1961). Furthermore, a state must furnish prisoners not otherwise able to obtain one with a transcript of prior hearings (*Long v. District Court,* 385 U.S. 192, 1966). In *Bounds v. Smith* (430 U.S. 817, 1977) the Court further asserted that prison authorities must "assist inmates in the preparation and filing of meaningful legal papers by providing prisoners with adequate law libraries or adequate assistance from persons trained in the law."

Inmates of various prisons operated by the Arizona Department of Corrections (ADOC) alleged that ADOC officials were furnishing them with inadequate legal research facilities and thereby depriving them of their right of access to the courts, in violation of *Bounds v. Smith.* In *Samuel A. Lewis, Director, Arizona Department of Corrections, et al., Petitioners v. Fletcher Casey, Jr., et al* (64 LW 4587, 1996) the court held in favor of the correctional department as the inmates failed to show widespread actual injury.

Bounds did not create an abstract, free-standing right to a law library or legal assistance; rather it acknowledged the right of access to the courts. Inmates have to prove that the alleged shortcomings in the prison library or legal assistance program hindered their efforts to pursue a non-frivolous legal claim. In addition, the Court relied on a constitutional principle that:

> ...prevents courts of law from undertaking tasks assigned to the political branches.... It is the role of courts to provide relief to claimants, in individual or class actions, who have suffered, or will imminently suffer, actual harm; it is not the role of courts, but that of the political branches to shape the institutions of government in such fashion as to comply with the laws and

the Constitution.... If—to take another example from prison life—a healthy inmate who had suffered no deprivation of needed medical treatment were able to claim violation of his constitutional right to medical care..., simply on the ground that prison medical facilities were inadequate, the essential distinction between judge and executive would have disappeared: it would have become the function of the courts to assure adequate medical care in prisons.

Bounds did not guarantee prison law libraries and legal assistance programs. They are only "one constitutionally acceptable method to assure meaningful access to the courts." There can be "alternative means to achieve that goal." An inmate has to show that access to the courts was so "stymied by inadequacies of the law library that he or she was unable even to file a complaint."

FOURTEENTH AMENDMENT

Prisoners bring their cases to the federal courts by accusing the prison systems of violating the First, Fourth, and Eighth Amendments and the due process clauses of the Fifth and Fourteenth Amendments of the U.S. Constitution. The Fifth Amendment provides that "no person" should "be deprived of life, liberty, or property" by the federal government "without due process of the law [legal proceedings]."

The Fourteenth Amendment states that no state should "deprive any person of life, liberty, or property without due process of law." Through a series of court cases the Supreme Court has ruled that the Fourteenth Amendment insures that the rights guaranteed to the people by the Bill of Rights, which applied originally only to the federal government, cannot be taken away by state governments. The following sections describe some prisoner rights cases.

FIRST AMENDMENT CASES

The First Amendment of the U.S. Constitution guarantees that:

> Congress shall make no law respecting an establishment of religion, or prohibiting the free exercise thereof; or abridging the freedom of speech, or of the press; or the right of the people peaceably to assemble; and to petition the government for a redress of grievances.

Censorship

In *Procunier v. Martinez* (416 U.S. 396, 1973) the Supreme Court ruled that prison officials cannot censor inmate correspondence unless they:

> ...show that a regulation authorizing mail censorship furthers one or more of the substantial governmental interests of security, order, and rehabilitation. Second, the limitation of First Amendment freedom must be no greater than is necessary or essential to the protection of the particular governmental interest involved.

Prison officials can refuse to send letters that detail escape plans or encoded messages but cannot censor inmate correspondence simply to "eliminate unflattering or unwelcome opinions or factually inaccurate statements." Because prisoners retain rights, when "a prison regulation or practice offends a fundamental constitutional guarantee, federal courts will discharge their duty to protect constitutional rights."

However, the Court recognized that it was "ill-equipped to deal with the increasingly urgent problems of prison administration." Running a prison takes expertise and planning, all of which, said the Court, is part of the responsibility of the legislative and executive branches. The task of the judiciary, on the other hand, is to establish a standard of review for prisoners' constitutional claims that is responsive to both the need to protect inmates' rights and the policy of judicial restraint.

In 1974 (*Pell v. Procunier*, 417 U.S. 817) the High Court held that federal prison officials could prohibit inmates having face-to-face media interviews. The Court reasoned that judgments regarding prison security "are peculiarly within the province and professional expertise of corrections officials, and in the absence of substantial evidence in the record to indicate that the officials have exaggerated their response to these considerations, courts should ordinarily defer to their expert judgement in such matters." Prisoners had other means in which to communicate with the media.

In 1985, in *Nolan v. Fitzpatrick* (451 F. 2d 545), the First Circuit Court ruled that inmates had the right to correspond with newspapers. The prisoners were limited only in that they could not write about escape plans or include contraband material in their letters.

The Missouri Division of Corrections permitted correspondence between immediate family members who were inmates at different institutions and between inmates writing about legal matters, but allowed other inmate correspondence only if each prisoner's "classification/treatment team" thought it was in the best interests of the parties.

Another Missouri regulation permitted an inmate to marry only with the superintendent's permission, which can be given only when there were "compelling reasons" to do so, such as a pregnancy. In *Turner v. Safley* (482 U.S. 78, 1987) the Supreme Court found the first regulation constitutional and the second one unconstitutional.

The court held that the "constitutional right of prisoners to marry is impermissibly burdened by the Missouri marriage regulation." The Supreme Court had ruled earlier that prisoners had a constitutionally protected right to marry (*Zablocki v. Redhail,* 434 U.S. 374, 1977), subject to restrictions due to incarceration such as time and place and prior approval of a warden. However, the Missouri regulation practically banned all marriages.

The findings in *Turner v. Safley* have become a guide for prison regulations in America. The High Court observed that:

> When a prison regulation impinges on inmates' constitutional rights, the regulation is valid if it is reasonably related to legitimate penological interests.... First, there must be a "valid, rational connection" between the prison regulation and the legitimate government interest put forward to justify it.... Moreover, the government objective must be a legitimate and neutral one.... A second factor relevant in determining the reasonableness of a prison restriction ... is whether there are alternative means of exercising the right (sic) that remain open to prison inmates. A third consideration is the impact accommodation of the asserted constitutional right will have on guards and other inmates, and on the allocation of prison resources generally.

Religious Beliefs

While inmates retain their First Amendment freedom to practice their religions, the courts have upheld restrictions on religious freedom when the corrections department needs to maintain security, when economic considerations are involved, and when the regulation is reasonable.

The legal definition of religion is not limited to mainstream faiths. The judiciary ruled that witchcraft qualifies as a religion, although the courts did not recognize an inmate-created sect called Church of the New Song, whose faith required them to be "served steak and wine from time to time." While prisoners have not brought any suits against correctional institutions for violating their freedom of beliefs, several have challenged prison authorities for prohibiting religious practices.

RELIGIOUS SERVICES. In general the courts have ruled that inmates have the right to practice their beliefs, subject to restrictions that correctional officials deem necessary for the safe running of the prison. The correctional administrators cannot arbitrarily prohibit practices of an established religion unless it can prove the customs create "a clear and present danger" to the operation of the facility.

The District of Columbia jail allowed, at public expense, interdenominational services, as well as services by Catholics, Jews, Protestants, Unitarians, the Salvation Army, and other religious groups. Public funds paid for Protestant and Catholic chaplains and for religious medals. An honorarium was paid to a rabbi when needed.

Several times in 1959 a group of Muslims requested permission to hold religious services. The Director of Corrections of the District of Columbia, Donald Clemmer, refused the requests because of his belief that "Muslims teach racial hatred." The director also confiscated a religious medal from the petitioner, William Fulwood, because Clemmer thought the medal was symbolic of a doctrine of hate and wearing it would promote racial tension in the prison. The jail administration also did not allow Fulwood to correspond with Elijah Muhammad, the leader of the Black Muslims, or subscribe to the Los Angeles *Herald Dispatch* because it carried a column by Elijah Muhammad.

In 1962 the U.S. District Court of the District of Columbia (*Fulwood v. Clemmer,* 206 F. Supp 370) ruled that, by allowing some religious groups to hold religious services and by conducting such services at public expense while denying that right to Muslims, the jail officials had discriminated against the Muslim inmates. These acts violated "the Order of the Commissioners of the District of Columbia No. 6514-B, dated Nov. 25, 1953, which requires prison officials to make facilities available without regard to race or religion."

The court held the same opinion on the distribution and wearing of religious medals. However, on the issue of correspondence and the newspaper subscription, the court stated that the judiciary "lacked general supervisory powers over prisons, and in absence of ... abuse of discretion by prison officials, courts should not interfere."

In 1972, in *Cruz v. Beto* (405 U.S. 319), Fred A. Cruz, a Buddhist serving in a Texas prison claimed that, while other prisoners were allowed use of the prison chapel, prison officials refused Buddhists the right to hold religious services. For sharing religious materials with other prisoners, Cruz was placed in solitary confinement on a diet of bread and water for two weeks.

The court stated that prison officials are "accorded latitude in the administration of prison affairs, and prisoners necessarily are subject to appropriate rules and regulations." However, prisoners have the right to petition the government for "redress of grievances," and the federal courts, while they do not "sit" to supervise prisons, must "enforce constitutional rights of all 'persons,' including prisoners." The court concluded that "reasonable opportunities must be afforded to all prisoners to exercise the religious freedom guaranteed by the First and Fourteenth Amendments without fear of penalty."

A five-to-four split Supreme Court, in *O'Lone v. Shabazz* (482 U.S. 340, 1987), declared that "state prison officials acted in a reasonable manner" and were not violating First Amendment freedoms when they did not allow inmates who were members of the Islamic faith to attend religious services held on Friday afternoons. "Prison policies were related to legitimate security and rehabilitative concerns, alternative means of exercising religious faith with respect to other practices were available, and placing Islamic prisoners into work groups so as to permit them to exercise religious rights would have adverse impact" on the running of the prison.

In the opinion of the four dissenters, however, when:

...exercise of the asserted right is not presumptively dangerous ... and where the prison has completely deprived an inmate of that right, then prison officials must show that "a particular restriction is necessary to further an important governmental interest...." The prison in this case has completely prevented respondent inmates from attending the central religious service of their Moslem faith....

The State has neither demonstrated that the restriction is necessary to further an important objective nor proved that less extreme measures may not serve its purpose.... If a Catholic prisoner were prevented from attending Mass on Sunday, few would regard that deprivation as anything but absolute, even if the prisoner were afforded other opportunities to pray, to discuss the Catholic faith with others, and even to avoid eating meat on Friday if there were a preference.

FOOD. Courts have ordered pork-free diets for groups whose religion forbids their eating pork, although they must make up a significant portion of the inmate population. However, pork does not have to be eliminated from the menu if a sufficient variety of other foods are offered.

In addition, there are limits to what a prison administration can be expected to do. In *Benjamin v. Coughlin* (708 F. Suppl. 570, 1989), a federal court in New York upheld the refusal of the New York Department of Correctional Services to meet the dietary conditions requested by the Rastafarians, a religion with origins in Jamaica.

Depending upon the sect of the religion, the group wanted no meats, no canned foods or dairy products, no food that had been grown with nonorganic pesticides or fertilizers, and food cooked in natural materials such as clay pots. The court ruled that meeting the demands would overburden the prison system both administratively and financially.

RELIGIOUS JEWELRY. In 1996 the U.S. 7th Circuit Court of Appeals, in *Sasnett v. Sullivan* (91 F.3d 1018), held that, under the Religious Freedom Restoration Act, the Wisconsin prison system could not prevent inmates from wearing religious jewelry. Prison officials had banned such items, arguing that they could be used as weapons. However, while the prison administrators had banned jewelry, they had not prevented inmates from having rosary beads, which could be used to strangle someone. The court concluded that "the burden of justification is on the state and it has not been carried."

HAIR AND DRESS. Michael G. Gallahan, a Cherokee Indian, practiced his religious beliefs, including having worn long hair since the age of five years. Tenets of his religion recognized hair as a "sense organ" and taught that loss of hair was equated to losing part of the body. Prison officials had established hair-length regulations because of the belief that long hair was a convenient place for hiding weapons, could obscure facial identification, and could cause sanitary problems.

In *Gallahan v. Hollyfield* (516 F. 2d 1004, 1981), a U.S. District Court in Virginia ruled "a prisoner is not stripped of all rights on incarceration; specifically, he retains those First Amendment rights that are not inconsistent with his status as a prisoner or with the legitimate penological objectives of the corrections system." The judges found that Gallahan "established a sincere belief in his religion" and that the state's reasons were "insufficient" to enforce the hair-length regulation, especially since Gallahan had agreed to wear his hair tied back in a ponytail.

On the other hand a 1992 appellate court decision, in *Scott v. Mississippi Department of Corrections* (961 F.2d 77), upheld haircut rules in a case involving a Rastafarian hairstyle. The court maintained that:

> it is not for us to impose our own ideas about prison management upon those who attempt the reasonable regulation of that nearly impossible task... [T]he loss of absolute freedom of religious expression is but one sacrifice required by ... incarceration.

The Sixth Circuit Court of Appeals, in *Abdullah v. Kinnison,* (769 F. 2d 345, 1985), ruled that a prison directive requiring practicing Muslims to keep white prayer robes in the institutional chapel rather than in cells was justified by security reasons and did not violate the First Amendment.

12-STEP PROGRAMS. As a precondition to his continued participation in a family reunion program, David Griffin had been required to participate in a substance abuse program modeled after Alcoholics Anonymous (A.A.), which makes references to "God" and a "Higher Power." He claimed that the requirement to participate in such a program violated his right to practice atheism under the First Amendment.

In 1996 the New York Court of Appeals, the state's highest court, in *Griffin v. Coughlin* (NY CtApp, No 73), concluded that:

> ...use of A.A. by the state correctional system as an essential component of an exclusive compulsory attendance ... program violates the Establishment clause.... Here, the state has exercised coercive power to advance religion by denying benefits of eligibility for the family reunion program to atheist and agnostic inmates who object and refuse to participate in religious activity.... No secular drug and alcohol addiction treatment program devoid of A.A.'s practices and doctrines is offered as a substitute.

The dissenters thought that, although the 12-step program may be perceived as:

> ...somewhat religious, [it] remains overwhelmingly secular in philosophy, objective, and operation.... The inmate was not compelled to participate in the ... pro-

gram. He voluntarily chose the course of action that placed his agnosticism and nonbeliefs at risk because he wished to receive something he is not unqualifiably entitled to from the state.

FOURTH AMENDMENT

The Fourth Amendment guarantees the "right of the people to be secure ... against unreasonable searches and seizures ... and no warrants shall issue, but upon probable cause...." The courts have not been as active in protecting prisoners under the Fourth Amendment as under the First and Eighth Amendments. In *Bell v. Wolfish* (441 U.S. 520, 1979) the Supreme Court asserted that:

> ...simply because prison inmates retain certain constitutional rights does not mean that these rights are not subject to restrictions and limitations.... Maintaining institutional security and preserving internal order and discipline are essential goals that may require limiting or retraction of the retained constitutional rights of both convicted prisoners and pretrial detainees. Since problems that arise in the day-to-day operation of a corrections facility are not susceptible to easy solutions, prison administrators should be accorded wide-ranging deference in the adoption and execution of policies and practices that, in their judgment, are needed to preserve internal order and discipline and to maintain institutional security.

Based on this reasoning the High Court ruled that body searches did not violate the Fourth Amendment. "Balancing the significant and legitimate security interest of the institution against the inmates' privacy interest, such searches can be conducted on less than probable cause and are not unreasonable."

In another Fourth Amendment case (*Hudson v. Palmer,* 46 U.S. 517, 1984), the Supreme Court upheld the right of prison officials to search a prisoner's cell and seize property.

> The recognition of privacy rights for prisoners in their individual cells simply cannot be reconciled with the concept of incarceration and the needs and objectives of penal institutions.... [However, the fact that a prisoner does not have a reasonable expectation of privacy] does not mean he is without a remedy for calculated harassment unrelated to prison needs. Nor does it mean that prison attendants can ride roughshod over inmates' property rights with impunity. The Eighth Amendment always stands as a protection against "cruel and unusual punishments."

Prisoners can sue for loss of their personal property. Also, to protect privacy, a federal court, in *Lee v. Downs* (641 F. 2d 1117, 1981) ruled that the prison staff must be of the same sex to supervise inmates during bathing or strip searches.

Sexual Misconduct

Due to the incidence of sexual misconduct involving correctional staff and inmates, by 1996 some 31 states, the

District of Columbia, and the federal government had passed legislation criminalizing such behavior in a correctional setting. According to *Sexual Misconduct in Prisons: Laws, Remedies and Incidence* (National Institute of Corrections, 2000), since 1996 additional legislation had been passed in 15 states. (See Table 13.1.)

In 1998, 11 departments of correction (DOCs) reported between three and five incidents of sexual misconduct among correctional staff and female inmates. Five DOCs reported more than five such incidents, six DOCs reported one to two incidents, and 14 DOCs reported that their facilities were incident-free in 1998. Of incidents involving male inmates in 1998, 12 DOCs reported one to two incidents, five reported three to five incidents, and five reported more than five such incidents. Fourteen DOCs reported no incidents in 1998. (See Figure 13.1.)

EIGHTH AMENDMENT

The Eighth Amendment guarantees that "cruel and unusual punishment [not be] inflicted." The Eighth Amendment has been used in cases involving overcrowding of prisons and the failure of prison officials to provide minimal conditions for health and protection from assault by other prisoners. The Supreme Court has established several tests to determine whether conditions or actions violated the Eighth Amendment:

- Did the actions or conditions offend concepts of "decency and human dignity and precepts of civilization which Americans profess to possess"?

- Was it "disproportionate to the offense"?

- Did it violate "fundamental standards of good conscience and fairness"?

- Was the punishment unnecessarily cruel?

- Did the punishment go beyond legitimate penal purposes?

Isolation Cells

In *Holt v. Sarver* (300 F. Supp 82, 1969) a U.S. district court in Arkansas found "solitary confinement or close confinement in isolation units of prisons not unconstitutional per se, but, depending on circumstances, it may violate the Eighth and Fourteenth Amendments." Isolation cells in an Arkansas prison were used for prisoners who broke rules, those who needed protective custody to protect them from other inmates, and those who were:

> ...general escape or security risks or who were awaiting trial on additional charges.... Confinement in isolation cells was not "solitary confinement" in the conventional sense of the term. On the contrary, the cells are substantially overcrowded.... The average number of men confined in a single cell seems to be four, but at times the number has been much higher (up to ten and eleven).

TABLE 13.1

Statutes prohibiting sexual misconduct involving correctional staff and inmates

	Legislation Passed 1996 or Earlier	New or Supplemental Legislation Passed Since 1996	Level of Offense
Alabama	None	No response to this question	
Alaska	✔		Felony
Arizona	✔		Misdemeanor
Arkansas	✔	✔	Misdemeanor
California	✔		Felony or misdemeanor
Colorado	✔		Felony (if coercive)
Connecticut	✔		Felony or misdemeanor
Delaware	✔		Felony
District of Columbia	✔		Felony
Florida	✔	✔	Felony
Georgia	✔		Felony
Hawaii	✔		Felony
Idaho	✔		Felony
Illinois		✔	Felony
Indiana	✔		Felony
Iowa	✔		Aggravated misdemeanor
Kansas	✔		Felony
Kentucky	None		
Louisiana	✔		Felony
Maine	✔		Felony
Maryland		✔	Misdemeanor
Massachusetts		✔	(Not specified)
Michigan	✔		Misdemeanor
Minnesota	None		
Mississippi		✔	Felony
Missouri	✔		Felony
Montana	None		
Nebraska		✔	Felony
Nevada	✔		(Not available)
New Hampshire		✔	Felony
New Jersey	✔		(Not available)
New Mexico	✔		Felony
New York	✔		Felony or misdemeanor
North Carolina	✔		Felony
North Dakota	✔		Misdemeanor
Ohio	✔		Felony
Oklahoma	✔		Felony
Oregon	None		
Pennsylvania		✔	Misdemeanor
Rhode Island	✔		Felony
South Carolina		✔	Felony
South Dakota	✔	✔	Felony
Tennessee		✔	Misdemeanor
Texas	✔	✔	Felony (if coercive)
Utah	None		
Vermont	None		
Virginia		✔	Felony or misdemeanor
Washington		✔	Felony or misdemeanor
West Virginia	None		
Wisconsin	✔		Felony
Wyoming	✔	No 1999 survey response	Felony (if coercive)
U.S. Bureau of Prisons	✔		Felony or misdemeanor (criminal if coercive)
Guam	None		
Puerto Rico	None		

SOURCE: "Table 1. Statutes prohibiting sexual misconduct involving correctional staff and inmates" in *Sexual Misconduct in Prisons: Laws, Remedies and Incidence,* National Institute of Corrections, U.S. Department of Justice, Longmont, CO, 2000

While the judges agreed that "if confinement of that type is to serve any useful purpose, it must be rigorous, uncomfortable, and unpleasant. However, there are limits to the rigor and discomfort of close confinement which a state may not constitutionally exceed."

The court found that the confinement of inmates in these isolation cells, which were "overcrowded, dirty, unsanitary, and pervaded by bad odors from toilets, constituted cruel and unusual punishment." The court also asserted that "prolonged confinement" of numbers of men in the same cell under unsanitary, dangerous conditions was "mentally and emotionally traumatic as well as physically uncomfortable. It is hazardous to health. It is degrading and debasing; it offends modern sensibilities, and, in the Court's estimation, amounts to cruel and unusual punishment."

In addition, those inmates who were not in isolation slept together in barracks where many of the inmates had weapons and attacked each other. While the court recognized that assaults, fights, and killings occurred in all penal institutions, the Arkansas Farm had not taken reasonable precautions. Prisoners should at least be "able to fall asleep at night without fear of having their throats cut before morning, and the state has failed to discharge a constitutional duty in failing to take steps to enable them to do so."

PUNITIVE ISOLATION. In the 1970s Arkansas sentenced inmates to punitive isolation in extremely small cells for an indeterminate period of time, with their status being reviewed at the end of each 14-day period. While most were released within 14 days, many remained in that status for weeks or months, depending upon their attitudes as appraised by prison personnel. Usually the inmates shared a cell with one other inmate, and at times three or four were together, causing them to sleep on the floor. Considering that these were violent men filled with "frustration and hostility," and that some were "dangerous and psychopaths," confining them together caused threatening situations that produced "a forcible response from prison personnel."

The lower courts found that the force used by the guards was excessive and declared that "confinement of prisoners in punitive isolation for more than 30 days constituted cruel and unusual punishment and was impermissible." In *Finney v. Hutto* (548 F. 2d. 740, 1977) the United States Court of Appeals agreed.

Medical Care

DELIBERATE INDIFFERENCE. On November 9, 1973 J. W. Gamble, an inmate of the Texas Department of Corrections, was injured while performing a prison work assignment. Although he complained numerous times about his back injury and was given pills, the guards accused him of malingering. In January the disciplinary committee placed Gamble in solitary confinement for

FIGURE 13.1

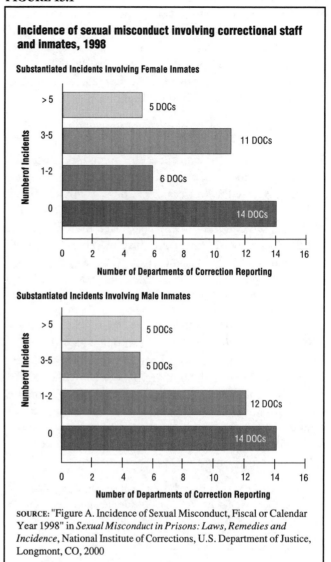

Incidence of sexual misconduct involving correctional staff and inmates, 1998

Substantiated Incidents Involving Female Inmates

(Number of Incidents vs. Number of Departments of Correction Reporting)
- > 5: 5 DOCs
- 3-5: 11 DOCs
- 1-2: 6 DOCs
- 0: 14 DOCs

Substantiated Incidents Involving Male Inmates

(Number of Incidents vs. Number of Departments of Correction Reporting)
- > 5: 5 DOCs
- 3-5: 5 DOCs
- 1-2: 12 DOCs
- 0: 14 DOCs

SOURCE: "Figure A. Incidence of Sexual Misconduct, Fiscal or Calendar Year 1998" in *Sexual Misconduct in Prisons: Laws, Remedies and Incidence*, National Institute of Corrections, U.S. Department of Justice, Longmont, CO, 2000

refusing to work. On February 4 he asked to see a doctor for chest pains and blackouts. Almost 12 hours later a medical assistant saw him and had him hospitalized.

The next morning after an electrocardiogram, he was placed on Quinidine for treatment of irregular cardiac rhythm and moved to administrative segregation. On February 7, after experiencing pain in his chest, left arm, and back, Gamble asked to see a doctor and was refused. The next day he was refused again. After finally seeing the doctor again on February 9 and being given Quinidine, Gamble swore out a complaint that the staff had "subjected him to cruel and unusual punishment in violation of the Eighth Amendment, made applicable to the states by the Fourteenth."

In past decisions the Court had concluded that "deliberate indifference to serious medical needs of prisoners constitutes the 'unnecessary and wanton infliction of pain'" (*Gregg v. Georgia,* 428 U.S. 153, 1976). This is true whether the indifference is displayed by prison doctors in their response to the prisoner's need or by prison guards who deny or delay access to treatment or interfere with the treatment. However, in *Estelle v. Gamble* (429 U.S. 97, 1976) the Supreme Court ruled that "every claim by a prisoner that he has not received adequate medical treatment" does not mean a violation of the Eighth Amendment.

An "inadvertent failure to provide adequate medical care" is not "an unnecessary and wanton infliction of pain" or "repugnant to the conscience of mankind.... Medical malpractice does not become a constitutional violation merely because the victim is a prisoner." Only deliberate indifference "can offend 'evolving standards of decency' in violation of the Eighth Amendment." Because Gamble saw medical personnel 17 times over three months, the court did not find this a violation of the Eighth Amendment. "A medical decision not to order an X ray or like measures does not represent cruel and unusual punishment."

FUTURE CONSEQUENCES. In *Helling v. McKinney* (509 U.S. 25, 1993) the Court ruled that a Nevada inmate had the right to bring a court action because he had been assigned to a cell with another prisoner who smoked five packs of cigarettes daily, and he had not been informed of the health hazards that he could incur by bunking with a heavy smoker. Quoting its earlier decision in *DeShaney v. Winnebago County Dept. of Social Services* (489 U.S. 189, 1989) the Court declared:

> [W]hen the state takes a person into its custody and holds him there against his will, the Constitution imposes upon it a corresponding duty to assume some responsibility for his safety and general well being.... The rationale for this principle is simple enough: when the state by the affirmative exercise of its power so restrains an individual's liberty that it renders him unable to care for himself, and, at the same time fails to provide for his basic human needs—e.g., food, clothing, shelter, medical care, and reasonable safety—it transgresses the substantive limits on state action set by the Eighth Amendment.

The justices asserted that prison administrators could not:

> ...ignore a condition of confinement that is sure or very likely to cause serious illness and needless suffering the next week or month or year. In *Hutto v. Finney* (437 U.S. 678, 1978) we noted that inmates in punitive isolation were crowded into cells and that some of them had infectious maladies such as hepatitis and venereal disease. This was one of the prison conditions for which the Eighth Amendment required a remedy, even though it was not alleged that the likely harm would occur immediately and even though the possible infection might not affect all of those exposed.... Nor can we hold that prison officials may be deliberately indifferent to the exposure of inmates to a serious, communicable disease on the ground that the complaining inmate shows no serious current symptoms.

The Supreme Court sent the case back to the district court for retrial, where McKinney had to prove his allegations to show that the Eighth Amendment was violated and that "society considers the risk that the prisoner complains of to be so grave that it violates contemporary standards of decency to expose anyone unwillingly to such a risk." However, in 1992, the director of the Nevada State Prisons had adopted a smoking policy restricting smoking to specified areas, which made McKinney's case virtually moot (a hypothetical case—only cases involving real injury can be considered by the courts).

Indifference Must Be Deliberate

In *Wilson v. Seiter* (501 U.S. 294, 1991) the Supreme Court upheld the judgment that prisoners "claiming that conditions of confinement constituted cruel and unusual punishment were required to show deliberate indifference on the part of prison officials." In *Estelle v. Gamble* the court had established that the Eighth Amendment could be applied to some "deprivations that were not specifically part of the sentence but were suffered during imprisonment."

However, the High Court emphasized that the prison staff had to "possess a sufficiently culpable state of mind." The court explained that "if the pain inflicted is not formally meted out as punishment by the statute or the sentencing judge, some mental element must be attributed to the inflicting officer before it can qualify" as a violation of the Eighth Amendment.

Guards Assaulting Prisoners

In 1983 Keith Hudson, an inmate at the state penitentiary in Angola, Louisiana, argued with Jack McMillian, a guard, who placed the inmate in handcuffs and shackles to take him to the administrative lockdown area. On the way there Hudson testified that McMillian punched him in the mouth, eyes, chest, and stomach. Another guard held him and the supervisor on duty watched. Hudson sued accusing the guards of cruel and unusual punishment.

A magistrate found that the guards used "force when there was no need to do so" and the supervisor allowed their conduct, thus violating the Eighth Amendment. The Court of Appeals for the Fifth Circuit, however, reversed the decision, ruling that:

> ...inmates alleging use of excessive force in violation of the Eighth Amendment must prove: (1) significant injury; (2) resulting 'directly and only from the use of force that was clearly excessive to the need'; (3) the excessiveness of which was objectively unreasonable; and (4) that the action constituted an unnecessary and wanton infliction of pain.

The court agreed that the use of force was unreasonable and was a clearly excessive and unnecessary infliction of pain. However, the Court of Appeals found against

Hudson because his injuries were "minor" and "required no medical attention."

The Supreme Court, in *Hudson v. McMillian* (503 U.S. 1, 1992), disagreed that the inmate had to suffer serious injury. In *Whitney v. Albers* (475 U.S. 372, 1986) the court had earlier ruled that guards, during prison disturbances or riots, must balance the need "to maintain or restore discipline" through force against the risk of injury to inmates. Those situations require prison officials "to act quickly and decisively" and allow guards and administrators leeway in their actions.

Under the *Whitney* decision the "extent of injury suffered by an inmate is one factor" considered to determine whether the use of force was unnecessary. However, the absence of serious injury, while "relevant ... does not end" the Eighth Amendment inquiry. The question must be asked whether the force applied was a "good faith effort to maintain or restore discipline, or maliciously and sadistically to cause harm." Although the circuit court termed the blows "minor," the Supreme Court viewed the extent of Hudson's injuries as no basis to dismiss his claims.

Private Officer Liability

Ronnie McKnight was a prisoner at the South Central Correctional Center (SCCC) in Tennessee. The Corrections Corporation of America (CCA) had a contract with Tennessee to operate some of its correctional facilities, including the SCCC. Under 42 U.S.C. Section 1983, McKnight sued two of CCA's correctional officers, Daryll Richardson and John Walker, for allegedly violating his Eighth Amendment constitutional right to be free from cruel and unusual punishment by holding him in restraints while transporting him to another prison. McKnight claimed that the restraints caused him serious medical injury requiring hospitalization, that Richardson and Walker ignored his protests, and that they ridiculed him after he complained about the restraints.

The two correctional officers filed a motion to dismiss the complaint on the grounds that they were entitled to qualified immunity as correctional officers (*McKnight v. Rees,* 88 F. 3d 417, 425, [CA 1996]). The district court denied the motion to dismiss. The U.S. Court of Appeals for the Sixth Circuit affirmed the lower court's decision, agreeing that Richardson and Walker were not entitled to qualified immunity as employees of a private, for-profit corporation.

As a rule, private parties are not granted qualified immunity because they do not serve the public interest. According to the court, privately employed correctional officers, while serving the public interest in operating a correctional facility, are not "principally motivated by a desire to further the interest of the public at large." Likewise, private corporations are not "principally concerned with enhancing the public good."

The court held that the private company and its employees have a greater motive to maximize profits by overstepping the bounds of constitutional rights. Therefore, the "increased threat of injury by violation of constitutional guarantees counsels against granting qualified immunity" to private correctional officers.

The court conducted a cost-benefit analysis and determined that private companies can include the increased threat of liability in their proposal when negotiating for state contracts, so "the state may pay more to obtain private correctional services, but less to monitor them on an ongoing basis." Moreover, the court found that qualified immunity is used as an incentive to encourage talented candidates to enter public service. The court concluded that this reasoning did not apply to this case, as private correctional officers are not public servants and are not motivated by the same intentions as a candidate for public office. The court held that "prison guards employed by a private firm are not entitled to a qualified immunity from suit by prisoners charging a Section 1983 violation."

Safety

Dee Farmer, a preoperative transsexual with feminine characteristics, had sometimes been in with the general prison population but sometimes had been segregated. He claimed to have been assaulted after being transferred from a lower level correctional facility to a higher security institution with more violent prisoners, where he was placed in the general population. Farmer brought suit alleging that the prison officials had acted with "deliberate indifference" to his safety.

The lower courts ruled in favor of the prison officials on grounds that they lacked "actual knowledge of a potential danger" and were not "reckless in a criminal sense." The Supreme Court, in *Farmer v. Brennan* (511 U.S. 825, 1994), returned the case to the district court for retrial because the lower court may have erred in placing "decisive weight" on Farmer's failure to notify the prison administrators of a danger.

The Supreme Court held that:

...a prison official may be held liable under the Eighth Amendment for acting with "deliberate indifference" to inmate health or safety only if he knows that inmates face a substantial risk of serious harm and disregards that risk by failing to take reasonable measures to abate it.

The Court further asserted that prison officials have a duty to:

...protect prisoners from violence at the hands of other prisoners. However, a constitutional violation occurs only where the deprivation alleged is, objectively, "sufficiently serious,"... and the official has acted with "deliberate indifference" to inmate health or safety.

Deliberate indifference entails something more than negligence, but is satisfied by something less than acts or omissions for the very purpose of causing harm or with knowledge that harm will result.... It is the equivalent of acting recklessly.

The Amendment outlaws cruel and unusual "punishments," not "conditions," and the failure to alleviate a significant risk that an official should have perceived but did not, while no cause for commendation, cannot be condemned as the infliction of punishment under the Court's cases....

However, this does not mean that prison officials will be free to ignore obvious dangers to inmates. Whether an official had the requisite knowledge is a question of fact subject to demonstration in the usual ways, and a fact finder may conclude that the official knew of a substantial risk from the very fact that it was obvious. Nor may an official escape liability by showing that he knew of the risk but did not think the complainant was especially likely to be assaulted by the prisoner who committed the act.

It does not matter whether the risk came from a particular source or whether a prisoner faced the risk for reasons personal to him or because all prisoners in his situation faced the risk. But prison officials may not be held liable if they prove that they were unaware of even an obvious risk or if they responded reasonably to a known risk, even if the harm ultimately was not averted.

On December 9, 1996, the U.S. Court of Appeals for the Seventh Circuit, in *Babcock v. White* (CA 7, No 94-3806) held that a prisoner cannot claim damages on the issue that prison officials failed to prevent exposure to a risk of harm. According to principles of law, the inmate has standing in a court only if the officials failed to prevent harm. However, this ruling does not exclude suits arising from a continuous disregard for a prisoner's safety or ones based on claims of psychological injury.

Court Orders to Improve Conditions

In 1971 four inmates, without the help of attorneys, brought a suit before the Federal District Court in Louisiana challenging the conditions in the state penitentiary at Angola. After hearing an investigator's report on the conditions of the facility, the judge issued an order for reforms. Finally, in 1999 after dramatic improvements at the maximum-security prison, a federal judge closed the case saying, "It is ordered that all court supervision over Louisiana State Penitentiary is terminated." The warden of the prison does not plan to change anything put in place by the court order, and the governor's office is committed to running the prison in a manner that the court would approve of.

Some states, such as Wisconsin, have had only one or two facilities under court orders, while others, such as South Carolina, have had their entire state prison system under court order. Some states have only one or two conditions to reform, while others have to correct "total conditions." The National Prison Project of the American Civil Liberties Union annually publishes *Status Report:*

State Prisons and the Courts, listing the states and territories under court orders.

In 1981 the Supreme Court, in *Rhodes v. Chapman* (45 U.S. 337), held that, "even if no single condition of confinement would be unconstitutional in itself, exposure to the cumulative effect of prison conditions may subject inmates to cruel and unusual punishment."

An Alabama Case

In *Pugh v. Locke* (406 F. Suppl 318, 1976) a U.S. district court in Alabama declared the:

...conditions of confinement in the Alabama penal system constituted cruel and unusual punishment where they bore no reasonable relationship to legitimate institutional goals and, as a whole, created an atmosphere in which inmates were compelled to live in constant fear of violence, in imminent danger to their physical well-being, and without opportunity to seek a more promising future.

The court also enjoined (stopped) the state from:

...maintaining a prison system that was not otherwise in compliance with constitutional requirements in respect to overcrowding, segregation and isolation, classification, mental health care, protection from violence, living conditions, food service, correspondence and visitation, educational, vocational work and recreational opportunities, physical facilities, and staff....

and ordered it corrected. The four main Alabama facilities housed anywhere from 200 to more than 400 inmates over capacity. The effects of overcrowding were "heightened by the dormitory style of arrangements." Bunks were packed so tightly that inmates could not walk between them. Sanitation and security were impossible to maintain. Overcrowding also caused inmates to sleep on mattresses in hallways and next to the urinals. Old and filthy mattresses helped spread contagious diseases and body lice. The buildings possessed inadequate heating and ventilation systems. The facilities were "overrun with roaches, flies, mosquitoes, and other vermin."

Plumbing was inadequate. In one facility, one toilet served 200 men. Toilets either did not flush or overflowed. Personal hygiene was impossible. The state supplied soap and razor blades. Only those who could afford to buy toothpaste, toothbrushes, shampoo, shaving cream, razors, or combs could obtain them. Household cleaning supplies were not available for the inmates to keep their living spaces clean.

Food service conditions were also unsanitary. Food was improperly stored in dirty storage areas and was often infested with insects. Dishwashers did not reach the minimum temperature for sanitation. Eating and drinking utensils were unsuitable; some inmates used tin cans for drinking containers. Inmates who worked in food services were not trained properly in sanitation methods. A U.S.

public health officer testified at the trial that he "found these facilities wholly unfit for human habitation according to virtually every criterion used for evaluation by public health inspectors."

Prisoners were assigned to various Alabama institutions on the availability of space and not on which facility was most appropriate for their crime or condition. Offenders suffering from mental disorders went unidentified and were housed throughout the prison population:

> Violent inmates are not isolated from those who are young, passive, or weak. Consequently, the latter inmates are repeatedly victimized.... Emotional and physical disabilities which require special attention pass unnoticed.

Understaffing of the facilities allowed inmates to:

> ...assume positions of authority and control over other inmates, creating opportunities for blackmail, bribery, and extortion.... [M]ost prisoners carry some form of homemade or contraband weapon, which they consider to be necessary for self-protection.... An inmate required to live in these circumstances stands no chance of leaving the institution with a more positive and constructive attitude than the one he or she brought in.... Further, this Court finds that these conditions create an environment that not only makes it impossible for inmates to rehabilitate themselves, but also makes dehabilitation [worsening of inmates' attitudes and abilities to cope with the outside world] inevitable.

The court also found fault with the lack of recreational programs to occupy free time and any "meaningful opportunities to participate in vocational, educational or work activities." Prisoners received 25 cents per week from the state without a way to earn extra money to purchase necessities for personal hygiene or to supplement the inadequate prison diet. However, the prison did little to control the flow of money, and those with money could also buy "drugs, alcohol, sex, changes in institutional records, and special privileges."

The court declared that the use of isolation and segregation cells was unconstitutional as they were overcrowded, had no beds, no lights, and no running water, and had a hole in the floor for a toilet, which could only be flushed from the outside. The inmates in punitive isolation got only one meal daily, were not permitted any exercise or reading material, and could shower only once every 11 days. Offenses for being placed in these cells ranged from swearing at the guards to murder.

Because of these conditions the court set up minimum constitutional standards for the entire penal system and appointed an independent committee to help the board of corrections make the changes. In 1984 the court stopped actively supervising the orders after "substantial compliance" had been achieved. In 1988 the court finally dismissed the case.

A Texas Case

Texas provided another major Eighth Amendment case. In 1980 a district court declared the entire state prison system unconstitutional on overcrowding and conditions and appointed a special master to correct the problems. In *Ruiz v. Estelle* (679 F.2d 115, 1982) the Fifth Circuit Court of Appeals upheld the ruling. The court asserted that, for the judiciary to find the totality of conditions of confinement unconstitutional, they must be cruel and unusual and "not merely harsh or restrictive."

The circuit court agreed with the district court that the correctional board had to reduce the overall inmate population and that each inmate should be provided with 40 square feet of space. The district judge thought the overcrowded conditions were a threat to the inmates' safety, fostered the lack of privacy, increased stress and tension, and furthered the possible spread of disease.

The Texas Department of Corrections argued that the inmates were not in the overcrowded cells or dormitories most of the day. However, the court found that many were idle in their living quarters because of a shortage of guards in the work fields. The threat to inmates in dormitories was great because potentially "assaultive inmates are present in great numbers in every dormitory" and the dormitories were "practically unsupervised." This resulted in a "constant threat to the inmates' personal safety." The circuit court also upheld the district court's appointment of special masters and monitors to supervise the implementation and compliance of its ruling, but declared the order "too sweeping" in that it permitted the master to give the district court reports based on his own observations without a formal hearing.

In May 1998 then-Texas Attorney General Dan Morales filed a motion requesting that a federal court release Texas from a final judgment from the lawsuit. The state made the request under the 1996 federal Prison Litigation Reform Act (PL 104-134). The act says that, if there are no ongoing constitution violations, states whose prison systems were subject to a final court judgment may seek to end that judgment two years after passage of the act. According to Morales, "Texas has run a constitutional prison system for more than a decade, with the past six years totally free of court supervision or oversight."

Following a 1999 ruling from the U.S. District judge not to dismiss the case, the Fifth U.S. Circuit Court of Appeals upheld the Prison Litigation Reform Act, limiting federal control of prison systems and lessening judicial involvement in inmates' complaints. This ruling paves the way for Texas to be released from federal supervision.

Restrictive and Harsh Punishment Is Constitutional; Wanton and Unnecessary Infliction of Pain Is Unconstitutional

In *Rhodes v. Chapman* (452 U.S. 337, 1981) the Supreme Court ruled that housing prisoners in double cells was not cruel and unusual punishment. The justices maintained that:

> ...conditions of confinement, as constituting the punishment at issue, must not involve the wanton and unnecessary infliction of pain, nor may they be grossly disproportionate to the severity of the crime warranting imprisonment. But conditions that cannot be said to be cruel and unusual under contemporary standards are not unconstitutional. To the extent such conditions are restrictive and even harsh, they are part of the penalty that criminals pay for their offenses against society.

The Court concluded that the Constitution "does not mandate comfortable prisons," and only those "deprivations denying the 'minimal civilized measure of life's necessities'" violate the Eighth Amendment.

DUE PROCESS COMPLAINTS

Due process (procedural fairness, fair hearings) in the prison setting usually concerns disciplinary procedures. Most of the time disciplinary action is taken on the word of the guard or the administrator, and the inmate has little opportunity to challenge the charges. Rules are often vague or not formally written out. Disrespect toward a guard is defined most of the time by the guards themselves.

The Supreme Court, however, has affirmed that procedural fairness should be used in some institutional decisions. In 1974, in *Wolff v. McDonnell* (418 U.S. 539), the Supreme Court declared that a Nebraska law providing for sentences to be shortened for good behavior created a "liberty interest." Thus, if an inmate met the requirements, prison officials could not deprive him of the shortened sentence without due process, according to the Fourteenth Amendment. (The Fourteenth Amendment states that "no state shall ... deprive any person of life, liberty, or property, without due process of law....") The High Court asserted:

> ...that due process required that prisoners in procedure resulting in loss of good-time or in imposition of solitary confinement be afforded advance written notice of claimed violation, written statement of fact findings, and the right to call witnesses and present documentary evidence where such would not be unduly hazardous to institutional safety or correctional goals....

> A prisoner is not wholly stripped of constitutional protections and though prison disciplinary proceedings do not imply the full panoply of rights due a defendant, such proceedings must be governed by a mutual accommodation between institutional needs and generally applicable constitutional requirements.

> However, the inmate at a procedural hearing does not have a right to have counsel (lawyer, advisor) in the proceedings. Silence at a hearing can be used against the inmate because it is a disciplinary hearing, not a criminal proceeding. If incriminating testimony by an inmate could be used in later criminal proceedings, then he

must be offered immunity if forced to testify (*Baxter v. Palmigiano,* 425 U.S. 208, 1975).

While the Supreme Court found dormitory bunking unconstitutional in certain cases (see above), in *Bell v. Wolfish* (441 U.S. 520, 1979) it ruled that putting two persons in a room intended for one did not necessarily violate the Constitution. At the Metropolitan Correctional Center (MCC), a federally operated short-term custodial facility in New York City designed mainly for pretrial detainees, inmates challenged the constitutionality of the facility's conditions. As this was a pretrial detention center the challenge was brought under the due process clause of the Fifth Amendment. The District Court and the Court of Appeals found for the inmates, but the Supreme Court disagreed. Chief Justice William Rehnquist argued that:

> While confining a given number of people in a given amount of space in such a manner as to cause them to endure genuine deprivations and hardship over an extended period of time might raise serious questions under the Due Process Clause as to whether those conditions amounted to punishment, nothing even approaching such hardship is shown by this record.

> Detainees are required to spend only seven or eight hours in their room, during most or all of which they presumably are sleeping. The rooms provide more than adequate space for sleeping.... While "double bunking" may have taxed some of the equipment or particular facilities in certain of the common areas, ... this does not mean that the conditions at the MCC failed to meet the standards required by the Constitution. Our conclusion in this regard is further buttressed by the detainees' length of stay (most are released in 60 days).

The High Court also ruled in *Bell* that the administrator could constitutionally prohibit inmates from receiving books that were not mailed directly from publishers, book clubs, or bookstores, and stop the delivery of packages of food and personal items from outside the institution. The administrator could also have body-cavity searches of inmates following contact visits with persons from the outside and require the detainees to remain outside their rooms during inspection.

EARLY RELEASE

Two cases decided in 1997 pertained to prisons releasing inmates early to relieve overcrowding and then later revoking their release status. Beginning in 1983 the Florida legislature enacted a series of laws authorizing the awarding of early release credits to prison inmates when the state prison population exceeded predetermined levels. In 1986 Kenneth Lynce received a 22-year prison sentence on a charge of attempted murder. In 1992 he was released based on the determination that he had accumulated five different types of early release credits totaling 5,668 days, including 1,860 days of "provisional credits" awarded as a result of prison overcrowding.

Shortly thereafter the state attorney general issued an opinion interpreting a 1992 statute as having retroactively canceled all provisional credits awarded to inmates convicted of murder and attempted murder. Lynce was arrested and returned to custody. He filed a *habeas corpus* petition alleging that the retroactive cancellation of provisional credits violated the *ex post facto* clause of the Constitution.

The Supreme Court agreed with Lynce. In *Lynce v. Mathis* (65 LW 4131, 1997) the Court ruled that to fall within the *ex post facto* prohibition a law must be "retrospective" and "disadvantage the offender affected by it" (*Weaver v. Graham,* 450 U.S. 24, 29), 1981). The 1992 statute was clearly retrospective and disadvantaged Lynce by increasing his punishment.

Oklahoma's Preparole Conditional Supervision Program took effect whenever the state prisons became overcrowded and authorized the conditional release of prisoners before their sentences expired. The Pardon and Parole Board determined who could participate in the program. An inmate was eligible for preparole after serving only 15 percent of a sentence, and was eligible for parole after one-third of the sentence had elapsed.

Ernest Harper was released under the preparole program. After he spent 5 apparently uneventful months outside prison, the governor denied him preparole. He was returned to prison without a hearing and on less than 5 hours' notice.

Despite his claim that his reincarceration deprived him of liberty without due process in violation of the Fourteenth Amendment, the Oklahoma Court of Criminal Appeals and the Federal District Court denied him *habeas corpus* relief. The corrections department argued that the Court had ruled that a hearing was not necessary to transfer a prisoner from a low-security prison to a higher-security one and that was what they were doing in this case.

The Tenth Circuit Court of Appeals, however, held that the preparole program was sufficiently like parole and a program participant was entitled to procedural protections. In *Leroy L. Young v. Ernest Eugene Harper* (65 LW 4197, 1997) the Supreme Court upheld the decision of the Tenth Circuit Court. It ruled that Oklahoma had violated Harper's due process rights by sending him back to prison without giving him a hearing to show that he had not met the conditions of the program.

HARDER TO BRING SUIT

In 1995 the Supreme Court, in *Sandin v. Conner* (115 S.Ct. 2293), made it harder for prisoners to bring constitutional suits to challenge due process rights. In a 5–4 decision the majority made it clear it was frustrated with the number of due process cases, some of which they felt clogged the judiciary system with unwarranted complaints such as claiming a "liberty interest" in not being transferred to a cell with an electrical outlet for a television.

Sandin v. Conner concerned an inmate in Hawaii who was not allowed to call witnesses at a disciplinary hearing for misconduct that had placed him in solitary confinement for 30 days. The Court of Appeals of the Ninth Circuit had held in 1993 that the inmate, Demont Conner, had a "liberty interest," allowing him a range of procedural protections in remaining free from solitary confinement. The Supreme Court overruled the Court of Appeals, affirming that the inmate had no "liberty interest." Due process protections play a role only if the state's action has infringed on some separate, substantive right that the inmate possesses. For example, Wolff's loss of good time credit was a substantive right that he possessed. The punishment Conner had received "was within the range of confinement to be normally expected" since he was serving 30 years-to-life for a number of crimes, including murder.

"States may create liberty interests which are protected by the due process clause," but these will be limited to actions that "impose atypical and significant hardship on the inmate in relation to the ordinary incidents of prison life." Being put in solitary confinement in a prison where most inmates are limited to their cells most of the day anyway is not a liberty-interest issue. Because there was no liberty interest involved, how the hearing was handled was irrelevant. The decision did not overturn any prior court decisions and did not discuss cases brought to the Court under the Eighth Amendment.

Based on this ruling, only when prison staff imposes "atypical and significant hardship on the inmate" should a federal court consider the complaint a potential violation of a prisoner's constitutional right to due process of law. Any other actions, such as mismanaged disciplinary hearings or temporary placement in solitary, are just complaints about the "ordinary incidents of prison and life and should not be considered violations of the Constitution."

Chief Justice Rehnquist asserted that past Supreme Court decisions have "led to the involvement of Federal courts in the day-to-day management of prisons, often squandering judicial resources with little offsetting benefit to anyone." Judges should allow prison administrators the "flexibility" to "fine tune" the ordinary incidents of prison life.

This decision continues the more conservative trend of the Supreme Court. Prior to the 1960s prisoners had few rights, but the climate of reform and protest in the 1960s brought about a rash of inmate cases, giving prisoners new legal power. The more conservative social milieu of the 1980s led to more judicial restraint as the courts sought to balance the constitutional rights of the prisoners with the security interests of the correctional administrators.

On February 11, 2000, U.S. Senator Patrick Leahy (Democrat-Vermont) introduced The Innocence Project Act, designed to allow individuals who believe they were wrongly convicted of a crime to have access to DNA evidence that may exonerate them. The proposed legislation would require that biological evidence in a criminal case be preserved long enough to allow the convicted individual to seek DNA testing in the courts. The bill would also provide for Federal funding to states to help ensure that indigent defendants in death penalty cases receive competent legal counsel.

In 1994 Congress, in the Violent Crime Control Act (PL 103-322), made it harder for the federal judiciary to "hold prison or jail crowding unconstitutional under the Eighth Amendment." The law made it illegal for federal courts to find, in general terms, that overcrowding is unconstitutional. The inmate must prove that the crowding caused the infliction of "cruel and unusual punishment" on that particular inmate.

In 1996 the passage of the Prison Litigation Reform Act of 1995 (PL 104-134) made it harder for prisoners to bring individual suits and class actions, and for the courts to take over the running of prisons if they found problems. For example, before an inmate can bring a suit, all administrative remedies must be "exhausted."

The law also prohibits a prisoner from bringing another suit if the "prisoner has had three or more actions in federal courts" that were "dismissed as frivolous." In addition, a prisoner's suit is also prohibited if it failed to "state a claim on which relief could be granted, or sought monetary relief from a defendant immune from such relief, unless the prisoner is under imminent danger of serious physical injury."

Is the 1996 Reform Law Constitutional?

This section may be challenged in the courts since it would appear to prevent any relief for actions when a prisoner no longer faces the threat of serious harm or property damages. In addition the law requires the courts to review prisoner complaints before putting them on the court docket or soon thereafter, and to dismiss the complaints if they seem frivolous or malicious or fail to state a claim on which relief can be granted.

Not only will the law limit the cases coming before the courts, but it will also limit the type of relief the courts

may order. Courts cannot give any relief to an inmate "unless the court finds that such relief is narrowly drawn, extends no further than necessary to correct the violation of the federal right, and is the least intrusive means necessary to correct the violation of the federal rights."

The law limited the court's "authority to release or prohibit admission of prisoners, or required that three-judge courts issue such orders." It limits the "court's authority to appoint special masters to conduct hearings and prepare findings of fact." The law also limits legal fees that can be paid. (*Resource Guide for Managing Civil Rights Litigation,* Federal Judicial Center, Washington, D.C., 1996.)

Cases contesting the constitutionality of the law have been filed throughout the country. For example, a district court judge in Iowa held that the "three strikes" limit on filings was unconstitutional. Also under discussion in the courts is the retroactivity of various features of the law and whether the law violates separation of powers by subjecting the court system to the control of Congress. In 2000 the Supreme Court of the United States ruled in *Miller v. French* that the law had not violated the separation of powers clause of the Constitution, but other legal challenges continued.

Making it more difficult for prisoners to get help in suits, the 1996 Federal Appropriations Act [sec 504(a)(15)] also prohibited recipients of funds from participating in any litigation on behalf of prisoners. As a result the Legal Services Corporation (LSC), which provides lawyers for impoverished litigants, adopted an interim rule effective as of August 29, 1996, prohibiting participation of LSC recipients in any litigation on behalf of a person incarcerated in federal, state, or local prisons.

In July, 1996, a federal judge eliminated decrees governing New York City jails that had stemmed from earlier lawsuits complaining of overcrowded, unsafe, and unsanitary conditions. Mayor Rudolph Giuliani had requested the court to do so after the Prison Litigation Reform Act had been signed. The mayor said that it would save the city millions of dollars once the court-supervised decrees were removed. In an interview in the *New York Times,* Robert Gangi, executive director of the Correctional Association of New York, an advocacy group, commented that, while inmates occasionally filed frivolous lawsuits, these decrees protected the rights of prisoners and corrected many problems that could return without the courts watching.

IMPORTANT NAMES AND ADDRESSES

American Bar Association
740 15th St. NW
Washington, DC 20005-1019
(202) 662-1010
FAX: (202) 662-1032
URL: http://www.abanet.org

American Civil Liberties Union Foundation (ACLU)
National Prison Project
733 15th St. NW, Suite 620
Washington, DC 20005
(202) 393-4930
FAX: (202) 393-4931

American Correctional Association
4380 Forbes Blvd.
Lanham, MD 20706-4322
(301) 918-1800
FAX: (301) 918-1900
(800) 222-5646
URL: http://www.corrections.com/aca

American Jail Association
2053 Day Rd., Suite 100
Hagerstown, MD 21740
(301) 790-3930
FAX: (301) 790-2941
(800) 222-5646
E-mail: aja@corrections.com
URL: http://www.corrections.com/aja

Amnesty International USA
National Office
322 8th Ave.
New York, NY 10001
(212) 807-8400
FAX: (212) 627-1451
http://www.aiusa.org

Bureau of Justice Statistics
810 7th St. NW
Washington, DC 20531
(202) 307-0765
FAX: (202) 307-5846

(800) 732-3277
E-mail: askbjs@ojp.usboj.gov
URL: http://www.ojp.usdoj.gov/bjs

Campaign for an Effective Crime Policy
514 10th St. NW, Suite 1000
Washington, DC 20004
(202) 628-1903
FAX: (202) 628-1091
E-mail: staff@crimepolicy.org
URL: http://www.crimepolicy.org

Criminal Justice Institute
213 Court St., Suite 606
Middletown, CT 06457
(860) 704-6400
FAX: (860) 704-6420
E-mail: cji@netcom.com
URL: http://www.cji-inc.com

Families Against Mandatory Minimums
1612 K St. NW, Suite 1400
Washington, DC 20006
(202) 822-6700
FAX: (202) 822-6704
E-mail: famm@famm.org
URL: http://www.famm.org

Federal Bureau of Investigation
935 Pennsylvania Ave. NW
Washington, DC 20535-0001
(202) 324-3000
FAX: (202) 324-4705
URL: http://www.fbi.gov

Federal Bureau of Prisons
320 1st St. NW
Washington, DC 20534
(202) 307-3198
FAX: (202) 514-6620
URL: http://www.bop.gov

Federal Judicial Center
1 Columbus Cir. NE
Washington, DC 20002-8003

(202) 502-4153
FAX: (202) 502-4077
URL: http://www.fjc.gov

Justice Research and Statistics Association
777 North Capitol St. NE, Suite 801
Washington, DC 20002
(202) 842-9330
FAX: (202) 842-9329
URL: http://www.jrsa.org

Juvenile Justice and Delinquency Prevention
810 7th St. NW
Washington, DC 20531
(202) 307-5911
FAX: (202) 307-2093
URL: http://www.ojjdp.ncjrs.org

NAACP Legal Defense and Educational Fund
1444 I St. NW, 10th Floor
Washington, DC 20005
(202) 682-1300
NY Office: (212) 219-1900
FAX: (202) 682-1312

National Center on Institutions and Alternatives
3125 Mt. Vernon Ave.
Alexandria, VA 22305
(703) 684-0373
FAX: (703) 684-6037
E-mail: ncia@igc-apc.org
URL: http://www.ncianet.org/ncia

National Conference of State Legislatures
1560 Broadway, Suite 700
Denver, CO 80202
(303) 830-2200
FAX: (303) 863-8003
URL: http://www.ncsl.org

National Council on Crime and Delinquency
685 Market St., Suite 620
San Francisco, CA 94105
(415) 896-6223
FAX: (415) 896-5109

National Criminal Justice Association
444 Capitol St. NW, Suite 618
Washington, DC 20001
(202) 624-1440
FAX: (202) 508-3859
URL: http://www.sso.org/ncja

National Criminal Justice Reference Service
P.O. Box 6000
Rockville, MD 20849-6000
(301) 519-5500

(800) 851-3420
URL: http://www.ncjrs.org

National Institute of Justice
810 7th St. NW
Washington, DC 20531
(202) 307-2942
FAX: (202) 307-6394
URL: http://www.ojp.usdoj.gov/nij
E-mail: askncjrs@ncjrs.org

National Legal Aid and Defender Association
1625 K St. NW, Suite 800
Washington, DC 20006-1604
(202) 452-0620
FAX: (202) 872-1031
E-mail: info@nlada.org
URL: http://www.nlada.org

The Sentencing Project
154 10th St. NW, Suite 1000
Washington, DC 20004
(202) 628-0871
FAX: (202) 628-1091
E-mail: staff@sentencingproject.org
URL: http://www.sentencingproject.org

U.S. Parole Commission
5550 Friendship Blvd., Suite 420
Chevy Chase, MD 20815-7286
(301) 492-5990
FAX: (301) 492-6694
URL: http://www.usdoj.gov/uspc

U.S. Sentencing Commission
1 Columbus Cir. NE
Washington, DC 20002-8002
(202) 502-4500
URL: http://www.ussc.gov

RESOURCES

The Bureau of Justice Statistics (BJS) of the U.S. Department of Justice is a major source of data and information concerning crime, sentencing, and inmates. *Correctional Populations in the United States, 1997* (2000) summarizes information on inmates in the nation's jails and prisons. Other valuable BJS publications include: *Truth in Sentencing in State Prisons* (1999); *Substance Abuse and Treatment, State and Federal Prisoners, 1997* (1999); *Prison and Jail Inmates at Midyear 2000* (2001); *Capital Punishment, 1999* (2000); *Prisoners in 1999* (2000); *State Prison Expenditures, 1996* (1999); *Juveniles in Adult Prisons and Jails: A National Assessment* (2000); *HIV in Prisons 1997* (1999); *State Court Organization 1998* (2000); *State Court Sentencing of Convicted Felons, 1996* (2000); *Medical Problems of Inmates, 1997* (2001); *Compendium of Federal Justice Statistics, 1998* (2000); *Health Treatment of Inmates and Probationers* (1999); *Incarcerated Parents and Their Children* (2000); *Women Offenders* (2000); *Profile of State Prisoners Under Age 18, 1985–97* (2000); *Defense Counsel in Criminal Cases* (2000); and *Drug Use, Testing and Treatment in Jails* (2000). The BJS also produced the *Sourcebook of Criminal Justice Statistics 1999* (2000), with the Hindelang Criminal Justice Research Center, State University of New York, Albany.

The National Institute of Justice (NIJ) researches criminal issues and publishes *The National Institute of Justice Journal,* whose article "Can Telemedicine Reduce Spending and Improve Prisoner Health Care?" (April 1999) was cited in this publication. Other NIJ publications used in this publication are *Research in Brief,* "Three Strikes and You're Out: A Review of State Legislation" (1997), and *Key Legislative Issues in Criminal Justice: Mandatory Sentencing* (1997).

The Federal Bureau of Investigation's *Crime in the United States—1999* (2000) provides the latest arrest statistics and crime rates and is an essential resource for those interested in studying crime across the country.

The U.S. government's Office of Juvenile Justice and Delinquency Prevention (OJJDP), an excellent resource on juvenile justice, produced *Juvenile Offenders and Victims: 1997 Update on Violence* (1999); *Detention in Delinquency Cases, 1988–1997* (2000); *Female Delinquency Cases, 1997* (2000); *State Custody Rates, 1997* (2000); *Juvenile Court Statistics 1997* (2000); and *Juveniles and the Death Penalty* (2000).

Information Plus thanks the Sentencing Project (Washington, D.C.) for permission to use information from its reports *U.S. Surpasses Russia as World Leader in Rate of Incarceration* (2000) and *Diminishing Returns: Crime and Incarceration in the 1990s* (2000) by Jenny Gainsborough and Marc Mauer. Information Plus also thanks the National Association of State Budget Officers for information from its publication *1999 State Expenditure Report* (2000).

The Criminal Justice Institute publishes *The Corrections Yearbook 2000: Jails* (Camille Camp and George Camp, Middletown, Connecticut, 2001). Information Plus also thanks the U.S. Census Bureau for use of information contained in *Statistical Abstract of the United States: 2000* (2001).

Other sources include: *The Impact of "Three Strikes and You're Out" Laws: What We Have Learned* (1996) from the Campaign for an Effective Crime Policy (Washington, D.C.); *The Case for Shorter Prison Terms: The Illinois Experience* (1994) from the National Council on Crime and Delinquency (San Francisco); and *Sexual Misconduct in Prisons: Laws, Remedies and Incidence* (2000), published by the National Institute of Corrections, Longmont, Colorado. Information Plus is grateful for the use of tables provided by the Correctional HIV Consortium, San Francisco, California, 1998.

The RAND Corporation, a "nonprofit institution that helps improve public policy through research and analysis," produced *Three Strikes and You're Out: Estimated Benefits and Costs of California's New Mandatory Sentencing Law* (Peter Greenwood et al., 1994) and *Mandatory Minimum Drug Sentences: Throwing Away the Key or the Taxpayers' Money?* (Jonathan P. Calkins et al., 1997). Information Plus thanks RAND for permission to use its material.

INDEX

Nevada, 41, 50, 102, 110, 112
New Hampshire, 27, 76, 83, 102
New Jersey, 17, 109, 122, 138
New Mexico, 29, 94, 109–110, 112
New York
    Auburn System, 3
    Brooklyn residential treatment program, 118
    decrease in prisoner population, 17–18
    Elmira Reformatory, 3
    juveniles incarcerated, 82
    New York City annual cost per prisoner, 13
    smoking ban, 138
    Stay'n Out program, 137
    truth-in-sentencing laws, 102
Nolan v. Fitzpatrick (1985), 141
North Carolina, 82, 83, 92, 94, 109
North Dakota, 85, 102, 109, 110

O

Ohio, 17, 85, 102
Oklahoma, 11, 18, 27, 29, 123
Oklahoma, Eddings v. (1982), 83
O'Lone v. Shabazz (1987), 142
Oregon, 94, 120–121, 127
Overcrowding, 16, 20, 27–28, 32, 37–38, 76–77

P

Palmer, Hudson v. (1984), 143
Parens patriae, 6
Parole. *See* Probation and parole
Pate, Cooper v. (1964), 139
Pell v. Procunier (1974), 141
Penitentiary Act of 1779, 2
Pennsylvania
    colonial abolishment of death penalty, 2
    early prisons, 3
    Graterford prison drug sweeps, 138
    largest jail jurisdictions, 17
    telemedicine consultations, 68(f6.5), 69f
    "three strikes" laws, 109, 110
Per diem fees, 22
Petersilia, Joan, 121, 122–123
Philadelphia Society for Alleviating the Miseries of Public Prisons, 2–3
Physical and sexual abuse of prisoners, prior to incarceration, 46–48, 66(t6.21)
Plea bargaining and "three strikes" laws, 113
Prison farms. *See* Work programs
Prison Litigation Reform Act of 1995, 152
Prisoners
    abused prior to incarceration, 46–48, 48t
    admitted to state prisons, by type of admission, 39(t4.19)
    adults under community supervision or in jail/prison, 85t
    with children, 48–50
    with children, by gender, 49(t5.11)
    with children, current offenses of, 51t
    with children, maximum sentence length and time to be served before release, 52t
    convicted felons receiving prison sentences, 37f

criminal history, by mental health status, 66(t6.20)
death row prisoner characteristics, 54(t5.18)
under death sentence and executed, 54(t5.17)
estimated number, by most serious offense, 126t
executed under civil authority, by sex and race, 53t
family background, by mental health status, 67(t6.23)
federal prisoners, 44–45
fees to, 14, 21
fights since admissions, by mental health status, 65(t6.18)
by gender, 43t
homelessness, employment, and income source, by mental health status, 67(t6.22)
jail inmates, 15–17, 15t, 18t, 19(t3.10)
living with their children at time of admission, 49(t5.12)
maximum sentence length and months served, by offense and mental health status, 68(t6.24)
most serious current offense, by mental health status, 65(t6.19)
number, by offense, 126f
parole revocation, 45(t5.4)
percent of sentenced prisoners, by most serious offense, 127(t12.2)
percentage, by offense, 38(t4.15)
persons under age 25 incarcerated, 80(t7.17)
with physical/mental impairment, 57(t6.1)
prison population, by year, 15t
in private facilities, by jurisdiction, 30t
program participation, 52, 82–83, 134
by region and jurisdiction, 26t
rights of, 139–152
sentence length and actual time served, 39(t4.17)
sentence time served, 38(t4.14)
sentenced, by gender, 27t
sentenced, by most serious offense, 46t
sentenced, by offense type, 45(f5.1)
sentenced, per 100,000 residents, 28(f4.1)
sentenced prisoners, total growth of, 38(t4.16)
state prisoners, 44
state prisoners, characteristics of, 81(t7.20)
state prisoners in local jails, 29, 32
victim characteristics, 64(t6.17)
See also Drug offenders; Health and medical care; Jails; Juveniles; Prisons; Probation and parole; Violent offenders; Women
Prisons, 25–42
    capacities, 31t, 32
    construction, 13, 28
    drug sweeps and drug trafficking, 137–138
    Federal Bureau of Prisons facilities, 33t–34t

jurisdictions, highest and lowest populations, 29(t4.4)
medieval, 2
population as a percent of capacity, 32t
population trends, 29(t4.5)
prisoners admitted, by type of admission, 39(t4.19)
reform, 2–4, 148–149
state and federal population, change in, 25t
state prison populations, youth and adult, 81(t7.19)
See also Health and medical care; Jails; Work programs
Privatization, 20–21, 28–29, 39–41
Probation and parole, 85–99
    adults on parole, 94t–95t, 96t
    adults on probation, 87t–88t, 89(t8.5)
    adults under community supervision, 85t
    community corrections among the states, 86t
    federal offenders under community supervision, by offense, 90t–91t
    gain time, 3–4
    good time accumulation, 97t–99t
    intensive supervision probation, 120–121
    persons under the supervision of the Federal Probation System, 89(t8.4)
    supervision termination, 92t–93t
    violators, 37
Procunier, Pell v. (1974), 141
Procunier v. Martinez (1973), 140–141
Program participation of prisoners, 52, 82–83, 134
Public opinion
    murder penalties, 6t
    rehabilitation and punishment, 5–6, 5(t1.1)
    U.S. prison systems ratings, 5(t1.2)
Pugh v. Locke (1976), 148–149

Q

Quakers, 2–3
Quinlan, J. Michael, 41

R

Race/ethnicity. *See* American Indians and Alaska Natives; Asian and Pacific Islander Americans; Black/African Americans; Hispanic Americans; White Americans
Rated capacity, 18
Redhail, Zablocki v. (1977), 141
Rees, McKnight v. (1996), 147
Rehabilitation, 3–6, 5(t1.1)
Rehnquist, William, 104, 105, 151
Religious beliefs. *See* First Amendment cases
Restitution centers, 118
Rhode Island, 9, 27
Rhodes v. Chapman (1981), 149–150
Rights of prisoners, 139–152
Rosenfeld, Richard, 136
Ruffin v. Commonwealth (1871), 139
Ruiz v. Estelle (1982), 149
Russia, incarceration rates, 25

S

prison population as a percent of capacity, 32t

prison sentence length and actual time served, 39(t4.17)

prisoner deaths, by cause, 61(t6.9)

prisoner fights since admissions, by mental health status, 65(t6.18)

prisoner percentage, by offense, 38(t4.15)

prisoner population, by year, 15t

prisoner victim characteristics, 64(t6.17)

prisoners, by gender, 43t

prisoners, by region and jurisdiction, 26t

prisoners abused prior to incarceration, 48t

prisoners admitted to state prisons, by type of admission, 39(t4.19)

prisoners executed under civil authority, by sex and race, 53t

prisoners in private facilities, by jurisdiction, 30t

prisoners living with their children at time of admission, 49(t5.12)

prisoners sentenced, by most serious offense, 46t

prisoners sentenced, per 100,000 residents, 28(f4.1)

prisoners tested for HIV, 63(t6.11), 63(t6.12), 63(t6.13)

prisoners under death sentence and executed, 54(t5.17)

prisoners with children, 50t

prisoners with children, by gender, 49t

prisoners with children, current offenses of, 51t

prisoners with children, maximum sentence length and time to be served before release, 52t

prisoners with physical/mental impairment, 57(t6.1)

prisons, change in state and federal population, 25t

profile of detained juvenile delinquency cases, 77(t7.10)

rehabilitation and punishment, public opinion, 5(t1.1)

sentence length and total time to expected release, 103(t9.3)

sentence time served, 38(t4.14)

sentenced prisoners, by offense type, 45(f5.1)

sentenced prisoners, number and rate, 27t

sentencing for convicted defendants by type of counsel, 103(t9.1)

sexual misconduct among correctional staff and inmates, 145f

state prison populations, youth and adult, 81(t7.19)

state prisoners under and over age 18, 78(t7.14)

substance abuse treatment, local jails, 132(t12.10)

substance abuse treatment history, 132(t12.9)

supervision termination, 92t–93t

telemedicine consultations, Pennsylvania, 68(f6.5), 69f

total growth of sentenced prisoners, 38(t4.16)

treatment for mentally ill, 68(t6.25)

truth-in-sentencing laws, 39(t4.18)

type of counsel for state and federal prisoners, 103(t9.2)

U.S. prison systems ratings, public opinion, 5(t1.2)

women, estimated number of who will be incarcerated, 44(t5.2)

women incarcerated, by region and jurisdiction, 44(t5.3)

Stay'n Out program, 137

Strike zone, 109

Stroud v. Swope (1951), 139

Substance abuse and treatment, 91–92, 120, 125–138

alcohol treatment, by prior alcohol use, 134t

drug/alcohol use at time of offense, 128(t12.5)

drug use, federal prisoners, 128(t12.4)

drug use, state prisoners, 127(t12.3)

drug use, testing, and treatment in jails, 129(t12.6)–130(t12.6)

levels of prior alcohol use, 131t

levels of prior drug abuse, 130(t12.7)

prisoners treated, 135t

probationers and parolees, 90–91

substance abuse treatment, local jails, 132(t12.10)

substance abuse treatment history, 132(t12.9)

treatment, by levels of prior drug use, 133t

See also Drug offenders

Substance Abuse and Treatment, State and Federal Prisoners, 1997 (BJS), 130–131

Sullivan, Sasnett v. (1996), 142

Supervised mandatory release, 92

Swope, Stroud v. (1951), 139

T

Telemedicine, 69–70

Tennessee, 17, 18, 102, 109

Texas

death penalty, 50, 83

expenditures, 11

fees to prisoners, 22

incarceration rates, 7, 27

largest jail jurisdictions, 17

prison reform, 149

private facilities, 28

probationers and parolees, 85

smoking ban, 138

truth-in-sentencing laws, 102

Webb County annual cost per prisoner, 13

Therapeutic communities, 136–137

Three Strikes and You're Out: A Review of State Legislation (National Institute of Justice), 109

"Three strikes" laws, 4, 109–114, 111t–112t

See also specific states

Todd, Larry, 138

Torture, medieval, 1

Transportation to penal colonies, 2

Truth-in-sentencing laws, 36–37, 39(t4.18), 102

See also specific states

Turner, Susan, 122–123

Turner v. Safley (1987), 141

"Two strikes" laws. *See* "Three strikes" laws

U

Unconditional prison release, 92

UNICOR, 42

Utah, 9, 50, 110

V

Vermont, 85, 110

Violent Crime Control Act (1994), 152

Violent offenders, 35–36, 47–48, 67–68, 81–82, 101

Virginia

death penalty, 50

mandatory life sentences with no parole, 109

parole abolishment, 13, 94

probationers and parolees, 85

smoking ban, 138

"three strikes" laws, 110

W

Washington

fees to prisoners, 22

mandatory life sentences with no parole, 109

parole abolishment, 94

probationers and parolees, 85

"three strikes" laws, 109, 112

work release programs, 122–123

Weekender programs, 19–20

West Virginia, probationers and parolees, 85

White, Babcock v. (1996), 148

White Americans

alcohol users, 132–133

correctional officers, 35t

criminal history of death row prisoners, 55(t5.20)

death row prisoners, 54(t5.18)

drug users, 129–130

jail inmates, 18t

juvenile residential placement by age and gender, 77(f7.3)

juveniles incarcerated, 82

prisoners executed under civil authority, 53t

prisoners with children, 50t

sentence lengths, 101

treated for substance abuse, 135t

See also Juveniles; Women

Whitney v. Albers (1986), 147

Wisconsin, mandatory life sentences with no parole, 109

Wolff v. McDonnell (1974), 150

Wolfish, Bell v. (1979), 143

Women

abused prior to incarceration, 46–48, 48t

alcohol users, 131

conviction status, adult, 19

correctional officers, 35t

court processing of juvenile offenders, 76(*f*7.2)

drug users, 129

estimated number of who will be incarcerated, 44(*t*5.2)

incarceration by region and jurisdiction, 44(*t*5.3)

increase in numbers incarcerated, 43–44

jail inmates, increase, 16

juvenile offenders, 78–79

offenses committed, 19(*t*3.11)

prisoners executed under civil authority, 53*t*

prisoners with children, 49*t*, 50*t*, 51*t*, 52*t*

sentence lengths, 101

sentenced prisoners, 28(*f*4.2)

shorter maximum sentences, 45–46

treated for substance abuse, 134–135, 135*t*

violent offenders, 36

Work programs
   Auburn System, 3
   jail industries, 22

prisons, 41–42

union complaints against, 4

work release, 122–123

See also UNICOR

Work Release: Recidivism and Corrections Costs in Washington State (Petersilia, Turner), 122–123

Wyoming, juvenile incarceration rate, 76

Z

Zablocki v. Redhail (1977), 141